Building for Air Travel

Building for Air Travel

Architecture and Design for Commercial Aviation

Edited by

John Zukowsky

With essays by

Koos Bosma, Mark J. Bouman, David Brodherson,
Robert Bruegmann, Wood Lockhart, Leonard Rau,
Wolfgang Voigt, and John Zukowsky

Prestel   Munich · New York

The Art Institute of Chicago

This book was published in conjunction with the exhibition "Building for Air Travel: Architecture and Design for Commercial Aviation," organized by The Art Institute of Chicago and presented in the museum's Kisho Kurokawa Gallery of Architecture from October 19, 1996, through January 5, 1997. The exhibition was also presented at the Museum of Flight in Seattle and the Galleries of San Francisco International Airport.

Contributions by Wolfgang Voigt translated from the German by Matthew Heintzelman, Chicago
Contributions by Koos Bosma translated from the Dutch by Wendy van Os-Thompson, Heemstede

Copublished by The Art Institute of Chicago, 111 South Michigan Avenue, Chicago, Illinois 60603-6110, and by Prestel-Verlag

Front cover: The NBBJ Group, with Leo A. Daly, architects. Sea-Tac International Airport, Seattle-Tacoma, 1992 (pl. 121).
Back cover: Aéroports de Paris, architects; Paul Andreu, chief architect. Charles de Gaulle International Airport, Roissy-en-France, 1972-94 (pl. 118).
Spine: Leo A. Daly, architects, with site adaption by Holmes and Narver, architects. Prototypical high-activity air traffic control tower, O'Hare International Airport, Chicago, 1993-95 (pl. 155).
Endpapers: (front) Delano and Aldrich, architects; aerial view of LaGuardia Airport, New York (pl. 45); (back) Giefer and Mäckler, architects; aerial view of Terminal 1, Rhein-Main International Airport, Frankfurt am Main, 1965–72 (pl. 101).
Frontispiece: Alfred and Heinrich Oeschger, architects. View of the airfield from inside the terminal at Zurich International Airport, 1946-53 (now altered), showing two Douglas DC-4 aircraft.

The exhibition and book were made possible by major funding from

The National Endowment for the Humanities

with additional support from

United Airlines
Lufthansa German Airlines
The Benefactors of Architecture at The Art Institute of Chicago
The Claridge Hotel, Chicago

This book is a publication of the Ernest R. Graham Study Center for Architectural Drawings at The Art Institute of Chicago.

Prestel books are available worldwide. Please contact your nearest bookseller or write to either of the following addresses for information concerning your local distributor:

Prestel Verlag · 16 West 22nd Street, New York, NY 10010, USA, Tel. (212) 627-8199, Fax (212) 627-9866; and Mandlstrasse 26, D-80802 Munich, Germany, Tel. (+49-89) 381 7090, Fax (+49-89) 38 170935

Edited by Robert V. Sharp, The Art Institute of Chicago, and Carol Jentsch Rutan, Chicago

Designed by Heinz Ross, Munich

Composition by Gerber Satz GmbH, Munich
Lithography by Horlacher & Partner, Heilbronn (plates)
and Gerber Satz GmbH, Munich (other illustrations)
Paper: BVS* matt, 150 gr./sq.m., acid-free, Papierfabrik Scheufelen, Oberlenningen
Printed by Peradruck Matthias GmbH, Gräfelfing
Bound by Kunst- und Verlagsbuchbinderei GmbH, Baalsdorf

Printed in Germany

ISBN 3-7913-1684-2 (hardcover edition)

Contents

Foreword

Although many of us might associate the development of aviation in America with notable sites on the east and west coasts, we would do well to remind ourselves that the Midwest has played an important role in its advancement. The Wright brothers, of course, conducted their landmark powered flight in Kitty Hawk, North Carolina, in 1903, but they further developed and tested their airplane at Huffman Field near Dayton, Ohio, on a site that is now within Wright-Patterson Air Force Base. The civil engineer and aviation pioneer Octave Chanute conducted numerous experiments in gliding flights on the Lake Michigan dunes just outside Chicago, and he was a profound influence on the Wrights well before they took up powered flight. Chicago has also witnessed important events integral to the development of aviation. For example, during the 1893 World's Columbian Exposition, the city hosted the country's first International Aeronautic Congress, co-organized by Chanute and aeronautical engineer Albert Zahm of Notre Dame University. Chicago also sponsored in Grant Park in 1911 (the year after Chanute's death) one of the first important air shows in America, and the 1944 meeting called by Franklin Delano Roosevelt and the United Nations to discuss postwar air transportation became known as "the Chicago Convention." Thus, Chicago's name appears frequently in the annals of aviation history. The enormous success of Chicago's Municipal Airport (renamed Midway Airport in 1950) propelled the demand for an even larger facility, and the rise of O'Hare International Airport to its present distinction as the world's busiest airport is now an intimate part of Chicago's very identity. Clearly, then, it is appropriate for an institution in Chicago to examine the history of commercial aviation, but why an art museum?

Artists and architects have long been fascinated with manned flight. Many modern artists saw this new and exciting invention as symbolic of what they were trying to do in shaping a new artistic vocabulary for a new era. The Cubist painter Georges Braque likened collaged constructions to early aircraft of wire, fabric, and wood. The architect Le Corbusier sketched airplanes in the 1920s, and his 1935 book *Aircraft* is filled with photographs of airplanes, aerial views of cities, and accompanying annotations that celebrate the dynamism and "new spirit" of manned flight and enable us to see cities from a distance and escape the limits of traditional urbanism. Futurists, such as Filippo Marinetti, likened flight to breaking the bonds of the ancient world, and Constructivists, such as El Lissitzky, painted airport plans as if they were abstract paintings. Now, almost three quarters of a century after the first airport terminals were built, some notable architectural achievements are beginning to receive the recognition they deserve, from the landmark status accorded two structures from the 1960s by Eero Saarinen, Dulles International Airport and the TWA Terminal at John F. Kennedy International Airport, to the current restoration of Washington's renowned National Airport of the early 1940s.

In addition, airports, airplane interiors, and aircraft assembly and maintenance buildings are among the most important forms of architecture and design in our century. For this reason it is appropriate that our Department of

Architecture should organize this examination of their impact on our society. Under the direction of John Zukowsky, Curator of Architecture at the Art Institute, this department has been at the forefront of examining architectural issues through creative exhibition installations and scholarly, yet accessible, publications. For this project, as for many others organized by his department, Mr. Zukowsky has generated substantial financial support from the public and private sectors. Once again, we are particularly grateful to the National Endowment for the Humanities for their generous support of this undertaking, and we acknowledge as well the important corporate sponsorship of United Airlines and Lufthansa German Airlines, and the assistance of the Benefactors of Architecture at the Art Institute. Their contributions have enabled us to experience the dynamic framework for the installation designed by Helmut Jahn and have also made it possible for us to produce this striking and informative book.

James N. Wood
Director and President
The Art Institute of Chicago

Acknowledgments

Planning for this project began in fall 1993, when Wolfgang Voigt, David Brodherson, and I met in Chicago to discuss our mutual interests in aviation and the architecture and design of airports. We quickly realized that we could turn this interest into an exhibition and book, and we were encouraged to do so by the Director of the Art Institute, James N. Wood, who also suggested that we pursue federal funding for this undertaking. With the advice of my two colleagues, I added several guest essayists to the team, and, working together with Art Institute staff members, we succeeded in receiving a major grant from the National Endowment for the Humanities (NEH). We especially appreciate the support given to us in this endeavor by Marsha Semmel, the former Director of Public Programs for the NEH, former Program Officer Virginia Wagner, and NEH Chairman Sheldon Hackney. The NEH award enabled us to attract additional corporate funds from the global partnership of United Airlines and Lufthansa German Airlines. Especially helpful in this regard were Regina Fraser, Promotions Representative, and Eileen Sweeney of Public Affairs, both for United Airlines, Hans Diessel, Regional Sales Manager, USA-Midwest, and Bahman Armajani, Marketing Manager of the Central Region, both for Lufthansa, and Charles Croce, Lufthansa's Director of Corporate Communications in New York. In addition to this generous federal and corporate funding, we are grateful to the Benefactors of Architecture at the Art Institute for the endowed funds that support our efforts here: J. Paul Beitler and Lee Miglin, John Buck, Charles Gardner, Sandi Miller, Stuart Nathan, Harold Schiff, and Richard Stein. Also, Michael Wathen of Chicago's Claridge Hotel generously provided lodging for a number of our special visitors for the opening of the exhibition and throughout the course of the Chicago showing.

With this firm base of public, corporate, and individual support, we were able to proceed with our research plans, with the assistance of a multitude of people whose help was essential to the success of this project. Over the course of planning this exhibition and book, more than 100 airports were contacted for information, and many people connected with these airports were generous with their resources. Among those who deserve our wholehearted thanks are: Patricia Eckert, Marketing Manager, Anchorage International Airport; Terry Morgan, Director of Corporate Communications, and Diane Faulks, Investor Relations Executive, British Airport Authority; Yod Ratananenya, Director of the Administrative Department, Airports Authority of Thailand; Wolf-Dieter Schultze of the Press Department, Berlin-Schönefeld Airport; Szilárd Szirmák, Head of International Relations, Air Traffic and Airport Administration, Ferihegy Airport, Budapest; Mario Cardozo Grimaldi, Press Director, Instituto Autonomo Aeropuerto Internacional de Maiqueta near Caracas; Walter Römer, Flughafen Köln Bonn; Bo Haugaard, Marketing and Public Relations Director, Copenhagen Airports; Angel Biasatti, Public Affairs Manager, Dallas-Fort Worth International Airport; John Gallagher, Press Officer, Aer Rianta, Dublin; Phyllis G. Van Aken, Director of Marketing Communications, Alliance Development Company, Alliance Airport, Fort Worth; Klaus Busch, Rhein Main International Airport, Frankfurt-am-Main; Raye Wyllie, Public Relations Officer, B.A.A. Scottish Airports, Glasgow; Clemens Finkbeiner-Dege, Press Department, Flughafen Hamburg; Birgit Lohuis, Press Department, Flughafen Hannover; Paul B. Gaines, Department of Aviation, City of Houston; Dennis L. Rosebrough, Director of Public Affairs, Indianapolis Airport Authority; John Starcke, Aviation Department, City of Kansas City; Susanne Trumpler, Flughafen Leipzig-Halle; Zew Blaufuks, Director of External Relations, Aeroportos e Navegação Aérea, Lisbon; Titus Johnson, Marketing Assistant, London City Airport; Ethel L. Pattison, Public Relations Division, City of Los Angeles Department of Airports; Josette Dany, Director of Marketing Communication, Aéroport International Marseille Provence; Claudio Mazzesi, Public Relations Manager, Società Esercizi Aeroportuali, Milan; Joan Beauchamp, Consultant in Public Affairs and Communiations, Aéroports de Montrèal; Joy Faber, Senior Information Officer, Office of Media Relations, Port Authority of New York and New Jersey; Chigusa Oshima, Chief, International Affairs Division, Kansai International Airport; Trine Lind, Director of Corporate Communications, Oslo Hovedflyplass; Michael J. Caro, Retail Operations Executive, BAA Pittsburgh Inc.; Petr Rychetsky, International Relations, Czech Airport Administration, Prague; Jorge Czajkowski, Secretaria Municipal de Urbanismo, Rio de Janièro; Gilson Campos, Press Relations Regional Head Officer, Empresa Brasileira de Infra-Estrutura Aeroportuária, Rio de Janièro; Elsa Cameron, Director, Bureau of Exhibitions and Cultural Education, and John Hill, Associate Curator, San Francisco International Airport; Barbara Stewart, Communications Specialist, Seattle-Tacoma International Airport; Elizabeth Malzacher of Luftfartsverket, Stockholm-Bromma Airport; Josep Barreiro Miró, Chief of Communications, Aeropuerto de Barcelona; Carlos Craido Alonso, Head of International Relations, AENA Aeropuertos Españoles y Navegación Aérea, Madrid, and Cándida Duqve and Angela Navarro, also in that office; Ramón Gómez Rodriguez, Director, Aeropuerto de Bilbao; Brenda G. Geoghagan, Public Relations Representative, Hillsborough County Aviation Authority, Tampa International Airport; G. Kajita, Public Relations Officer, New Tokyo International Airport Authority; Ewa Czesnik and Assistant to the Director Maciej Kalita, Warsaw Airport-Okecie; J. Gurure, for the Airport Manager, Harare Airport, Zimbabwe; Andreas Meier, Public Relations Department, Zurich Airport Authority – Flughafen Zürich.

In addition, a variety of architects, designers, airline employees, and employees of aircraft manufacturers were very generous with their time and resources, and they merit our gratitude as well: Admiral René M. Bloch in Paris and Claude Lenseigne, formerly with Aerospatiale; Brian J. Losito, Audio-Visual Specialist for Air Canada; Eugene Asse, architect in Moscow, who arranged the cooperation of Aeroproekt; Air France employees, particularly P. Guillaume Acolas, the General Manager of the North Central Region; Lee Young of the Chicago office; Jacques Bankir, Vice President of Fleet Schedules and Economics; Patrick de Brébisson, CDG Project Manager; and Dominique Hymans, Musée Air France; several staff members of Aéroports de Paris (ADP), including Paul Andreu, chief architect and Vice President of Projects; Serge Salat, Senior Engineer Architect, and Catherine Antoine, his secretary; Didier Hammon, Vice President of Corporate Communications; and Bernard Lamourere, Technical Relations, both from ADP; Kathy Friske, Corporate Communications, American Airlines; David Kaye of Ove Arup and Partners, and David J. Brown, Publications Coordinator; Ronald Sutell, Director of Facilities, Alaska Airlines; Terry Arnold, Manager Tiltrotor Communications, Bell Helicopter Textron; Hanna Benthem of Benthem Crouwel Architekten; Laurie Haefele of William Nicholas Bodouva and Associates;

Brian Taylor of William Brazeley and Associates Ltd.; Ronald L. Peters, Senior Principal, Design, BPLW; Ron Paquet of Canadair-Bombardier; Robert J. Price, former Vice President for Charles Butler Associates; Patricia Robbins of C & D Interiors; Paul Collier with Santiago Calatrava; Michael J. Riordan, Associate of Leo A. Daly, and Richard Clarke, Design Partner; Uwe Schneider, Head of Industrial and Graphic Design and Michael Lau of his office, Dietmar Plath, Head of Public Relations, and his assistant Monika Kock, all with Daimler Benz Aerospace Airbus; Sandy Smith, Communications Manager, Airbus Industrie of North America, and Arthur Howes, Deputy Vice President Communications, and Françoise Trupiano, Promotional Materials Controller, Airbus Industrie, Toulouse; Boeing staff members, particularly Tom Lubbesmeyer of Boeing Historical Archives; Brian Ames, Communications Manager for the 747-767 Program; Stephanie J. Mudgett, Communications Specialist for the 777 Division, and Steven Thieme, Communications Manager of the Renton Division; Bradford Agry, Jason Machado and Jim Ryan, all of Henry Dreyfuss Associates; Curtis W. Fentress and Jennifer Barry of C.W. Fentress J.H. Bradburn and Associates; Chas. Willits, a former industrial designer with the Douglas Aircraft Company, now with NASA; Charles Forberg; Tom Ernst of Ford and Earl; Katy Harris of Sir Norman Foster and Partners; Kim Drummond, Marketing Director, Gad Shannan; Barbara McCarthy, Manager of Corporate Communications for Gensler and Associates; Meinhard Von Gerkan, Bernd Pastuschka, and Bettina Ahrens of GMP; Daniel McKelvie, Director of Marketing for Holmes and Narver; Steven M. Reiss, Executive Vice President of HNTB; Kate Nigl of Aviation Marketing for Hellmuth, Obata and Kassabaum and architects there, particularly Carmelo Monti and Ripley Rasmus, Design Director; Michael Itkis, CEO and Managing Director of Interactive Flight Technologies, Inc.; Naoko Takanashi of Toyo Ito and Associates; Sylvia Sanders, Librarian of Albert Kahn Associates and Deborah Ferriss, Marketing Director; Yoshiko Takanawa and Junko Nukui of Kisho Kurokawa and Associates; Ilona Ryder of KPF; Toshihiko Sakow of KSA; Ronald J. Hoffman, Executive Director of Landor Associates and Public Relations Associate Lori Rosenwasser; Eric Schulzinger, Manager of Corporate Photography for Lockheed; numerous people at Lufthansa, especially Gernot Hübl, Vice President of North American Cargo and Marianne Arnold; Marlies Heitmann, Manager, Business Sales and Services, Chicago; Werner Bittner, Archive Director; Hans Besser, Project Manager, Lufthansa Terminal, Frankfurt; Barbara Dziedzic, Advertising and Public Relations Manager, LOT Polish Airlines; Linda Folland and Richard Rutledge, Archives and Records Direction, Corporate Communications, Herman Miller, Inc.; Keith H. Palmer, Murphy/Jahn; Rohn K. Price, Principal Associate and Chapin A. Ferguson III, Director of Corporate Communications, Odell Associates; Fred Ouweleen, Jr., President of Pacific Miniatures; Janet Adams Strong, Pei, Cobb, Freed and Partners; Janet Hagan and Jack Gold, Public Relations and Marketing, Cesar Pelli and Associates; Barbara Klingbeil of Roberts and Schaefer; Joy McElroy of Smith, Hinchman and Grylls Associates; Ronald Rhodes; G. Phillip Smith of Smith and Thompson; Lisa Glover, formerly of Albert Speer and Partner; Gretchen Banks, John Ravitch, Craig Hartman, Joseph Gonzalez, Anna Maria Dueñas, and Maggie Diab of Skidmore, Owings and Merrill; Andrew Zdzienicki, Senior Vice President, TAMS Consultants, Inc; Tom Granzow, Product Development Manager, Sundberg-Ferar Inc; Mark Coleman, Vice President of Marketing for TWA; staff at Teague Associates, especially now retired senior designer Paul Phillips, Vice Presidents Robert Welsh, Kenneth Dowd, and Larry Stapleton, and Design Director Jim Bergman; David Rolland, Kenzo Tange Associates; numerous people at United Airlines, especially Larry Clark, Vice President of Properties; Thomas H. Brown, Manager of Airport Planning; and Mary Sue Thyfault and Gayle Schimpf, both in the Creative Services Department; and Sharon Kent Freeman, Publicist for Western Pacific Airlines.

Beyond all the gracious assistance from airports, airlines, aircraft companies, and architects and designers, people at a variety of other institutions helped us, especially as regards access to specific historic documents and photographs. We also appreciate their work on our behalf: Alice Birney and Donna Ellis, both with the Library of Congress; Ewa Jasienku, Curator of Architecture, the Museum of Architecture, Wrocław; Holly Wells, McDermott Library, University of Texas at Dallas; Georgia Smith, Girard Foundation; Curtis Wilcox, Harry Ransom Humanities Research Center, University of Texas at Austin; Dennis McClendon, Chicago Cartographics; Janet Parks, Avery Architectural Library, Columbia University, New York; Russell Flinchum and Elizabeth Horwitz, both from the Cooper Hewitt National Museum of Design; John King, Croydon Airport Society; Cathleen R. Latendresse, Access Service Coordinator, Henry Ford Museum and Greenfield Village; Dennis Parks, formerly Library Director, and Donna M. Bushman, Photo Department, EAA Aviation Center; Georgia Wolf, Jeppesen Sanderson, Inc., Englewood, Colorado; Elizabeth Thurlow, Research Collections Manager, Museum of Flight; Ronald J. Bulinski, Assistant Archivist, San Diego Aerospace Museum; Brian Nicklas, Michelle Corey, Ralph Strong, and Karen Whitehair, Archives Division, National Air and Space Museum, Smithsonian Institution; Eileen Flanagan, formerly of the Graphics Department, Chicago Historical Society; Erica Stoller at ESTO; Anna Eavis, Architectural Information Services Manager, National Monuments Record; Robert Elwall, Photographs Curator, and Jacqueline Wilkinson, Student Library Assistant, British Architectural Library, Royal Institute of British Architects; B.A. Newman, First Lieutenant, U.S. Marine Corps, Joint Public Affairs Office, Marine Air Station Tustin; Judith Walters, Naval Aviation History; William E. Brown, Head of the Archives and Special Collections, University of Miami; Lawrence Okrent, Okrent Associates, Chicago; Akira Kiyokawa, Director, Hideaki Saitoh, Manager of Public Relations, and Satomi Kohinata, Public Relations Department, Tokorozawa Aviation Museum; Joshua Stoff, Curator, Cradle of Aviation Museum; and D. Sibanda and William Tekede, National Archives of Zimbabwe.

Other individuals outside the Art Institute should be thanked for helping to make the exhibition this volume accompanied an exciting reality. Architect Helmut Jahn, with the assistance of Duane Carter of Murphy/Jahn, created a very exciting installation for the exhibition which was built by Gene Young Effects, who also restored the cutaway aircraft models of the B307, B314, DC6, and Boeing 747 that were lent by the Cradle of Aviation Museum, Fred Ouweleen, Jr., and Lufthansa. Colin Morris of Morris Associates in London prepared the model of Gatwick Airport lent by the Croydon Airport Society. Ralph Bufano, Director, Joan Piper, Director of Programs, and John Summerford, Exhibits Manager, all from the Museum of Flight; and Elsa Cameron, Director of the Exhibitions and Cultural Exchange Division, San Francisco International Airport, are to be thanked for their efforts to have this exhibition travel to their institutions.

Last, but not least, we want to thank a number of staff members of the Art Institute for their efforts on behalf of this project. First and foremost among them are Karen Victoria and Greg Perry, Director and Associate Director, respectively, of Government Relations, who were then assisted by Maria Titterington, and Greg Cameron, Director of Corporate and Foundation Relations with Meredith Miller, his Associate Director. Their help was essential to secure sufficient funding to implement this project. The Department of Architecture staff devoted long hours and conscientious labor to make this complex project a reality. Martha Thorne, formerly of Madrid, Spain, and now Associate Curator of Architecture, assisted in acquiring documentation on Spanish airports.

Research Assistant Annemarie van Roessel helped to compile relevant data and curated an adjunct exhibition of related drawings from our permanent collection. Luigi Mumford, the department's Technical Specialist, supervised the preparation of works in the adjunct exhibition on architectural drawings from aviation facilities within our permanent collection, with the assistance of interns and volunteers. Secretary Linda Adelman typed the checklist and relevant materials published here.

Over the past fifteen years, the museum's Publications Department, especially its Associate Director, Robert V. Sharp, has collaborated closely with the Department of Architecture to produce a number of titles that have contributed to the field of architectural history. Robert and his co-editor Carol Jentsch Rutan worked diligently to bring this book into existence, interacting with authors, searching out and selecting illustrations, and coordinating the project with our copublisher, Prestel-Verlag. They were assisted in their efforts by Andrea Arthurs. The staff at Prestel are to be thanked for their cooperation with our Publications Department. Staff in the Ryerson and Burnham Library, particularly Architectural Archivist Mary Woolever and Senior Library Assistant Susan Perry, also helped with catalog research and photograph requests. Annie Morse and Annabelle Clarke of the Department of Imaging and Technical Services assisted in providing photographs for the essays. We are also extremely grateful to the authors of these essays; they have contributed substantially to this volume and to our understanding and appreciation of airport architecture. Advice and assistance regarding the financial operations for the exhibition were provided by Robert E. Mars, Executive Vice President for Administrative Affairs; Calvert W. Audrain, Assistant Vice President for Administrative Affairs-Operations; and Dorothy M. Schroeder, Assistant Director for Exhibitions and Budget. Executive Director of Registration Mary Solt, with the assistance of Darrell Green, Associate Registrar for Loans and Exhibitions, insured that the pieces on loan were appropriately recorded, and they organized the complex shipping arrangments for the works on display. Reynold V. Bailey, Manager of Art Handling, and his staff carefully installed the objects, working closely with Ronald Pushka, Assistant Director of Physical Plant, and his staff. Joseph Cochand, Senior Graphic Designer in the Department of Graphic Design and Communication thoughtfully prepared the graphics for the exhibition installation, signage, and press materials. The Public Affairs Department, under Executive Director Eileen Harakal and with the assistance of John Hindman, promoted the exhibition to a wide audience. Jane Clarke, Associate Director of Museum Education, and Barbara Scharres, Director of the Film Center of the School of the Art Institute, are to be thanked for creating exciting interpretive programs and film series to relate to themes in the exhibition and this book. Finally, Amy Laukkanen, the Project Director for the museum's Architecture and Design Society, organized the preview of the exhibition and that evening's related activities.

John Zukowsky
Curator of Architecture
The Art Institute of Chicago

John Zukowsky **Introduction**

"Please fasten your seat belts, and see that your tray tables are stowed and your seatbacks are in the upright position." How many times have we heard these words as part of what will be a less than memorable event? Things were not always that way. Indeed, air travel used to be an exciting experience, and certainly it has influenced the architecture and design of our century to a perhaps greater degree than anything else, including even the automobile. Yet, because we have grown accustomed to the experience of flying, the airport and airplane now take on almost consistently negative connotations, as unsafe, noisy, and overcrowded. This is witnessed by recent criticism of airlines, airports, and the entire air traffic control system in our local and national press.[1] How could our perception of air travel have soured so thoroughly less than a century after that famous first flight by the Wright brothers in 1903? A brief examination of the roots of air travel might begin to explain what has happened to it and its public image over the past decades.

A look at early airports, aircraft factories, and airliners themselves reveals that their design vocabulary reflected designers' efforts to counter society's feelings of ambivalence and insecurity toward this new mode of transportation. Although visionary projects early in this century by Antonio Sant'Elia, Tony Garnier, Le Corbusier, and Hugh Ferriss, and airport competitions, such as that sponsored in 1929 by Lehigh Portland Cement (see Brodherson, p. 68), all urged the development of airports within existing transportation matrices, the projects that were realized provided familiar rather than radical solutions. Initially, designers drew upon forms established in rail transportation before they developed design and planning solutions particular to aviation. Thus, such early terminals as those at Glendale and Burbank, California, from 1928-30 (see pls. 11 and 13) projected the image of a suburban railway station: the Glendale facility was even called "Grand Central Terminal." Airplane factories and hangars from this era often took their design cues from the railyard shed, and airplane interiors, such as that of the Boeing 80A from 1928-31, imitated that of a Pullman railroad car (see pl. 17). The latest aircraft were even put on display in railroad stations, in publicity stunts that were intended to entice more affluent and sophisticated travelers to this new means of transportation, especially as air travel was directly tied to an air-rail transcontinental service provided by Transcontinental Air Transport and the Pennsylvania and Santa Fe railroads (fig. 1). Passengers flew by day and traveled in railroad sleeping cars at night, on cross-country trips that lasted two days and two nights. Direct reliance on the railroad, however, and a dependence on familiar imagery to allay passenger fears eventually gave way to the simplified wall planes, open spaces, and structural expressiveness of International Style modernism, which served as the norm for airport design before and after World War II. In the interiors of their airliners, air carriers nonetheless often continued to pay homage to the luxurious sleeping compartments and lounges of streamlined railroad trains until well into the postwar period. As recently as the "jumbo jet" era of the late 1960s, airlines held on to their elaborate lounges, and the very latest ideas from British Airways offer first-class passengers their own private compartments.

1 Gary Washburn, "FAA Retirements Could Lead to More Glitches," *Chicago Tribune* (July 26, 1995), sec. 2, pp. 1-2, and Gary Washburn and Ginger Orr, "FAA Finds a New Flaw in Computer," *Chicago Tribune* (July 27, 1995), sec. 2, pp. 1, 6; "How Safe is this Flight?" *Newsweek* (April 24, 1995), pp. 18-28; Joan Beck, "Heaven Help Us with the Airlines," *Chicago Tribune* (July 27, 1995); Pico Iyer, "Where Worlds Collide: In Los Angeles International Airport, the Future Touches Down," *Harpers Magazine* (Aug. 1995), pp. 50-57; Timothy Smith, "Why Air Travel Doesn't Work," *Fortune* (April 3, 1995), pp. 42-56; and Michael J. McCarthy, "The Zombie No. 19603 Flies after 27 Years' Service to a Number of Airlines," *Wall Street Journal* (Aug. 9, 1995), pp. 1, 4. These are but a few recent articles.

Fig. 1 Transcontinental Air Transport's Ford Tri-Motor inside New York's Pennsylvania Railroad Station, 1929-30.

Airports took on the role of spurs to regional development well before World War II, and planners often sited new air facilities in relation to rail lines and highway interchanges. Gatwick Airport south of London is a good example of the former (see Voigt, fig. 25), and Frankfurt's Rhein-Main of the latter; both were built in 1936 (see pls. 32 and 92). Yet it was the postwar period that witnessed a real boom of regional growth around airports, particularly evident in the case of large airports, such as Chicago's O'Hare International, the world's busiest with 66 million passengers in 1994, and now worth billions of dollars annually to Chicago and the surrounding suburban communities (see the essay by Robert Bruegmann in this volume). Moreover, airports and air transport have played an important social role in the twentieth century. On one level they have served, and continue to serve, as sources of pride and technical accomplishment. In many cases, Europe took the lead immediately after World War I with state support of airlines, aircraft manufacturers, and airports. Germany was the early leader, and she serves as a good case study of aviation in relation to national pride.

Weimar Germany became the first country to build a permanent airport and terminal when it constructed one in Königsberg (now Kaliningrad) in 1922 (see pl. 1 and Voigt, figs. 7-8) in East Prussia, in order to connect the city with the rest of Germany after it had been separated by territory ceded to Poland at the end of World War I. Other airports soon followed, the most famous being Berlin's Tempelhof of 1923 (see pls. 3-4 and Voigt, figs. 9-10). Despite Germany's defeat in World War I, her hegemony in aviation should not come as a surprise. In his recent history of German aviation, Peter Fritzsche discussed the integral nature of aviation to national consciousness in Wilhelmine, Weimar, and Nazi Germany, stating that this relatively new nation-state, regardless of its political outlook, actively supported air travel – the symbol of modernity – so as not to play a subordinate role in the modern world order.[2] Even the Bauhaus, the much-vaunted avant-garde architecture and design school in Dessau (1925-32), sought the cooperation of the Dessau-based Junkers Aircraft Company, specialists in metal aircraft, in fabricating their early tubular-steel chairs.

Prominent German airports thus existed several years before comparable examples were built elsewhere in Europe and the United States. In the U.S. the Air Commerce Act of 1926 authorized the creation of civil airlines, but airport construction was left to local authorities until the 1938 Civil Aeronau-

2 Peter Fritzsche, *A Nation of Flyers: German Aviation and the Popular Imagination* (Cambridge, Mass., 1992).

tics Act provided some funding for airports as a matter of national defense. Although such American aircraft as the Boeing 247 (1933; see pls. 22-24) and the Douglas DC-3 (1935-36; fig. 2) paved the way for streamlined modern airliners – at least when compared with traditional Zeppelins and the more conservatively designed Junkers Ju 52-3m (1931-32; see pl. 32) – it was Germany that held many world records in aviation. These included that for non-stop trips by commercial aircraft: in 1938 the 26-passenger Focke-Wulf FW200 *Condor* undertook two such flights, between Berlin and New York, and Berlin and Tokyo (fig. 3). This feat prefigured the significant role that land-based aircraft would play in the development of post-World War II commercial air transport, as opposed to the important prewar role played by flying boats and airships (see pls. 25-28, 42-44). Germany also led the world in passenger use of airports in its showpiece of the mid-1930s, the much-enlarged Tempelhof in Berlin (see pls. 5-7) which, in 1938, was among the world's busiest with 204,116 passengers on 26,950 flights. Likewise, German aircraft factories were among the most advanced, even offering extensive health facilities for workers, as at the Heinkel factory near Oranienberg from 1935. All this changed with Germany's defeat in World War II. In the postwar era the victors clearly took the lead, with new showcase airports at London's Heathrow (1955; see Bosma, fig. 3), New York's Idlewild (1957; see pl. 71-72), and Orly in Paris (1961; see Bosma, fig. 4).

These new facilities of the 1950s and 1960s featured the most modern of design environments, which not only catered to travelers, but also increased recreational usage by families on weekends. Such visitors came to see the new jet aircraft from the large glass windows of the terminal or from the observation decks; or they could take the airport's sightseeing tour, dine in the restaurant overlooking the field, and even, as at Orly, visit an art gallery and movie theater. The introduction of fare discounts in the 1950s and 1960s and the appearance of the Boeing 747 (1968-69) and subsequent "wide body" planes, seating 300 to 500 people, in the 1970s and 1980s further democratized air travel, as did the Airline Deregulation Act of 1978. But this popularity made air travel, airports, and airplanes major targets for terrorists in the 1970s and 1980s, the most infamous incident being the destruction of a Pan Am 747 over Lockerbie, Scotland, on December 21, 1988. Intensified security measures changed the planning of airports, deliberately cutting up the open

Fig. 2 United Airlines Douglas DC-3 (1935-36) in flight over Chicago, showing the new markings developed by Zay Smith, c. 1940.

Fig. 3 Kurt Tank, chief engineer and designer. Focke-Wulf FW200 *Condor*, 1937, at Floyd Bennett Field, Brooklyn, after its 24-hour, 57-minute flight from Berlin to New York (photo Aug. 11, 1938).

flow of space, screening passengers at various stages, and eliminating casual sightseers from outdoor observation areas. With airports' recreational function thus restricted, architects and planners paid greater attention to developing passenger amenities in terminals of the 1980s, particularly with regards to shopping areas, which now provide airport management with ways to make their facilities both more attractive to visitors and, in turn, more profitable.

Although stores and services existed in airport terminals as early as the 1920s, the application of retail shopping-center management principles to the design of airport stores is a relatively recent phenomenon, reaching a sophisticated level with the opening of Pittsburgh's new airport in 1992. The "Airmall" at this facility, developed by British Airports Authority (BAA), features well-respected national and local merchants charging the kinds of competitive prices one finds in suburban shopping areas. BAA is planning to build an aviation theme park at Gatwick Airport – a 120,000-square-foot building to house a museum of aviation, interactive displays, flight simulators, and an amusement park ride based on baggage handling.[3] These efforts are being planned to lure more visitors and their expendable incomes to the airport for recreational purposes, a return to an activity common in the 1950s and 1960s.

Thus, the social significance of the airport has changed since the mid-1920s. The airport has served as an outpost of civic and national pride, a mechanized processor of mass transit, a catalyst to urban and suburban growth, and an example of free-market enterprise trying to redefine itself and find a place within society beyond its functional purpose. This last, most recent development is clearly a consequence of postwar social values, an expression of the public's search for secure, controlled environments for entertainment in suburban malls, sports facilities, and even theme parks located within easy access of their homes. The essays and annotated plates in this volume provide the reader with a multifaceted survey of the development of airports and related facilities. However, since these building types would not exist were it not for the airplanes themselves and the companies that fly them, the rest of this introduction will look at the development of aircraft and airline design, especially as manifested in airplane interiors and corporate imagery. This discussion may then provide an appropriate context for the essays that follow.

Although there have been several publications on the architecture of airports including hangars – references to which can be found throughout the notes that accompany the essays in this book – very little has been written on airline corporate imagery or aircraft interiors in terms of design history, aside from a smattering of brief articles, and even few of these accurately identify the designers of aircraft spaces from the 1920s to the 1940s. It is hard to tell, for example, when the first architect, interior designer, or professional industrial designer planned the interior of an airliner. Airliners of the late 1920s and early 1930s often have interiors credited to the designer of the airplane, usually the factory's chief engineer. Though some of these engineers clearly drew on Modern Movement vocabulary, it seems as if the first architects and designers to execute aircraft interiors did so in the mid to late 1930s. Fritz August Breuhaus de Groot, a society architect and interior designer, with Cäsar Pinnau as his office designer, executed the interiors of a Heinkel 70 commuter plane for Lufthansa, as well as the interiors of the famed airship *Hindenburg*, both from 1935 (see pls. 29-31). Breuhaus was also responsible for the more conservatively styled interiors of Hermann Göring's Junkers Ju 52-3m airplane, presumably at the same time.[4]

Fig. 4 Edward Wells, chief designer, with Howard Ketcham, interior designer. Cutaway view of a Boeing 307 *Stratoliner*, the Pan American Airways *Clipper "Flying Cloud,"* 1938-39.

3 Christopher Lloyd, "Airport Rides Ready for Takeoff," *Sunday Times* (London), (July 10, 1994), sec. 3, p. 10.

4 Fritz August Breuhaus de Groot, *Bauten und Räume* (Berlin, 1935), and John Zukowsky, ed., *The Many Faces of Modern Architecture: Building in Germany between the World Wars* (Munich and New York, 1994), pp. 14-16. For the few articles on aircraft interior design that are not particularly detailed on "designer history," see Aaron Betsky, "Changing Flight Patterns," *Metropolis* (Sept. 1994), pp. 33-37; Kenneth Gaulin, "The Flying Boats: Pioneering Days to South America," *Journal of Decorative and Propaganda Arts* (Winter/Spring 1990), pp. 78-95; J. Gordon Vaeth, "Zeppelin Decor: The Graf Zeppelin and the Hindenburg," *Journal of Decorative and Propaganda Arts* (Winter/Spring 1990), pp. 48-59. Gerald Nason, "Inside-Up: Interior Design and the Airliner," *The Architectural Review* (Dec. 1966), pp. 413-22, does not mention the name of any early interior designers, even though, of the articles cited, his contains the most thorough historical survey.

Fig. 5 Howard Ketcham, designer. Interior of the Boeing 307 *Stratoliner* for Pan American Airways, 1938-39.

Fig. 6 Raymond Loewy, designer. Interior of the Boeing 307B *Stratoliner* for TWA (Transcontinental and Western Air, later Trans World Airlines), 1938-39.

5 Bel Geddes's interiors of the *China Clipper* were published in Sheldon Cheney and Martha Candler Cheney, *Art and the Machine* (New York, 1936, rpt. 1992), pp. 96, 101, and Linda Wellesley, "Flying DeLuxe," *The Airwoman* (Feb. 1935), p. 7. Documents relating to their creation are in the Bel Geddes Collection, the Harry Ransom Humanities Research Center, the University of Texas at Austin. The Dreyfuss studies from 1936 for United's DC-3 are part of his microfilmed records in the collection of the Cooper-Hewitt National Design Museum. A comparable Dreyfuss interior for a corporate plane was published in "Planning for Intensive Use of Space," *Architectural Forum* (April 1936), pp. 238-39. In the Board of Directors Minutes, January 1, 1937, to December 31, 1937, for the 1939 New York World's Fair, Raymond Loewy listed himself as designer of the interiors of the Douglas DC-3 sleeper (DST) and the Boeing *Stratoliner*. His claims, however, could not be corroborated in Loewy's archives in the Library of Congress nor in Boeing's archives. The 307 *Stratoliner* interiors can be found in Angela

Across the Atlantic, a number of important designers were involved in airplane projects: Norman Bel Geddes executed the interiors for Pan American's famous *China Clipper* of 1934-35 (see pls. 25-26); Henry Dreyfuss designed living-room environments (which probably remained unexecuted) for lounge chairs in United Airlines' DC-3s of 1936; and, in 1938-39, Raymond Loewy designed the interior of the Boeing 307 *Stratoliner* for TWA, while Howard Ketcham styled the same plane for Pan American.[5] But all this activity belongs to the prehistoric era of designers and architects working with the aircraft industry. Breuhaus, Pinnau, Bel Geddes, Dreyfuss, and Loewy had active careers beyond their work for commercial aircraft, and they are perhaps best known for their other contributions to design. Ketcham, unfortunately, has drifted into obscurity. In all these examples it is hard to say what exactly the designer did beyond being a stylist or decorator. It seems that Bel Geddes, Loewy, and Ketcham did not establish much of the structural and spatial arrangements (for example, windows, bulkheads, and so forth) in their respective aircraft, which are more likely to have been the responsiblity of engineers. Rather, their work, particularly in the case of Loewy and Ketcham, dealt with selecting the seat fabrics, window coverings, and some of the materials for the manufacturer-designed spaces of the aircraft (figs. 4-6).

This relationship changed with World War II, especially as the postwar period brought a boom in commercial air travel. Architects working for the military created spectacular camouflage ensembles for aircraft factories (fig. 7) and, more importantly, designed and built what would be prototypical

Fig. 7 The Austin Company, architects. Boeing Plant 2 on East Marginal Way, Seattle, 1939-43, camouflaged with a canvas and wood mock-suburban subdivision on top.

Fig. 8 Charles M. Goodman, architect.
International terminal, built of wood, in
Washington, D.C., for the Air Transport
Command, c. 1943-44 (probably now
demolished); from *Architectural Forum*
(March 1945).

Schönberger, ed., *Raymond Loewy:
Pioneer of American Industrial Design*
(Munich, 1990), pl. 5, and Howard
Ketcham, "Designing Interiors for Air
Travel," *Interior Design and Decoration*
(June 1940), pp. 55-56. Ketcham's article
also illustrates Loewy's studies for the
Curtiss-Wright *Substratosphere* transport
(1936-40) which were probably not
produced since the aircraft became the
C-46 *Commando* transport during the war.
Ketcham was also the color advisor for
the interiors of Pan American's Boeing
314 (see pls. 49-51), as documented in
"Atlantic Clipper Has Modern Interiors,"
Life (Aug. 23, 1937), pp. 39-41. N. S.
Lechter and R. S. Rosé, "Styling Aircraft
Interiors," *Aero Digest* (Oct. 1941),
pp. 55-57, 399-400, discuss the role of the
"engineering stylist" (as opposed to an
architect, interior designer, or industrial
designer) in planning aircraft interiors
and sleeping berths of long-range aircraft
by two employees of Lockheed. One of
the very few other references to airliner
interiors that exist in architecture
magazines of the 1930s is Sune
Lindström, "Inredning AV eff trafikflyplan
Fokker FXXII för ab Aerotransport,"
Byggmästaren (May 21, 1935), p. 152.

6 For the Dreyfuss proposal to convert B-24
bombers, see "Industrial Design: Using
New Materials," *Interiors* (May 1944),
pp. 59-61, 85, and "Postwar Transport
Plane," *Architectural Forum* (July 1944),
pp. 91-96. For a military air transport
terminal as a modernist prototype for
postwar developments, see "International
Air Terminal: Air Transport Command,"
Architectural Forum (March 1945),
pp. 97-105. For thin-shell concrete
hangars during and after World War II,
see "Naval Air Stations," *Architectural
Concrete* 8, no. 2 (1942), cover and p. 8;
Anton Tedesko, "Wide-Span Hangars for
the U.S. Navy," *Civil Engineering* (Dec.
1941), pp. 697-700; and "Reinforced
Concrete Shells Span 257 Ft. Wide
Airplane Hangars," *Architectural Forum*
(Sept. 1948), pp. 138-39. The postwar
boom in commercial aviation was
predicted by Francis R. Meisch, "Archi-

modernist airports (fig. 8) and hangars (see pls. 56-57) for the new postwar
age. And a designer such as Henry Dreyfuss attempted to promote the recycling of bombers into airliners by using some of the new materials that had
been developed during the conflict, for instance, lightweight alloys and
polarizer filters for the windows (figs. 9-10).[6]

At the end of the war, established industrial designers such as Dreyfuss
and Walter Dorwin Teague began a lifelong relationship with aircraft manufacturers: Dreyfuss designed the compartmentalized, room-like interior space
(a Dreyfuss visual trademark) of Lockheed's sleek *Super Constellation* (1951),
and Teague created the open, spacious, clean-lined interior of Boeing's
Stratocruiser (1946-49; see pls. 62-64). Still others at this time, for example,
E. Gilbert Mason, did comparable work for the spaces of the Douglas entry
into the postwar commercial airline business, the DC-6 (1947). Mason continued his career in aviation interiors with Dreyfuss at Lockheed (see pls. 67-68)
and, later, ran his own aviation seating company. The postwar travel boom
intensified in the mid-1950s with the introduction of a variety of jet-powered
aircraft; these housed interiors by brand-name architects and designers, and
constituted a "golden age" of design for commercial aviation. Among those

Figs. 9-10 Henry Dreyfuss, designer.
Proposed conversion of a Consolidated B-24
bomber into an airliner, 1944; from *Architectural Forum* (July 1944).

tecture and Air Transportation," *Pencil Points* 24 (Nov. 1943), pp. 36-69, and idem, "Air Terminals for Mass Air Travel," *Pencil Points* (Nov. 1944), pp. 42-85. See also "Airplanes, Airports Make the Great Air Age," *Architectural Record* (Dec. 1944), pp. 78-83, 128; "Globe Girdling Airways," *Architect and Engineer* (March 1943), pp. 13-18; and the special issue "Airports and Hangars," *Architectural Record* (July 1943). Surprisingly, very little about the wartime impact on postwar architecture and design for commercial aviation can be found in Donald Albrecht, ed., *World War II and the American Dream* (Cambridge, Mass., 1994). Invaluable information about the prewar and wartime periods can be found in Wayne Biddle, *Barons of the Sky* (New York, 1991).

7 Society of Industrial Designers, *U.S. Industrial Design 1949-50* (New York, 1950), pp. 104-05, for Teague's design of the Boeing 377 *Stratocruiser* and pp. 108-09 for Mason's design of the DC-6. Teague's *Stratocruiser* interiors received coverage in other sources, such as *Interiors* (Jan. 1945), pp. 10, 12, and *Interiors* (July 1947), p. 20. For Dreyfuss's work on the interiors of the Lockheed *Super Constellation* (1951), see Henry Dreyfuss, *Designing for People* (New York, 1955), pp. 130-35, 170-71. For Mason's work on the later Lockheed *Electra*, see pls. 67-68, and also "Living Room Aloft for New Turboprop Planes," *Interiors* (June 1957), pp. 122-23, and "Dreyfuss Designs the Electra," *Industrial Design* (Oct. 1957), pp. 88-92. For Mason's own seat company, see "High Chairs," *Industrial Design* (Feb. 1961), pp. 52-59, esp. 58-59. Rietveld's work on the F27 and other interiors for KLM is dealt with in Ludo Van Halem, "Kleur tussen hemmel en aarde: de vliegtuiginterieurs van Gerrit Rietveld, 1955-58," *Jong Holland*, no. 2 (1955), pp. 44-61. Although Frank Jackson, "The New Air Age: BOAC and Design Policy, 1945-60," *Journal of Design History* 4, no. 3 (1991), pp. 167-85, suggests that coordinated interior design for Britain's commercial aviation industry was an American innovation, the full story of professional designers and architects working on Continental European aircraft interiors has yet to be told, as witnessed by Van Halem's recent article on Rietveld and my own discussions with architect Gustav Peichl about his design of *Caravelle* interiors for Austrian Airlines.

Fig. 11 George R. Edwards, chief designer. Vickers *Viscount* turboprop airliner, 1948-53, at Halifax International Airport (photo 1960).

active here were the famous Dutch architect Gerrit Rietveld,[7] such established designers as Teague (see pls. 75-77) and Dreyfuss (see pls. 67-68), as well as a newcomer such as Charles Butler. Butler offers an interesting case study of the difficulties involved in documenting the work of aircraft interior designers who are not among the "superstars" of architecture and design.

A student of designer Alexey Brodovitch at the Pennsylvania Museum School of Industrial Design (now the Philadelphia College of Art), Charles Butler worked for Raymond Loewy from 1944 to 1948, before becoming a partner in Butler and Zimmerman. Their first jobs were styling Northwest Airlines' model of the *Stratocruiser* (1948) and the interiors of Martin 404s for Eastern Airlines and TWA (1950). Butler made his first really independent contribution with the redesign of the Vickers *Viscount* turboprop airliner (1948-53). The standard *Viscount* interior had contoured bucket seats akin to those in a sports car, with writing tables in front of some. The interiors designed by British architect and exhibition designer James Gardener for British European Airways (BEA) softened the sculptured contours of the seats and, curiously, de-emphasized the overhead hat racks by using netting, a familiar feature in trains and in earlier planes, such as the Boeing 247 (pl. 23). When Trans-Canada Airlines (TCA) and, then, Capital Airlines ordered these new British turboprop planes in 1953-54 (fig. 11), they hired Butler to "Americanize" the interiors. Butler's solution hid the large round fuselage ribs with a flattened roof of Fiberglas covered with PVC (Duracote) and included a cantilevered aluminum hat rack padded with Duracote (fig. 12). He incorporated more modernist straight lines in the seats and designed light-colored fabrics of beige, brown, and soft green, new plastic surfaces, and folding trays that fitted into the backs of lightweight folding seats. Further modifications for Capital included built-in shelves for carry-on baggage just behind the cockpit at the airliner's entrance, colored Melmac dinnerware, and a color-scheme of watermelon, beige, and light green with drapes in what Butler termed "Mt. Vernon plaid" – appropriate furnishings for an airline based in the nation's capital (fig. 13).

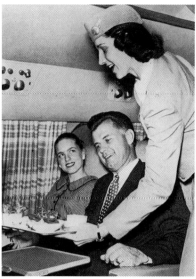

Fig. 12 Charles Butler, designer. Interior of the Trans-Canada Airlines *Viscount* airliner, 1955.

Fig. 13 Charles Butler, designer. Interior of Capital Airlines *Viscount*, showing plaid curtains and Melmac tableware, 1955; from *Monthly News Bulletin of the American Cyanamid Company* (Sept. 1955).

The *Viscount* was a hit in North America. Its quiet Rolls Royce *Dart* turboprop powerplants gave it a cruising speed of 320 to 350 miles per hour, and the 40 to 49 passengers aboard had excellent views through the large, distinctively oval windows. The success of this British-made plane led Lockheed, prompted by American and Eastern Airlines, to develop the turboprop *Electra* (1957; see pls. 67-68) on an accelerated 39-month production schedule so that these two airlines would again be competitive with Capital.[8] The success of the *Viscount* brought Butler many other aviation-related projects, including work on the interiors of Continental's *Viscounts* in the late 1950s, and this, in turn, led to numerous design commissions for that airline in the jet era of the 1960s. Because of Butler's achievements in designing interiors for the *Viscount,* much of his firm's work was with British aeronautical companies as the design consultant for interiors of airliners such as TCA's Vickers *Vanguard*, Vickers VC-10, British Aircraft's BAC-111, Hawker-Siddeley's *Trident*, and the British Aerospace *Concorde*, most from the early to late 1960s (see fig. 14). A number of these designs were produced by Butler's London office – Charles Butler Associates Design for Industry – in conjunction with his New York headquarters. Butler received numerous commissions for executive jet interiors throughout the 1960s as well as for airline corporate design, particularly for Canadian Pacific Airlines in the early 1960s and, in 1970, for TWA's standard ticket counters, its updated, twin-globes logo (a modification

8 "Enter the Viscount," *Industrial Design* (Aug. 1955), pp. 27-33. I am indebted to Robert J. Price, the former Vice President of Design for Charles Butler Associates, for a summary of the firm's history, access to photographic material, and a variety of references to magazine articles and offprints of such: see George L. Christian, "Design Firm Gives Planes New Look," *Aviation Week* (April 12, 1954), n. pag.; "How TCA Revamped the *Viscount,*" *Aviation Age* (April 1955), n. pag.; "First Look Inside Capital's *Viscounts,*" *Aviation Week* (Nov. 8, 1954), p. 99; and "Melmac is High Fashion," *Monthly News Bulletin of the American Cyanamid Company* (Sept. 1955), pp. 10-12.

Fig. 14 Seated, left to right, Robert Peach, president of Mohawk Airlines, with Charles Butler, in Butler-designed seats for the British Aircraft Company BAC-111, c. 1964-65.

Figs. 15-16 Harley Earl, designer, with Dorothy Draper, decorator. Interior and lounge of the Convair 880, 1960.

Fig. 17 J. A. Graves, designer. Interior of the Canadian Pacific Airlines variant of a DC-8, here styled by Charles Butler, 1960.

9 Information about Butler's career came from former associates in his office, namely Arque Dickerson, Rod Fyfield, and especially Robert J. Price (see note 8). Butler's corporate jet interiors have been published in Edward Carpenter, "Baby Jets for Business," *Industrial Design* (July 1962), pp. 24-33, esp. 27, 29-31. See also Barbara Allen, "Mess Halls in the Air," *Industrial Design* (May 1968), pp. 28-33. For Butler's design philosophy in relation to that of Dreyfuss, Teague, and Loewy, see George Christian, "Comfort in Airline Cabin Design Makes Dollar Sense," *Aviation Week* (May 14, 1956), n. pag. See also "Cooperation for Comfort: Charles Butler Associates Design for Industry," *Flight* (Jan. 27, 1961), pp. 111-12. Articles by Charles Butler include "The CPA Jet Empress," *Jet Age Airlanes* (June 1961), pp. 15-16, and "What's Wrong with Aircraft Interiors," *Airlift* (April 1959), n. pag. Butler's concept for TWA lasted, with minor alterations, through the 1970s and 1980s, up to the airline's complete redesign in 1995 using concepts provided by the St. Louis advertising agency of D'Arcy, Masius, Benton & Bowles. See *Airways* (Jan./ Feb. 1996), p. 9.

Fig. 18 Walter Dorwin Teague Associates, designers. Wide-body styled interior of an Argentine Airlines Boeing 737, 1968-69 (photo Oct. 18, 1974).

Fig. 19 Interior of an Ilyushin IL-62 showing Soviet adaptation of the wide-body look, 1971-72 (photo Aug. 2, 1972).

of Raymond Loewy's design from the early 1960s), and even the remodeling of Eero Saarinen's Trans World Airlines Terminal at Kennedy Airport. After his death, Butler's office closed in December 1975; his designers were scattered across the country, and information about the firm was equally dispersed, making it rather difficult to reconstruct his active practice.[9]

As American carriers entered the jet age from the mid-1950s to the early 1960s, the major American manufacturers – among them, Boeing, Convair, and Douglas – all strove to capture the market for these new high-speed machines. Convair hired General Motors stylist Harley Earl, already a design stylist for Eastern Airlines, to create the interiors of their Convair 880 (figs. 15-16). His overhead interior racks had forms reminiscent of the stylized dashboards of automobiles from the 1950s. The Douglas team, led by designer J. A. Graves, with such staff designers as Chas. Willits and Harvey Bjornlie, all under the supervision of chief engineer E. F. Burton, planned the DC-8 interiors to feature seats that had all passenger controls for ventilation and light conveniently built in, and not overhead and difficult to reach as in other airliners (fig. 17; cf. fig. 15). Few of these historical details have ever been known outside of selected aviation circles. Although the work of Walter Dorwin Teague and his successors at Teague Associates on Boeing airliners from 1945 to the present has long been recognized within the industry, the public knows very little about it, automatically attributing the design of aircraft interiors to the manufacturer or the respective airline, not to a designer. Long-time employees of the Teague office, such as Frank Del Guidice, sometimes rate a mention in aviation histories, occasional articles, or newspaper obituaries.[10] Yet, because of Boeing's continued success with airliners since the introduction of the 707 in the mid-1950s, Teague and his office, more than designers for Convair and Douglas, have shaped our notions of aircraft interiors, with imitations seen around the world. A case in point is the so-called "wide-body look" of sculptured, spaceship-like ceilings, enclosed overhead storage units, and molded walls, which Teague introduced in the 747 "jumbo jet" (1968-69) and which was subsequently applied to smaller, standard size 727 and 737 interiors (fig. 18). This, in turn, influenced Soviet manufacturers to incorporate comparable design features in their jetliners (fig. 19), and even seems to have had an impact on Douglas's designs of the DC-10 and on the work of Sundberg-Ferar in styling the Lockheed L-1011 (1970; see pls. 107-09).[11] The latest Teague designs for Boeing testify to the manufacturer's enduring satisfaction with their work (see pls. 161-67).

Fig. 20 Uwe Schneider, chief of industrial design, Daimler-Benz Aerospace Airbus. Interior of the A310 mockup, 1982.

Boeing's and Teague's major competitor is the industrial design team at Daimler-Benz Aerospace Airbus, headed by Uwe Schneider. A veteran designer, responsible for the interior of the somewhat unorthodox VFW-614 commuter jet (1962-71) and of BMW's highly popular 700 series autos in the early to mid-1970s, Schneider became part of Deutsche Airbus (now Daimler-Benz Aerospace Airbus) in the early 1970s. He worked on the mid-1970s design of the A300 and on the A310 of the late 1970s and early 1980s. Originally, Airbus had developed the interiors of the A300 by having their German design team at Deutsche Airbus in Munich work with Eliot Noyes and Associates, Raymond Loewy's office, and David Ellis, but in the end many of the suggestions from these American designers were not implemented. In a way comparable to Charles Butler's work on the *Viscount*, Airbus was initially worried about entering the Boeing-dominated U.S. market; they wanted a designer to "Americanize" their aircraft before soliciting sales from U.S. carriers. In a way that typifies their non-conformist approach to making airplanes, Airbus invited several prominent industrial designers to submit proposals and, eventually, for the interior of the A300B they hired the small New Jersey-based design firm of Toshihiko Sakow, whose work with aircraft was untested. Sakow's design featured enhanced lighting to create illusions of greater space, and modified overhead storage bins with doors that opened up and back into the storage areas.[12] Aspects of this interior were used in Eastern Airlines' A300B aircraft, but the A300 design in service today is the work of Schneider and his team. They have also designed the cabin of the A310 (1978; in service 1983) with comparable interiors that feature gently curved ceilings and walls divided into bays that visually break up the longitudinal tube into compartments below (fig. 20), a trademark of all later Airbus interiors (see pls. 142-44).

Although it is relatively easy to document Teague's work for Boeing and the work of the Airbus interior design team because both are actively in busi-

10 Frank Del Guidice headed Teague's work for Boeing. See his obituary in *The New York Times* (Oct. 24, 1993). See also Allen (note 9), p. 33; "How a Big Design Office Works: Walter Dorwin Teague Associates," *Industrial Design* (1956), esp. p. 36; and "Design for Air Travel," *Industrial Design* (Oct. 1970), pp. 26-49, esp. p. 41, where Del Guidice is quoted on the interiors of the 747. Other Teague designers since then are the recently retired Senior Aircraft Designer Paul Phillips, their current Design Director Jim Bergmann, and Vice Presidents Robert P. Welsh and Kenneth J. Dowd. For the extraordinary, full-scale mockup that Teague did for the Boeing 707 in a New York loft building, see "Million-Dollar Modelmaking," *Industrial Design* (Aug. 1956), pp. 64-67. Regarding records on the interiors of other American jetliners from the mid to late 1950s: Consolidated Vultee/Convair materials are in the San Diego Aerospace Museum, and the Detroit industrial design firm of Ford and Earl (successors to Harley Earl) informed me that they gave photographs and slides of their Convair 880 interiors in 1991 to the Henry Ford Museum. Throughout the course of research on this topic, the Douglas archives remained inaccessible to me, though Chas. Willits did inform me about the DC-8 interiors. See "How Designers Serve Aviation," *Industrial Design* (Oct. 1957), pp. 86-87, on the role of Harley Earl at Convair and on Douglas's own design team. Dorothy Draper's study for the lounge of a Convair 880 is in the Cooper Hewitt Museum (1977-106-1) and serves as the basis for my attribution of fig. 16. See also Carleton Varney, *The Draper Touch: The High Life and High Style of Dorothy Draper* (New York, 1988), pp. 262-63.

11 Scott Kelly, "MoTown's Transit Paradox," *Industrial Design* (May 1968), pp. 22-27.

12 "Earning Their Wings," *Industrial Design* (Jan./Feb. 1974), pp. 34-37.

13 "The Flying Billboards: Western Pacific Airlines Takes Advertising to a New High," *Airways* (Jan./Feb. 1996), pp. 30-34. The Bel Geddes papers in the Harry Ransom Humanities Research Center of the University of Texas at Austin contain a proposal to Juan Trippe of Pan American (April 1, 1935) that

Fig. 21 InnoVision, designers, with Tramco, design executors. Western Pacific Airlines Boeing 737-300, 1995, logo jet for Stardust Las Vegas Resort and Casino, showing Aki the Showgirl on the tail.

Fig. 22 InnoVision, designers, with Tramco, design executors. Western Pacific Airlines Boeing 737-300, 1995, logo jet for *The Simpsons*, showing characters from the popular Fox Television program.

outlines Bel Geddes's ideas for corporate imagery for that airline while he executed the *China Clipper* interiors for them in 1934-35. It is not known whether these proposals were accepted, and the lack of further documents about them in the archive suggests that they were not implemented. Zay Smith's work for United is documented in an unpublished letter of Dec. 22, 1986, that he sent to Howard Lovering, Executive Director of the Museum of Flight, Seattle, the original of which is in the archives of that museum. Also, see Smith's obituary in the *Chicago Tribune* (May 2, 1995). The firm of Nowland and Schladermundt may also have done a comparable, large-scale image redesign for Chicago and Southern Airlines just after World War II, but this requires further research that may not be possible, since neither the airline (absorbed by Delta in 1953) nor the design firm still exists. See Harold Van Doren, *Industrial Design* (New York, 1954), p. 39. For Otl Aicher's work and that of his followers for Lufthansa, see *Ulm Design: The Morality of Objects* (Cambridge, Mass., 1991), pp. 146-47, 270, and "Dinnerware in Flight," *Industrial Design* (Jan. 1965), pp. 60-63. For Girard's work for Braniff, see "New BI Design Program," *Industrial Design* (Jan. 1966), pp. 12, 15, and "Out-Maneuvering the Plain Plane," *Interiors* (Feb. 1966), pp. 100-05.

ness, research on other important designers, such as Charles Butler, is difficult, especially when office records have been dispersed. This difficulty is compounded by the inaccessibility of the corporate archives of some leading aircraft manufacturers in America and Britain as a result of mergers, corporate restructuring, or changes in the type of product they create (for example, from commercial to military aircraft). Study of the work of designers who shape airline corporate identity is similarly affected by this inaccessibility.

Since its 1967 design for Alitalia Airlines, Landor Associates of San Francisco has been recognized as a leader in the field of airline corporate identity, particularly after its recent work for British Airways (see Rau, pp. 237-38, and pls. 151-54). The BA job ranged over several thousand items on a variety of scales, from logo and stationery design to a redesign of the *Concorde* interiors that was undertaken slightly earlier than Air France's 1993-94 revamp of their *Concorde* interior by the noted interior designer Andreé Putman. A marked trend in airline corporate imagery of the 1990s has been to use the planes for advertising, an idea that began with Southwest Airlines' Shamu-Sea World plane and continued with planes honoring states in Southwest's market area (see pls. 133-34). This idea has found dramatic expression, in 1995-96, with Western Pacific's "logo jets." These are, essentially, flying billboards that advertise a variety of things, such as the popular Fox Television show *The Simpsons*, the Broadmoor Hotel in Colorado Springs, and the Stardust Casino in Las Vegas, thereby generating additional revenue for the carrier and publicity for both the advertiser and the airline (figs. 21-22). Researchers can cite very early examples of airline advertising and corporate consciousness, such as Berlin architect Otto Firle's 1918 design of the Lufthansa crane (see pl. 2), Bel Geddes's 1935 proposal to Pan American (presumably not accepted) for revitalizing their logo, ticket offices, and airway stations, or architect Zay Smith's 1937-40 redesign of the logo, aircraft markings, and uniforms and interiors of United Airlines' Boeing 247D (see pls. 22-23) and DC-3 (see fig. 2). Most design buffs and historians, however, believe that the comprehensive shaping of airlines' corporate identity dates back to the early to mid-1960s, to the work done by Otl Aicher at Lufthansa and by Alexander Girard at Braniff (see pls. 86-90), followed by that done by the Dreyfuss firm for American Airlines in the late 1960s and early 1970s.[13] Another all-encompassing identity project to be carried out at this time was, in fact, the image program devised by Charles Butler for Canadian Pacific Airlines in 1960-61, which included aircraft interiors, dinnerware, logos, and uniforms. And there are even earlier documented efforts to achieve complete corporate redesign, such as those undertaken by Raymond Loewy for United, or by Edward Larrabee Barnes and Charles Forberg for Pan American – programs that were implemented because in the mid-1950s these carriers were about to enter the new era of the jet age.

Pan American Airways used Barnes's services, in 1955, to shape a new corporate image that would include the Boeing 707 and Douglas DC-8 jet transports they had ordered. Pan American wanted an image that they could use for a long time (what they referred to as "maintainability"), and they wanted that image first applied to existing ticket offices and aircraft and then expanded to embrace all aspects of their corporate identity as the new jets were delivered. Barnes, who had been one of the Dreyfuss staff working on Consolidated Vultee aircraft towards the close of World War II, followed his graduation from Harvard by opening his own practice in New York in 1948. Forberg, also trained as an architect at Harvard and, for a time, a teacher of design at Chicago's Institute of Design, joined Barnes in 1955 just after the latter had received the Pan American commission. Together, Barnes and Forberg retained Pan American's globe from its previous logo, but enlarged and gridded it (without the traditional Pan American wing) in a lighter blue color (see pl. 81). They chose a chiseled typeface and also created the abbreviated "Pan Am" in response to the popular public nickname given to the airline. In addition, they modified Teague's layout of the Boeing 707, selecting the seats and introducing the light blue color into the aircraft's ceiling and, in consultation with the famous textile designer Jack Lenor Larsen, the seat fabric. Although Pan American did not accept some of Barnes and Forberg's ideas (including the colorful ground crew uniforms and the molded plastic flight bags), the famous logo and color schemes remained design trademarks of that carrier until competition resulting from deregulation of the airlines in 1978 and other factors eventually forced it into bankruptcy in 1991-92.[14]

While Pan Am was searching for a new look in the jet age, United engaged Raymond Loewy in 1954 to reshape its corporate image and, as of 1955, to assist in selecting and designing their forthcoming jet equipment. Loewy started on existing DC-6B and DC-7 aircraft, and he then moved to create standard ticket offices, flexible-track interior seating arrangements for the airline's new DC-8 jets (1959), serving trays and table settings, aircraft livery – indeed, all corporate imagery, even the flight crew and stewardess uniforms (fig. 23). As Barnes and Forberg had introduced lighter blue hues to Pan Am's livery, so Loewy chose pale blues mixed with metallic gold highlights for United's interiors, a matching pale blue for the uniforms, and a patriotic red, white, and light blue for the aircraft exteriors (see pl. 69). TWA took notice of Loewy's successful work for United and they, too, hired him in 1960 to reshape their corporate design as they planned their jet-age terminal at Idlewild Airport (now John F. Kennedy International; see pls. 84-85).[15]

That airlines and aircraft manufacturers hire industrial designers, architects, and corporate design specialists has thus become an increasingly established fact of commercial aviation since the end of World War II. The airlines need the services of these design specialists as much as they do their frequent flyer programs, computer reservations systems, or group sales agents, if they are to remain up-to-date in what is a very competitive, multibillion-dollar business. And the designers, in turn, prove that there is more to architecture and design for commercial aviation than airport terminals and airplane hangars. All are part of an integrated attempt to project the image of efficient modernity to potential customers. Indeed, this obsession with what is most modern is both a strength and a weakness, since it often causes the industry

14 "Pan American Expresses a New Personality for a New Kind of Travel," *Industrial Design* (March 1959), pp. 30-41. The demise of Pan American is discussed in terms of deregulation in Barbara Sturken Peterson and James Glab, *Rapid Descent: Deregulation and the Shakeout in the Airlines* (New York, 1994).

15 "Loewy Launches Design Program for United Airlines," *Industrial Design* (April 1956), p. 18, and "Transportation by Air," *Industrial Design* (Dec. 1959), p. 111, for Loewy's tray design for United. See Raymond Loewy, "DC-8 Jet Mainliner: United Air Lines Case Study," unpublished paper of Oct. 2, 1961, presented to the Council of Industrial Design (original in the Loewy Archives, The Library of Congress).

Fig. 23 Raymond Loewy, designer. United Airlines flight crew, with uniforms and corporate imagery by Loewy, in front of a new DC-8 (photo Oct. 1959).

to ignore or discard things that are not the latest in design or technology. Hence, it is difficult to reconstruct precisely the story behind the works of some of these aircraft and airline design consultants from what the industry must perceive as the ancient history of the 1940s and 1950s. This disregard for history and this overemphasis on modernity are especially apparent if one considers the number of airports and aircraft facilities that have been demolished or extensively altered in past years. Although efforts have recently been made to restore sensitively, and to expand, Saarinen's famed Dulles International Airport and to restore the historic terminal of Washington National Airport from the early 1940s (see Brodherson, figs. 16-17), these same years have also witnessed the demolition of the original United Airlines headquarters of 1938 by Albert Kahn at Chicago's Midway Airport; TWA's resistance to making their Saarinen-designed building at Kennedy Airport a landmark; and continued plans to demolish potential landmarks of aviation history, from Myron Goldsmith's famous hangar of 1958 at San Francisco International (see pls. 94-95) to the 1928-29 terminal of Hamburg's airport — the oldest functioning airport terminal in the world (see pl. 18 and Voigt, fig. 13). In an industry that often views its aircraft and their interiors, its logos, and other design features as ephemeral, it is no wonder that the same attitude applies to buildings that serve air transport. It is our hope that the essays that follow will make us all more aware of the importance of commercial aviation to our designed environment and, in turn, make those whose livelihood is commercial aviation as sensitive to their heritage as they are to the needs of the present and future.

Wolfgang Voigt

From the Hippodrome to the Aerodrome, from the Air Station to the Terminal: European Airports, 1909–1945

We know quite well how to build a railway station or a seaport, but we're still feeling our way with the airport.

A. B. Duval, 1929[1]

I wish to express my thanks to Neil Bingham of the R.I.B.A., Werner Bittner and Ilse Ludewig from the Lufthansa Archives, Koos Bosma, Pergiacomo Bucciarelli, Jean-Louis Cohen, Hartmut Frank, John King, and John Zukowsky.

1   A. B. Duval, "Les Ports aériens," *Illustration* (Aug. 17, 1929), p. 155.
2   An overview of the issue is offered in Wood Alexander Lockhart, "Airport Development and Design: A New Architectural Problem" (Ph.D. diss., Northwestern University, 1972).
3   For the history of ideas in aviation, see Wolfgang Behringer and Constance Ott-Koptschalijski, *Der Traum vom Fliegen: Zwischen Mythos und Technik* (Frankfurt am Main, 1991); on Lana di Terzi, see pp. 280-82.
4   Le Corbusier, *Aircraft* (London and New York, 1935), p. 7.

When civil air traffic began in Europe in spring 1919, following the end of World War I, there were already hundreds of airfields, but no consensus as to what an airport should look like, no shared image of the form and architecture suitable to an airport.[2] The airplanes themselves and the amount of air traffic were changing rapidly, and as a result, the parameters for the ground stations of this new type of transportation changed constantly as well. It took a decade before a functional typology was really developed, and there were airports throughout Europe that had to be completely rebuilt twice within fifteen years because the old installations had become obsolete at an alarming rate.

For a long time, there was no agreement even on what to call this "thing." The term *airport* and its synonyms in other languages (*aéroport, aeroporto, aeropuerto, Flughafen, luchthaven*, etc.) became generally established only in the 1930s after a period in which several expressions had existed side by side (*aerodrome, airdrome, airport*; French: *port aérien, port avion*). French had been the lingua franca of flight ever since the first manned balloon ascent by the Montgolfier brothers in 1783, and it was to remain so until World War I. The verbal confusion, with words generally borrowed from French, reveals the cultural and technical models that were the force behind the evolution of flight. Today, some of the vocabulary still comes from the sport of racing, some from agriculture, some from the language of railways; most of it, however, is derived from the iconology of sailing, which had shaped the idea of manned flight as early as the seventeenth century, when a writer such as Francesco Lana di Terzi dreamed up imaginary *airships*, in which bold *aeronauts* sailed across the *sea of air*.[3]

The year 1909 was crucial for aviation in Europe. Louis Blériot's successful crossing of the English Channel in a homemade monoplane on July 25 marked the breakthrough of motor-driven, heavier-than-air flight, which now finally passed the testing phase. The immense enthusiasm for flight spread far beyond the borders of France. It caught up architects, too, occasionally unleashing false hopes. Architect Auguste Perret, as reported by Le Corbusier, his colleague in those days, stormed into his studio waving a newspaper in his hand and shouting: "Blériot has crossed the Channel! Wars are finished: no more wars are possible! There are no longer any frontiers!"[4]

Air meetings, first organized this same year, played a major role in the future of flying by providing an effective stage for the pioneers of flight, who were quickly becoming public stars. These pioneers were usually a combination in one person of builder, test pilot, and often even stunt flier. Setting the style for future meetings were the events held at the first French *port avion* in Juvisy near Paris, built in 1908; especially influential, however, was the *Grande Semaine de l'aviation de la Champagne* organized by French businessmen in the last week of August 1909, near the city of Reims. A ten-kilometer-long, quadrilateral circuit course was pegged out on an open field, using pyramid-shaped wooden pylons. On the short side of the quadrilateral a row of hangars was erected with workshops and three comfortable stands, on which the Parisian high society gathered (fig. 1). The *Grande Semaine* was

Fig. 1 Air meeting near Reims, France, 1909, showing observation stands with hangars in the background; from *Livre d'or de la conquête de l'air* (1909).

a social event of the first order, attracting to Reims not only the president of the French Republic, but also foreign guests, such as British Chancellor of the Exchequer David Lloyd George and former President Theodore Roosevelt.[5] The festival's managing corporation built its own railway line to provide transportation for spectators numbering in the hundreds of thousands.

Only a few weeks separated the event in Reims from a similar air show at Brescia in northern Italy, which the writer Franz Kafka attended as a press observer,[6] and from a flying exhibition by two pioneers, the American Orville Wright and the Frenchman Hubert Latham, held simultaneously at Tempelhof field in Berlin. An even more important event, however, was the *Internationale Flugwoche*, which opened in October 1909 at Johannisthal near Berlin, on the capital city's first airfield outfitted by a private company specifically for this purpose.[7] The meetings of those years resembled an international traveling circus, for the trophies and prize money offered everywhere caused aviation pioneers to make frequent appearances, with which they financed the improvement of their machines.

In terms of urban development, the facilities were essentially the same in Juvisy, Reims, Brescia, and Johannisthal; these were grassy places with simple, lightweight buildings erected on the periphery: wide viewing stands, along with hangars placed some distance away, in unpretentious order and without a precise plan. The architectural language was rooted in the world of sports and racing, with airplane hangars – modest wooden buildings – replacing the racing stables. The terms *aerodrome* and *airdrome*, used early on in the history of airports, owe their creation to their relationship with *hippodrome* and its more recent variant, *autodrome* (coined about 1900).

The air shows soon left behind traces in visionary projects by architects from various countries, who – apparently without being in contact with each other – took up the theme of flight, each in his own manner. The Frenchman Eugène Hénard started things off in 1910 with his rather fanciful design of a highly modern "street of the future" (fig. 2).[8] Like many of his contemporaries, Hénard dreamed of an airplane for everyone, and he graced the roof of his new, six-story, metropolitan apartment house with a *terrasse*

5 On the meeting at Reims, see Robert Wohl, *A Passion for Wings: Aviation and the Western Imagination, 1908-1918* (New Haven and London, 1994), pp. 100-10; in addition, see Owen S. Lieberg, *Les Premiers Hommes-oiseaux: La Grande Semaine de Reims* (Paris, 1975).

6 On Kafka and the meeting at Brescia, see Wohl (note 5), pp. 111-14; in addition, see Felix Philipp Ingold, *Literatur und Aviatik: Europäische Flugdichtung, 1909-1927* (Basel and Stuttgart, 1978), pp. 28-29.

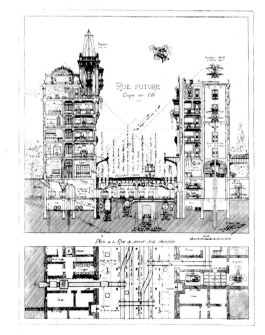

Fig. 2 Eugène Hénard, architect. Sectional view and plan of the "street of the future," 1910, with rooftop platform for airplanes; from *L'Architecture* (1910).

7 On the air meetings at Tempelhof and Johannisthal, see Werner Schwipps, *Riesenzigarren und fliegende Kisten: Bilder aus der Frühzeit der Luftfahrt in Berlin* (Berlin, 1984); in addition, see Michael Hundertmark, "Flugplatz Johannisthal: Wiege der deutschen Luftfahrt," in Museum für Verkehr und Technik, *Hundert Jahre deutsche Luftfahrt: Lilienthal und seine Erben* (Berlin, 1991), pp. 21-38. For the planning history of Johannisthal, see Harald Bodenschatz and Jans-Joachim Engstfeld, "Berlin Johannisthal/Adlershof," *Bauwelt* 84 (1994), pp. 2646-55.

8 Eugène Hénard, "Les Villes de l'avenir," *L'Architecture* (1910), suppl. no. 46. See also Alain Guiheux, "Eugène Hénard et Tony Garnier: Le Règne de la circulation," in Jean Dethier and Alain Guiheux, eds., *La Ville, art et architecture en Europe, 1870-1993* (Paris, 1994), pp. 153-54.

9 Hendrik Christian Andersen and Ernest M. Hébrard, *Creation of a World Centre of Communication* (Rome, 1913).

10 See David van Zanten, "Walter Burley Griffin's Design for Canberra, the Capital of Australia," in John Zukowsky, ed., *Chicago Architecture, 1872-1922: Birth of a Metropolis* (Munich and Chicago, 1987), pp. 319-43; for Agache's design, see pp. 321, 332-33. On Agache, see Catherine Bruant, "Louis Bonnier, Donat-Alfred Agache, Marcel Auburtin," in Dethier and Guiheux (note 8), p. 158.

11 See the figure in Dethier and Guiheux (note 8), p. 154.

12 Tony Garnier, *Une Cité industrielle: Etude pour la construction des villes* (Paris, [1917]).

d'atterissage, no larger than a room, which was supposed to make it possible for small flying machines to take off and land. After landing, the machines would be brought by elevator to a subterranean garage, which extended behind the building out into the garden zone, and which also housed automobiles.

The earliest visions of a municipal airfield were created by two of Hénard's compatriots, the Beaux-Arts urban designers Donat-Alfred Agache and Ernest Hébrard. In 1912 Agache received third prize in the international competition for a new federal capital of Australia – the present-day Canberra. In the same year Hébrard designed the International World Centre with the Danish sculptor Hendrik C. Andersen. This metropolis of the future with its pacifist imprint was to be located near Rome and to be dedicated to the peaceful cooperation of nations.[9] An airfield appears in both designs in the green periphery outside the blocks comprising the inner city. As an integral part of the urban infrastructure, the airfield was not treated any differently from the municipal exhibition park or the railway station. In Agache's work it takes the shape of a traditional architectural space with monumental Beaux-Arts forms, dominated by a symmetrical group of three domed administrative buildings, which could just as easily belong to a school or a court of law (fig. 3).[10] The rest of the facilities follow the scheme of the buildings at the Reims meeting, with the addition of three airship halls. The rectangular form of the rural airfield, however, is reduced to the dimensions of a parade ground: such a cramped space alone would have made the installation unusable, but this does not diminish Agache's accomplishment, for he succeeded in presenting aviation as a new theme for urban development. His colleague, Hébrard, already knew how to avoid this shortcoming, by concentrating the buildings on one side of his hexagonal *port aviation*.

A few years later, Tony Garnier, city architect of Lyon, also responded to the new challenge. His social utopia, an idealized design of a modern industrial city, had already been graced with an automobile raceway in its earliest, 1901-04 version.[11] In the version developed during World War I, published in Garnier's famous book *Une Cité industrielle* (1917), we find this space expanded. Now, adjacent to a test track for automobiles, lies a half-mile-long trapezoidal airfield with hangars for airplanes and airships (*dirigeables*) at either end, the whole site arranged logically on the edge of the industrial zone.[12] Part of the space occupied by large railway workshops in the first version has now been given over to an airplane factory. There are no viewing stands and no bothersome peripheral structures, with the exception of small

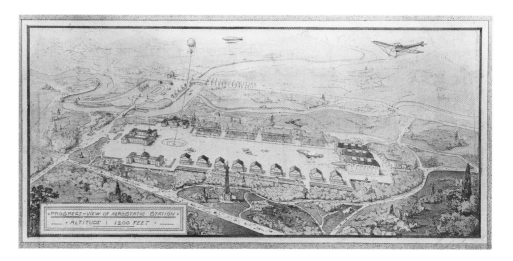

Fig. 3 Donat-Alfred Agache, architect. Bird's-eye view of a proposed airfield, part of a competitive design for the new capital of Australia, Canberra, 1912.

Fig. 4 Erich Mendelsohn, architect. Hangar with workshops for airships and airplanes, 1914; from *Erich Mendelsohn: Das Gesamtschaffen des Architekten – Skizzen, Entwürfe, Bauten* (Berlin, 1930).

hangars and airship halls, which are placed so that the approach and take-off zones remain free of buildings. Garnier's project was, like Hébrard's, aeronautically conceived and even realistically sized. In keeping with the theme of his book, however, it reflected his view of aviation as a promising means of transportation, within the overall framework of the city, rather than as a vehicle of public spectacle.

Meanwhile, in Germany a young architect by the name of Erich Mendelsohn was occupied with granting the new building type an up-to-date form using the latest technology. Among his sketches from 1914 are some versions of a massive reinforced concrete building that was to be 1,300 to 1,600 feet long, which he later published under the name *Aerodrome* (fig. 4).[13] The tall central section was to provide space for six airships, while slightly curved wreaths of low airplane hangars with workshops occupied both long sides. The dynamically flowing form anticipates Mendelsohn's organically expressive architecture, especially as it was realized after the war in his Einstein tower near Berlin. Flight remained a theme in Mendelsohn's later work, even though he himself never received a commission in this field. As we shall see, some of his employees subsequently did receive such commissions.

Closely related in spirit to Hénard's and Mendelsohn's designs are the contemporaneous metropolitan and skyscraper visions created by the Milanese architect Antonio Sant'Elia. In 1914 his revolutionary *Stazione Aerplani Treni* illustrated his "Manifesto of Futuristic Architecture." Sant'Elia's transportation junction begins with a metropolitan railway station as its foundation, thus linking the nineteenth-century means of transit with the airplane, the Futurists' prized symbol of the new age.[14] Rising from railway platforms, elevators move passengers to the roof area of an axially symmetrical, terraced structure with protruding twin towers, under which the tracks and roads for autos disappear into tunnels. A rooftop terrace with low hangars on the sides serves as the take-off and landing platform for airplanes. Sant'Elia assigns them a status they had not yet acquired, for in his vision they are a normal means of transportation, just like the automobile and the train.

Passenger flights already existed at this time in Germany – not with airplanes, however, but with Zeppelin airships. From 1910 to the outbreak of the war, regular flights with up to twenty-four passengers started from Graf Zeppelin's airship base in Friedrichshafen on Lake Constance, and returned to the point of departure, after stopovers in Düsseldorf, Hamburg, Berlin, and other places.[15] These flights, though, cannot be viewed as air traffic in the current sense, since they were really nothing but round-trip excursions for airship enthusiasts. The airplane as a means of transportation was still a dream for the future. The cruel reality was to be four years of war from 1914 on, to which the volunteer infantryman Sant'Elia himself fell victim.

World War I made a reality of the "War in the Air" that the British writer H. G. Wells had depicted in his eponymous novel of 1908, with all its horrors of cities attacked from the air.[16] At the meeting at Reims, military observers from various countries had already sat in the stands and contemplated the military viability of the newfangled flying apparatuses.[17] Now, each of the

13 On the original sketches this is still designated "Aeroplan Werkstatt und Hangars"; see *Erich Mendelsohn: Das Gesamtschaffen des Architekten – Skizzen, Entwürfe, Bauten* (Berlin, 1930), p. 56; see also Sigrid Achenbach, *Erich Mendelsohn, 1887-1953: Ideen, Bauten, Projekte*, exh. cat., Kunstbibliothek Berlin (Berlin, 1987), pp. 41-42.

14 Vittorio Magnago Lampugnani, ed., *Antonio Sant'Elia: Gezeichnete Architektur* (Munich, 1992), pp. 47, 180-82.

15 Kenneth Hudson, *Air Travel: A Social History* (Bath, 1972), p. 62.

16 H. G. Wells, *The War in the Air* (London, 1908); on the novel, see Wohl (note 5), pp. 70-76.

17 Wohl (note 5), p. 101.

18 Figures according to Behringer and Ott-Koptschalijski (note 3), p. 419.

19 Georg Steinmetz, *Grundlagen für das Bauen in Stadt und Land*, vol. 3 (Munich, 1922), pp. 250-60.

20 A picture of Peter Behrens's airplane hall for the *Waggonfabrik* in Hanover appears in Walter Müller-Wulckow, *Deutsche Baukunst der Gegenwart: Bauten der Arbeit und des Verkehrs* (Königstein im Taunus and Leipzig, 1929), p. 80.

21 See AEG Aktiengesellschaft, "Die AEG-Fabriken Hennigsdorf," in *Informationen aus der AEG Geschichte 3/91* (Frankfurt am Main, 1991), pp. 6-8.

22 On the military airfields of World War I, see Lockhart (note 2), p. 13.

23 First cited in P. Nutt, *The Future of Aviation* (1919); quoted here from John Myerscough, "Airport Provision in the Inter-War Years," *Journal of Contemporary History* 20 (1985), p. 41.

24 For the beginnings in Germany, see Günther Ott, "Pioniere der Verkehrsluftfahrt: Deutscher Luftverkehr 1919-1945," in Museum für Verkehr und Technik (note 7), pp. 61-79. On the first air route between Berlin and Weimar, see also Helmut Conin, *Gelandet in Berlin: Zur Geschichte der Berliner Flughäfen* (Cologne, 1974), p. 55.

warring parties had its own air fleet, which grew to gigantic proportions; in France, for example, the number of military aircraft swelled from 138 in 1914 to 6,870 by the end of the war.[18]

By 1910 some manufacturers had already moved from the sheds and garages of the first hobby builders to the hangars of those airfields where meetings took place. These sites soon functioned, in fact, as a type of fair at which the airplanes were not only presented, but were also sold. Johannisthal near Berlin offers a German, Brooklands Aerodrome an English, example of this development. Thus, the hangars at Johannisthal, which had been rented to foreign fliers at the first aviation week in 1909, a short while later housed four domestic airplane makers, among them Edmund Rumpler, the creator of the most famous German airplane of the prewar period, the Rumpler *Taube*.

Airplane works were being created everywhere in Germany during the war years, and for the first time architects associated with the Modern Movement and with the Deutscher Werkbund were involved. Georg Steinmetz designed a factory with adjoining workers' quarters in East Prussia.[19] Peter Behrens, through whose studio such architects as Mies van der Rohe, Walter Gropius, and Le Corbusier had passed, built an airplane works in Hanover in 1915[20] and a second in Hennigsdorf near Berlin for AEG (Allegemeine Electrizitäts-Gesellschaft), which had previously concentrated on the production of electrical appliances and equipment. Behrens had been the artistic consultant for AEG since 1907. The four-aisled hall in Hennigsdorf (fig. 5), with its steel skeleton and brick covering, differed from his neighboring locomotive factory only in its extremely wide folding doors, necessary to accommodate planes whose width usually exceeded their length.[21]

It was no longer the meetings, but the provisional airfields behind the war fronts that formed the image of the airfield—grassy areas of at least 500 yards in diameter, which ideally would be either round or elliptical, with a slight downward incline from the center to the outer edge. This arrangement allowed the flier to take off even against the wind. On the edge of the field, barracks and light hangars were set up, often consisting of nothing more than large tents. The first standardized hangars on the Allied side were prefabricated wooden buildings that could be assembled quickly.[22]

"Pre-war aviation was a sport; during the war it was a military weapon; after the war it will be one of the transport industries."[23] This prediction from 1918 by the Frenchman d'Aubigny was soon to be fulfilled. But the "industrial" mass air traffic of our time was still a long way off and the beginnings were quite modest. On February 6, 1919, an airplane of the Deutsche Luft-Reederei flew from Berlin's Johannisthal airfield to Weimar with two pilots, one passenger, 40 letters, and 140 lbs. of newspapers on board. This was to become the first civil air route operated on an established flight plan.[24] In

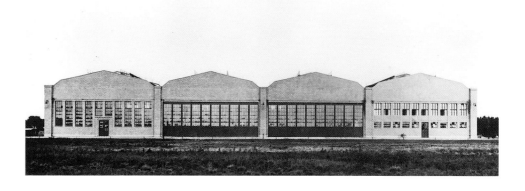

Fig. 5 Attributed to Peter Behrens, architect. AEG Airplane Factory at Hennigsdorf near Berlin, 1915.

Weimar in those days the German National Assembly was meeting to give the young republic, which took its name from the city, a democratic constitution. In order to escape from post-revolutionary disturbances, the political meetings had been moved from Berlin to a safe place in central Germany. Because of the great success of this air route – 120 flights in only four weeks – by March three additional air routes connected Berlin with Hamburg, Munich, and Warnemünde. The first international civil air route followed on August 25, 1919, with a two-and-a-half-hour flight of the Air Transport and Travel Ltd. from Hounslow airport near London to Le Bourget near Paris. The airplane used was a single-engine De Havilland DH-4A biplane, carrying one passenger![25]

The birth of civil air traffic was a logical consequence of the immense upswing of flying during the war. By 1918 there existed across Europe airplanes with strong engines and larger weight capacities which had little in common with the fabric-covered flying machines of the prewar era. The first postwar machines on the air routes were rebuilt bombers, with windows cut into the fuselages and small passenger cabins built in. The infrastructure of a future air traffic network was also in place, for many cities already possessed military and factory airfields. And there were a lot of unemployed pilots and unnecessarily large airplane industries that faced an unavoidable downsizing. Thus, manufacturers such as Farman in France, Airco/De Havilland and Handley Page in England, and Junkers, Rumpler, and AEG in Germany seized the initiative by forming civil air services that created a new market for their airplanes. Airco and AEG were particularly farsighted, in that each provided especially early for a parallel institution; for Airco, it was the Air Transport and Travel Ltd., established in 1916,[26] and for AEG, the Deutsche Luft-Reederei (est. 1917), which, joined with other companies, was to emerge as Lufthansa in 1926.[27]

On many first-generation airfields, the first airline companies were much like tenants, tolerated by the military. At Hounslow, for example, the passenger processing and passport and customs formalities took place in a hangar left over from the war. At Le Bourget commercial aviation was allowed to set up on the eastern side of the airfield, where barracks and hangars that had been vacated by the military were made available. Le Bourget, located seven-and-a-half miles from Paris, was not only one of the very first commercial

25 Hudson (note 15), p. 18.
26 Ibid., p. 16.
27 Ott (note 24), p. 61.
28 On the alterations to Le Bourget in 1921-22, see Louise Faure-Favier, "De Paris à Lausanne: Comment on inaugure une ligne aérienne," *L'Illustration* (Nov. 19, 1921), p. 462; in addition, see L. Hirschauer, "L'Aviation commerciale en 1921," *L'Illustration* (Sept. 10, 1921), pp. 219-21.
29 On the airport at Königsberg, see Müller-Wulckow (note 20), p. 82; Magistrat der Stadt Königsberg, *Königsberg in Preussen* (Berlin, 1926), p. 44; *Die Verwaltung der Stadt Königsberg i. Pr. nach dem Kriege* (Königsberg, 1924), pp. 112, 139-40.
30 The designer of the terminal, which received little attention at the time, did not achieve greater fame until thirty years later, as one of the architects of the Stalin-Allee in Berlin, the first "Socialist" boulevard of the German Democratic Republic in the 1950s. For the career of Hanns Hopp, see *1945: Krieg – Zerstörung – Aufbau: Architektur und Stadtplanung 1940-1960*, Schriftenreihe der Akademie der Künste, vol. 23 (Berlin, 1995), p. 371.

Fig. 6 Architects of the Sous-Secretariat de l'Aéronautique. Bird's-eye view of the air station at Le Bourget Airport near Paris, 1922; from *L'Illustration* (1929).

Fig. 7 W. Eisenblätter, artist. Bird's-eye view of the airport at Königsberg, East Prussia (now, Kaliningrad, Russia), 1921-22; drawing based on an aerial photograph.

airports, it was also the showplace of the first attempt at giving shape to a new type of building—the terminal, which was called the *air station* or *airway station* (*Aérogare*, *Flugbahnhof*, or *Luftbahnhof*) because its function was comparable to that of reception buildings at railway stations. The word *terminal* also came from the world of railways; it first appeared in the mid-1930s alongside these other terms, ultimately replacing them after 1945.

The barracks crammed in between the Bessonneau hangars of Le Bourget appeared inappropriate to the postwar era, so the national undersecretary for aeronautics started planning new buildings in 1921-22, though he made the mistake of making a long-term situation out of a provisional one.[28] Thus, an ensemble of neoclassical pavilions replaced the barracks, but they retained the impractical division of functions and institutions (administration, passport and customs control, weather service, telegraph service, airlines) between various buildings (fig. 6). A neo-Baroque *jardin à la française* filled the free space between the buildings, preparing arriving passengers for the mood of the French capital city.

The terminal was being re-invented at precisely the same time as in Paris – albeit with more success – in the East Prussian city of Königsberg (today, Kaliningrad).[29] On a 1,300-by-2,000-foot-long rectangular airfield near the neighborhood of Devau, work started with the construction of two hangars, placed at right-angles to each other in the corner of the field closest to the nearby main road. The *air station*, completed in 1922 to designs by Hanns Hopp,[30] was erected at an angle between the ends of the hangars (pl. 1; fig. 7). Hopp's terminal united the splintered program of Le Bourget in a single,

Fig. 8 Hanns Hopp, architect. Terminal at Königsberg Airport, 1921-22.

symmetrical building, with symmetrically staged terraces on flat roofs and a façade with heavy protruding pillars, greatly influenced by Behrens's verticalism (fig. 8). That the first modern airport was built in the most out-of-the-way corner of Germany, and not in the capital city, had political justification. After the Treaty of Versailles, East Prussia was separated from the rest of Germany by the so-called Polish corridor. The airport, partly financed by the state, was intended to help mitigate this isolation, and it made Königsberg for a decade-and-a-half into the distribution point of the rapidly growing air traffic from Berlin to the Baltic and Finland, as well as to the Soviet Union.

An architectural type for the terminal had now become apparent, an important moment in the history of European airports. The buildings, almost always placed on the periphery, are not simply lined up, but rather arranged according to a recognizable plan. Thus begins the second generation of airports, following immediately after the first, but still belonging to what Reyner Banham called the "pastoral phase,"[31] for these were still flat, omnidirectional, grassy fields, which, however, were now laid out for civil air traffic. These sites, measuring 800 to 1,000 yards in diameter, required expensive care and had to be drained. A paved surface, the so-called apron, was permissible only in front of the terminal and the hangars. To allow for easier orientation from the air, it was common to demarcate the airfield with a white circle 150 feet in diameter, as well as with the name of the place in giant letters. At the end of the 1920s the most important airports – among them, London's Croydon, Amsterdam's Schiphol, and Berlin's Tempelhof – even had illuminated airfields, which allowed for flying at night.

Königsberg was but the prelude to the building of Tempelhof, the Berlin commercial airport that opened in 1923 on a former parade ground as a replacement for Johannisthal. It was to become a model for many other airports.[32] The symmetrical scheme of hangar-terminal-hangar, which was invented in Königsberg, reappears here on a substantially larger scale, although in a linear fashion with only a slightly concave curve on the northern periphery of the airfield. The curve followed the fence of a cemetery, one of whose corners protruded into the airport grounds and thus prevented a straight border. This originally unintentional form was later adopted at many other airports, because it satisfied an organic ideal that an airfield be circular: it was as though the arriving airplanes were received by the buildings with open arms.

As in Königsberg, work began on the hangars, in 1924; in 1925 a radio office followed, placed on the middle axis of the complex, directly on the apron. It represents an early form of the freestanding control tower, which was not further pursued at that time, and found successors only after World War II. A command platform with a cylindrical glass house in the center topped off the octagonal pavilion. This is where flight monitoring took place in bad weather, an improvement over the open platform on the central structure of the terminal in Königsberg.[33] The airplanes were given clearance for take-off from here via a light signal that was directed straight at the pilot's open seat or, in newer models, toward the side window of the cockpit.[34]

The terminal, erected from 1926 to 1929 between the street and the radio office to a competition design by the architects Paul and Klaus Engler, contained administrative offices, passenger processing facilities, and a large restaurant for spectators (pl. 3; fig. 9).[35] The street façade of the long, slightly curved, flat-roofed building is especially impressive. Its three-story brick front was divided quite simply from corner to corner with continuous hori-

31 Reyner Banham, "The Obsolescent Airport," *Architectural Review* 132, no. 788 (Oct. 1962), p. 252.

32 On the history of Tempelhof, see Conin (note 24); Werner Treibel, *Geschichte der deutschen Verkehrsflughäfen: Eine Dokumentation von 1909 bis 1989* (Bonn, 1992); John Walter Wood, *Airports: Some Elements of Design and Future Development* (New York, 1940), pp. 194-201; Hans-Joachim Braun, "The Airport as Symbol: Air Transport and Politics at Berlin-Tempelhof, 1923-1948," in William M. Leary, ed., *From Airships to Airbus: The History of Civil and Commercial Aviation*, vol. 1, *Infrastructure and Environment* (Washington, D.C., and London, 1995), pp. 45-54.

33 Fritz Bräuning, the municipal architectural counsel of the municipal district of Tempelhof, provided the design.

34 John Wegg, "The Development and Emergence of Air Traffic Control in the United Kingdom and Europe, 1919-1939," in Leary (note 32), pp. 115-26.

35 Paul and Klaus Engler, "Empfangsgebäude des Flughafens Tempelhof," *Deutsche Bauzeitung* 63 (1929), pp. 345-48.

36 John Dower, "Some Aerodromes in Germany and Holland," *Journal of the Royal Institute of British Architects* 38, no. 11 (April 4, 1931), p. 351.

37 Conin (note 24), p. 107.

Fig. 9 Paul and Klaus Engler, architects. Terminal at Tempelhof Airport, Berlin, 1926-29 (now demolished).

zontal bands of windows. John Dower, an English architect who traveled to German and Dutch airports in 1931, spoke of its "real architectural merit."[36] The Englers' design was the first terminal that allowed for expansion of the complex, since it could easily be lengthened at both ends. Of the four sections, however, only two were built, because it later became apparent that the plan drawn up in 1923 would have to be altered to accommodate the rapid increase in air traffic at Tempelhof in the 1930s.[37]

On the west side, the first of two hangar groups had been built in 1924-25 using structural steel, with a workshop integrated in the middle (fig. 10).

Fig. 10 Heinrich Kosina and Paul Mahlberg, architects. Hangars with workshop at Tempelhof Airport, Berlin, 1924-25 (now demolished); from Gescheit and Wittmann, *Neuzeitlicher Verkehrsbau* (1931).

The dominant horizontal lines on the front side run into the vertical windows illuminating the workshop; angling toward the top, these continue in the slanted roof surface. It is not accidental that this figure is reminiscent of Mendelsohn's sketches, for the architects, Heinrich Kosina and Paul Mahlberg, both started out in Mendelsohn's studio.

Hangars, of course, are worthy of an essay of their own, but we must limit ourselves here to a few comments. The surprisingly large hangar capacity at early commercial airports can be explained by the winter break, a months-long practice that was still common in 1925. During this break the whole air fleet required a safe roof. The lightweight airplanes, often constructed of wood, were not strong enough to withstand a harsh storm in the air or on the ground, for there was always the danger that they would be blown away and smashed, as happened in 1928 during a windstorm at Tempelhof.[38] The fleet of planes was like a herd of sheep, and the size of the stall was dictated by the fact that all must fit inside. The word *hangar*, borrowed from French, in fact designates a shed for hay and other things that was open on one side and built onto a farmhouse.

Hangars retained the same basic form as in Reims and Johannisthal – simple boxes without disruptive supports on the inside and with a latchable opening toward the airfield offering the greatest possible width. What did develop over the course of several decades were subtle technological changes in construction and, of course, the dimensions, for hangars grew in width along with increases in aircraft wingspan. The hangars at Tempelhof by Kosina and Mahlberg, for example, had an unhindered opening 96 feet wide, which could be closed off with automatic folding doors. A hangar built in 1927 at the Hamburg airport under the direction of Fritz Schumacher, utilizing a dual-arm steel-frame construction, offered an opening 260 feet wide, expecting to receive the "giant airplanes" announced at the time.[39] This facility remained a standard model for years to come, until the imposing hangar at Linate near Milan (1937) expanded the opening to a width of 459 feet.[40] This was possible only by hanging the roof on two powerful steel girders in the form of a bow-shaped bridge, a design that anticipated the construction principles of the new "jumbo hall" in Hamburg (designed by Von Gerkan, Marg and Partners, 1992-94; see pl. 130).

Natural lighting was necessary for servicing and repair work. One extreme solution in this regard was presented in Karl Johann Mossner's hangar at the first Munich airport, at Oberwiesenfeld (1928-29; fig. 11). The roof trusses of this hangar, which could be opened on three of the four sides, rested on eight

38 Ibid., p. 152.
39 Hartmut Frank, ed., *Fritz Schumacher, Reformkultur und Moderne* (Stuttgart, 1994), p. 272. See there also Schumacher's hangar for the land-sea airport at Travemünde, p. 275. For more on hangars, see Alfred Mehmel, "Aeroplane and Seaplane Hangars," *The Architect and Building News* 151 (July 5, 1937), pp. 168-70.
40 See Wood (note 2), p. 233.
41 Mossner created the design in cooperation with the chief architect of the city of Munich and the company that carried out the project, Seibert Eisenhochbau- und Brückenbau G.m.b.H.; see "Der neue Flughafen München-Oberwiesenfeld," *Die Baugilde* 11 (1929), pp. 1474-79.
42 The locations were Orvieto, Orbetello, and Torre del Lago; see Pier Luigi Nervi, *Bauten und Projekte* (Stuttgart, 1957), pp. 28-43.
43 Dower (note 36), p. 354.
44 See "Terminal Station of the Hamburg Airport," *Architectural Forum* 53 (July 1930), pp. 43-48; Manfred F. Fischer, "Fuhlsbüttel: Ende eines Denkmals?" in Hamburgische Architektenkammer, ed., *Architektur in Hamburg* (Hamburg, 1994), pp. 106-19. For the competition, see Monika Nerlich-Girlich, "'Helios': Der Wettbewerb für den Flughafen Fuhlsbüttel," in Ulrich Höhns, ed., *Das ungebaute Hamburg: Visionen einer anderen Stadt in architektonischen Entwürfen der letzten hundertfünfzig Jahre* (Hamburg, 1991), pp. 234-41.

Fig. 11 Karl Johann Mossner, architect. Hangar at the Oberwiesenfeld Airport near Munich, 1928-29 (now demolished), showing Fokker-Grulich F-III and Rohrbach Roland RO VIII aircraft of the late 1920s.

Fig. 12 Pier Luigi Nervi, architect. Hangar at the Air Force base at Orvieto, Italy, 1935; from *Moderne Bauformen* (1939).

square towers of steel skeleton, which contained the stairs and hid the folding doors. All of the wall areas around the steel were filled in with hollow glass blocks, which bathed the interior in bright daylight.[41]

Hangars were specialized industrial halls, and their often very distinct forms had much to do with the fact that they had to be inexpensive. Unlike in the U.S., decorated façades, such as that at Speke near Liverpool (1937-38; pl. 41), were the exception. While British and German architects usually built hangars of steel and wood, in France after 1900 a highly developed style of construction using reinforced concrete predominated. Eugène Freyssinet had introduced this in 1917 in his great airship halls at Orly with their parabolic profile. These, however, were of military origin, and thus are beyond the scope of our discussion, as are the hangars erected between 1935 and 1941 at military airports in Italy by Pier Luigi Nervi (fig. 12). The latter's vaulted roofs of prefabricated concrete achieved admirable proportions and, as extraordinary examples of the genre, they deserve to be mentioned in this context.[42]

The city of Hamburg erected the most innovative terminal of the 1920s at its Fuhlsbüttel Airport, which in Dower's judgment represented "a very close rival of Berlin for the first place in Europe ... architecturally, indeed, it is the finer of the two."[43] The brick construction, completed in 1929 to a competition design by the architects Friedrich Dyrssen and Peter Averhoff, continued the concavely curved outline of Tempelhof, along with its location between the two large hangars on the periphery of the airfield (pl. 18).[44] For the first time, the various functions of the interior were strictly separated into different zones, a feature without which every present-day terminal would imme-

Fig. 13 Dyrssen and Averhoff, architects. Terminal at Fuhlsbüttel Airport, Hamburg, 1928-29 (now altered).

Fig. 14 Hans Wittwer, architect. Restaurant at Halle-Leipzig Airport, 1929 (now demolished), with original terminal and hangar in the background.

diately cease to operate. Rooms for luggage and freight were located on the lower level, the lobby with all the furnishings for passenger processing was on the ground level, while the second floor was reserved for the restaurant and the third floor for the administrative offices. A sophisticated arrangement of ramps and stairways inside and outside the building made it possible for travelers to remain separate both from spectators and restaurant customers and from the flow of luggage and freight. The view from the airfield was unusual: here, the façade was broken into a series of terraces, reminiscent of an amphitheater (fig. 13). No terminal shows the typological legacy of the hippodrome and of the first air meetings as clearly as Fuhlsbüttel. It was hoped that the terraces and an adjacent spectator garden in front of and next to the terminal would hold up to 35,000 spectators during air shows; this number was never achieved, although at times the number did reach into the thousands.

The architecture of the building at Fuhlsbüttel exposes the financial dilemma of these airports, which were as modern as they were generously dimensioned. Air traffic was indeed growing steadily, but, until after World War II, the capacity remained too scant to cover the costs of these buildings, which were paid for out of public funds. Popular air shows with paying spectators were a German specialty in the 1920s, for it was here more than in neighboring countries that "aviation was the love affair of ordinary people," a passion that had commenced with German enthusiasm for the Zeppelin airships before World War I.[45]

A notably modern construction strictly for spectators was erected at the airport serving the two cities of Halle and Leipzig, which were only twenty-one miles from each other. They gave up their own airports in 1926 in order to share the costs of a larger, modern airport.[46] The restaurant, sited next to the terminal, was built in 1929 to a design by Hans Wittwer, the office partner of Hannes Meyer, who at that time was the director of the Bauhaus in Dessau. Above the ground floor rose a seemingly weightless dining area that was completely surrounded by a glass curtain (fig. 14). The cantilevered roof was held up by five middle supports of reinforced concrete. The extended arms tapered slightly upwards towards the ends, evoking an image of flapping wings.[47] This restaurant was the first building erected at an airport to refer allegorically to flight in its actual construction, rather than simply in applied ornamentation. Today architects still produce designs of this nature, but not all of these can be considered as successful as the Halle-Leipzig structure.

45 Approximately 400,000 people came to Tempelhof when the "ocean fliers" Köhl and von Hünefeld, who had completed the first non-stop crossing of the Atlantic in the east-west direction together with the Irishman Fitzmaurice, arrived in Berlin on June 20, 1928; see Peter Fritzsche, *A Nation of Flyers: German Aviation and the Popular Imagination* (Cambridge, Mass., 1992), p. 150.
46 On the Halle-Leipzig airport, see Wood (note 32), pp. 202-05.
47 See *Bauwelt* 21, no. 33 (1931), pp. 17-27.

48 For the figures for Hamburg, see Treibel (note 32), p. 219; for Berlin, see Conin (note 24), p. 350. The cited numbers are average values, however. On the peak days in the summer months, the number in Berlin could rise to 1,500 passengers with 100 scheduled aircraft arriving and departing on a single day; Wood (note 32), p. 198, cites this figure for 1939.

49 State subsidies for the French airlines for 1920-21 are quoted at 60 to 80 percent of the income; see Hirschauer (note 28), p. 220. The state subsidies for Lufthansa in 1926 amounted to 65 percent and in 1939 were still at 32 percent; see Behringer and Ott-Kopschalijski (note 3), p. 432.

50 Source for the U.S.A.: *Aircraft Year Book 1928*, cited from Dominick A. Pisano, preface to *American Airport Designs* (reprint of the 1930 edition; Washington, D.C., 1994), p. v; source for Germany: Myerscough (note 23), p. 48.

51 Fritzsche (note 45).

52 R. E. G. Davies, *Lufthansa: An Airline and its Aircraft* (New York, 1991).

53 It should be noted, however, that in this area, even before Hitler broke the terms of the Treaty of Versailles, i.e. from the early 1920s, a secret cooperation with the Soviet Union had been underway; see Karl-Heinz Völker, "Die Entwicklung der militärischen Luftfahrt in Deutschland 1920-1933," in Militärgeschichtliches Forschungsamt, ed., *Beiträge zur Militär- und Kriegsgeschichte*, vol. 3 (Stuttgart, 1962), pp. 123-289.

54 The conduct of the military towards the ambitions of the civil flier competition was difficult, and could go as far as outright obstructionism; for Great Britain, see the informative report by Myerscough (note 23), p. 45.

The statistics on air travel in the late 1920s — the number of actual passengers as distinct from the mass of spectators — may strike us as surprisingly low. Landings and take-offs in Hamburg in 1928 — that is, just before the completion of the terminal — averaged no more than 62 passengers per day. In Berlin this figure was 113 passengers per day. In 1938, after a decade of often dramatic increases in air travel, there were in Hamburg still only 125 passengers daily, and in Berlin — at the time one of the greatest airports of the world, alongside London, New York, and Chicago — 678 passengers per day.[48] Two things are clear: first, flight was still the luxury of a small elite, and, second, the income from this business was insufficient either for the construction and maintenance of modern airports or for the financing and servicing of the national air travel fleets. The deficits incurred had to be offset by large subsidies to the airlines. In addition, financial support was necessary for the construction of airports, and national and municipal participation was vital to support the airport operating companies. The principle put forward in 1920 that this burgeoning industry "must fly by itself" — as expressed by Winston Churchill, the minister of air travel in the British government at the time — was not to be realized anywhere. The state aid granted in Europe for the airlines in the early years reached 60 to 80 percent of their income, only to drop to rates around 30 percent by 1939.[49] Massive state support was also the only reason for the headstart that European air traffic maintained over that of the United States in the mid-1930s. In the U.S. in 1928 no more than 52,394 transported passengers were counted at all airports, compared with 151,000 in Germany in 1927.[50]

Probably the strongest support for flight was in Germany, which Peter Fritzsche in his recent book has called "a nation of flyers," because it played the role of draft horse in European civil air traffic right from the beginning, and it held onto this role until the 1930s.[51] It was in Germany in 1919 that the first completely metal airplane developed specifically for commercial air flight, the Junkers F-13, was put on the market (see pl. 1). Germany possessed the largest airline in Lufthansa, the densest air network, the most commercial airports serviced according to a flight schedule, and a modern, stylistically formative aeronautical architecture that was a major influence on that of other countries.[52] It may come as a surprise that the primary loser of World War I should have achieved this rank, but it is doubtless correct to relate this fact to the stance that this highly industrialized country took to modernity, which also manifested itself in the strong avant-garde architecture produced during the Weimar Republic. A decisive factor, however, without which history would have taken a different course, was article 1 of the Treaty of Versailles, which denied the German Reich the maintenance of a military air fleet.[53] The involvement in civil air traffic offered Germany a way of retaining part of its aeronautical infrastructure, and it gave the German public the chance to compensate for the shame of defeat through successes in civil aviation. The Versailles limitation promoted this path by freeing German commercial aviation from military considerations. Thus, the leeway in the 1920s was clearly larger than in Great Britain or France, when it came to using existing airfields or planning and building new airports.[54]

An important factor in commercial aviation turned out to be the competition between German cities, which, afraid of losing their connection to the means of transportation of the future, became engaged somewhat earlier than the cities of neighboring countries in trying to outdo each other in the construction of airports and of sometimes clearly outsized terminals. Cooperative efforts such as that between Halle and Leipzig, which provided the model for later joint airports at Minneapolis-St. Paul, Dallas-Fort Worth, Cologne-Bonn, and so forth, remained the exception. Completely national airports, which usually served a capital city – such as Croydon or Le Bourget or Evere in Brussels, or the Prague-Ruzyne airport – were unknown in Germany, so that even Tempelhof was owned by the city of Berlin, albeit with the participation of Prussia and the Reich.[55]

The airport at Croydon lay eleven miles south of London on the site of an airfield that had existed since 1915, and that had been used jointly by the Royal Air Force and the National Aircraft Factory. In order to put an end to the rather makeshift arrangement at the Hounslow airfield, Croydon – where a former RAF officers' mess had been transformed into a hotel, and where there were hangars[56] – was opened in 1920 as the new *air port* of London; at the same time, it was the *customs port* of the country, from which international air routes proceeded. This was the base of Imperial Airways, founded in 1924, which connected the motherland with its colonies overseas. On the eastern side of the airfield a two-story administration building was erected in 1926-28 that was covered with cast stone in the style of stripped classicism. The Directorate of Works and Buildings in the Air Ministry was responsible for its design.[57] It was the largest terminal of its time, clearly surpassing Tempelhof and Fuhlsbüttel, although the actual size was not immediately apparent owing to the compact style of construction.[58]

An unusual feature of this building, which remained in use until 1959 and is now a registered landmark, is the control tower, the first of its kind truly to deserve this name. As though intended to guard the British Empire, it grew out of the airfield façade like the fortified tower of a city wall (fig. 15). The Air Ministry described its purpose in a highly revealing manner: "Its functions may be said to combine those of the 'bridge' of a battleship and the 'traffic office' of a railway."[59] On the top floor, the officer on duty kept watch on a rotating gallery, assisted by two radio operators inside the tower, who established contact with arriving planes.[60] The technology was exciting and new, but the designers thought and sketched in the familiar categories of castle, ship, and railway. That is especially evident in the rounded arch of

Fig. 15 Architects of the Air Ministry. Terminal at Croydon Airport near London, 1926-28.

55 In 1925 Prussia and the Reich each held 24 percent of the Berliner Flughafen-gesellschaft; the city of Berlin had 52 percent; see Treibel (note 32), p. 54.
56 See Hudson (note 15), p. 22.
57 For the airport at Croydon, see Wood (note 32), pp. 158-63; Lockhart (note 2), pp. 55-56.

Fig. 16 Architects of the Air Ministry. Terminal at Croydon Airport near London, landside entrance, 1926-28.

58 Croydon totaled 1,000,000 cubic feet, vis-à-vis 800,000 cubic feet in buildings of roughly the same size at Hamburg and Berlin; see Wood (note 32), pp. 159 and 207.

59 Air Ministry, ed., *Guide to Croydon Aerodrome (The Air Port of London)* (London, 1929), p. 7.

60 On the technology of flight control in the control tower at Croydon, see Wegg (note 34), p. 119.

61 John Dower, "Aerodromes," *Journal of the Royal Institute of British Architects* 39, no. 13 (April 30, 1932), p. 511.

62 Dower (note 36), p. 362.

63 For the history of the airline and Dutch transit aviation, see A. van Kampen, *Plesman: Grondlegger van de gouden KLM 1919-1969* (Bussum, 1969).

64 U. F. M. Dellaert, "De Gemeente-Luchthaven van Amsterdam," *Het Vliegveld* (1929), no. 11, pp. 406-11, and no. 12, pp. 436-43; Wood (note 32), pp. 226-31.

65 On Schiphol, see also Lockhart (note 2), p. 53, although he—just like Wood (note 32, p. 227)—incorrectly ascribes the design to the municipal architects of the city of Amsterdam, only to assign it at the same time to the "Rotterdam School."

66 An exception is the last volume of the *Storia universale dell'Architettura*, written by Francesco dal Co and Manfredo Tafuri, which was published in 1979. Here, at any rate, Sagebiel's Berlin airport from 1939 is reproduced (German edition: *Weltgeschichte der Architektur: Gegenwart* [Stuttgart, 1988], p. 66).

the main portal leading to the booking and waiting hall (fig. 16).[61] Anyone driving up in front of this would have imagined him- or herself at a railway station, not at the ground station of a revolutionary new means of transportation. John Dower was especially harsh in his judgment: "Croydon is a dull and grim sobriety and does not express aviation at all."[62]

The Netherlands boasted the oldest airline in the world, KLM (Koninklijke Luchtvaart Maatschappij), which was founded in 1919, one year before Schiphol, Amsterdam's municipal airport and the home port of KLM since the earliest days. From the outset, Schiphol was one of the busiest transit sites on the Continent.[63] Until the middle of the nineteenth century the area, thirteen feet below sea level, had been occupied by the ever-expanding Harlemmer-meer, a large lake that was finally drained to protect Amsterdam and Leiden from flooding. Next to a constantly enlarged group of hangars on the southeast periphery, a single-story, brick-covered terminal was erected in 1929. Its L-shaped plan deviated from the symmetrical designs of its German counterparts.[64] Dirk Roosenburg, an earlier employee of Hendrik Berlage and the designer of Holland's early aviation buildings, including factories for Fokker airplanes, provided the design. The control tower, with its semi-circular, protruding, glassed-in turret and viewing platform, followed the style of the modern railroad signal towers then being built in Germany and Holland (fig. 17). The brick building, in a modernized version of the "Amsterdam School" style, represents a successful melding of various influences—it was regional-istic like the terminal in Hamburg, modernistic in its dynamic mass development, and functionalistic in that its outline resulted from adherence to a set of specific requirements.[65]

A striking disparity exists between the airports that were actually created in the interwar years and those airport projects conceived at the same time in the circle of avant-garde architects. The terminals and hangars built at the early commercial airports are absent from the great works of modern architectural history, in which recognition of airport architecture seems to begin with the hangars by Nervi and, in the case of terminals, with Eero Saarinen's TWA terminal in New York from 1961 (see pls. 84-85).[66] Instead, one encounters Le Corbusier's famous 1922 metropolitan vision of the *ville contempo-*

Fig. 17 Dirk Roosenburg, architect. Aerial view of the Terminal at Schiphol Airport near Amsterdam, 1929 (now demolished), with Fokker F-VII aircraft.

raine for three million residents, with its – from the viewpoint of aviation safety – rather absurd *Aéro-Port*, which is directly linked to the vision of Sant'Elia.[67]

Le Corbusier's airport lies directly at the center of his city on the roof terrace of a grandiose central station serving all means of transportation – street, rail, and air – stacked up in six levels (see Bruegmann, fig. 1). Its location turns it into a city crown dedicated to movement and speed. At the same time, it is the pulsing heart of the urban structure, which sends the transportation streams through the body of the city and thus keeps it alive. One problem, of course, is posed by the array of 50-story skyscrapers, standing about 1,000 feet apart, directly on the periphery of the flight terrace, for each landing and take-off would have faced the greatest of danger between such high obstacles (the helicopter had not yet been invented). Le Corbusier's own commentary was disarmingly naive, even arrogant: "The technology of landing large international airplanes has not yet been sufficiently perfected."[68] So it was not Le Corbusier who had proposed an unusable airport, but rather the airplane builders who had not yet done their work!

Such disregard for the realities of aviation is surprising in an architect whose rhetoric placed so great a value on airplanes: he dedicated a whole chapter to them in his legendary major work *Vers une architecture* (1923), and later even a whole book (*Aircraft*, 1935). It took eight years before, in 1930, Le Corbusier silently retreated from his dream in order to place his airport in the *ville radieuse*, a modified version of his urban utopia, on a round surface on the periphery of the skyscraper quarter.[69] Immediately after World War II he adopted a completely opposite point of view when, in 1946, he pledged allegiance to the new model of the "naked" prairie airport in open country, on which one should build to a maximum height of eight-and-a-half feet above the ground – everything else, he believed, would damage the complete harmony of the "biology of modern airplanes."[70]

Le Corbusier was not the only one in the 1920s and 1930s to indulge in fantasies in the style of Hénard and Sant'Elia. The closest possible connection between the airport and the ideal of a skyscraper city – as learned from America – remained a goal to be pursued, in which, as a rule, the airport was placed not at the foot of the high-rise buildings, but rather on a platform in the roof area. Platforms for the roofs of high-rises were planned between 1928 and 1935 in Hamburg, London, Milan, and Leipzig. An important source of inspiration was El Lissitzky's *Wolkenbügel* (his "cloud hanger utopia") from 1924, whose tall construction on stilts spread out to a great width at a great height.[71] The most popular interpretation of the theme was presented in 1926 through the architecture in Fritz Lang's film *Metropolis*, which was designed by architect Erich Kettelhut. Beneath the top of the powerful tower that dominated the city of Metropolis – a modern version of the myth of the tower of Babel – rested a platform with five prong-shaped launching ramps: an impressive image that fascinated not only the general public, but also architects (fig. 18).[72] Late fruits of this recurrent reverie are those helicopter landing platforms on high-rises that are used only sparingly because they are so dangerous, such as that on the Pan Am Building in New York (Walter Gropius with the Architects Collaborative, 1958-63) and that on the new Ministry of Finance office in Paris (Paul Chemetov, 1989).

When the first decade of civil air travel was over, parallel discussions began in several countries about the shortcomings and perspectives in the building of airports. The debate was especially lively in Britain and France –

67 Le Corbusier, *Urbanisme*, Collection de l'Esprit Nouveau (Paris, 1924), pp. 157-84.

68 Cited from ibid., pp. 180-81. Until the larger airplanes were perfected, small shuttle planes were to establish a connection to an airport on the edge of town; ibid., p. 172. Yet even these would not have been able to land.

69 Le Corbusier, *La Ville radieuse* (Boulogne-sur-Seine, 1935). His competition design, also created in 1930, for the development of the left bank of the Schelde in Antwerp envisaged a "normal" airport in accordance with current technological standards; see Le Corbusier (note 4), p. 109, for a reproduction of the Antwerp project. In another text written in 1930 ("One returns to Paris") he praised the limits on building heights in the periphery of Tempelhof Airport, which naturally excluded high-rises; see Le Corbusier, *Précisions sur un état présent de l'architecture et de l'urbanisme* (Paris, 1929; 2nd ed., Paris, 1960); cited here from the German edition, *Feststellung zu Architektur und Städtebau* (Berlin, Frankfurt am Main, and Vienna, 1964), p. 235.

70 Le Corbusier expressed these opinions at the first French aviation congress held after the war, in 1945; he chaired the session on "Infrastructure." See "1946: L'Architecture et les aéroports modernes," in Le Corbusier, *Œuvre complète 1938-1946* (Zurich, n.d.), pp. 190-91.

71 Christoph Bürkle, *El Lissitzky: Der Traum vom Wolkenbügel*, with an essay by Werner Oechslin (Zurich, 1990).

72 On the phenomenon of rooftop landing sites, see Wolfgang Voigt, "Luftdroschken auf dem Dach und eine Bandstadt für Flugzeuge," in Höhns (note 44), pp. 242-45.

Fig. 18 Erich Kettelhut, architect. Tower with rooftop airport, design for the film *Metropolis,* 1926; from Dethier and Guiheux, eds., *La Ville, art et architecture en Europe, 1870-1993* (Paris, 1994).

interestingly, those countries that earlier than most had their own high-level administration for aviation. The British Air Ministry had existed since 1917, and the French, under the Secretary of Aviation, since 1920 (transformed into the Ministère de l'Air in 1928); Italy followed suit in 1925, but it was not until 1933 that Germany established a comparable organization. It was precisely in the two first-named countries that the inadequacy in the number, design, and furnishing of commercial airports was most obvious.

The leaders of the discussion in Britain were architects and their associations, who now discovered the significance of a building type that they had previously left to the military and to government officials. The Royal Institute of British Architects took the initiative in the fall of 1928 with a competition for young architects, who were invited to design the ideal airport of a metropolis like London for a point in time in the not-too-distant future, the year 1943.[73] Dissatisfaction with the recently opened Croydon terminal was widespread, and not even the representatives of the ministries were immune to it, for they voluntarily cooperated on an R.I.B.A. committee that examined the shortcomings of existing facilities.

In 1931 the committee sent reporters to the other side of the Channel and to the United States, where great advances in the construction of airports were being made after Charles A. Lindbergh, who had become a national hero overnight in 1927, had harshly criticized the weaknesses in this area. Squadron leader Nigel Norman and architect Graham Dawbarn flew across the U.S., gathering experiences that would later stand them in good stead as the designers of outstanding buildings at the airports at Brooklands (1932), Jersey, Channel Islands (1937), and Birmingham (1938-39).[74] "The Continent generally is employing architects for its aerodrome work everywhere, and, indeed, have employed them from the start," asserted John Dower, who toured the Continent and in the process became acquainted with the high standards of the larger airports in Germany and the Netherlands.[75] The committee was in agreement: if they were to be suitably built for the future, modern airports represented a complex planning problem that began with the selection of a

73 See "R.I.B.A. Aerodrome Competition," *The Architects' Journal* 69 (Jan. 30, 1929), pp. 208-11, and "R.I.B.A. Competition for a Design of an Aerodome," *Journal of the Royal Institute of British Architects* 36, no. 8 (Feb. 23, 1929), pp. 325-26.

74 For the airport buildings by Norman and Dawbarn, see Alastair Forsyth, *Buildings for the Age: New Building Types 1900-1939* (London, 1982). For an oral version of Nigel Norman's report, see Nigel Norman, "Aerodrome Design," *The Architectural Association Journal* 48, no. 555 (May 1933), pp. 359-74.

75 Dower (note 36), p. 362.

proper site, for the gain in travel time in the air would be squandered if the transit connections on the ground did not work properly. Thus, the future of commercial air travel would be decided not in the air, but on the ground – through the construction of attractive airports whose positive image would also attract more people to use airplanes.[76]

The increase in flight movements and passengers and the quickly growing weight of commercial aircraft (rising between 1927 and 1937 from an average of ten tons to twenty tons)[77] required new concepts both for the buildings and for the whole airfield, and it is with the latter that the third generation of airport construction announced itself. The heavier airplanes destroyed the turf, whose days were numbered as a result. Expensive take off and landing strips with paved surfaces, as had been standard at all airports in the U.S. since 1928, now became inevitable in Europe too.[78] The airplanes themselves relied on wind strengths to a much greater degree than the jets of today with their high thrust, so that a virtual compass of usually four or more strips was planned in order to be prepared for various wind directions; in 1935 the airport at Bromma near Stockholm became the first to be equipped in this way (see pl. 20).

After it was discovered that, within a few years, many airports could not be expanded because their edges had been cluttered with hangars and other buildings, doubts arose concerning the common practice of building on the periphery. From the criticism leveled at the airport at Le Bourget, the French engineer A. B. Duval developed a principle, introduced in 1929, of a wedge-shaped building zone, which projected forward from the edge into the center of the airfield, so that more than 80 percent of the periphery could remain undeveloped.[79] In the 1930s the wedge scheme dominated many unrealized projects; it was put into effect, however, in 1931 at the airfield of Lyon and in 1937 at Birmingham and Helsinki.

The limits of the terminals of the older type very quickly became clear at the large airports. They strongly resembled single-track railway stations – conceived for a plane to be prepared individually so that it came to a stop in front of the building for loading freight and passengers, and afterwards rolled to the runway. The path of the passengers into the airplane cabin was short and safe in the beginning; with the rise in traffic, this became less so, as the number of aircraft present simultaneously increased. In 1936 there were al-

76 See the concluding report by the secretary of the committee, John Dower (note 61); see also the remarks by Dower and Norman before the Architecture Club, "Cities as Airports," *The Builder* 141, no. 4637 (Dec. 18, 1931), p. 993, and "Town Planning and Aviation," *The Builder* 141, no. 4638 (Dec. 25, 1931).

77 Carl Pirath, *Flughäfen: Raumlage, Betrieb und Gestaltung*, Forschungsergebnisse des verkehrswissenschaftlichen Instituts für Luftfahrt an der Technischen Hochschule Stuttgart, no. 11 (Berlin, 1937), p. 14.

78 Before the outbreak of World War II they were constructed at only a few places, for example, Stockholm (see below), Amsterdam, Helsinki, Moscow, Bremen, and Bordeaux.

79 Duval (note 1).

80 Pirath (note 77), pp. 13-14.

81 Braun (note 32), p. 49.

82 See "R.I.B.A. Aerodrome Competition" (note 73).

83 L. F. Bouman, "Droog Instappen," *Het Vliegveld* (May 1933), pp. 138-41.

84 On Armstrong's seadromes, see J. T. W. Marshall, "Transatlantic Flying a Commercial Reality through Man-Made Islands," *The American Architect* 138, no. 2590 (Dec. 1930), pp. 30-31, 68, 70, and R. E. G. Davies, "The Armstrong Seadrome (1923-1943)," in *Fallacies and Fantasies of Air Transport History* (McLean, Va., 1994), pp. 22-30.

85 *F. P. 1 antwortet nicht* was produced by the UFA in Berlin, and distributed to theaters in 1932. Erich Kuttelhut, who had also worked on *Metropolis*, designed the film's architecture, clearly influenced by the example of such seadromes.

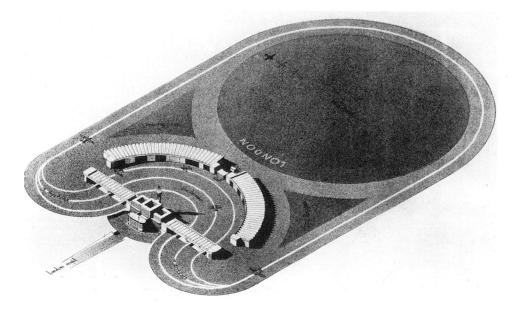

Fig. 19 D. H. McMorran, architect. Royal Institute of British Architects competition for a design for an airport in the year 1943, 1928; from *The Architects' Journal* 69 (Jan. 30, 1929), p. 209.

Fig. 20 Henry J. Gielow, engineer. Manmade island ("seadrome") to service transatlantic airplanes, after an idea of Edward R. Armstrong, 1930; from *The American Architect* 138 (Dec. 1930), p. 30.

Fig. 21 André Lurçat, architect. Project of an airport in the River Seine, Paris, 1932; from *L'Architecture d'Aujourd'hui* (1932).

ready ten take-offs and landings per hour at Tempelhof and Croydon during peak hours.[80] There were two options to increase capacity and save time: either the airplanes approached with their motors running, or they would be prepared next to each other in parallel positions.

In 1930 the Berlin airport company granted commissions for measurements of time and studies of movements, in order to determine whether rationalization could increase the efficiency of the airport.[81] And as early as 1928-29 the entries in the Lehigh and R.I.B.A. competitions had included practical recommendations for more subtle systems of boarding passengers, arrangements that were supposed to untangle the confusion on the apron by creating two levels: by means of passenger tunnels that led directly to the waiting airplanes, or by means of bridges from which one descended to airplanes waiting in parallel formation. Both alternatives had the additional advantage that everything could take place under a protective roof, as in D. H. McMorran's competition project for a London airport in the year 1943 (fig. 19).[82] Individual ideas from these two competitions reappear, as we shall see, in the new terminal buildings of the 1930s. In the public sphere, interestingly enough, they did so under the slogan of comfort, of "dry boarding."[83] No mention is made of the fact that more was involved than shielding the flying elite from wind and rain: passengers had to be protected from life-threatening contact with rotating propellers and rolling airplanes.

One area of insecurity for the future of airports was intercontinental traffic, since no one could say for certain which technology would eventually win out – the land airplane or the seaplane, or even the airship, which had no competition in terms of passenger comfort, and had re-entered the race after the first successful transatlantic crossing of the Zeppelin LZ 127 in 1928. In order to shorten the distances on the Atlantic for land airplanes, the American engineer Edward R. Armstrong recommended from 1923 on his frequently improved system of floating *seadromes* (fig. 20), which were copied from the first aircraft carriers of the U.S. Navy. Eight such artificial islands with flight platforms measuring 1,100 feet in length and up to 340 feet in width were to be anchored to the sea floor on a route that led from New Jersey via the Azores to the coast of Brittany.[84] Armstrong's seadromes were never realized, but they inspired architects and even film directors, such as the German Karl Hartl, whose sound film about one such "floating platform," *F.P.1 antwortet nicht* (F.P.1 is not answering), became a worldwide success.[85]

In the same genre, André Lurçat produced a project for a new Paris airport located in the middle of the Seine, which he unsuccessfully presented to the French air ministry in 1932 (fig. 21). A more central location than the Ile

Fig. 22 Norman and Dawbarn, architects. Terminal building at Elmdon Airport near Birmingham, 1938-39; from *The Architect and Building News* 159 (Aug. 18, 1939).

des Cygnes, in the river south of the Eiffel Tower, could simply not be imagined. Lurçat wanted to convert the 2,700-foot-long island into an air platform, with a connection to the Métro, as well as hangars and auto garages on the lower level, and a catapult system to launch the airplanes into the air independently of the wind, just as is done on aircraft carriers.[86]

The introduction of flying boats led to a boom in amphibian airports, those land-sea airports on coasts, at which one could transfer to a land airplane. For example, in order to cater for traffic from Central Europe to Scandinavia, the airports at Stettin and Travemünde were set up on the German Baltic coast. From the airport at Marignane near Marseilles, which had existed since 1922, a route extending all the way to Saigon in French Indochina was opened in 1931 using flying boats.[87] At all of these places there were cranes or airplane slips that could lift the aircraft onto the land; they were then pulled into the hangar for repairs. Probably the most extensive land-sea airport was built in 1937 – quite far from the coast – at Linate near Milan, where a 3,900-foot-long and 450-foot-wide basin was dug specifically for seaplanes.[88] The buildings designed by Gianluigi Giordani made Linate one of the most elegant airports on the continent. The terminal, placed on stilts in order to provide protected parking space for autos, and the separate administration building were plastered, reinforced-concrete buildings with large glass windows in the Italian rationalist style of the 1930s. The passengers left

Fig. 23 D. Pleydell-Bouverie, architect. Terminal at the Municipal Airport of Ramsgate, 1937 (now demolished); from *Architectural Review* (July 1937), p. 3.

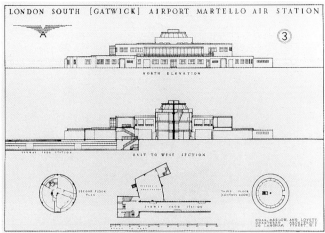

Fig. 24 Hoar, Marlow and Lovett, architects. Terminal building at Gatwick Airport, 1936, with tubes connecting to aircraft.

Fig. 25 Hoar, Marlow and Lovett, architects. Elevation, section, and plans of Gatwick Airport, 1936.

86 André Lurçat, "Projet pour un aéroport-relai au centre de Paris," *L'Architecture d'Aujourd'hui* no. 3 (April 1932), pp. 86-89. Planes were also catapulted from German ocean liners, such as the *Bremen*, as early as 1929; see Davies (note 52), p. 35.

87 On Marignane, see Wood (note 32), pp. 181-86.

88 On Linate, see Wood (note 32), pp. 232-37.

89 For Birmingham, see Forsyth (note 74) and "Birmingham Airport," *The Architect and Building News* 159 (Aug. 18, 1939), pp. 187-92.

90 "Ramsgate Municipal Airport," *Architectural Review* (July 1937), pp. 3-6.

91 The film, directed by William Cameron Menzies, was based on H. G. Wells's 1933 novel, *The Shape of Things to Come*.

92 John King, *Gatwick: The Evolution of an Airport* (Gatwick, 1986).

the terminal via two ramps, which led them to either the apron or the water basin, depending upon their destination.

Some of the most striking airport buildings of the time were created in Great Britain, which worked successfully to make good its earlier shortcomings in this field. At the municipal airport of Birmingham, for instance, the principle of a wedge-shaped building zone was realized in 1938-39 in an especially evocative form. The four-story terminal, designed by Norman and Dawbarn, lies like the hull of a ship on the tip of the wedge, where it is surrounded on three sides by the airfield (fig. 22). The building's shape was the result of an attempt to protect cargo and passengers from the weather and to allow passengers access to either of two waiting airplanes. Thus, two fifty-foot canopies balance each other and are directly connected with the steel-frame construction that leads right through the building. The front view provides a somewhat romantic allegory of flight, for the building seems to have sprouted wings, under which the airplanes that have landed gather like chicks around the hen.[89]

In this same direction lay the terminal at the small airport at Ramsgate, completed in 1937, a jewel of the whole genre which was inexplicably razed in the 1980s. The architect D. Pleydell-Bouverie had been commissioned to create a landmark that would be recognizable both on the ground and from the air.[90] His solution was a streamlined pavilion that was fully glassed in on the airfield side and tapered towards each end (fig. 23). This was surmounted by a protruding concrete platform, above which there was a control room resembling a cockpit in the middle. The building's distinctive shape calls to mind fantasy projects such as "wing-only airplanes" with cabins in the wings, examples of which could be admired in the British science fiction film *Things to Come* (1936).[91] Probably nowhere else did the playful melding of a seemingly simple airport construction with the image of an airplane succeed so perfectly as here.

A forward-looking construction was the terminal completed in 1936 at the commercial airport of Gatwick (fig. 24), which, lying twenty-five miles south of London, was rather far removed from the city it served. As compensation, however, Gatwick was the first European airport with a direct railway connection. A pedestrian tunnel led from the railway station to a circular "island" in a corner of the airfield, designed by architects Hoar, Marlow and Lovett (fig. 25).[92] The circular arrangement guaranteed optimum use of space: circled around the structure, six airplanes could be processed at once, their sides up against the building and their noses facing in a counterclockwise direction.[93] The passengers left the terminal via *gates* and reached the airplane through six telescoping passageways that spread out like rays from the building. These were moved forward and back on rails, using electric motors. Such passageways had already been in use in California (at Oakland, Berkeley) since the end of the 1920s, but here, for the first time, they were worked into an intelligent system. Popularly known as the "beehive," the building remained in operation until 1956 and, with the exception of the telescoping passageways, is still standing (see pl. 92).

In its adherence to function, this completely unpretentious, modern building at Gatwick was ahead of its time, though contemporary critics could not have understood this when they pointed out that its circular form was incapable of expansion.[94] They never imagined that many "beehives" would later be combined into single complete units. Gatwick is thus the ancestor of the terminal systems of the 1960s and 1970s, when airports were forced to offer an increasingly larger number of positions for handling passengers. Insular types in the style of Gatwick were created in Los Angeles (1961), Toronto (1964), Geneva (1968), and Paris (1974), although always as a subsystem of a main terminal. To some degree, the satellite systems of Houston (1964), Cologne-Bonn (1970), and Newark (1973) can be traced back to Gatwick. That this type found successors only a quarter-century later may be the result of the paradoxical fact that at Gatwick a problem was solved before it had been clearly formulated – for in comparison with the jet age, the spatial and organizational problems of the airports around 1935 were but a preliminary skirmish.

When the buildings at the Paris airport began to be inadequate at the beginning of the 1930s, a debate began in France concerning alternatives to Le Bourget; the debate produced, among other responses, the previously mentioned proposal of André Lurçat.[95] Urbain Cassan presented his project for an intercontinental land-sea airport near Versailles, for which he would have to construct an artificial lake like that at Milan-Linate.[96] The aviation ministry, however, held out for the expansion of the existing airport and concentrated on a new terminal, which was to be appropriately representative of France at the world's exposition to take place in Paris in 1937. In response to criticism from architects, the ministry permitted a public competition, which was held in 1935. Georges Labro, who had emerged as one of the winners in the 1927 competition for the League of Nations Palace in Geneva, received first prize and the commission.[97] His three-story Beaux-Arts modern building, clad in natural stone, with streamlined elements, was expandable on both sides, a feature considered especially valuable (see pls. 38-39). The reception hall, stretching nearly the entire length of the building, is generously proportioned and elegant. It receives natural lighting through glass bricks in the concrete-shell roof. In the middle of the 722-foot-long, terraced airfield façade, dominated by horizontal lines, is a balcony, the tip of which housed the flight control under a glass dome. The building was three times the size of that at Croydon, and thus the largest terminal in Europe, if only for a short time.

In Germany, too, a record-setting construction was in progress: under the direction of the Imperial Aviation Ministry (Reichsluftfahrtministerium or RLM), the existing complex at Tempelhof was to be completely replaced. The architect, Ernst Sagebiel, had been office director for Erich Mendelsohn until 1933. Among the works of his that were realized as a result of his being a member of the RLM's building department were, along with Tempelhof, the massive RLM building on Wilhelmstrasse in Berlin (1933-36), and the airports

93 According to Wood, the Gatwick design was influenced by the 1934 competition for the Stockholm airport, in which Sven Markelius participated with a terminal in a circular shape; see Wood (note 32), p. 165.
94 For example, Wood (note 32).
95 On this debate, see the issue of *L'Architecture d'Aujourd'hui* dedicated to this topic, vol. 7, no. 9 (1936), pp. 2-57.
96 "Exemple d'un grand aéroport mixte: Le Projet Paris-Versailles," ibid., pp. 54-57.
97 Charles Clement-Grandcour, "La Nouvelle Aérogare du Bourget," *La Construction Moderne* 53 (1937-38), pp. 75-84.

98 For the planning history of the second airport at Tempelhof, see Braun (note 32), pp. 49-51; Conin (note 32), pp. 181-201; Treibel (note 32), pp. 58-59; see also the analysis of the building by Manfred Hecker, "Heimatkunde," *Bauwelt* 85, no. 46 (1994), pp. 2543-44.

99 "Der Weltflughafen Tempelhof: Ein Blick auf das Werden eines grossen Werkes," *Bauwelt* 28, no. 9 (1938), pp. 1-16.

100 See Lars Olof Larsson, *Die Neugestaltung der Reichshauptstadt: Albert Speers Generalbebauungsplan für Berlin* (Stuttgart, 1978), p. 25.

101 Wood (note 32), p. 201.

at Stuttgart-Echterdingen and Munich-Riem (both 1936-39). Tempelhof now received a larger, elliptical airfield with a ring-shaped, paved runway, which was tripled in size in the direction of the city (1,333 acres), so that the airport, which had already been unsurpassed in the 1920s because of its proximity to the city, was now only two miles from the center of Berlin on its northwest side (see pls. 5-7).[98]

It was on this side that, beginning in 1936, Sagebiel erected his new terminal, on a monumental circular plaza that was connected to the North-South axis planned by Albert Speer at the same time, but never realized (see Bruegmann, fig. 3).[99] The façades, with light limestone cladding, evince a simplified classicism that all but obscures the architect's avant-garde origins. The path of passengers arriving from the city is quite effectively staged – they come from a broad plaza to the courtyard of honor, enter the reception hall, and finally the departures hall. The space, traversed in a straight line, is thus gradually narrowed, only to open out again in a very broad arc towards the airfield. The giant 3,870-foot-long concave airfield front is impressive. It resembles a crescent in which the architect, for the sake of effect, unites all the functions of the airfield. Of unusual dimensions is the 40-foot-high canopy, which cantilevers out 170 feet along the entire length of the building. This extraordinary building not only generously covers the 1,246-foot wide handling zone for the airplanes, but also the adjoining hangars at the sides. One part of the roof surface was intended as a raised stand for 65,000 spectators. Of this, only 14 staircases leading to the roof were built, which give the arc-shaped construction a rhythmic division on the reverse side.

Adolf Hitler, who personally directed the renovation projects of the capital city, which he saw as the center of a world power, justified this unusual size to the city and to the airport managers in 1934 as follows: the beauty and size of this construction was intended to "silence any condescending criticism of Germany"; besides which, the second Tempelhof airport was supposed to be usable until the year 2000, the first one having been unable to fulfill its purpose after only ten years.[100] The American airport expert John Walter Wood, who reviewed 40 European airports in 1939, did not find anything objectionable in the dimensions either: "Extremely large installations are needed, since … the potential air traffic of the future is enormous." However, he did criticize the expensive waste of space in the canopy, whose goal could have been achieved by much simpler means.[101] Nevertheless, Tempelhof as a type of construction was a dinosaur condemned to extinction, for the future belonged to the successors of the small type of terminal, such as that at Gatwick.

When World War II broke out, the development of new commercial airports ceased, and commercial facilities everywhere were seized for use by Allied and Axis military powers alike. The end of the war naturally witnessed a boom in the construction of commercial airports, new terminals, and expanded facilities. The unfinished building at Tempelhof was made operational in a makeshift manner. It was not completed until after 1945, by the American occupational force, which repaired the damage inflicted by the war, and provided the airport with a provisional paved runway. Tempelhof became the primary scene of the Berlin Airlift during the Soviet blockade of the West Berlin enclave, which began in 1948 and lasted nearly a year. Thus, an important prestige object of the Third Reich – one of the few that were actually built! – experienced a truly unprecedented reinterpretation as a symbol of Western freedom, and this symbol was … an airport.

1 Francis R. Meisch, "Architecture and Air Transportation," *Pencil Points* 24 (Nov. 1943), p. 43.
2 John Thackara, *Lost in Space: A Traveller's Tale* (Haarlem, 1994), p. 8.

Koos Bosma

European Airports, 1945–1995: Typology, Psychology, and Infrastructure

In the course of the last half century, aviation has become a global processing system, operating from its own artificial environment. The large postwar airport is a megastructure, wherein urban traffic is smoothly converted into airborne traffic. It is also a place that converts the traveler into a passenger with automated behavior (fig. 1). In present-day mass transport, every passenger is an anonymous cargo, to be shifted over the globe as comfortably as possible. This view was expressed even at the time of World War II: "The passenger, a mobile unit, must be controlled and guided for safety and operating efficiency, in his own interest."[1] For the passenger, of course, the airport is too often a mysterious circulation system, with an unknown number of entry and exit points. Yet, more than a billion travelers were moved over the world by scheduled flights in 1993,[2] and if the ambitions of an expanding facility like Paris's Charles de Gaulle International Airport in Roissy-en-France are taken seriously – 100 million passengers a year – even greater numbers of the world's population will be going from one airport to another.

In the worldwide network of airlines and airports, the transfer points are of primary importance, not the spaces in between. At the final destinations and transit locations, we are required to change speed. Ultimately, an airport's success is measured by the ease, speed, and efficiency with which travelers switch from one means of transportation to another. The logistics involved are complex, and in the past century the right architectural expression has been found only with great difficulty. Linear continuity, separation of passenger flow, prevention of intersecting paths, optimum signage, and separate stationary areas (lounges, restaurants, waiting areas, and shops) make considerable demands on the architectonic setup of airport terminals. The logistics of an airport, of course, are geared to getting passengers through the terminal as fast as possible; nonetheless, the commercial factor of their "dwell time" must also be shaped.

Fig. 1 Frederick Gibberd and Partners, architects. Heathrow International Airport, London, begun 1947, showing interior view of Terminal 2, 1955, remodeled in 1975 by Pascall and Watson with Murdoch Design Associates (photo Oct. 1984).

The design of the architectonic core of the airport, the terminal, is generally essential to its image, but it is also, as one would expect, fundamental to the airport's success. This vast complex of buildings – housing all the facilities for passenger, baggage, and cargo handling – has three functions. First, tickets, passports, and bags must be checked quickly to keep circulation flowing. Then, the terminal must have "storage" capacity for all the persons, baggage, and mail it has received. And, lastly, the terminal must provide, in the transport interchange, protection from extreme climatic conditions, noise, and dirt.

Airport Typology

In industrialized societies individual mobility is of vital importance. The parking garage, the regional shopping center, and the airport are, for good reason, the main new buildings types of the twentieth century.[3] And all three of these types have coincided in the last ten years at the largest European airports. Naturally, any airport can be classified according to the type of aircraft landing and taking off there, and the type of service it provides – in other words, according to its status in the established hierarchy of airports (see the essay by Mark J. Bouman in this volume). But since this is a discussion of the architecture of large European airports, it makes more sense to base the classification on the operational system, planning, and design that give the airport its identity.

Large airports have been the subject of an ongoing study, covering many years, conducted by teams of researchers and designers. The question that these planners and architects have been addressing all this time is whether essentially static architecture can shape such unstable surroundings. After all, the tension between the continuing changes in the transport process and the architectonic monumentality of the transfer centers is considerable. Nevertheless, there are a number of fixed programmatical demands for an airport: safety and convenience, walking distances, parking and access, to name a few. These demands still allow for substantial design leeway, although this too is restricted by current views on other criteria – like flexibility and scope for expansion, centralization and decentralization – which are inherent in airport design and determine what type of airport a country or municipality decides to build. In order to be competitive, airlines tend to cultivate the decentralized unit system: a series of individual stations connected by a corridor. Expansion is possible, but management becomes increasingly difficult given the immense distances spanned by large airports. The centralized variant, on the other hand, assembles all the airline counters, waiting areas, and baggage handling in one main section, keeping walking distances down and enabling passengers to transfer relatively quickly and easily from one airline to another.[4] The most extreme form of decentralization occurs when terminals are located in the actual city, and passengers are bused to the planes.[5]

As a result of the tremendous advances in aviation during World War II, there was growing awareness in the immediate postwar period that new types of commercial aircraft, carrying eighty to a hundred passengers at a time, would overwhelm the arrival and departure halls of existing facilities, and thus change the organization and composition of airport buildings. The tonnage, speed, and size of the new planes, as well as their relatively slight reaction to crosswinds, made tarmacked runways and aprons absolutely

3 Michael Brawne, "Airport Passenger Buildings," *Architectural Review* 132, no. 789 (Nov. 1962), p. 341.

4 See "Basic Airport Types" in the special issue "Airport Terminal Buildings," *Progressive Architecture* 34 (May 1953), p. 87.

5 Jacques V. Block, "L'Homme, l'aéroport, l'environnement," *L'Architecture d'Aujourd'hui*, no. 156 (June/July 1971), pp. 4-9.

6 Reyner Banham, "The Obsolescent Airport," *Architectural Review* 132, no. 788 (Oct. 1962), p. 252.

7 K. K. Perlsee, "Ein neuer Flughafentyp mit Relais-Omnibussen," *Werk* (July 1952), pp. 222-23.

8 Edward G. Blankenship, *The Airport: Architecture—Urban Integration—Ecological Problems* (New York and Washington, D.C., 1974), p. 32.

essential. The location of buildings along the airport's perimeter was now pointless. Thus, the second and third generations of airports, often called the "green marinas" – monumentalized before the war at London's Croydon Airport, Paris's Le Bourget, Berlin's Tempelhof, and Hamburg's Fuhlsbüttel (see Voigt, figs. 6, 9, and 13) – were pensioned off. From the postwar perspective, these were ruins of a bygone era, monuments that in terms of practical use were obsolete from the moment they were designed.[6]

Airport construction and modernization in Europe only really got going in the 1950s. This was partly due to the vicissitudes of postwar reconstruction and partly to the fact that in Germany airfields were the responsibility of the Allies until 1955. The frontal system of air terminal design, also known as the transporter configuration, dominated throughout Europe. In this design, the aircraft stood out on the aprons, separate from the terminals, and passengers had to walk out across the tarmac to the planes. The early postwar Zurich International Airport in Switzerland, designed by architects Alfred and Heinrich Oeschger, provides an excellent example of such a facility (frontispiece; fig. 2; pls. 58-59). But these terminals, of course, could not keep up with the rapid increases in the amount of postwar air travel, and as the planes stacked up farther out on the hardstand, passengers found themselves walking ever greater distances, in all kinds of weather. There was clearly a "missing link." Before long, shuttle services were available, and such special amenities as mobile lounges or buses were used to bridge distances and transport passengers to and from the airplanes.[7] The reason given when buses were introduced in the 1950s – first used at Amsterdam's Schiphol Airport – was flexibility. Differing sizes of aircraft and "doorstep" heights were added problems, though these too could be overcome.[8] But when jets came on the scene, the problem of the "missing link" became acute. The new planes were not simply bigger: they needed much more space at or near the terminal, and their size was evidence of the increasing volume of mass transport. Furthermore, passengers could no longer be subjected to the noise of jet engines and the danger of their air displacement. Not only did jet noise cause alienation between airport and town, but it also brought about the necessity for an enclosed interchange between terminal and aircraft.

Fig. 2 Alfred and Heinrich Oeschger, architects. Airside of terminal at Zurich International Airport, 1946-53, with view of a Swiss Air Lines DC-3; from *Werk* (Feb. 1954), p. 41.

The search for new types of airport illustrates the fact that the organization of countless airport amenities was far from programmatical or set down in design standards. A wide variety of facilities had to be provided, to help offset the costs of running the ever-expanding terminal buildings: washrooms plus hairdressers, dentists, a nursery and a mortuary, hotel, nightclub, cinema and exhibition rooms, reception and conference rooms for state visits, quarantine quarters for animals, safes, and nuclear shelters.[9] And all these extras made airports even more complicated. The accumulation of program elements, and the transport of greater numbers of passengers which jet planes facilitated, made it essential to find less monumental and more functional spatial models for the modern airport.

The physical segregation of aircraft from terminal is not the only feature of the fourth generation of airports – another important aspect is the concentration of passenger buildings on an island in a central section of the airport. Runways are grouped in constellations or arranged tangentially around the terminal. The central building has a circular platform for planes heading for their parking bays, and a central core with buildings, roads, and car parks. A tunnel or underpass gives access to the island. This configuration means that landside activities can penetrate into the airport's very heart. The result is architecture on a grand scale, and a complete split between the airport and its surroundings. This generation of airports anticipates an increase in air traffic and a growing demand for aircraft positions and gates, which are often added to existing buildings by means of corridors. Yet, once again, additions mean that passengers have to cover greater distances on foot. The prototypes of the fourth generation are London's Heathrow Airport and Paris's Orly. Heathrow, used as an airfield for the Royal Air Force during World War II, is one of the earliest extant examples. The airport, encased in a star-shaped system of runways, was opened in 1946 (see Lockhart, fig. 10), but the first permanent buildings were finished only ten years later, after a design by Frederick Gibberd and Partners (see fig. 3).

The terminal at Orly (1957-61), designed by Aéroports de Paris, headed by Henri Vicariot, is a rectangular box, 660 feet long and 230 feet wide, consisting of a concrete frame with curtain walls in front. The eight-story building has been extended on the east and west sides, with a two-story, linear "finger" that makes the façade on the airside 2,300 feet long (see fig. 4). The architecture of Orly is monumental and monolithic, in gray, black, and white. Massiveness is expressly avoided, in favor of transparency, in the true modernist tradition of Ludwig Mies van der Rohe. The building is the perfect embodiment of the terminal as a showcase (fig. 5).[10]

Fig. 3 Frederick Gibberd and Partners, architects. Aerial view of Heathrow International Airport, London, showing Terminal 2, 1955, and later additions of Terminal 1, 1968, and Terminal 3, 1970; not visible in this aerial photograph is Terminal 4, 1986.

Fig. 4 Aéroports de Paris, architects; Henri Vicariot, chief architect. Aerial view of Orly Airport, Paris, opened 1961, showing original terminal now called Orly South; not visible in this aerial photograph is the terminal called Orly West, 1971.

Fig. 5 Aéroports de Paris, architects; Henri Vicariot, chief architect. Interior view of main hall of the terminal at Orly Airport, Paris; from *L'Architecture d'Aujourd'hui* 32 (Sept. 1961), p. 52.

Fig. 6 NACO (Netherlands Airport Consultancy), with M. Duintjer, architects. Aerial view of Schiphol Airport, Amsterdam, with, left to right, piers C, D, and E, 1963-67 (photo May 8, 1967).

9 Heinrich Kosina, "Bauliche Anlagen der Luftfahrt," *Baukunst und Werkform* 15 (Feb. 1962), pp. 61-62.
10 Andre Lortie, "Paris-CDG: l'aeroporto e la città," *Casabella*, no. 604 (Sept. 1993), p. 22.
11 "Aéroport international de Rome Fiumicino," *L'Architecture d'Aujourd'hui* 32 (Sept. 1961), pp. 56-63; on Linate Airport in Milan, see "Aéroport de Milan Linate," *L'Architecture d'Aujourd'hui* 32 (Sept. 1961), p. 68; on Copenhagen, see "L'Aéroport de Copenhague, Danemark," *L'Architecture d'Aujourd'hui* 34 (Oct./Nov. 1963), pp. 92-99; for information about the architect at Copenhagen, see J. Bertelsen, ed., *Vilhelm Lauritzen: A Modern Architect* (Holte, 1994).
12 Wood Alexander Lockhart, "Airport Development and Design: A New Architectural Problem" (Ph.D. diss., Northwestern University, 1972), p. 208.

Finger- and star-shaped terminals appeared in the 1950s in the United States and soon afterwards in Europe. Passengers could be brought together in a central area and then divided up into arrival and departure lounges right beside the aircraft standing next to the pier. When two floors are used, it is possible to separate different functions. The first European example of the fifth generation of airports is the terminal at London's Gatwick Airport (1958), a rectangular building with one finger (see pl. 91), to which another two were added in 1964. Such big European cities as Rome, Milan, Copenhagen, London, and Amsterdam adopted the system too.[11] Amsterdam's Schiphol Airport is, in fact, the ultimate expression of the finger, with passengers proceeding along moving walkways. Adjustable gangways or jetways protrude from the fingers and are designed to enable planes to taxi to the gates under their own steam (see figs. 6-7).[12]

The finger and star terminals provided not only a clever means of expansion for existing airports, but also an excellent opportunity for new airports to link up better with parking facilities. In order to reduce the walking distance between parking lot and plane, a decentralized setup of separate gates was opted for, and central passenger handling was abolished. Decentralized terminals, or satellite configurations, make the most of aircraft maneuverability. Among the first satellites constructed in North America was that in Toronto; planning began in 1957, construction was underway by 1961, and the circular terminal enclosing a seven-story parking garage was opened in 1964 (fig. 8). Elongated terminals, whether straight or curved, forming a cir-

Fig. 7 NACO, with M. Duintjer, architects. Terminal at Schiphol Airport, Amsterdam, pier D, with view at center of DC-8 stretch version (photo Sept. 27, 1967).

cle or polygon, enable aircraft to taxi right up to the gates and stay there: the drive-in airport. The first European example of a satellite system was created at Geneva's Cointrin Airport (opened in 1968), followed by Cologne-Bonn Airport in 1970 (fig. 9).[13] The plethora of cars searching for somewhere to park in the airport's vicinity gave rise to the idea of using elevators and escalators for all connections with the airport, thus reducing walking distances. At Heathrow and Schiphol, parking garages are an integral part of the overall plan. The cheapest airport is one huge infrastructural node, with minimal distances, limited spatial requirements, and low construction costs.[14] The main terminal at the Otto Lilienthal International Airport at Berlin-Tegel (the winning entry by Von Gerkan, Marg and Nickels in 1965; completed in 1974) and Terminal 1 at Paris's Charles de Gaulle Airport – often called Roissy I (designed by Aéroports de Paris, headed by Paul Andreu; 1967-74) – served as models for a new series of terminals in which parking was treated as a central issue. In an elaboration of Paul Schneider-Esleben's studies into drive-in terminals ("stacked" parking), begun in 1960, Von Gerkan, Marg and Nickels designed a simple main form (a hexagon), in which the idea of the shortest route from car to plane has been carried to its extreme: the terminal as a roundabout (fig. 10).

Roissy I comprises a round main building with seven trapezoidal satellites, where the planes stand (fig. 11). Studies for this airport were started in 1966. Paul Andreu, now principal designer with Aéroports de Paris, has concentrated his energy on the operations, the geometrical organization of space, and the constructive severity of the building.[15] He and his team have designed a facility at Roissy that is the absolute opposite of Paris Orly: they strove for maximum concentration of space, with, instead of a rectangular box, a cylinder – a continuous omnibuilding, in which traffic and the other functions are bunched together vertically. Roissy I is twice as big as Orly, but distances for traffic there have been cut to a minimum, using separate approach roads for cars, and parking on the upper floors and roof of the terminal. After the passenger has parked in the vertical garage, he takes the elevator and escalator to the departure hall, hands over his luggage, and then walks through a tunnel to the appropriate satellite, where he waits for boarding in a departure lounge.[16] The central concourse in the terminal covers two stories and contains the necessary facilities. Roissy I is an advanced high-tech variant of the roundabout-type terminal: a machine for boarding aircraft. The layout of the roads around Roissy has supplied a number of landmarks – the road network, water tower, air traffic control tower, and terminal – making the airport a vast architectonic network.

Fig. 8 John B. Parkin, architect. Aerial view of Lester B. Pearson International Airport, Toronto, showing Terminal 1 (satellite), 1961-64, and Terminal 2, 1968-72 (photo 1972).

Fig. 9 Paul Schneider-Esleben, architect. Aerial view of Cologne-Bonn International Airport, 1962-70.

13 See, for instance, G. K., "Flughafen Köln-Bonn fertiggestellt," *Bauwelt* 61 (Nov. 1970), pp. 406-07; "Bonn-Cologne," *L'Architecture d'Aujourd'hui*, no. 156 (June/July 1971), pp. 30-34; Werner Treibel, *Geschichte der deutschen Verkehrsflughäfen: Eine Dokumentation von 1909 bis 1989* (Bonn, 1992), pp. 283-316.
14 Z. Striszic, "Airports," *Architectural Design* 43, no. 4 (1973), pp. 224-39.
15 Serge Salat and Françoise Labbé, *Paul Andreu: Metamorphosis of the Circle*, trans. Ronald Corlette Theuil (Milan and Paris, 1990), p. 30.
16 Ibid., p. 46.

Fig. 10 Meinhard von Gerkan, with Volkwin Marg and Klaus Nickels, architects. Aerial view of terminal with parking at Otto Lilienthal International Airport, Berlin-Tegel, 1969-74 (photo Aug. 1976).

Fig. 11 Aéroports de Paris, architects; Paul Andreu, chief architect. Aerial view of Terminal 1 and its satellites at Charles de Gaulle International Airport, Roissy-en-France, 1967-74; from *L'Architecture d'Aujourd'hui* (March 1974), p. 28.

The central building is connected with the seven satellites by two-story tunnels, some 800 feet in length (see fig. 12). The complex is built of reinforced concrete and does not really have a façade. Andreu has thus interpreted one of the doctrines of Le Corbusier – that an airport be built as a naked phenomenon – in such a way that the concrete acquires a fitting fundamental expression, which also reassures the passengers: a clear architectonic idiom and unconfused passage through the empty center to the gates.

The fundamental concept of the fifth generation of airports – minimal distance between landside and airside – came under great pressure in the 1970s, when international terrorism surfaced. Since then airports have had to meet strict safety regulations. One of the main features of the sixth generation of airports is the bottleneck principle. The arrival and departure halls are once again centrally located (often on separate floors), but there is a strict division between the "secure" area (following passport inspection and body search) and the "open" area. Well-devised terminal concepts guarantee the discreet transition from public area to a zone with differentiated security, thus avoiding any feeling of restricted freedom. The consequence of the new safety regulations is, once more, longer walking distances, and passenger handling is again the focus of attention. An airport with optimum security is the prime objective and so the simple handling logistics receive special focus.

In the 1980s and 1990s an attempt has been made to capitalize on the new programmatical demands, forcefully deploying architectural means to turn the airport into a pleasant place, with its own identity. This may explain in part the attention currently being paid to the large concourse, often reminiscent of a hangar. It is interesting to note that high-tech terminals, in which the construction elements are on enthusiastic display, score well with visitors and architectural critics. In hangars the space framework – whether steel trusses or concrete ribs – has always been visible, but the shed has never featured very high on the list of architectonic priorities, since elevations and space formation are not accorded much room. The choice of the hangar as a source of inspiration for the design of a terminal raises the question as to whether the elements that the modernist architectural tradition considers to be of secondary importance (ordonnance and detail by means of ornament, color, and material) really are of minor importance, and whether the con-

Fig. 12 Aéroports de Paris, architects; Paul Andreu, chief architect. Section of main building, satellites, and tunnels of Terminal 1 at Charles de Gaulle International Airport, Roissy-en-France, 1967-74.

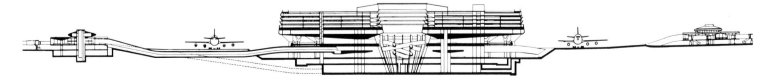

struction does in fact determine the essence of the building. Le Corbusier was guilty of this same reductive approach. In his view, the biomorphic and magnificent expression of airplanes could only be offset by the architecture of the "naked" airport, that is, with concrete buildings. Le Corbusier viewed the skeleton as the essence.[17]

Be that as it may, the passenger terminals of the sixth generation of airports – from the new facility at Stansted Airport north of London (fig. 13) to the totally new Kansai International Airport in Japan (see pls. 128-29) – are designed as vast open spaces. But these are spaces to pass through, with ambiguous social connotations, in that they are collective spaces without a feeling of communality. The space itself calls forth associations with a transparent tube or station concourse: a mixture of street and interior.[18] Architects strive to show the construction as a universal structure, but that structure also has to be unique for the location. The spaces are bathed in brilliant light, filtered through the transparent walls. The terminal roof, often easier for passengers to observe than the other elevations, becomes a fifth façade, and as such, is an essential part of the spatial composition.

The new terminal at Hamburg's Fuhlsbüttel, for example, designed by Von Gerkan, Marg and Partners (1986-94) is one of the finest celebrations of the concourse concept (see pls. 131-32). All possible typological interpretations that can be attributed to a concourse apply here: passage, hangar, and nineteenth-century railway station.[19] Characteristically, Von Gerkan's office has also designed a maintenance hangar at Hamburg for Lufthansa's jumbo jets (see pl. 130) recalling a prewar hangar at Milan's Linate Airport from 1937.[20] In terms of its use of space, the new Hamburg terminal resembles a simple frame without façades. The only façade is the roof, which is shaped like an airplane wing. The roof is borne by six pairs of sturdy, reinforced concrete pillars. Each pillar supports four slender, diagonal steel tubes that hold up the roof construction. The dynamics of the wall-less curved roof contrasts with the two static rectangular office buildings, which clamp the hall in between them. The glass façades of the terminal and the window bands in the roof serve to filter light through the roof into the hall. In the late afternoon and at night the hall is lit indirectly by way of the roof.

The new terminal at Stansted Airport, designed by Sir Norman Foster (1986-91), pursues an emphatically formal likeness with the traditional aircraft hangar. In terms of typology, postwar hangars have undergone the few-

17 Le Corbusier and Pierre Jeanneret, Œuvre Complète, 8 vols. (Zurich, 1930-70), vol. 4 (1938-46), pp. 190-91.

18 An extreme imitation of the nineteenth-century railway station hall: "Julio Lafuente: Ostiense New Air Terminal, Rome, Italy," Architecture and Urbanism (May 1992), pp. 96-105; M. A. Arnaboldi, "Una stazione per l'aereo: Fly by rail," L'Arca 54 (1991), pp. 78-83.

19 Klaus-Dieter Weiss, ed., Von Gerkan, Marg und Partner: Unter grossen Dächern (Braunschweig and Wiesbaden, 1995), p. 136.

20 J. G. Wattjes, "Vliegtuighal van het vliegveld te Linate, architect D. Torres," Bouwbedrijf en Openbare Werken 14 (1939), pp. 184-86.

21 Lockhart (note 12), p. 228.

22 Important articles about Stansted include Architecture and Urbanism (Nov. 1991), pp. 42-128; Jean-Claude Garcias, "Norman Foster: Ossature, membranes et fluides," L'Architecture d'Aujourd'hui, no. 276 (Sept. 1991), pp. 66-73; B. L. [Béatrice Loyer], "Aéroport de Stansted, GB," Techniques et Architecture, no. 398 (1991), pp. 134-41; see also the special issue "Stansted," The Architectural Review 189, no. 1131 (May 1991), pp. 36-82.

Fig. 13 Norman Foster and Partners, architects; with Ove Arup and Partners. Baggage claim area inside the terminal at Stansted Airport, near London, 1986-91.

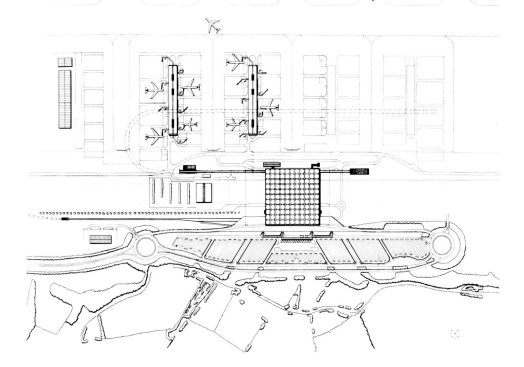

est changes of all airport buildings. They continue the basic prewar principle of space, the only difference being the measurements: an unobstructed floor plan and unlimited lengthwise expansion, with no use of columns.[21] Apart from concrete arch constructions – which are really variants on constructions in steel – trusses also started to be made of concrete. Since the 1960s, however, large airports have switched to the cantilever system and steel space frame, and the popularity of concrete arch-work has waned. The dawn of the jet age has, in fact, served only to refine certain matters of design, though it has, of course, also required adjustments in dimensions: namely, superhangars. The hangar concept, combined with the logic of the large nineteenth-century railway terminus, was the deliberate starting point for London's Stansted terminal (fig. 13).[22] High-tech architecture is not only an end in itself there, but also a logistic structuring of the visual. Unlike Heathrow and Gatwick, Stansted was conceived as an airport that functions as a unit, offers passengers a clear pedestrian route, and is flexible enough to allow expansion without fragmentation into a series of independent buildings. The key to understanding this white edifice – with its immense roof of over 400,000 square feet – lies in analysis of its construction (fig. 14). All the public amenities are located on one floor, with an unambiguous concourse, at which departures and arrivals take place. The technical aspects, such as climate control, baggage handling, public transport, and parking, are housed in the base of the building. The projecting trussed roof and branching groups of pillars rhythmically follow a 400-square-foot grid, and immediately catch the eye (fig. 15). These "tree structures" support canopy-like skylights that also

Fig. 16 Aéroports de Paris, architects; Paul Andreu, chief architect. Landside roadway to Terminal 2 at Charles de Gaulle International Airport, Roissy-en-France: module B, 1972-81; module A, 1972-83; module D, 1985-89; module C, 1987-94.

regulate the penetration of daylight. On the one hand, Stansted makes the impression of a minimalist square glass box, standing, pavilion-like, in its surroundings, while, on the other hand, it is a bold statement of the expressionist celebration of construction.

The complexity of the most recent terminal at Charles de Gaulle, familiarly called Roissy II, designed by Aéroports de Paris, headed by Paul Andreu (module B, 1972-81; module A, 1972-83; module D, 1985-89; module C, 1987-94), does not arise from the building but from the road system (fig. 16). The airport has been conceived as a structure of pathways, with choices required at every bend. It starts while you are still in the car. Roissy II is one of the airports with a linear setup, inspired by the Dallas-Fort Worth type: an expansion or multiplication of an elongated building, with parking facilities right beside the aircraft (see pls. 111, 113, 116, 118). The linear system integrates all the means of transport in one line, and then disperses passengers and goods over the different functional levels. The advantages of this model are the straight movement of planes, speedy transfer in the airport's integrated traffic systems, drive-in facilities for various types of transport, the shortest possible distances to public transportation facilities, and the human scale of the buildings.[23] Roissy II has used the integration of the megastructure into the urban environment to maximum effect.

Airport Psychology

Air travel has done away with the impediments of geographical dispersal and allowed the difference between here and there to be exploited. The modern air traveler is a nomad who wants to feel at ease everywhere in the world community, with a minimum of baggage. This breakaway from his environment has affected his individuality. Air space, with its tele-facilities, has become an extension of his home and office; the plane is his mobile home.

We experience an airport as a logistical machine, steered by information panels and signs: an impressive creation, but alarming too. If we look more closely at the worldwide network of airports with their air corridors, we get the impression of a permanent maelstrom, which sucks us in without exposing us to the climatological conditions of a normal sojourn on land: wind, rain, and daylight. In the maelstrom, flowing movements are more important than objects or buildings. Flowing space has its own physical and visual climate – an optically static environment, its own code of discipline (hard and

23 Striszic (note 14).
24 "Der Flughof Kloten-Zürich," *Werk* (Feb. 1954), p. 42.

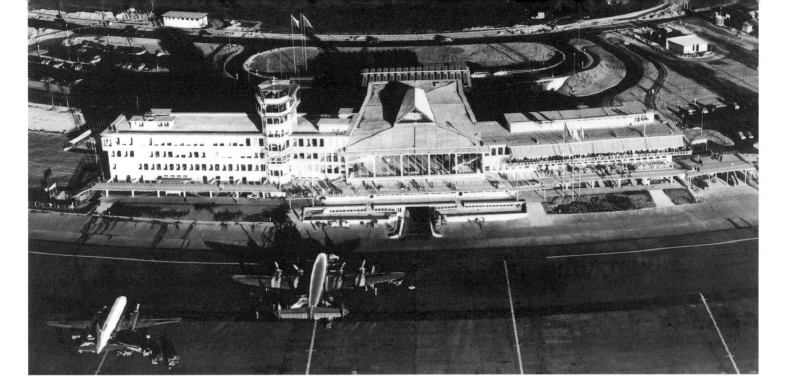

Fig. 17 Alfred and Heinrich Oeschger, architects. Aerial view of Zurich International Airport showing cone-shaped main terminal, 1946-53, with view of a Lockheed *Constellation* and a Convair 240 (or 340).

soft pressure) with check-in counters, baggage depots, and uniformed staff. A flight is a minor drama with a prologue and an epilogue. This staged drama contains set elements: excitement, emotional encounters, colorful uniforms worn by ground and air staff, baggage-laden trolleys, endless queues of waiting travelers, and constant bustle. The space between one climax – the moment of touchdown – and another – entry into a new city or country – is the realm of the design team: a regular flow in which nodes, contrasts, and surprises are shaped.

Airport buildings not only supply comfort, but also satisfy emotional and symbolic needs. We unconsciously associate air travel with speed, adaptability, light, air, comfort, and service. It is the architect's job to reinforce that unconscious desire, with the use of plenty of glass, muted colors, comfortable furniture, and perfect treatment of the passenger. The space surrounding the flowing movement should radiate not only an atmosphere of comfort and luxury, but also one of reassurance and mild euphoria, against a backdrop of necessary facilities presented in a simple and efficient design. Transparency of organization and styling suggests minimal resistance. Architecture is also part of the airports' and airlines' marketing strategy. It is vital that airports be different, and that difference must be expressed in their architecture. The visitor must also be convinced that the socio-economic disruptions caused by air traffic – dangers, disasters, pollution, noise, smell, traffic jams, jet lags – are outweighed by the advantages of the megastructure. In addition, architecture has the symbolic function of an optimistic reference to the myth of Icarus. At most airports there is a profusion of associations with winged or more abstract nautical shapes.

But of equal importance is the adoration of light, the best architectonic medium of them all. At the early 1950s airport in Zurich, for instance, the entrance is conically shaped, suggesting various associations with space (fig. 17). At the airside the terminal becomes progressively wider and lighter, providing departing passengers with the "well tempered spatial state of mind" and "a glimpse of the wide world" (see fig. 18 and frontispiece).[24] In architects' rhetoric, light can even lend an area an identity of its own. The design for the new Franz Josef Strauss International Airport in Munich (design team headed by Hans-Busso von Busse; opened in 1992) is, according to the

Fig. 18 Alfred and Heinrich Oeschger, architects. Interior view of the terminal at Zurich International Airport, 1946-53, looking towards the airfield.

designer, contained in a white structure, based on the play with light colors characteristic of South German Baroque (see fig. 19).[25] Even at a decidedly high-tech airport like Stansted, the construction also serves to guide the passenger from darkness to light: "The arrival is in a huge cave from which the passenger gradually ascends to a huge luminous tent. After passing through clearly organised stages of preparation, and arriving at a point where the initiate can contemplate the heavens, he is plunged underground again to arrive at a jetty whence he boards his aerial vessel."[26]

At Roissy I, one walks from the darkness of the parking garages and basements to the light of the satellite. Andreu has sought to achieve an axial composition of masses and a sensitive encounter of light and material. The concrete cylinder of the terminal has an empty core that calls for a moment of reflection (fig. 20). On the first floor a fountain plays. Moving staircases have been installed diagonally through the empty area, transporting passengers from the dark, through the emptiness, to the light. The building is not an object that is easy to observe: the feeling of passage, the impression of open and closed spaces, the intelligent manipulation of interior and exterior are more important than one set viewpoint. This is an organism without a façade. Forms follow one another like a seamless assembly.[27]

Roissy II has abandoned the monolithic approach of Roissy I, and a more layered relationship between the whole and the parts has been achieved. The ellipse is the supporting formal theme. Inside nothing touches the ceiling, nothing goes in that direction or is suspended from it. For architect Paul Andreu, the roof is a shield from the heat, noise, and light, but it is also a metaphor for the heavens.[28] For many other airport designers as well, architectonic design is subservient to the idea of the gateway, which affords a view of the journey to the light.

Airport Infrastructure

Although lip-service was already being paid in the postwar years to the theory that airport planning was a regional matter,[29] with a bus terminal, railway station, rent-a-car service, and infrastructural connections integrated in the plan, it took several decades for the theory to be put into practice. The way in which airports fit into the surrounding region after the war was roughly a three-stage process: fourth and fifth generation airports were based on the island concept, and in those days the airport was a comfortable

25 "Hans-Busso von Busse + Claus Baldus. Interview: Space, Light, Structure – A Kind of Subdued Passion," *Architecture and Urbanism* (Feb. 1993), p. 84.
26 Peter Davey, "Stansted," *The Architectural Review* (note 22), p. 45.
27 Salat and Labbé (note 15).
28 Ibid.
29 See, for instance, J. Gordon Carr, "Airports of the Future," *Architectural Record* (July 1943), pp. 66-70 and special issue (April 1945); see "Airport Terminal Buildings" (note 4), pp. 69-121.

Fig. 19 Hans-Busso von Busse and Partner, architects. Interior view of the main hall of the terminal at Franz Josef Strauss International Airport, Munich, 1976-92.

Fig. 20 Aéroports de Paris, architects; Paul Andreu, chief architect. Bird's-eye view of the central core of Terminal 1 at Charles de Gaulle International Airport, Roissy-en-France, 1967-74.

village. But by the time the sixth generation was ready to be built, the village was becoming a veritable town, even though the logistics were geared to the vast numbers of car owners. Since the 1980s, large airports have been functioning as infrastructural nodes of national, sometimes international, importance. National spatial planning policy enables the various forms of transport to link up with flights. In Paris, for example, the high-speed train (TGV) makes a great loop around the city, stopping at Euro-Disney as well as at both major airports, Orly and Charles de Gaulle.

These stages illustrate the airport's insatiable appetite for land. Moreover, it is becoming increasingly clear that their very scale ensures that they contrast sharply with, and make demands on, their urban surroundings. The amount of space needed and the way in which it is used by Schiphol illustrates this galloping development: in 1920 it was one field in the Harlemmermeer polder; in 1945 a couple of runways on a small corner of the polder; in 1967 a conglomeration of central buildings and four runways taking up about a quarter of the polder; and between the start of its most recent expansion in 1994 and its projected completion date sometime around 2005, this airport will grow to encompass five runways and an immense infrastructure of roads and railways, with environmental problems affecting the entire conurbation of western Holland (see fig. 21).

After a period of thirty years in which air transport had built up a monopoly in terms of speed, safety, and comfort, a crisis broke out around 1970, attended by social and financial problems and declining service. The crisis was connected with competition from high-speed trains for the favors of short-haul passengers. The failure to include airports in regional planning (in terms of adequate connections with other means of transport and proper integration of landside activities) came in for strong criticism. But the oil crisis of the early 1970s and increasing environmental awareness also played a part. The controversy over Runway West 18 at Rhein-Main Airport in Frankfurt was a notorious example. The decision to build this addition was made in 1965, but it was not constructed until 1981, only after countless objections had been obviated. The main objection was that around five acres of woodland had to be chopped down. And only after twenty years of political, administrative, and legal battling could Munich's new airport eventually be built.

It was not until the 1990s that the full direct and indirect consequences of airport operations were to attract attention. In 1991, for example, the air-

Fig. 21 Aerial view of Schiphol Airport, Amsterdam (photo July 6, 1992), with view of pier F by NACO (Netherlands Airport Consultancy), with M. Duintjer, architects, 1977, and, at the far right, pier G and new arrival hall by NACO, with Benthem and Crouwel, architects, 1989-93 (see also fig. 6).

Figs. 22-23 Helmut Jahn of Murphy/Jahn, architects. Kempinski Hotel at the Munich Airport Center, Franz Josef Strauss International Airport, Munich, 1991-94.

line Swissair was courageous enough to take "ecological stock" of the effects of airport-related activities on the environment. Swissair's 55 airplanes were emitting 429 tons of nitrogen, 99 tons of hydrocarbon, and 280 tons of carbon monoxide a day into the immediate environment of the Zurich Airport. Passengers, the people bringing and collecting them, visitors, and employees were covering 970,000 km a day in cars, producing emissions in a 20-km radius around the airport of 240 tons of nitrogen oxide, 151 tons of hydrocarbon, and 803 tons of carbon monoxide.[30]

Airports have enormous impact on their communities in terms of employment. Frankfurt's airport (pls. 101-02), for instance, provides jobs for 40,000 people (21,000 of whom work for Lufthansa); London's Heathrow employs around 55,000 people. More than 1,000 flights each day keep British meteorologists, air traffic controllers, pilots, cabin crews, cleaners, caterers, check-in staff, baggage handlers, technicians, firemen, police, and security officials on the go. Thousands of supply companies employ at least another 300,000 people.[31] These days commerce on the ground often makes more money for airports than international flights. Gatwick Airport, for example, has plans for an "airport theme park," intended to attract a million visitors a year. Interestingly enough, their journey will take them no further than the airport itself.[32] Not only do airports provide recreation, but they also meet the international business community's requirements: conference rooms, hotels, galleries, showrooms, business centers: "These multiple programmes and agendas – operational, commercial, political – are one reason why writers have started talking about airports as cities – cities of the air. Both cities and airports cover large areas; both are a complex of intersecting transport systems, economies, buildings, and people. But there is one crucial difference: cities have inhabitants. At airports everyone is transient."[33] So it is better to see airports as rampant metropolitan fragments. The connections between these megastructures and the surrounding metropolis must be optimal, because an airport generates an extraordinary amount of traffic. That is why its deployment in a regional and even continental context, with its hinge function, is of crucial importance. In 1961 the Greek planner Konstantinos Doxiades introduced the concept of "Ecumenopolis, the up-and-coming city which will cover the entire world."[34] In that universal city, airports function as city squares.

The new economic perspective can be found beside infrastructural intersections. In Great Britain, for example, more than 30 million square meters of commercial floor space was created between 1980 and 1990. It consists of horizontal buildings with an abstract architectonic vocabulary, covered euphemistically by the term "big sheds."[35] Airports are the most extreme

30 Otto Goedecke, "Flughafen München II," *Baumeister* 71 (1991), p. 31.
31 Deyan Sudjic, *The 100 Mile City* (London, 1992), p. 150.
32 Thackara (note 2), p. 13.
33 Thackara (note 2), p. 15.
34 *Ekistics* (Oct. 1961).
35 M. Pawley, "Stansted and the Triumph of Big Sheds," *Architecture and Urbanism* (note 22), p. 47.
36 Sudjic (note 31), pp. 149-69.
37 E. Swyngedouw, "De produktie van de Europese maatschappelijke ruimte," in W. Zonneveld and F. D'hondt, eds., *Europese ruimtelijke ordening: Impressies en visies vanuit Vlaanderen en Nederland* (Ghent and The Hague, 1994), p. 51.

manifestations in this category, the ultimate example being London's Stansted. These structures are parachuted into what was once farm land, embedded in a new infrastructure of public and private transport. Investments in urban functions at and near airports – stopover (hotels), shopping (malls), work space (technology parks and multinational offices) – act as magnets in the region (see figs. 22-23).[36]

Competition between the European airports has led to a reorganization of flight movements. In the present European market at least three hundred regions are fighting strategic battles for capital and jobs. Cities with traffic interchanges play a key role in national economies. In today's superstructure, London, Paris, and Frankfurt have the most important airports, followed by Amsterdam's Schiphol. The economic importance of an internationally competitive airport is confirmed by the huge investments that it generates. At Schiphol, for instance, in order to safeguard that airport's position for the future, billions of dollars are being invested in a fifth runway and some twenty-five concomitant infrastructural projects. The reorganization of European airspace in turn ties in with the geopolitical creation of trans-European networks, geared to improving existing development axes (see the essay by Leonard Kau in this volume). These axes are characterized by intensive traffic flows and a highly dynamic pattern of business premises and family dwellings. All the macroprojects, intended to get inert Europe moving, create immobile spatial structures: terminals, stations, and office parks, which are "geared to better, but ever-speculative and uncertain monetization of the space."[37]

The inadequate absorption of airports in the surrounding region and the consequences of aviation for the environment, combined with the indisputable economic significance of national airports as job-providers, constitute a Gordian knot that is forcing the powers that be, nationally and internationally, to become involved in the design and construction of airports. This worldwide complexity, which has overtaken us sooner than expected, will once more have vast consequences for airport architecture. One thing is certain: design trends are so subject to change that the prototype of the twenty-first-century airport cannot, as yet, be admired anywhere in the world.

"An Airport in Every City":
The History of American Airport Design

David Brodherson

Like the characters in the old children's parable "The Little Red Hen," my father, Sam, and my aunt, Rose, helped "sow the wheat" for this research. Unfortunately, they are unable to enjoy the "harvest." I miss them; this is in their memory. Grants from the National Endowment for the Arts, the Graham Foundation for Advanced Studies in the Fine Arts, and the New Jersey Historical Commission have supported this research. I also wish to thank John Zukowsky, John Reps, Michael Tomlan, and Robert Sharp, who, in varying fashion, have guided this research.

1   Reprinted from a radio address in *The United States Aviation Quarterly* 1 (June-Aug. 1929), pp. 10, 67-68.
2   For a study of the origins of airport policy, see David Brodherson, "What Can't Go Up Can't Come Down: The History of American Airport Policy, Planning and Design" (Ph.D. diss., Cornell University, 1993); see also Lawrence Chimerine and Gregory Stanko, "Stop the Subsidies to Europe's Airlines," *New York Times* (Nov. 27, 1994), sec. 3, p. 11.

In 1928 Secretary of Commerce and presidential candidate Herbert Hoover, anticipating an era of prosperity that never materialized, made his now famous pledge assuring every American family of "a chicken in every pot." Approximately a year later, President Hoover's Assistant Secretary of the Navy, Ernest Lee Jahncke, echoed these words when he promised "an airport in every city."[1] In reality, America was a long way from fulfilling either promise, although the public and private sectors had been engaged in an array of aeronautical activity well before this time. The United States Post Office Department, for example, developed and operated airmail service from 1918 to 1925 (see fig. 1) and, after the passage of the Contract Air Mail Act of 1925, gave many private entrepreneurs and companies a start in commercial aviation. But the passage of the Air Commerce Act of 1926 initiated an important, formative period in the evolution of public policy promoting and regulating the development of airports in cities across the country. The coordination of federal, state, and local policies established between 1926 and 1929 ensured the proper environment necessary for airlines to operate large aircraft profitably, safely, conveniently, and comfortably.

The Air Commerce Act created a national air transportation network modeled after the United States maritime system. Unlike the development of other federally sponsored programs affecting infrastructure throughout the country, however, these laws delegated responsibility for the design of airports largely to local governments, though in accordance with federal standards. But the national government retained responsibility for the creation of the aids to navigation and airways, much as it had overseen lighthouses and ship channels, which are keys to federal control of interstate commerce. The development of American air transportation policy contrasted starkly with Europe, where the responsibility for forming airlines, building navigation aids, and constructing airports nearly always rested in the hands of each country's central government.[2]

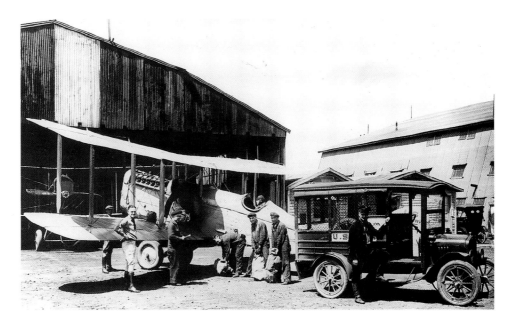

Fig. 1 United States Post Office Department airmail service, Checkerboard Field, Roosevelt Road and 1st Avenue, Maywood, Illinois, c. 1921, with a De Havilland DH-4 mail plane.

Although changes in commercial aviation have occurred since the Air Commerce Act, local governments in the United States are still primarily responsible for airport development. Nonetheless, important exceptions or anomalies exist. First, although the authors of legislation establishing air transportation policy followed maritime models, airport designers generally borrowed their ideas from the architects and engineers of railway terminals. Second, for a brief period of time, private enterprises such as Pan American Airways and the Curtiss-Wright Corporation built their own networks of airports in chains crossing the country and girdling the globe. The designs of these privately owned facilities were indistinguishable from municipal airports. Third, though the agency assumed responsibility long after other cities were well on their way with airports, the Federal Aviation Administration (under various names) has directly overseen the design of the airports serving the nation's capital, Washington, D.C., from 1938 until 1985. But wherever located and however managed, airports have become important public works, indispensable to urban economies; they are our urban gateways, and as symbols of civic pride they surpass in importance even our tallest skyscrapers.

The stimulus for the creation and development of early airports came from several sources. Certainly, the foundation of public policy that encouraged the creation of airports was one important influence. But so were events like the 1929 airport design competition sponsored by the Lehigh Portland Cement Company of Allentown, Pennsylvania. This competition received 257 entries that tried to address the practical requirements of the modern municipal airport in the planning of landing areas, the design of terminals and service buildings, and the integration of the entire facility into the fabric of the city (see fig. 2).[3] The competition gathered worldwide attention and spurred considerable discussion and review of airport planning. Finally, the stimulus of American aeronautical engineers who designed aircraft with greater capacity flying at lower cost and at higher speeds has also, over the decades, compelled architects, planners, and engineers to build bigger airports. These airport and terminal designs evolved in four slightly overlapping stages.

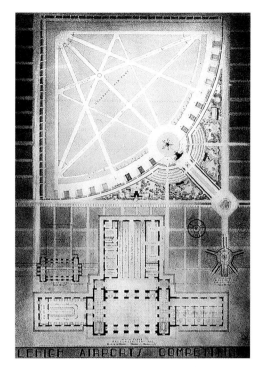

Fig. 2 A. C. Zimmerman and William H. Harrison, architects. Design for Lehigh Airports Competition, first prize winner, 1929; from *American Airport Designs* (New York and Chicago, 1930), p. 14.

The Era of Experimental Airport Design, 1926–1929

The late 1920s constituted an extraordinary era of experimental design that affected the core components of the air travel system. Two different concepts for the design of airport terminals, for example, suggested the uncertainty of the future of this transportation medium. In the interior, seating provided for waiting passengers and guests was similar to that of an austere, inexpensively furnished club room, or perhaps a private living room. Hangars adapted the civil engineering of train sheds employing three-pin-truss or column-and-truss systems with some architectural ornament referring to flight. Away from the airport, ticket offices were little more than comfortably furnished store fronts with a counter for a clerk to sell tickets, give information, and provide surface transportation to the airport.

One of the two terminal types developed in this era, the "depot hangar," or "lean-to hangar," combined a waiting room and office facilities with the aircraft hangar; this form was used in airports across the country in such places as Newark, Chicago, Wichita, and Los Angeles. The clear, dry weather of the Los Angeles metropolitan area, its growing population, and the booming film industry created ideal conditions for the growth of the air trans-

3 Lehigh Portland Cement Company, *American Airport Designs* (New York and Chicago, 1930).

4 "Airports in Pictures," *Airports* 3 (Aug. 1929), p. 29; Daniel Bluestone and Harold J. Christian, "The Ford Airport Hangar," *Historic Illinois* 8 (Aug. 1985), pp. 1-6; Henry V. Hubbard et al., *Airports: Their Location, Administration and Legal Basis*, Harvard City Planning Studies (Cambridge, Mass., 1930).

Fig. 3 Gable and Wyant, architects. Airside of Curtiss-Wright Depot Hangar No. 1, Mines Field, 1929, now the site of the cargo office of Los Angeles International Airport.

portation industry (see pls. 11-13). In 1926 the Los Angeles Chamber of Commerce made a preliminary selection of thirteen possible locations for a municipal airport. Eventually, the city chose the site that is now Los Angeles International Airport for the construction of its first air terminal. The city leased a 640-acre tract that William M. Mines had used as an airfield. Gable and Wyant, locally popular architects, designed the Spanish Colonial Revival facility, Hangar No. 1, which contractors erected in 1929 (fig. 3). In 1966 the Los Angeles Cultural Heritage Board designated this depot hangar a local monument; in 1992 it was listed on the National Register of Historic Places as a significant structure despite later improvements. Today the facility serves as an air freight office.[4]

At the same time, architects began modeling the "simple terminal" after the railroad station. In the late 1920s, the Curtiss-Wright Corporation – one of the premier aircraft manufacturing companies – began building its own, domestic, air transportation system, linking a dozen airports and some thirty-five service bases from New York and Baltimore on the East Coast, through Chicago, Milwaukee, St. Louis, and other cities, to Los Angeles and San Francisco on the West Coast. While Curtiss-Wright focused on a domestic system of airports, Pan American Airways concentrated its effort upon an international network of airports linked extensively by flying boats that it purchased from three major manufacturers, Boeing, Martin, and Sikorsky. Pan American built one of the earliest terminals in its system in Miami, Florida, in 1928, a

Fig. 4 Delano and Aldrich, architects. Airside of Pan American Airways Terminal, Miami, 1928 (now demolished), with a Ford Tri-Motor.

facility that served initially as a landplane gateway for Ford Tri-Motors carrying fourteen passengers to destinations in Cuba and the Caribbean (see pls. 8-9, 27-28). The airline employed the New York architectural firm of Delano and Aldrich, who would later design terminals for the airline as it began to extend routes across the Atlantic and Pacific oceans and to South and Central America. This first Miami terminal, no longer extant, was located at the north edge of what is now the city's international airport. The two-story, simple Mediterranean style stucco terminal had two "gates" or access routes to and from aircraft (fig. 4).[5]

Although the United States Congress crafted the Air Commerce Act of 1926 to establish a viable system of local airport development, the federal government ironically decided against providing adequately for an airport in the nation's capital. Congress debated the issue until passing the Civil Aeronautics Act of 1938, which President Franklin D. Roosevelt signed into law. This act allowed the United States government to build an airport in the capital city. Although Congress remained indecisive, Roosevelt quickly used this new power in conjunction with money from the Works Progress Administration (WPA) and the Public Works Administration (PWA) to build Washington National Airport.[6]

During this protracted period of governmental inaction, private-sector businessmen constructed rival air transportation facilities on what ultimately became the site of the Pentagon. In 1925 organizers of the Philadelphia Sesqui-Centennial Exposition established a committee on aviation to promote commercial air transportation. Thomas Mitten, a local streetcar magnate active in the fair organization, formed the Philadelphia Rapid Transit Air Service carrying visitors from Norfolk, Virginia, to Philadelphia with a stop in Washington, D.C. For this intermediate stop Mitten's staff selected a "gypsy field" at the west end of the Highway Bridge near the shore of the Potomac River. With the permission of the Secretary of Commerce, Mitten named his facility Hoover Field. His company built comfortable but unassuming terminals that could accommodate passengers flying on ten-passenger Fokker F-VII trimotor aircraft. Though he had made a great investment in this system, Mitten closed the line soon after the conclusion of the Sesqui-Centennial.

5 "Pan American Airways System: Miami Terminal to Incorporate Most Advanced Ideas in Airport Design and Operation," *Airway Age* 9 (Nov. 1928), pp. 34-37; Roger W. Sherman, "Planning for Airport Buildings," *Architectural Forum: Transportation Building Reference Number* 53 (Dec. 1930), p. 731.

6 John Stuart, "The Washington National Airport," *Pencil Points* 21 (Oct. 1940), pp. 602-13; Ellmore A. Champie, "Washington National Airport, 1941-1971: Three Decades of Public Service," Unpublished Historical Files, Federal Aviation Administration, Washington, D.C.; Charles S. Rhyne, *The Civil Aeronautics Act Annotated with the Congressional History Which Produced It, and the Precedents upon Which It Is Based*, Scotus Series, with a Foreword by Pat McCarran (Washington, D.C., 1939).

Fig. 5 Holden, Stott and Hutchinson, architects. Airside of Washington Airport, Washington, D.C., 1930 (now demolished).

Fig. 6 Holden, Stott and Hutchinson, architects. Interior view of the waiting room of Washington Airport, 1930 (now demolished).

7 "Philadelphia Sesqui-Centennial Exposition," *Aviation* 19 (Nov. 2, 1925), p. 638; Sam Milner, "Washington National Airport: Origins and Development, 1776-1976," National Airport Documentation, Archives, Library National Air and Space Museum, Smithsonian Institution, Washington, D.C.; "Air Transport in Rapid Spread," *Railway Age* 83 (Dec. 3, 1927), pp. 1, 116; Donald Duke, *Airports and Airways: Cost, Operation and Maintenance* (New York, 1927); "Commercial Airports Near the Capital," *U. S. Air Services* 14 (May 1929), pp. 48, 50.

8 "Airport News Supplement: Land and Sea Terminals at Washington," *Airports* 3 (Aug. 5, 1929), p. 3; "Airports in Pictures, Washington," *Airports* 3 (Sept. 1929), p. 32; "Commercial Airports Near the Capital," *U. S. Air Services* 14 (May 1929), pp. 48, 50; "Building a Port for the Nation's Capital," *Airports* 4 (Jan. 1930), pp. 49, 51; "Washington Airport: Nation's Capitol Boasts a Model Airport," *Airports* 5 (Aug. 1930), pp. 20-21, 36; "Proposed Development of Washington Airport for Washington Air, Terminals, Inc., Washington, D. C.," *American Architect* 135 (May 20, 1929), pp. 677-78; Sherman (note 5), pp. 735-36.

9 There are numerous articles in the clipping file in the Martin Luther King, Jr., Memorial Library, Washington, D.C.; Talbot F. Hamlin, "Airports as Architecture," *Pencil Points* 21 (Oct. 1940), p. 640.

Lacking the stability of a public enterprise, International Airways operated the facility briefly before Atlantic Seaboard Airways purchased the airport for its operations in 1929.[7]

By late 1929, the Washington Terminal Corporation, a subsidiary of the Federal Aviation Corporation, began plans to build a new terminal at Washington Airport, a competing facility that was separated from Hoover Field by only a heavily trafficked road. The corporation employed the architects Benjamin Wistar Morriss and Lansing C. Holden, Jr., who prepared an elaborate master plan for a seaplane and landplane port. After scaling back these plans, the architectural firm of Holden, Stott and Hutchinson received approval from the United States Fine Arts Commission, the District of Columbia's architecture and planning "watchdog." Contractors began construction in January 1930, and builders finished the project late that spring (fig. 5). The structure was two stories high with a passenger waiting room on the first floor (fig. 6). With a linoleum tile floor and decorative cove moldings of an aircraft, the waiting room was equipped with enough rattan furniture for approximately a dozen people – essentially the capacity of the largest airliners at that time.[8]

Forced out of business by the Depression, the two separate companies that operated the adjoining Hoover Field and Washington Airport sold the facilities to a single company, the National Aviation Corporation, in 1933. National Aviation quickly combined the two fields, and the following year expanded the terminal by approximately 50 percent with new wings for passengers and a modestly sized control tower on the third floor. Despite such substantial changes, in 1941, upon the opening of the federally owned Washington National Airport on the nearby Potomac River at Gravelly Point (see fig. 16), the War Department acquired the old airport tract for construction of the Pentagon. Before demolition, architectural historian Talbot F. Hamlin endearingly described the terminal as "the little old station in the old Washington airport…a small rectangular structure pleasant in proportion and without ostentation, and quite adequate for the embryonic air traffic for which it was designed."[9]

In this era of air transportation, visual navigational devices were indispensable. These ranged from simple signs painted on roofs, to illuminated rotating beacons or "lighthouses" guiding airplanes *en route*, to floodlights illuminating airfields for nocturnal operations. Although the Aeronautics Branch of the United States Department of Commerce did not finance the construction of many of these navigation aids, the aviation agency did establish standards of design to assure maximum visibility. Although the painted signs in chrome yellow and black have disappeared, one beacon erected around 1928 still stands in the Bronx atop a highrise building at 958 University Avenue (fig. 7). Largely ignored by local, state, and federal historic preservation agencies, this navigation beacon, resembling a small and simple but distinctive lighthouse, once guided aircraft over the ridges of Washington Heights in Manhattan and University Heights in the Bronx and across the Harlem River valley.[10]

In this early period of airport history, still other entrepreneurs financed airport development of unusually elaborate design. In Missouri and Kansas, for example, Fairfax Airports, Inc., operated a small chain of airports. The Fairfax Airport in Kansas City, Kansas, was important for its rich architecture and its distinctive landscaping. The corporate board of directors spared little expense in the construction of this mid-continent facility. Architect Charles A. Smith designed the hangars and the unusually large and ornate Art Deco passenger terminal (fig. 8). Landscape architect Ernest Herminghaus collaborated on the plantings, which were even more distinctive than the terminal architecture. Many architects and planners believed that airports should be designed with the aerial perspective in mind, although most experts argued that the airport should somehow blend with its surroundings. Herminghaus, however, intended that the landscaping be beautiful and just as evident to aviators and their passengers in the air as it was to pedestrians on the ground. In accordance with his design theory, Herminghaus conceived an elaborate "modernistic" landscape as an obvious navigation aid to help pilots locate the airfield, while satisfying the need for beautification on site. He thought that pilots and their passengers could see objects on the ground only in two dimensions, length and breadth, and that they could more readily see large-scale, formal, geometric designs employing yellow and orange in massive floral beds, rather than the delicate subtleties of most picturesque gardens. He therefore designed a bold, symmetrical, formally patterned landside environment. Despite the changes of airplane size and scale of operation, this kind of landscaping would still be visible today in the best weather, though barely, from craft flying many times higher at cruising elevations of approximately thirty-five thousand feet.[11]

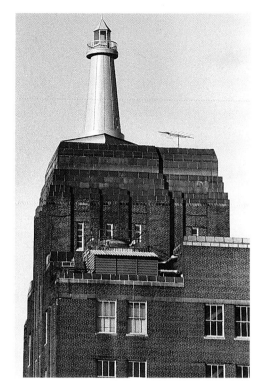

Fig. 7 Architect unknown. Navigation beacon, University Heights, Bronx, New York, c. 1928.

Airport Design in the Era of Economic Uncertainty, 1929–1941

Despite the economic ravages of the Great Depression, air transportation grew; federal relief programs through the WPA and the PWA funded local efforts to improve existing airports or build new ones. Despite later modifications of air commerce law, the relationship between designer and client or local government remained stable. Local, governmentally owned airports began dominating. The introduction of land-based aircraft with greater range, capacity, and speed, such as the Boeing 247 (see pls. 22-24) and the later Douglas DC-3 (see Zukowsky, fig. 2), provided a stimulus to focus work relief efforts on airports. In contrast, aeronautical engineers employed by the Boeing, Martin, and Sikorsky aircraft manufacturing companies believed that flying boats were the best solution for large, profitable, and safe ocean cross-

Fig. 8 Ernest Herminghaus, landscape architect, and Charles A. Smith, architect. Night view of the airside of Fairfax Airport, Kansas City, Kansas, 1929, showing a Ford Tri-Motor.

ings. Although the construction of these "ocean liners of the air" also provided a stimulus for the construction of new or better airports, these airports had to be on the shores of large bodies of water to serve both types of craft. Architects continued to derive ornament from aviation imagery, and building types often represented regional styles and incorporated other design concepts then in vogue. Navigation aids such as air traffic control towers grew slightly, becoming a more pronounced projection from the roof of the terminal. Radio aids to navigation began to supplement visual aids, though the buildings that served these radio aids were austerely unattractive structures adjacent to the steel-truss antennae towers. As during the preceding experimental era, hangars, too, were steel-truss buildings, but their size increased to house more and larger aircraft. Likewise, architects continued to design downtown ticket offices as comfortably furnished store fronts with ticket counters, airline route maps, and advertising posters.

10 Department of Commerce, Aeronautics Branch, *Air Marking*, Aeronautics Bulletin No. 4 (Washington, D.C., 1929); "What Architects Are Talking About," *American Architect* 136 (July 1929), p. 63; Department of Commerce, Aeronautics Branch, *Construction of Airports*, Aeronautics Bulletin No. 2 (Washington, D.C., 1928); Harry H. Blee, "Notes on Airport Lighting," Department of Commerce, Aeronautics Branch, Washington, D.C., April 15, 1929.
11 Francis Keally, "Architectural Treatment of the Modern Airport," *Airports* 2 (June 1929), pp. 39-40, 47; Ernest Herminghaus, "Landscape Art in Airport Design," *American Landscape Architect* (July 1930), pp. 15, 17-18; Hubbard (note 4), pp. 135-38.

Soon after the City of Los Angeles began the development of Hangar No. 1 at Mines Field, the Austin Company, a design-and-build firm still currently engaged in design, engineering, and construction of air transportation facilities, developed United Airport in nearby Burbank. The Austin Company designed and built this facility in 1930 for the vertically and horizontally integrated Boeing Air Transport Company, an aviation conglomerate that was later divided into Boeing Aircraft Company and United Airlines in 1934 with the passage of the Air Mail Act, which required that aircraft manufacturers divest themselves of their airline holdings. Despite this private ownership, the airport and its buildings were similar to municipal facilities of the era as a result of federal efforts to standardize airport and terminal design (pl. 11; fig. 9). Passengers boarding planes walked directly through the building entrance,

Fig. 9 The Austin Company, architects. Aerial view of United Airport, Boeing Air Transport Company, Burbank, California, 1930 (now altered).

through the waiting room, past a ticket office on the side, and out under a gable-roofed pergola to a telescoping canopy. This canopy, a precursor of the modern "Jetway," extended and retracted to protect and control movements of passengers enplaning and deplaning. The Austin Company also designed two hangars in 1930 to flank the terminal. These were steel-truss structures with overhead doors that opened almost the full length of each of two sides of the building. The hangars, which measured 260 feet by 300 feet, had clear spans almost long enough to house two football fields side by side. Bold block letters on a dark background on the roofs of the hangars proclaimed "Burbank" and "United" to approaching pilots and passengers.[12]

At the other end of the country, Miami, Florida, had grown as a result of Henry Flagler's efforts to make the city a railroad resort; by 1929, four seaplane bases in Biscayne Bay also served the city. This population would in turn be the foundation for Juan Trippe's development of Miami as a Pan American Airways resort or gateway leading to still other resorts and adventures in the Caribbean as well as Central and South America. For several years in the late 1920s, the New York-Rio-Buenos Aires Airline, later acquired by Pan American, operated from a dock on shore and a barge floating in Biscayne Bay. In 1931, after Pan American had merged with this airline, the new company built hangars on land at Dinner Key and made plans for the construction of an elaborate flying boat terminal (pl. 27). This complex was located on land previously acquired with an unusual governmental grant of the power of eminent domain to a private-sector enterprise. Delano and Aldrich of New York designed the terminal, completed in approximately 1934. The terminal was located on a traffic circle at the end of a landscaped drive inset into the slope of the shore. Passengers entered at grade, passed through a rather simple, cruciform-plan building, and exited down stairways leading to the water-level boarding area. The facility accommodated four flying boats at a time, accessible under the protection of telescoping canopies. The center of the waiting room featured a large globe – originally intended to adorn the roof – and other ornament such as a winged clock and ceiling beams painted with semi-abstract images of aircraft (pl. 28). The exterior, too, was ornamented with a bas-relief frieze of the corporate aviation theme. Although Pan American Airways established a central business district service and a corpo-

12 Sherman (note 5), pp. 702, 717, 719, 720; Marc Goodnow, "Architectural Aspects of Pacific Airports," *Architect and Engineer* 103 (Nov. 1930), pp. 29–42.

13 Rufus Steele, *Miami: An Air Capital* (Miami, 1929), p. 5; "The Miami Airport International Air Terminal of the Pan American Airways System, Delano & Aldrich Architects," *Architecture* 71 (April 1937), pp. 195-202; Mary K. Evans, "National Register of Historic Places Inventory-Nomination Form," Miami, 1974.

Fig. 10 Philip Barnum, architect. Interior view of Pan American Airways central business district ticket office, Miami, c. 1934.

Fig. 11 H. G. Chipier, architect. San Francisco Airport, 1937 (now demolished).

rate presence in Miami, the airline did not appoint the ticket office as luxuriously. Local architect Philip Barnum designed the facility in the mid-1930s (fig. 10). In 1974 the State of Florida designated the Dinner Key airport a landmark. The original exterior is largely intact, but the interior has been modified.[13]

In contrast with this privately developed system on the East Coast, the Public Utilities Commission of the City and County of San Francisco developed a new airport in the late 1930s. In the Bay Area, and in a substantial number of other cities, including Pittsburgh, Boston, St. Louis, Chicago, New York, and Newark, in-house teams of talented civil servants designed airports for their local governments. In 1937, after a seven-year postponement of construction, the Public Utilities Commission finally erected a new facility. Structural engineer George D. Burr oversaw the work of architect H. G. Chipier, who designed the passenger terminal (fig. 11). The design team located the airport and its terminal to serve both flying boats and land-based aircraft. For building what was conceived as a public utility, they employed concrete, incorporating earthquake resistant features. They used this material because it enabled them to engage in architectural expression economically in a modern Spanish style. Although Burr claimed that this public facility cost only $155,000, its interior revealed that the building intended to serve the activity of a wealthy clientele (fig. 12). The building measured 80 feet airside to

Fig. 12 H. G. Chipier, architect. Interior view of the waiting room at San Francisco Airport, 1937 (now demolished; photo Dec. 24, 1937).

landside and 206 feet from wing to wing. The terminal had many of the same amenities as a railroad station: a spacious waiting room, ticket counter, telegraph office, and restaurant. The wrought iron ornament, patterned flooring, and painted beams in the two-and-one-half-story-high waiting room were the building's richest display of the Spanish influence. The waiting room had only a few pieces of furniture, leather couches and upholstered chairs.[14]

Like San Francisco, the City of New York embarked upon a campaign to build a major airport, Floyd Bennett Field, that would serve both amphibians and land-based aircraft. In 1928 the famed transatlantic flyer and aeronautical engineer Clarence D. Chamberlin consulted with the Department of Docks of the City of New York on the master plan, but the new airport was inadequate almost from completion in 1931. First, it was poorly located in a remote section of southern Brooklyn. Then, efforts to install pneumatic tube systems to carry mail quickly to city post offices and plans to construct a rapid transit system to Manhattan both failed. Despite the construction of an attractive Georgian Colonial passenger terminal, the airport languished. Today the terminal and adjacent hangars stand in Gateway National Park.[15]

Injuring the civic pride of the World War I ace and recently elected mayor of New York, Fiorello LaGuardia, Newark Airport across the Hudson River served New Yorkers much more conveniently than did Floyd Bennett Field. In response, New York City officials began to plan in 1934 to locate a new municipal airport at North Beach in north-central Queens on an airfield owned by the Curtiss-Wright Corporation. Oddly enough, this site on Bowery Bay had been rejected by the city only a few years before in favor of Floyd Bennett Field. Recognizing that the Newark Airport better served the entire metropolis, the United States Post Office in 1935 designated it the airmail terminus for the region. Further irked by this, Mayor LaGuardia intensified efforts to develop the Municipal Airport, renamed LaGuardia Airport in his honor in 1947, and currently operated by the Port Authority of New York and New Jersey. The mayor incorporated this project into a citywide Depression-era program for transportation improvements, which included parkways, tunnels, and bridges. On September 3, 1937, President Franklin D. Roosevelt approved the project for the new airport, co-sponsored by the WPA. Ushering ground-breaking ceremonies into the mechanical age, the flamboyant Mayor LaGuardia pitched the first load of dirt with a steam shovel six days later. Delano and Aldrich, already widely known, had gained even greater prominence and experience in airport architecture while designing the infrastructure of the Pan American system in such places as Guam, before beginning work on the Municipal Airport at North Beach in 1937. They designed not one passenger terminal but two: one to serve passengers flying in land-based aircraft on domestic routes and the other to accommodate passengers traveling in flying boats on international transatlantic routes (see pls. 42, 44-45). Likewise, Delano and Aldrich designed two sets of hangars for these two types of craft — fewer but larger hangars for the flying boats at the west end of the field adjacent to the Marine Terminal. The airport opened in 1939.[16]

Both terminals have been considered extraordinary achievements. Although passengers moved through the Marine Terminal much as they would through a railroad station, they did so in a building whose circulation, massing, and lighting are similar to the Pantheon in Rome. Both the Pantheon and the Marine Terminal have blocky but well proportioned rectilinear façades, behind which stands the drum-shaped major portion of the building (see pl. 43). Likewise, the interior of the Roman structure and the airplane terminal

14 George D. Burr, "Airport Administration Building," *Architectural Concrete* 3, no. 4 (1937), pp. 21-24. For an explanation of the role of the city architect in the design of airports in these other urban centers, see, for example, David Brodherson, "'All Airplanes Lead to Chicago': Airport Planning and Design in a Midwest Metropolis," in John Zukowsky, ed., *Chicago Architecture and Design, 1923-1993: Reconfiguration of an American Metropolis* (Munich and Chicago, 1993), pp. 75-97.

15 Letters and other documents pertaining to Floyd Bennett Field and the Mayor's Committee on Aviation can be found in the City of New York, Department of Records and Information Services, Municipal Archives (hereafter, NYC Archives).

16 Relevant correspondence of Mayor Fiorello LaGuardia, press releases, and other documents can be found in NYC Archives; see also "Program of Events, New York Municipal Airport Dedication, North Beach, Long Island, Sunday, October Fifteenth, 1939," Drawings and Archives Collection, Delano and Aldrich-McIlvaine Collection, Idlewild Airport, Queens, N. Y., Avery Architectural and Fine Arts Library, Columbia University; "The Development of Airports," *Pencil Points* 21 (Oct. 1940), pp. 630-31.

17 Delano and Aldrich with Alexander D. Crosett, Municipal Airport No. 2, North Beach, City of New York, Department of Docks, Sea Plane Hangar, First Floor Plan, March 23, 1938, Delano and Aldrich Collection, New York Municipal Airport, Drawings and Archives Collection, Avery Architectural and Fine Arts Library, Columbia University.

Fig. 13 Delano and Aldrich, architects. Aerial view of Marine Air Terminal and hangar, Municipal Airport No. 2, North Beach, later renamed LaGuardia Airport, New York, 1937-39 (photo 1944).

open from small areas to a grand, circular, domed space. Where the Pantheon has a dramatic oculus in the center of the dome of the drum, the Marine Terminal has a similarly placed skylight. Delano and Aldrich, steeped in the Beaux-Arts tradition, self-consciously adapted the ancient to the aeronautical. Despite this historicism, the architects also included contemporary ornamental references to aviation. A glazed terracotta frieze of flying fish rings the exterior of the second floor. Wood benches, otherwise like furniture in a railroad station, had contrasting inlays of propellers. The Marine Terminal was designated an historic structure in 1980 by the Landmarks Preservation Commission of the City of New York. Furthermore, as a result of restoration and careful adaptive reuse, under the operation of the Port Authority, the terminal still serves flyers.

Also at LaGuardia, a flying boat hangar with a later addition still stands (fig. 13). Delano and Aldrich with consulting engineer Alexander D. Crosett designed the maintenance facility. The pentagonal plan of the hangar required a modest but innovative modification of the steel trusses. Normally, as for the landplane hangars, engineers designed a series of parallel roof trusses each supported by a pair of columns. Each truss also had smaller, linking members to help stiffen the structure. At LaGuardia, however, the civil engineer configured the main trusses of the marine hangar to radiate from a center point at one side of the pentagonal plan behind a façade of offices and smaller shops. A column and truss marked each of the angles of the pentagon creating mammoth clear spans for the doors and the interior of the hangar.[17]

As outstandingly massed and ornamented as the landplane terminal was, its passenger circulation was far more innovative. The terminal combined the best in railroad station design with important elements that became common features in later decades. In addition to the luxurious upper-level dining, observation, and service facilities, enplaning and deplaning passengers moved through the terminal to and from automobiles on two levels, similar to the layout of many major contemporary airports. A "loading platform," where aircraft parked on the apron, extended approximately 750 feet at ground level from the center line of the terminal. At the outset this enabled as many as twenty-one airplanes to load simultaneously from a partially enclosed area. In general, enplaning passengers entered the second story of the terminal from the upper-level roadway, walked through the terminal, and proceeded down stairs into the ground-level loading platforms. Deplaning passengers could board surface transportation after walking back to the terminal, through the lower level, and out to waiting automobiles and taxis (see pl. 45).[18] Alternatively, passengers could walk a short distance across the loading platform from the airplane to waiting automobiles.

While the City of New York was redeeming its pride as a progressive, urban center, capturing the position as an airmail terminus, a consortium of airline companies—Transcontinental and Western Air, United Airlines, Pan American Airways, Eastern Airlines, and American Airlines—began planning to improve one vital link in the route between Manhattan and LaGuardia Airport. In 1937 this group began negotiations to plan a shared ticket office in the city's central business district. The airlines employed architect John B. Peterkin, the consulting engineering firm of Clark, MacMullen and Riley, and the interior design firm of Walter M. Ballard Company. Builders finished construction of this extraordinary five-story limestone ticket office in late 1940. Caught in the fever of political rhetoric, the periodical *Interior Design and Decoration* hailed the building "not only as an expression of American Faith but also as a symbol of Democracy at work." The building was indeed a feat of aviation enterprise, but it was also distinctively engineered and styled, from the massive eagles capping the Forty-Second Street entrance, to the aviation motifs on the carpet in one of the restaurants, and even to the internal automobile ramp and elevator system that enabled limousines to whisk passengers to and from the airport. Limousines traveling in a one-way circulation system rolled in with city-bound passengers on one level and out with airport-bound travelers on another level. Transportation motifs appeared throughout the passenger spaces of the terminal, but the most exciting application was on the restaurant's carpeting, designed by the Walter Ballard Company. The carpet pattern was composed of a grid formed by propellers with other stylized aviation motifs filling the interstices (fig. 14). Sometime around 1979, after the terminal had languished for almost a decade, the Philip Morris Company purchased the tract and demolished the terminal to build a new corporate headquarters. Recognizing the significance of the eagles and beacon capping the façade, they employed Malcolm Holzman of the architectural firm of Hardy, Holzman and Pfeiffer to arrange salvage of this sculpture. He organized the removal of these and oversaw their acquisition for display as outdoor sculpture at an entrance to the Best Company building in Richmond, Virginia.[19]

Far removed from Manhattan, the City of Albuquerque, New Mexico, played a seminal role in the development of ground facilities crucial in the earliest transcontinental air service. In the late 1920s and through the 1930s, airports adjacent to the Rockies in the west and the Appalachians in the east were particularly important as aids to aircraft flying through nearby breaks in these mountain chains. Airports such as Albuquerque and Cheyenne, Wyoming, to the north became less important as aeronautical engineers developed airplanes capable of safely making longer, higher leaps. Before these innovations in airplane design, in Albuquerque between 1928 and 1938, two privately owned airports served Transcontinental Air Transport and Western Air Express. In 1936, after almost ten years of effort, the City of Albuquerque finally succeeded in funding the construction of an airport with the assistance

18 Ibid.
19 "Hope's Windows," *Pencil Points* 22 (March 1941), p. 16; "The Airlines Terminal by John B. Peterkin," ibid., pp. 144-62; "Where Airlines Meet," *Interior Design and Decoration* 16 (Feb. 1941), pp. 22-25, 52, 54; Bigelow-Sanford Carpet Company, "In the Restaurant of the Airlines Terminal...Carpet by Bigelow!" ibid., p. 14; interview with Malcolm Holzman, Hardy, Holzman and Pfeiffer, New York, Oct. 6, 1995.

Fig. 14 John B. Peterkin, architect. Forty-Second Street entrance of Airlines Terminal, New York, 1937-40 (now demolished); from *Interior Design and Decoration* 16 (Feb. 1941), p. 14.

Fig. 15 Ernest H. Blumenthal, architect. Postcard view of airside of Albuquerque Municipal Airport, New Mexico, 1936-39.

of the WPA and Transcontinental and Western Air, predecessors of Trans World Airlines. The airport was the largest component of New Mexico's Depression-era relief projects, employing an average of 350 men per month from the start of construction in 1936 until opening in 1939 (fig. 15). City Architect Ernest H. Blumenthal, who had completed other municipal buildings in the Pueblo Revival style, also adapted this regional idiom to the airport terminal. Adobe block, for example, coats the contemporary structural support of reinforced concrete. Even the heavy wood furniture was a reminder of the locale's Spanish heritage. The terminal still stands, with a few historically sympathetic additions, but it no longer serves air transportation. Following the opening of the new airport in 1965, the original, 1939 structure has housed, first, the Albuquerque Museum, then the Junior League, which has worked to preserve this monument of early commercial aviation.[20]

Although our nation's capital acted much more slowly than such other American cities as New York, Newark, Los Angeles, Seattle, Denver, and Albuquerque, the federal government finally proceeded to develop one of the finest airports of the era. In 1938, against the advice of his cousin Frederic Delano, who was Chairman of the National Capital Park and Planning Commission, President Roosevelt selected the Potomac River site that serves today as the home of Washington National Airport. That same year, under the supervision of Colonel Sumpter Smith, head of the Civil Aeronautics Authority, the federal government finally began development of Washington National on hydraulic fill at Gravelly Point on the Potomac. Howard Lovewell Cheney, who had previously been a consultant to the Chicago Tribune and program advisor for its tower competition, as well as consulting architect to the National Advisory Committee on Aeronautics, was the "Consulting Architect directly responsible for the planning and design" of the airport complex.[21]

In addition to the standard programmatic requirements of airport design, Cheney and his staff faced several stiff challenges. Designing a building that would stand visibly at the head of the recently constructed Mount Vernon Parkway, Cheney was compelled to create a terminal based on the architecture of George Washington's home, while also acknowledging the Capitol across the river. Air travelers were to be able to see the vista of the city, but people on the opposite shore were to be unable to the see the airport in the

20 David J. Kammer, "United States Department of the Interior, National Park Service, National Register of Historic Places, Registration Form," Albuquerque, New Mexico, 1989; Junior League of Albuquerque, *Old Albuquerque Airport Terminal* (Albuquerque, New Mexico, 1979).

21 "Washington National Airport: Historical Highlights," Office of Public Affairs, Washington National Airport, Metropolitan Airports Authority, Washington, D.C.; "Hydraulic Fill Runways for Swampland Airport," *Engineering News-Record* 123 (Aug. 31, 1939), pp. 42-45; Ms. Leslie O'Brien, AIA Archives, telephone conversation with the author, Feb. 2, 1990.

skyline. The Interdepartmental Engineering Commission, three design review committees, and several private-sector architectural and engineering firms, including Fellheimer and Wagner, in addition to the Commission of Fine Arts, the National Capital Park and Planning Commission, and President Roosevelt, who was unusually interested in the architecture of the capital, all scrutinized Cheney's work. Other renowned architects and landscape architects, such as Aymar Embury II of New York, George Howe of Philadelphia, and Philip B. Maher of Chicago, were among the members of the Architectural Advisory Committee, which periodically met to review the design. Of the numerous participants in the design development, consultant Alfred Fellheimer was the most outspoken, even publishing his ideas in *Architectural Forum*. Fellheimer was primarily responsible for master planning, and it was he who suggested the most innovative concepts for inclusion in the project, such as telescoping loading gangways that were almost identical to today's ubiquitous "Jetway," as well as a terminal plan with extended fingers. Although Cheney provided for the later addition of such loading devices, he and other advisors rejected many of Fellheimer's suggestions. Roosevelt, allegedly, even provided the basic scheme for the elevation facing the parkway leading to Mount Vernon.[22]

Construction began in May 1940. Not surprisingly, an undertaking of such magnitude in the nation's capital received unusually wide coverage in the popular and professional presses. When the airport opened a year later, these publications almost unanimously acclaimed the design. Respected architect and architectural educator Joseph Hudnut, writing in *Architectural Forum*, was unusual in his criticism of the terminal, deriding its "glorification of travel" as well as its passenger circulation.[23] A marriage of streamlined Art Deco and Mount Vernon, the terminal was built of reinforced concrete and steel, with a striking wall of glass facing the airside and the panorama of the city across the river (figs. 16-17). Initially the design team planned twelve aircraft gates at 120-foot intervals with provision for expansion. The architects separated passenger circulation horizontally: enplaning travelers stepped from automobiles into the terminal through an entrance at the south end, while deplaning passengers exited the terminal from the north end. Since the terminal was inset into a hillside, all passenger movements required a change of stories within the building from the level of surface transportation to the lower level, where aircraft waited. The Civil Aeronautics Administration intended the airport to be a model of operation and design, from which local governments could learn. Interior designer Ethel Pilson Warren selected the furnishings, surfaces, and colors in many areas of the terminal, including even the linens, cutlery, and china in the second-story dining room and con-

22 Frederick Gutheim, *Worthy of the Nation: The History of Planning for the National Capital* (Washington, D.C., 1977), p. 221, explains that Cheney only "nominally designed" the building; Gutheim claims that Charles Goodman was primarily responsible for the building. Whatever the case, evidence exists indicating that Goodman played an important, if lesser, part in the project; Charles W. Elliot, 2nd, "The George Washington Memorial Parkway," *Landscape Architecture* 22 (April 1932), pp. 190-200; "Members and Alternates of the Interdepartmental Engineering Commission, Who Were the Final Arbiters on the Design of the Airport," *The Federal Architect* 11 (April-June 1941), p. 9; other records related to Washington National can be found in the Washington National Records Center, Suitland, Maryland, the Federal Aviation Administration, and the National Archives, Washington, D.C.; "Projected Airport, Fellheimer & Wagner, Architects, L. L. Odell, Aviation Consultant," *Architectural Forum* 73 (Aug. 1940), pp. 85-87; John Stuart, "The Washington National Airport," *Pencil Points* 21 (Oct. 1940), pp. 602-13; and reprinted in *The Federal Architect* 11 (April-June 1941), pp. 15-19.

23 For information on Washington National Airport, see the special issue of *The Federal Architect* 11 (April-June 1941); "New Buildings: Washington National Airport," *Architectural Record* 90 (Oct. 1941), pp. 48-57; Hugh Ferriss, "National Airport," *The New Pencil Points* 23 (Aug. 1942), pp. 71-72; "Washington National Airport," *Architect and Building News* 168 (Nov. 28, 1941), pp. 132-35; "Washington National Airport," *Architects' Journal* 94 (Dec. 11, 1941), pp. 387-90; Joseph Hudnut, "Washington National Airport," *Architectural Forum* 75 (Sept. 1941), pp. 169-76.

Fig. 16 Howard Lovewell Cheney and Charles M. Goodman, architects. Washington National Airport, Washington, D.C., 1941.

Fig. 17 Howard Lovewell Cheney and Charles M. Goodman, architects. Night view of airside of Washington National Airport, 1941, with a DC-3.

necting terrace. A modestly sized tower stood on the roof of the terminal. Despite numerous additions to the original terminal and steel-truss hangars, their historic fabrics are evident. These original facilities still serve the heart of business of this city and our country.[24]

Airport Design in the Postwar Era, 1945–1958

The airports of the post-World War II era have terminals that sprawl in one of several configurations. They function as indispensable components of what has become a mass transportation system. With the exception of their innovative footprint or plan and the obvious presence of aircraft around back, many of these buildings – even the greatest ones – could be mistaken for other types of structure, such as shopping centers, office parks, and other urban complexes. The "pier finger" terminal, for example, has one- or two-story fingerlike appendages that project from a central "landside" ticketing area. The fingers feed passengers to and from long rows of aircraft parked on the apron at the edge of the "airside." Likewise, the "satellite" terminal, whether one or two stories, is a separate building on the apron of the airfield with airplanes clustered around, the satellite itself connected to the main terminal for passenger ticketing and baggage claim by a hallway either above or below grade. The "linear" or "gate arrival" terminal is akin to a long membrane with modular units stretching between surface and air transportation vehicles. Its greater length and shallower depth is intended to hasten the interchange between aircraft and automobile.

Although the aphorism "hurry up and wait" was coined to describe the processing and movement of soldiers during World War II, it also has important implications for the amount and design of seating in airports. During the period from 1945 to 1958, interior designers, architects, and industrial designers began to conceive specialized chairs, benches, and tables manufactured by such firms as the Herman Miller Company and the Knoll Group. Like the army, airports and airlines became human processing and distribution systems, warehousing masses of people, even if only briefly. Unlike the army, however, the air transportation system has had a tradition of pampering its passengers, even now after access to air travel has proliferated downward through the socio-economic strata as a result of fare wars. The changes resulting from the great postwar economic boom rippled through every aspect

24 W. E. Reynolds, "The Concrete Work at the Washington National Airport," *The Federal Architect* 11 (April-June 1941), pp. 44-46; Howard L. Cheney, "Washington National Airport," *Architect and Engineer* 150 (Sept. 1942), pp. 29-36; Donald H. Connolly, "[Introduction]," *The Federal Architect* 11 (April-June 1941), p. 11; "Capital's New Airport Plan Hailed as National Model," *U. S. Air Services* (Nov. 1938), p. 22; "At the Washington National Airport," *Interior Design* 17 (Nov. 1941), pp. 36-41.

Fig. 18 Paul Gerhardt, Jr., architect. Presentation rendering of Municipal Airport, later Midway Airport, Chicago, 1945.

of the air transportation industry. Architects started to construct air traffic control towers as separate specialized buildings rather than merely as small projections from the roof of the passenger terminal. Hangars, of course, also grew in size. In addition to employing steel-truss structural systems in these mammoth buildings, engineers began to apply such previously uneconomical structural methods as thin-shell concrete, folded-plate concrete, and cantilevers – all with unimaginably high and long clear-span interiors.

Much as Chicago's location made it an important transportation hub for the railroad, the automobile, and truck transportation, the city has also played a major role as a commercial aviation center. Although initially little more than an open field, from which barnstormers operated in the early 1920s, Chicago Municipal Airport, later renamed Midway Airport in honor of the success of American naval air forces in the Battle of Midway Island, became one of the most important air transportation facilities in the United States. After two years of study a commission appointed by the Chicago City Council decided to enlarge the existing municipal airfield, established in 1922 by the Chicago Aeronautical Bureau in the southwest corner of the city. The City of Chicago dedicated the new airport on December 13, 1927.[25]

Although the Department of Public Works, Bureau of Parks, Recreation and Aviation constructed an airport terminal designed by City Architect Paul Gerhardt, Jr., in 1931, the distinctive International Style concrete facility quickly became inadequate. Even before the end of the Great Depression, air transportation throughout Chicago and the nation had grown so quickly that the airport required a larger terminal. Yet, the Depression and World War II stalled the city's plans to build a new, higher capacity passenger terminal.[26]

Eventually, the Department of Public Works began to erect a new building, which Gerhardt designed in 1945 (fig. 18). Gerhardt located the terminal at the northeastern corner of the one-mile-square airport, approximately a mile closer to the city's downtown business district than the original. Expecting rapid but unpredictable change in the airline industry, Gerhardt created a low-cost building that was to be amortized in less than ten years of operation. The terminal could serve only fifteen aircraft simultaneously, and each airline independently operated a similar portion of the terminal preparing passengers for arrival and departure. This facility, which processed passengers on a single, ground-floor level, had a modified asymmetrical horseshoe plan. The units or modules were strung together in one long, thin building, the predecessor of the now common "linear" or "gate arrival" terminal.[27]

Perhaps drawing on his own column-entry to the Chicago Tribune competition, Gerhardt punctuated the linear terminal with oversized column

25 Brodherson (note 14).

26 Ibid.

27 Ibid.

28 Gerhardt submitted three entries to the Chicago Tribune competition, but see his final one in the official record, *The International Competition for a New Administration Building for the Chicago Tribune* (Chicago, 1923), pl. 160.

29 Eric Pace, "Anton Tedesko, 90, an Expert in Uses of Reinforced Concrete," *New York Times* (April 3, 1994), sec. L, p. 27; for a history of the development of the art of engineering, see David Billington, *The Tower and the Bridge: The New Art of Structural Engineering* (Princeton, N.J., 1985); an "Official U. S. Navy Photograph" of the Tedesko hangar is on the cover of *Architectural Concrete* 8, no. 2 (1942); Boyd G. Anderson, "American Airlines Hangar, Chicago Municipal Airport," *Engineering News-Record* (July 22, 1948); for an essay on the construction of the American hangar by the "resident engineer," see Nomer Gray, "Form on Traveler Speeds Arch Concreting," *Engineering News-Record* (Aug. 19, 1948); Charles S. Whitney also wrote about the history and technology of concrete; see "Reinforced Concrete Thin Shells," *Journal of the American Concrete Institute* (Feb. 1953); on the various materials and methods of hangar construction, see Fred N. Severud, "Hangars Analyzed," *Architectural Record* 101 (April 1947), pp. 114-24. Ammann and Whitney designed similar hangars for TWA at Lambert St. Louis Airport.

drums.[28] These drums dramatically break up the long façade; they also emphasize the air traffic control tower and entries to the building on both the airside and the landside. Ever since contractors finished the terminal in 1947, the city and individual airlines have had to continue to make improvements to increase capacity at Midway Airport.

Soon after the city finished the passenger terminal, the airlines began erecting new hangars on the north edge of the airfield. Two pairs of these were reinforced thin-shell concrete structures, designed by Charles Whitney, a pioneering concrete specialist and a partner of the renowned engineering firm of Ammann and Whitney (fig. 19). Architect Aymar Embury II assisted Whitney at least in the design of the first two hangars for American Airlines in 1948. In 1953 Trans World Airlines erected two similar hangars. Although Anton Tedesko, a leading civil engineer specializing in concrete structures with the Chicago engineering firm of Roberts and Schaefer, had designed a similarly shaped hangar in the early 1940s (see pl. 52), this differed substantially from the hangars at Midway. On one hand, the structural system of Tedesko's concrete ribs springing from the ground are a far more apparent expression of the structural art of engineering as measured by the efficiency, economy, and elegance of the structure; the thin shells between the ribs had little or no importance as structural elements helping to support the hangar as a whole. On the other hand, Whitney perfected a thin-shell hangar, making the ribs of smaller cross-section with less concrete and, consequently, greater economy. The Whitney ribs are so thin that they are much less noticeable and more subtly express the art of the engineer. Underlying this structural art is a deceptively simple yet significant engineering innovation that contributes to this more elegant, more economical, and more efficiently constructed form: in Whitney's innovation the shell is at mid-height of the rib, not "hanging" at the bottom of the rib as in the earlier Tedesko design. In this modified location at mid-rib, the shell responds to stresses together with the rib to bend and support the whole building, reducing the load placed on the ribs. The thin shell itself bears a part of the structural loading, so the ribs may be smaller without sacrificing the overall strength of the hangar.[29]

Naturally, the opening of new terminals at Chicago's O'Hare International Airport in 1963 greatly diminished the importance of Midway. But as O'Hare itself has begun to approach capacity — even with substantial improvements — Midway has been regaining some of its former importance, serving more and more air travelers. The hangars still stand, but these buildings, which are worthy of historic preservation or documentation, are inadequately

Fig. 19 Aymar Embury II, architect, with Ammann and Whitney, engineers. Hangars at Midway Airport, Chicago, 1953.

maintained. Likewise, parts of Gerhardt's terminal design are still obvious, though substantial additions to the terminal have made the entire structure unworthy of historic preservation. In 1995 the City of Chicago commissioned the architectural firm of Howard Needles Tammen and Bergendoff (HNTB) to design a new terminal that will replace the old facility.

Unable to expand Midway Airport into its densely urbanized environs, local civic groups and the City of Chicago began to search for a site for a new airport during World War II. In 1946 the city acquired Orchard Field, just beyond the city's extreme northwestern limits, where the Douglas Aircraft Company had occupied a manufacturing plant designed by the Austin Company (see Lockhart, fig. 4). That year Mayor William Kelly employed the recently retired City Engineer Ralph Burke to prepare a new master plan, finalized in 1952 (see Lockhart, fig. 1). Burke's design is, in part, the basis for what stands at O'Hare today, and his first terminal even had what may well have been the first modern "Jetway." But when Burke died before the completion of the project, Mayor Kelly's successor, Richard J. Daley, hired architects Naess and Murphy to finish the airport. With the assistance of the Cincinnati-based airport consulting firm of Landrum and Brown and other advisors, the re-formed architectural firm of C.F. Murphy Associates began finishing the O'Hare design in 1957. Although they retained the fundamental elements of Burke's concept, such as the pier fingers, the provision for a light rail transit system to and from the Loop, as well as the multilevel passenger circulation system with aircraft loading gangways, the new staff of private-sector consultants modified the proportions, sizes, quantities, and construction timetables of each of these elements. The terminal, completed in 1963, was composed of four semi-autonomous buildings with fingers. A drum-shaped restaurant building of reinforced concrete with a cable-suspended roof contrasted with these other three gray-glass and black-steel structures (see pl. 83). Architects and engineers designed the terminal with a dual-level roadway – the lower for surface transportation for deplaning passengers and the upper for surface transportation of enplaning travelers (see pl. 82). Baggage claims were on the lower level; airlines processed boarding passengers on the upper level of the two-story circulation system.[30]

For the upper level of the O'Hare terminal, Charles Eames designed the tandem sling seat in 1962 (fig. 20). Despite later stiff competition from seating developed by industrial designer Niels Diffrient and manufactured by the Knoll Group, the Eames design has become a classic. Tandem sling seating, manufactured by the Herman Miller Company, holds waiting-wearied passengers in numerous airports, from Washington's Dulles International Airport to John Wayne Airport, in Orange County, California.[31]

Down the Mississippi River, residents in nearby St. Louis were competing to make their city an air transportation center for the Midwest. World War I aviator and Listerine heir Albert Bond Lambert, his friend Charles Lindbergh, and another World War I aviator – and the founder of a local aeronautical engineering company – William B. Robertson had been pushing for the development of a commercial airport as early as 1927. In response, the City of St. Louis opened a Georgian Colonial passenger airport terminal that City Architect Albert A. Osburg designed. But the story is a familiar one: in less than fifteen years this terminal became inadequate to handle increased air transportation traffic despite additions.[32]

Around 1942 the City and County of St. Louis began to employ consultants, such as the engineering firm of Horner and Shifrin and the planning

Fig. 20 Charles Eames, architect and industrial designer for Herman Miller Company. Tandem sling seating, O'Hare International Airport, Chicago, 1962.

30 Brodherson (note 14). For the "Jetway" at O'Hare, see "Aero-Gangplank," *Aviation Week* (June 24, 1957), p. 84.

31 Knoll Group, *Knoll Office Chairs* (New York, 1993), pp. 2, 30-31.

32 "Corner-Stone Dropping Marks Formal Opening of Local Field," *St. Louis Globe Democrat* (July 13, 1923); see also the correspondence in Charles A. Lindbergh Papers and planning documents in the Albert Bond Lambert Papers, Archives, Missouri Historical Society, St. Louis (hereafter MHS); A. Osburg, City of St. Louis, Terminal Building, St. Louis Airport, Natural Bridge and Bridgeton Station Roads, December 1931, Department of Planning/Engineering/ Architecture, Lambert St. Louis International Airport, St. Louis.

33 Ralph Caplan, "Caplan on Nelson," *I.D.* (Jan.-Feb. 1992), pp. 76-83; Herman Miller, *Nelson Modular Seating* (Zeeland, Michigan, 1974).

34 Horner and Shifrin, *Airport Sites in St. Louis County* (St. Louis, 1942); Harland Bartholomew and Associates, "A Preliminary Report upon a Comprehensive Major Airport Plan. . . ," 1943; Metropolitan Plan Association for the St. Louis Region, *News Letter*, Aug. 25, 1944; Harland Bartholomew, "Significant Metropolitan Area Public Improvements to Meet Post-War Needs," 1945, Lambert Papers, MHS; George Hellmuth, telephone conversation with the author, Sept. 16, 1995; Charles Clifton Bonwell, "Technology and the Terminal: St. Louis's Lambert Field, 1925-1974" (Ph.D. diss., Kansas State University, 1975); William C. E. Becker, "St. Louis Air Terminal: Intersecting Ribs Carry Concrete," *Civil Engineering* 430 (July 1955), pp. 58-61; sources granting credit for the design of the concrete shells are inconsistent.

35 Letter from David E. Leigh to the author, July 4, 1994; letter from the author to David E. Leigh, Dec. 5, 1994.

firm of Harland Bartholomew, to suggest solutions to the insufficient airport and passenger terminal capacity. Instead of building a wholly new airport at another site, the city decided to construct a new terminal on the southeast edge of the airport. In 1951, after much discussion, the City Airport Commission of St. Louis employed the young architectural firm of Hellmuth, Yamasaki and Leinweber, who, in turn, consulted with architect Edgardo Contini, local civil engineer William C. E. Becker, and civil engineer Anton Tedesko on the merits of their design. Contini played a major role in the conception of the roof's concrete shell; Becker, a more conservative engineer, fearing that the thin shell might sag, helped finalize Contini's concept by adding edge beams and groin ribs to the design. Tedesko was the engineer in charge of dome design. Workers began construction in 1953, and the spectacular terminal opened in 1956 to great acclaim (pls. 73-74). Even before the terminal's completion, *Progressive Architecture* praised it as "one of [the] two best-designed public buildings" of 1953. Inspired by Roman architecture, the structure is a series of cross vaults, which could be extended by the removal of huge windows at the east and west ends and the addition of cross vaults. These austerely grand vaults were the anteroom to passenger loading and unloading areas in fingers extending from the center and the two ends of the multi-level terminal. Unfortunately, the Airport Commission followed this extraordinary but costly scheme only in expansions through 1967; thin shells became too expensive to create and were abandoned. Seating inside the new St. Louis terminal was designed by George Nelson and manufactured by the Herman Miller Company (see pl. 74). Nelson, an architect and architectural journalist turned industrial designer, created the "Nelson Chair" to accommodate large numbers of people in units holding as many as six individuals. These banks of chairs had cushioned seats and a raking back supported by a metal frame and legs. Architects at Idlewild Airport – now John F. Kennedy International Airport – employed a similar, trimmer two-seat version of this furniture with vinyl upholstery.[33] The furnishings at St. Louis, particularly the ticket counters – a programmatic requirement of all airport terminals – lessen the transparency of the impressive window walls.[34] Despite the praise accorded the St. Louis terminal, no historic preservation agency has designated the facility a landmark. Some experts believe, moreover, that recent additions have compromised the appearance of this terminal, once extolled as the "Grand Central of the Air."[35]

As in St. Louis, officials in New York were formulating their own airport plans for the postwar era; unlike the St. Louisans, however, Mayor LaGuardia led the decision to build a new airport, which, as mentioned earlier, was sited on a plot of ground rejected in 1930 when Floyd Bennett Field was undertaken. In November 1941, in response to the City Planning Commission's advice to develop a new airport, LaGuardia announced plans for an international airport at Idlewild golf course, on the eastern edge of Jamaica Bay. From December 1941 through June 1945, the city purchased, filled, and stabilized with beach vegetation approximately 4,600 acres for what is now John F. Kennedy International Airport. The city employed several private-sector consultants including renowned landscape architect and planner Gilmore Clarke and architects Delano and Aldrich, later replaced by Harrison and Abramovitz. Financial and technical exigencies prohibited implementing many of their recommendations. After extensive negotiations with a newly created City Airport Authority headed by Robert Moses and the Port of New York Authority led by Austin Tobin, Mayor William O'Dwyer signed a lease

with the regional planning agency to operate the airport in 1947. In the course of contentious and competitive lease negotiations, both public authorities presented master plans.[36]

Despite the battles of the titans of regional planning, Robert Moses and Austin Tobin, shifting political oversight and consequent changes of design consultants in the 1940s, the city and the Port Authority still created an important infrastructural foundation for international air service to and from the metropolitan area for the postwar era. In 1945 Delano and Aldrich had designed the temporary terminal, which contractors for the Port later quickly completed. The building that opened in 1948 was an unassuming concrete block terminal with a small glass-walled air traffic control tower capping the roof of the long shallow building. The Port Authority also developed three steel, triple-hinged arch hangars, which stood side by side. Designed by Roberts and Schaefer, these were 218 feet by 300 feet, some of the largest of this structural system built. Such impressive hangars descended directly from the civil engineering of the great train sheds of the nineteenth and early twentieth centuries.[37]

In 1952, six years after the Port of New York Authority began operating Idlewild Airport, Thomas S. Sullivan, the Director of the Aviation Planning Division, and consultant Wallace K. Harrison of the architectural firm of Harrison and Abramovitz led the finalization of the master plan. This plan incorporated the concept of "unit terminals": a cluster of several smaller, independent facilities, of various terminal types. These passenger terminals and related structures in the middle of the airport have become the template for the airport today. A "terminal city," a city within a city, stands there as a

Fig. 21 Aerial view of John F. Kennedy International Airport (originally Idlewild Airport), New York, opened 1948 (photo April 12, 1991).

36 Herbert Kaufman, "Gotham in the Air Age," in *Public Administration and Policy Development: A Case Book*, ed. Harold Stein (New York, 1952), pp. 143-97; Dudley Karlson, "Analysis of Airport Sites, Boro of Queens, Secretary, Board of Estimate," 1930, NYC Archives; Office of the Comptroller, *Report to the Board of Estimate of the City of New York to Accompany the Proposed Leases at the Municipal Airport at Idlewild* (New York, 1945); Department of Marine and Aviation, City of New York, *Municipal Airport at Idlewild* (New York, 1945); "New York's Airport for World Commerce, Part I: Plan, Layout, Access and Financing," *Engineering News-Record*, Jan. 24, 1946; Downer, Green and Carillo; Clarke, Rapuano and Holleran; and Harrison and Abramovitz, *The New York Municipal Airport at Idlewild* (New York, 1946); "Two Variations on a Theme," *Architectural Record* 101 (Feb. 1947), pp. 22-23.
37 "New York International Airport," *Airports and Air Carriers* 14 (Aug. 1948); *Report to the Board of Estimate* (note 36), p. 82; Dudley Hunt, Jr.,

"Idlewild: Architectural Engineering, Aircraft Maintenance and Service Facilities," *Architectural Record* (Sept. 1961), pp. 180-83; "Report on Port Authority Operations of La Guardia and New York International Airports, January 1, 1948- December 31, 1948," The Port of New York Authority, Archives, Library, The Port Authority of New York and New Jersey (hereafter PANYNJ); conflicting information about the design and construction of the earliest hangars at Idlewild exists; these hangars may have been designed and built by the Arch Roof Construction Company employing "Davidson Patented Steel Arches."

38 Port of New York Authority, "New York International Airport Control Tower," Sept. 16, 1952, PANYNJ.

39 Dudley Hunt, Jr., "Idlewild: How Idlewild Was Planned for the Jet Age," *Architectural Record* (Sept. 1961), pp. 152-56; Geoffrey Arend, *Kennedy International*, revised ed. (New York, 1987); The Port of New York Authority, *New York International Airport: Aerial Gateway to the United States* (New York, 1957); Rem Koolhaas, *Delirious New York: A Retroactive Manifesto for Manhattan* (New York, 1978).

Fig. 22 Tippetts-Abbett-McCarthy-Stratton, architects, with Ives, Turano and Gardner, associated architects. Pan American Airways Terminal, John F. Kennedy International Airport, New York, 1960 (renovated 1973; currently the terminal for Delta Air Lines).

Fig. 23 Ammann and Whitney, engineers. Aerial view of Pan American hangar at John F. Kennedy International Airport, New York, 1957-58.

result (see fig. 21). Eventually this city comprised nine passenger terminals (see fig. 22), an air traffic control tower, a heating, ventilating, and air conditioning plant, parking lots, a huge plaza landscaped with an illuminated fountain, a Tri Faith Plaza with three chapels, peripheral industrial districts with "animalport," aircraft maintenance hangars (see fig. 23) and air cargo facilities, a charter airline terminal, a bank, a general aviation terminal, an automobile service station, and a hotel, as well as countless concessions and services in its urban core and the "suburb" that surrounds it. Beginning operation on September 16, 1952, the new air traffic control tower at Idlewild was among the first buildings completed in this new aviation city. The tower was located at the center of the airport, which had grown to a 4,900-acre tract. Oddly attractive, the 150-foot-tall structure with an exposed steel frame was purported to be the tallest and was certainly one of the earliest freestanding air traffic control towers in the world.[38]

John F. Kennedy International Airport served as the most important international gateway in the United States until the Airline Deregulation Act of 1978 and the development of new jet craft with greater range enabled other new large-scale facilities to compete. The airport has also felt the impact of shifting trade routes, which now emphasize the Pacific rim and West Coast facilities. Still, JFK has been the aerial portal to international personages and celebrity figures whose arrival has been the stuff of daily papers and nightly news. This aviation city, like any great urban center, though lacking its unifying street wall of skyscrapers, is a place of great architectural vibrancy, resulting from competing yet complementing styles that form a setting for frenetic activity. Each airline planned its own terminal, much like a skyscraper, to be a corporate symbol. And, despite recent complaints, the "delirious airport" is still a great match to the social, architectural, and economic whirl of the "Delirious New York" it serves.[39]

Although airport architecture, planning, and engineering have evolved here and elsewhere in succeeding years, the airport city has become a model and veritable museum of modern airport passenger terminal and hangar design. A number of widely respected design firms or individuals have crafted outstanding individual buildings or their interiors: Skidmore, Owings and

Merrill, Tippetts-Abbett-McCarthy-Stratton, Ammann and Whitney, I. M. Pei and Associates, Eero Saarinen and Associates, Florence Knoll, Dorothy Draper, and Roberts and Schaefer. Skidmore, Owings and Merrill, for example, designed the International Arrivals Building and the adjacent departure wings, the first of these passenger terminals to be constructed (see pls. 71-72). The Port of New York Authority contractors began foundation preparation in October 1955; the International Arrivals Building opened with dedicatory ceremonies two years later as the central focus of this urban complex.[40]

In 1962 Trans World Airlines occupied their new terminal, an expressionistic, widely acclaimed, thin-shell concrete building, which Eero Saarinen and Associates and Ammann and Whitney began to design in 1956 (see pls. 84-85). Yet, sadly, despite the wide recognition TWA and their designers have received for this terminal, neither the airline nor the Port Authority has maintained this property adequately. In 1989 the airline commissioned the architectural firm of Perkins and Will to prepare an expansion plan for this international terminal. Their ideas included restoration of this splendid building and a linkage between it and the airline's domestic terminal to the south, another innovative structure originally designed by I. M. Pei and Associates for the now-defunct National Airlines. As a profit motivated but responsible corporate citizen, TWA wished "to capitalize on the renowned nature of the architecture of the existing buildings" and a complementing distinctive addition. These together would "restore the TWA/JFK complex as one of the most recognized airline facilities in the world" with "substantial marketing value and corporate identity." But for reasons it has been unwilling or unable to explain, TWA has not implemented this historically sensitive expansion plan. The airline resisted efforts of the Land Use Committee of the Council of the City of New York to designate their terminal a landmark, particularly the interior and the boarding areas. TWA's legal counsel, Marvin Mitzner of the firm of Davidoff and Malito, perhaps ignoring that a process exists for the negotiation of modifications of landmark designs, has incorrectly claimed that such designation "really prevents us [TWA] from modernizing the terminal in a way we believe is necessary." Over the airline's objections, the city council approved this designation soon after public hearings on October 18, 1994. Although the whole airport — like this individual building — has faced growing pains, it remains a remarkable — and improving — air transportation facility with many of its original features intact.[41]

Airport Development in the Era of Mass Air Transit, 1958–1996

The past forty years have witnessed the introduction of whole families of commercial aircraft. And, as aeronautical engineering companies continually strove to develop bigger, faster aircraft offering greater economies of scale, they also spun off many of their innovations into the development of smaller commuter craft and regional jets, such as the Boeing 727 and 737, the Douglas DC-9, and the Fokker 100. Increased traffic carried by this wider range of aircraft stimulated the redevelopment of airports large and small or the construction of completely new ones. Architects, engineers, and planners have designed new modestly sized terminals for local governments in far-flung places, such as Westchester County, north of New York City, Centennial Airport in Arapahoe County, Colorado, near Denver, and Dead Horse Airport at Prudhoe Bay, in the northernmost reaches of Alaska.

40 Port of New York Authority, "Fact Sheet, International Arrival Building and Airline Wing Buildings in 'Terminal City,' New York International Airport, April 1956," April 30, 1956, PANYNJ; *New York International Airport* (note 39).

41 For an interesting journalistic narrative of the design and construction process of the TWA terminal, see George Scullin, *International Airport: The Story of Kennedy Airport and U. S. Commercial Aviation* (Boston, 1968), especially pp. 153-79; Perkins and Will, *TWA JFK: Gateway USA, Executive Summary Draft* (Chicago, 1990), unpaginated; for the controversy over landmark designation, see David Dunlap, "T.W.A.'s Hub Is Declared a Landmark," *New York Times* (July 20, 1994), sect. B, p. 1; Herbert Muschamp, "Architecture View: Stay of Execution for a Dazzling Airline Terminal," *New York Times* (Nov. 6, 1994), sect. H, p. 31.

Fig. 24 Howard Needles Tammen and Bergendoff (HNTB), architects. Night view of New Hanover International Airport, Wilmington, North Carolina, 1985-90.

To serve the largest airplanes, architects have created ways to divide the terminal – much like the assembly area of a high-capacity factory – into areas of specialized labor, here serving landside and airside activity. In the largest city airports, in such hubs as Chicago, Seattle, Atlanta, Denver, Washington, D. C., Tampa, and Pittsburgh, landside and airside buildings were further apart but linked by internal transit systems. In still other urban air transportation facilities, designers continued to employ concepts first implemented in the earlier postwar era. In either case, airport buildings became dynamic distribution systems rather than static architecture; and many of these terminals sat in the middle of newly configured parallel runways. Meanwhile, in order to economize upon the cost of designing and engineering separate air traffic control towers at each different site, the Federal Aviation Administration periodically commissioned designers to formulate prototypes that could readily be modified or adapted.

During this same period, historic preservationists, airport managers, and their private-sector consultants have begun to recognize the great achievements of their predecessors. Unfortunately, too few of these specialists are striving to increase the capacity of existing airports while preserving or recording the extraordinary features of older facilities prior to their demolition. In addition, changes to existing facilities have occurred so quickly and so frequently that, despite the youth of these building types, the record of them is too often scant and historic preservationists have failed to locate them.

Remarkably, in recent decades, architects working in smaller towns have often created more attractive facilities that better serve their users than their colleagues working in the largest cities. Of the countless smaller airports, several stand out either because their designers created attractive and functional terminals that transcend the mundane image of high technology associated with the pedestrian glass and steel of the International Style; or because they overcame certain limitations or restrictions or responded to issues of historic preservation as a challenge rather than an impediment. Howard Needles Tammen and Bergendoff (HNTB), for example, a large-scale architectural firm, has designed a half dozen or more smaller airport terminals. In 1985 the firm designed the New Hanover International Airport in Wilmington, North Carolina (figs. 24-25), which is notable for several reasons. First, the architects did not site the building on the main axis of the approach road. Instead the postmod-

Fig. 25 Howard Needles Tammen and Bergendoff (HNTB), architects. Interior view of New Hanover International Airport, Wilmington, North Carolina, 1985-90.

ern terminal stands picturesquely on an axis forty-five degrees off the main access road. Although this location diminishes the monumentality of the terminal, it facilitates future expansion without interruption of operations in the existing terminal. Second, the terminal is inset into an artificially constructed hill: the grade for the automobile loop is higher than the grade for jet aircraft waiting on the other side of the terminal. This difference in grade enables passengers to circulate through the building on one main level and enplane or deplane through a loading gangway as in a major hub airport.[42]

In the Northwest, Alaska Airlines serves numerous small communities and it frequently flies a Boeing 737 combi, the nickname of a plane designed to carry an equal, if not greater, proportion of cargo than passengers. Alaskan island villages like Wrangell and Petersburg on the panhandle of Alaska are accessible only by air or, infrequently, by water transportation. Residents view the airline's provision of terminals as a lifeline and a civic commitment, not just a profit-making enterprise. The airline employed the Seattle-based architectural firm Edberg, Christiansen and Associates to design similar pre-engineered buildings erected on these two sites in 1993 (fig. 26); both were expansions to existing structures. As in most Alaskan locales, the airline and its architects faced an unusual array of challenges in the design of these two terminals. First, they were limited to building materials that could readily be barged to the site from Seattle and erected quickly in that region's brief construction season. Second, both sites face unusual geotechnical conditions affecting various aspects of the projects. The town of Wrangell, for example, could not supply water to the terminal. Consequently, architects incorporated a rainwater collection, treatment, and storage system. The unusually rainy weather in the region also required flooring inside the terminals that could withstand moisture tracked in from outside. But for all their focus on function, the architects did not ignore stylistic flourishes. To make the interiors of the terminals a bright attractive environment, particularly during the infamously gray Alaskan winters, they incorporated a variant of the Palladian window that complements the gable roof and admits a large amount of light into the building; a band of windows also stretches along the airside.[43]

In a more temperate region, Centennial Airport, a "reliever" facility operated by the Arapahoe County Public Airport Authority serves general avia-

42 HNTB, *Airport Design, Architects, Engineers, Planners* (Kansas City, Mo., n.d.); Steven Reiss, "HNTB, Architects, Engineers, Planners," Washington, D.C., 1994.

43 Ronald P. Suttell, "Airport Building Inventory, Alaska Airlines," Seattle, 1994; Gordon Edberg, telephone conversation with the author, Sept. 27, 1995.

44 "A Good Way To Build a Tower," *FAA World* (Feb. 1986), pp. 8-9.

Fig. 26 Edberg, Christiansen and Associates, architects. Pre-engineered Alaska Airlines Terminal, Wrangell, Alaska, 1993.

Fig. 27 Gale Abels Associates, architects.
Air traffic control tower and administration
building, Centennial Airport, Arapahoe
County, Colorado, 1985.

tion in Englewood, Colorado, a suburb of Denver. Intending to alleviate the
congestion that general aviation caused at the nearby Stapleton International
Airport, the Arapahoe County airport agency employed local architect Gale
Abels Associates in 1985 to design a new air traffic control tower and administration building. From plan to elevation this unusual complex is the greatest general aviation facility of its type in the country (fig. 27), amply
demonstrating the symbolic power of architecture. Abels monumentalized the
control tower and placed it in the center of a plaza formed by the distinctive,
crescent-shaped administration building. If its placement there inadequately
communicates the importance of the tower in the safe operation of the airport, then the formal location of this complex as the terminal vista of an approach boulevard should convince even the most dubious flyer.[44]

Among the largest airports in the country, new terminals, air traffic control towers, and other facilities have brought distinction to Chicago's O'Hare
International, Washington's Dulles International and Washington National,
and the newest of all, Denver International. Although possibly not the first of
their type, these transportation projects far more dramatically display many
of the same features of pioneering airports located in Tampa, Atlanta, and
other cities. Although the Washington airports have a lower volume of traffic than the others named here, they are important as the portals to the home
of our national government.

In 1966, three years after contractors finished construction of the terminal designed by C. F. Murphy Associates, the Federal Aviation Agency began
planning a new air traffic control tower at O'Hare. In response to earlier advice from master planners Landrum and Brown, the FAA employed I. M. Pei
and Associates to adapt their standardized air traffic control tower to O'Hare
(fig. 28). Construction of this austerely graceful, pentagonal tower was completed in 1971. Unfortunately, two years later the airport opened a hotel and
multi-level parking lot. Although these facilities increased the convenience of
the airport, the two structures obstructed motorists' and visitors' view of the

Fig. 28 I. M. Pei and Associates, architects.
Air traffic control tower, O'Hare International
Airport, Chicago, 1966-71.

The History of American Airport Design   91

tower, the most important symbol of safe air transportation. Approximately fifty similar towers designed by Pei's firm stand, for example, at Detroit City Airport, Great Falls International Airport in Montana, Lambert St. Louis International Airport, Tampa International Airport, and even at two military fields, Elmendorf Air Force Base in Anchorage, Alaska, and Andrews Air Force Base in Camp Springs, Maryland. Pei's design was the first in a series, which the Agency and the successor Federal Aviation Administration have commissioned periodically to reduce the costs of design and construction through the development of standardized structures. Welton Beckett, Golemon and Rolfe, and Leo A. Daly, for example, have also designed such standardized towers. At O'Hare the firm of Holmes and Narver has recently adapted the latest prototype design by Leo A. Daly. Construction on this facility, which will replace the Pei tower, began in 1993 (pl. 155). As attractive and as necessary as the new tower is, its operation may result in the demolition of a tower that already deserves landmark designation. Elsewhere in the country, despite the quality of these standardized designs, other airports have preferred to erect unique even if more costly structures – as, for example, at Los Angeles and Kennedy international airports (pls. 156-57).[45]

At the same time that a new hotel and parking structure opened at O'Hare, C. F. Murphy Associates began conducting master plan studies for the expansion of passenger facilities. This firm, renamed Murphy/Jahn, began finalizing their ideas in 1981. Their effort provided the conceptual foundation for the master plan by O'Hare Associates – a team led by Murphy/Jahn. This firm then created the grand spaces and rich finishes of the United Airlines Terminal that opened in 1988 (fig. 29) and sparked the development of the new, more modestly sized International Terminal by Perkins and Will, begun in 1989 and opened four years later (fig. 30). The site for United's terminal, which serves 70,000 passengers daily, was large enough to allow it to develop two high-capacity buildings linked by an internal transit system under an active aircraft ramp: one building doubles as a landside and airside terminal with facilities for passenger ticketing and baggage checking on the upper story and baggage claims on a lower story with a two-level approach road to serve both stories; the second building, a long, narrow, parallel satellite primarily for enplaning and deplaning travelers was distantly located in the middle of the ramp. Internal transit systems, such as the moving walkways at the United Terminal diminish the impact of long terminals on the harried traveler. In contrast with these moving walkways, other airports, such as Atlanta's Hartsfield, Tampa, Pittsburgh, and most recently Denver, employ rubber-wheeled vehicle transit systems that are akin to urban mass transportation systems. These were first designed by the Westinghouse Electric Corporation of Pittsburgh in 1963 and are now developed by AEG.[46]

Fig. 29 Murphy/Jahn, architects. United Airlines Terminal, O'Hare International Airport, 1983-88.

45 Brodherson (note 14), p. 90; [I. M. Pei and Associates], "Air Traffic Control Tower, Federal Aviation Agency, Various Cities, USA," New York, c. 1968; "Pei Designs Standard Control Tower for FAA," *Architectural Record* 12 (Dec. 1962), p. 10; "Slipform: Design and Construction," *Architectural and Engineering News* (Nov. 1964), pp. 58-60, 63-67; Federal Aviation Administration, *Airport Traffic Control Tower and Terminal Radar Approach Control Facility Design* (Washington, D.C.: Department of Transportation, Federal Aviation Administration, 1988); Welton Becket and Associates, *FAA National Standard Major Activity Level Airport Control Tower* (Los Angeles, n. d.); I am indebted to Mr. David Henderson of the FAA, who responded to numerous inquiries about towers; C. Lee Harper and Joseph M. Madda, "Airport Towers: A New Generation," *Civil Engineering* (Nov. 1993).
46 Brodherson (note 14), pp. 91-93; AEG Transportation Systems, Inc., *Automated Transit Systems, AEG* ([Pittsburgh], [1993]).

Fig. 30 Perkins and Will, architects. Airside of the International Terminal, O'Hare International Airport, Chicago, 1989-93.

Fig. 31 Eero Saarinen and Associates, architects. Dulles International Airport, outside Washington, D.C., 1958-62.

47 Brodherson (note 14), p. 94.
48 United States Congress, House of Representatives, *Site for a New Airport in the Vicinity of the District of Columbia: Message from the President of the United States*, 85th Congress, 2nd. sess., 1958; "Washington, D.C. Needs Additional Airport Facilities," *Civil Engineering* 19 (Nov. 1949), pp. 53-54; correspondence and various papers in the archives of Metropolitan Washington Airports Authority, Chantilly, Virginia; Kevin L. Kramer, "The Burke Airport Issue: A Case Study in Public Policy and Citizen Opposition" (M.S. thesis, Johns Hopkins University, 1975); "News: Washington — Washington Jet Airport Site Selected," *Architectural Forum* 108 (March 1958), pp. 8-9; letter from Boyd Anderson to the author, March 26, 1989; Arven H. Saunders, "Operational Experience at Dulles Airport," *Journal of the Aero-Space Transport Division, Proceedings of the American Society of Civil Engineers* 90 (Oct. 1964), pp. 53-58; "Airport Development Planning," *Progressive Architecture* 42 (Nov. 1961), pp. 158-63; James B. Lyttle, "Unique Roof Construction at Dulles Airport," *Journal of the American Concrete Institute, Proceedings* 60 (July 1963), pp. 835-50; Federal Aviation Agency, *Dedication Program: Dulles International Airport, Chantilly, Virginia, November 17-18, 1962* (Washington, D.C., 1962); Edgar Kaufmann, Jr., "Our Two Largest Airports: Dulles International Airport, O'Hare International Airport," *Progressive Architecture* 44 (Aug. 1963), pp. 86-111; "Portico to the Jet Age," *Architectural Forum* 119 (July 1963), pp. 72-83; interview with Morgan Williams, Hellmuth, Obata and Kassabaum, Washington, D.C., July 12, 1995.

As part of this spate of expansion, which United Airlines undertook to strengthen its competitive position through its hub in Chicago, the company also added a new hangar. This impressive structure, designed by a team of Austin Company engineers in 1987, has a steel column and roof truss structural system with a clear span of 250 feet that swallows a Boeing 747 whole, or on a different day, a DC-10 and two Boeing 737s.[47]

From the outset of development of Washington National Airport in the prewar era, the Civil Aeronautics Administration envisioned the need for an expanded facility or a second airport to serve the capital. In January 1958, President Eisenhower stopped the endless studies and rancorous debate with affirmation of the selection of the "political dark horse," Chantilly, Virginia, as the site of Dulles International Airport. Resisting involvement on the part of such influential Washingtonians as Senators Lyndon Johnson and Hubert Humphrey, the CAA selected a joint venture group headed by Boyd Anderson, partner in the engineering firm of Ammann and Whitney. On April 29, 1958, the design team, which included architects Eero Saarinen and Associates, engineers Burns and McDonnell, and local architect Ellery Husted, signed an agreement to develop almost everything from the master plan and approach roads to the architecture of individual buildings and even light standards. Despite resistance from the airlines, the CAA accepted the design team's recommendation to build a terminal employing "mobile lounges," which allowed Saarinen and his colleagues to design a grand terminal with minimal walking distances (fig. 31). The mobile lounges were overheight, oversized, bus-like vehicles designed by the Chrysler Corporation. They shuttled between the terminal and the aircraft parked out on remote hardstand to facilitate convenient aircraft loading and unloading while protecting passengers from inclement weather. The airport opened in 1962 to wide acclaim. Since that time, two firms — Skidmore, Owings and Merrill and Hellmuth, Obata and Kassabaum — have designed several additions and temporary modifications to the original building and its environs. Hellmuth, Obata and Kassabaum is finishing a new midfield terminal, which will further separate the functional division of labor in passenger processing, as in Atlanta's Hartsfield International Airport and at the new Denver International Airport. Eventually, a rubber-wheeled rail system will link the airside and landside terminals. Although these architects, engineers, and planners have added to this air transportation system and increased its capacity, they have generally left intact the distinctive features of this landmark airport and terminal.[48]

Closer to the central governing district of the national capital, other architects have similarly been modifying Washington National Airport. Master planning began in 1982, and after some congressional legislation shifting responsibility for the airports from the FAA to the Metropolitan Washington Airports Authority, the firm of Howard Needles Tammen and Bergendoff was able to complete master planning in 1988. HNTB advised the design of a major new terminal with three fingers to the north of the existing terminal; preservation of the original Art Deco facility with its functional but mundanely styled additions of the 1960s and 1970s; and construction of new parking structures, approach roads, and other amenities. The two terminals would provide forty-four gates, all equipped with loading bridges. Thirty-two of the gates will be in the new terminal. The two terminals will be linked of course; and the new one will be only 200 feet from the Washington Metro, providing convenient access to Capitol Hill and the suburbs (fig. 32).[49]

With modest changes to the master plan, a team led by design architect Cesar Pelli and Associates, including architect-of-record Leo A. Daly, two associate architects, Pierce Goodwin Alexander and Linville as well as Sulton Campbell Britt and Owens, and landscape architect Balmori Associates began work in 1990. The new terminal is an exposed steel structure adapting domes and arches from the Capitol. Its layout, too, adapts features of the original terminal, such as the dramatic view of the airfield with the city across the river and a consistently located ticket area to ease passenger movements. The new terminal is expected to open in 1997. Despite the transfer of responsibility from a federal agency to an independent authority; and as a consequence of the intense competition that has existed in the airline industry since the Airline Deregulation Act of 1978, those now responsible for this public infrastructure face unusual scrutiny – and for good reason. Architecture serving the District of Columbia, a focus of national attention, must be distinctive; at the same time, distinctiveness is pointless if the costs of this public architecture negate the benefits of affordable air transportation and economic development. This balance requires careful negotiations between designers, local governmental airport developers, and airport users, airlines included – and it is a process generally hidden from view and is therefore ill-understood in even the smallest towns in America.[50]

Although far from the limelight of Washington, D.C., the new Denver International Airport has also faced its share of unusual scrutiny. The public discourse to determine whether or not to build a new airport or expand the congested old Stapleton International designed by architect Paul Reddy began in 1977. In 1989 Denver employed the Perez Group of New Orleans as the prime architect on the project; dissatisfied with their design, however, Mayor Federico Peña replaced them with the architectural firm of C. W. Fentress,

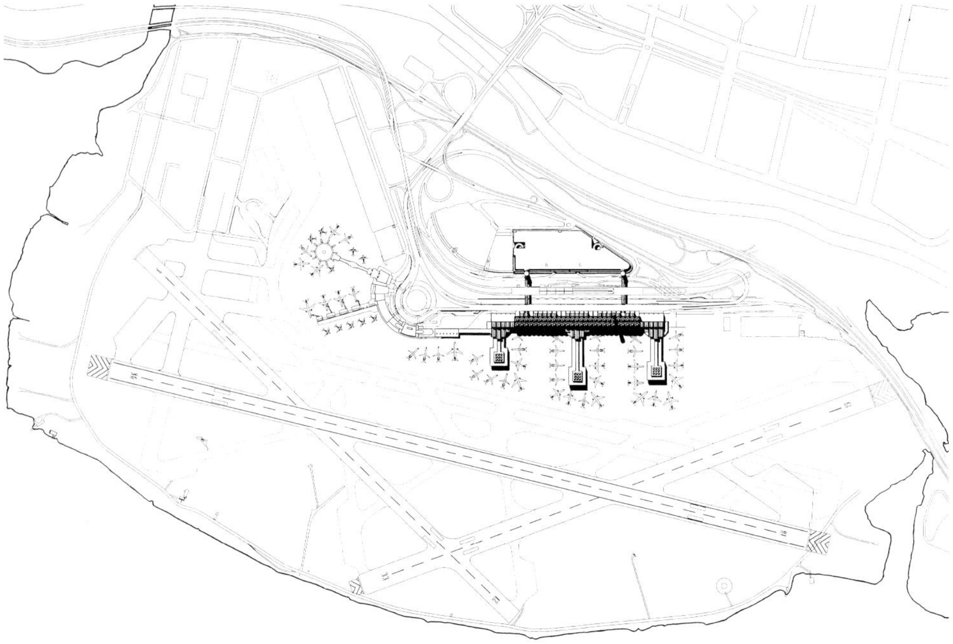

49 Howard Needles Tammen and Bergendoff, *Washington National Airport Master Plan: Summary Report* (Washington, D.C., 1992).

50 Interviews with Cesar Pelli, Jack Gold, Marc Shoemaker, Cesar Pelli and Associates, Inc., New Haven, Connecticut, June 21, 1994; interview with Dan Feil, Metropolitan Washington Airports Authority, New Haven, Connecticut, June 21, 1994; Jack Gold for Cesar Pelli and Associates, Inc., "Fact Sheet: New North Terminal, Washington, National Airport, 1990-1996," typescript, 1994; Dan Feil, telephone conversation with the author, Dec. 20, 1994.

51 Curt Fentress, Fentress Bradburn and Associates, telephone conversation with the author, Oct. 5, 1995.

52 Michael Fumento, "Federico's Folly," *American Spectator* (Dec. 1993), pp. 42-44ff; Bob Ortega, "More Good Reasons Not to Fly into Denver," *Wall Street Journal* (March 31, 1995), sect. B, pp. 1, 13; Ms. Jacqueline Middlebrooks, Dow Jones and Company, telephone facsimile to the author, Oct. 5, 1995.

Fig. 32 Howard Needles Tammen and Bergendoff (HNTB), architects of the master plan for terminal addition, 1984-88; Cesar Pelli and Associates, architects, with Leo A. Daly. Site plan of the expanded Washington National Airport, Washington, D.C., 1992-96.

Fig. 33 C. W. Fentress, J. H. Bradburn and Associates, architects. Aerial view of Denver International Airport, 1989-95.

J. H. Bradburn and Associates in 1989. Fentress and Bradburn retained the original circulation concept; but inspired by the technology of the Haj Terminal in Jeddah, Saudi Arabia, designed by Skidmore, Owings and Merrill (see pl. 105), Fentress, Bradburn and Associates utilized a tensile, fabric structural system to fashion a roof symbolizing Denver's heritage as a western mountain gateway (figs. 33-34). The roof could be readily manufactured in a factory and quickly assembled on site, cutting cost and time of construction. Inside the terminal, enplaning passengers circulate from the parking lots into a richly finished ticketing area. Enplanees travel from this balconied top level downward five more stories past an array of diversions and amenities to an AEG rubber-tired subway transit system. In a configuration similar to Hartsfield and Pittsburgh international airports, the underground transit system carries passengers along a main central axis between the landside terminal and three distant International Style midfield terminals. The midfield terminals, designed at the same time by the joint venture of Allred, Seracuse, Lawler/TRA, are parallel to each other and perpendicular to the subway. The airport is configured to facilitate expansion from the current level of service, handling thirty million passengers a year, to approximately 100 million a year.[51]

Attractive as the structure is, and important as it – and other new airports – will prove to be as an economic development engine, the press, particularly the conservative magazine *American Spectator,* unfairly vilified the project as "Peña's Plane Stupidity" and "Federico's Folly." Since the passage of the Air Commerce Act of 1926, which established the very foundation of commercial air transportation, observers and officials at all levels of government have criticized the development of public airports. Yet, the Dow Jones Transportation Average, which began indirectly measuring the importance of airports in 1970, presents a very different picture. Today this economic indicator lists eight passenger and freight carriers among the top twenty companies it tracks. This affirms the significance of the continuing development of new aviation infrastructure in Denver and the 1928 goal of "an airport in every city." We may not have reached this level of proliferation, but our local governments and their architects, engineers, and planners have created an extraordinary system of air transportation ground facilities permitting the operation of aircraft profitably, safely, and conveniently in large cities and small villages.[52]

Fig. 34 C. W. Fentress, J. H. Bradburn and Associates, architects. Landside of United Airlines entry to terminal at Denver International Airport, 1989-95.

The annotations in the plates section were contributed
by Koos Bosma, Mark Bouman, David Brodherson,
Robert Bruegmann, Wolfgang Voigt, and John Zukowsky.

Plates

1 Hanns Hopp, architect. Königsberg
Airport, 1921-22 (now demolished).

2 Otto Firle, designer. Design for the
corporate logo of Deutsche Lufthansa
Airlines, 1918.

It was an architect, Otto Firle, who designed the
first airline logo – three stylized cranes in flight,
later reduced to a single bird in a circle. Firle, a
Berlin architect and a member of the German air
corps during World War I, created it in his
capacity as advertising manager for Deutsche
Luft-Reederei (the German Air Shipping
Company). In 1926, Deutsche Lufthansa airlines
emerged out of this company. In 1922, the
world's first completely developed commercial
airport opened in Königsberg (now, Kaliningrad,
Russia), in former East Prussia, intended to serve
exclusively civil purposes. For the first time, all
functions of passenger processing were combined
in one terminal, flanked on each end by a hangar.
In the foreground of the picture a Junkers F-13
awaits its continued flight; this plane had entered
the market in 1919 as the first completely metal
commercial airliner in the world, and more than
300 were built over a twelve-year period.
The airport at Königsberg served as a stopover
and distribution point, and the air route from
Königsberg to Moscow (with a connection to
Berlin) shortened the travel time from 56 hours
by rail to only eight hours.   W.V.

3 Paul and Klaus Engler, architects.
   Night view of the terminal at
   Tempelhof Airport, Berlin, 1926-29
   (now demolished).

4 View of Tempelhof Airport in the
   mid-1930s, showing aircraft with
   the early hangar of 1924-25, left
   background, and the Engler terminal
   of 1929, right background (both now
   demolished).

Tempelhof Airport, laid out in 1923, arose
on a military training parade ground that
lay well within the city limits of Berlin. Its
proximity to the heart of the city (two-and-
a-half miles) in part kept it from being super-
seded by any other Berlin airport or airfield,
such as the Zeppelin field of Berlin-Staaken,
which had been in operation since 1919.
With 29,991 passengers in 1927, and 34,057
by 1932, Tempelhof was the busiest airport
in the world. The first buildings erected, in
1924-25, were the west hangars. Between
1926 and 1929 the modern terminal,
designed by Paul and Klaus Engler, was
added. This structure was noted for its
characteristic curved outline and a façade
towards the city that was completely defined
by horizontal lines. Around 1930, Tempelhof
appears in contemporary domestic and
foreign literature as a model of efficiency
and punctuality. But the steep rise of air
traffic (204,116 passengers in 1938) forced
the airport authority to triple the size of the
airfield and abandon all existing buildings
in the mid-1930s.
                                        W.V.

5-7 Ernst Sagebiel. Model of the new Tempelhof Airport, Berlin-Tempelhof, 1936–39 (now slightly altered), with a photograph of the terminal under construction from "Vom Werdegang der Stahlbau-werke" (1939), and a site plan of the airport from John Walter Wood, "Airports" (1940).

Owing to its characteristic arc-shape, architect Ernst Sagebiel's building at

Tempelhof Airport has often been called the "clothes hanger." It unites the terminal and hangars in a powerful complex, and it remained the world's largest airport construction until the 1950s. The 3,870-foot-long canopy on the airfield side rests on a costly steel construction that supports a dramatic 118-foot-long cantilever. Not only were passengers expected to board without getting wet ("dry boarding"), but even the largest airplanes of the day were expected to find room under the protective roof as well. During the Berlin airlift of 1948–49, C-47/

DC-3 and C-54/DC-4 cargo planes of the U.S. Air Force took off and landed at Tempelhof, delivering tons of food and supplies to the encircled West Berliners. Tempelhof was reopened in 1951 as a civil airport in the American sector of Berlin. The location in the city – once prized – soon became a dis-advantage: problems with jet noise and runways that could not be lengthened forced the airlines to move to Tegel Airport in 1975. Since 1990 Tempelhof has again been in operation as a regional commercial airport for small planes.

W.V.

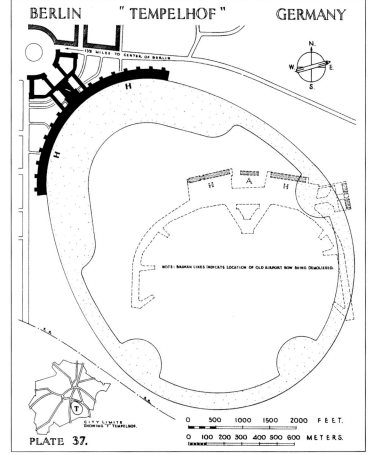

8-9 William Mayo, chief engineer. The Ford Tri-Motor 4AT-5AT, 1926-31.

Although not as successful as the Fokker VII-3m and the Junkers 52-3m, the Ford Tri-Motor is the best-known American example of a three-engine aircraft from the 1920s and 1930s. The inventor of the plane, William B. Stout, promoted the use of all-metal construction, instead of the more prevalent fabric-covered wood and steel (see pls. 14-17). Stout had approached both Henry Ford and his son Edsel in 1921 for funds to undertake his venture, telling them, "You will never get your money back." Both men supported him nonetheless. Stout ultimately raised $20,000 to build the 2-AT in 1924 (AT stood for Air Transport). The plane's corrugated aluminum-alloy skin over a metal frame was light, strong, and corrosion resistant. In 1925 Ford bought Stout's company, and the Ford Tri-Motor was a direct outgrowth of Ford's interests to make air travel accessible to a wider public. Some 199 of these planes were built. Dubbed the "Tin Goose," the aircraft seated twelve to fourteen people. Special editions of the plane were outfitted for Admiral Byrd's Antarctic expedition of 1929, and Franklin Delano Roosevelt used it in his presidential campaign of 1932.

J.Z.

10 Albert Kahn Associated Architects and Engineers, architects. Ford Airport, Dearborn, Michigan, 1927 (now partly demolished and altered).

In the late 1920s private enterprisers began to form large corporations involved in several facets of air transportation. Unlike other aerial entrepreneurs, however, Henry Ford created his system to inspire flyers and investors as well as to transport people engaged in his company's automotive business. Using the now famous Ford Tri-Motor introduced in 1926, Ford's airline shuttled passengers and cargo between factories in Dearborn, Michigan, outside Detroit, and Lansing, Illinois, a Chicago suburb. Albert Kahn and his associates, who had been the architects for several aviation buildings at Langley Field, Virginia, in 1917 and numerous automobile assembly plants, designed the terminals and hangars at both ends of the route. Both facilities stand today although modified. The Dearborn passenger terminal has been adapted as a hotel, whereas the Lansing facility, primarily a hangar, still serves aviation. The Dearborn hangars are located on a Ford test facility inaccessible to the public. Following the completion of these early aviation buildings,

the Kahn firm expanded or developed numerous new aircraft assembly plants for World War II; in 1966 the architects designed the City of Detroit Air Terminal Building.

D.B.

11-12 The Austin Company, architects. United Airport, Burbank, California, 1930 (now altered), with a site plan of the airport from John Walter Wood, "Airports" (1940).

13 Henry L. Gogerty, architect. Grand Central Terminal, Glendale, California, 1928 (now slightly altered).

Not surprisingly, the history of air transportation and the movies have long been intertwined in a symbiotic relationship in southern California. Movie director Cecil B. DeMille built three airfields in the Los Angeles area for his airline, the Mercury

Aviation Company, and as staging areas for his productions in 1918 and 1919. The warm, dry climate was optimal for aeronautical engineering and flight testing by such aviation pioneers as Donald Douglas and Howard Hughes. Of the approximately fifty airports and airfields that once served the Los Angeles area, the architecture of the Grand Central Terminal in Glendale and the United Airport in Burbank stand out. Once the bastions of only the wealthiest travelers, these buildings were richly ornamented with regional Spanish Colonial and Mission elements. Henry L. Gogerty's unorthodox but dramatic and functional design at Glendale was more akin to a hacienda and mission than a transportation depot. In contrast, the United Airport Terminal had the more commonplace but convenient cruciform plan, and its well-proportioned setback massing was similar to other passenger terminals. The terminal was part of a vertically and horizontally integrated system, from which the Boeing Air Transport Company, the precursor of United Airlines, and the Boeing Aircraft Company operated. Despite the changes to these two historic air terminals, their original appearances are preserved in Hollywood films shot on location in the 1930s.

D.B.

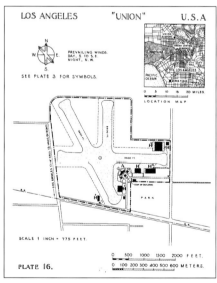

LOS ANGELES   "UNION"   U.S.A

PREVAILING WINDS.
DAY, S. TO S.E.
NIGHT, N.W.

SEE PLATE 3 FOR SYMBOLS.

LOCATION MAP

SCALE 1 INCH = 775 FEET.

0   500 1000 1500 2000 FEET.
0   100 200 300 400 500 600 METERS.

PLATE 16.

14-15, 17 Claire Egtvedt, chief engineer and designer. Boeing 80A, 1928. Exterior and interior views of a restored example in the Museum of Flight, Seattle, and a photograph of a United Airlines version of the Boeing 80A in flight over Chicago, 1928.

16 Interior view of the Boeing factory, Seattle, showing model 80 aircraft under construction, July 7, 1928.

Boeing built a total of sixteen models 80 and 80A airplanes to serve an increasing demand for space reserved on its "B-Line" route between Chicago and San Francisco. These flights were conducted by its own airline, Boeing Air Transport. This aircraft provided transcontinental travel in thirty-two hours. Unlike the all-metal Ford Tri-Motor (see pls. 8-9), the Boeing 80 was constructed with the conventional fabric skin over a metal and wood frame. The plane seated twelve people, while the model 80A, with more powerful engines and a redesigned tail, held up to eighteen. On May 15, 1930, United Airlines, at that time a subsidiary of Boeing, introduced the first stewardess—a registered nurse who could allay passenger fears in case of rough weather, as well as serve beverages and a hot meal. The plane's wood-paneled interiors, lavatory, soundproofing, and leather-covered seats led many to nickname it the "Flying Pullman," likening its amenities to those found in safe and swift rail travel. Model 80A was withdrawn from service by United Airlines in 1933, being replaced by the Boeing 247 (see pls. 22-24).

J.Z.

18 Dyrssen and Averhoff, architects. Fuhlsbüttel Airport, Hamburg, with Junkers F-13 and G-38, 1928-29 (now altered).

19 Luis Gutiérrez Soto, architect. Barajas Airport, Madrid, 1929-31 (now greatly altered).

20-21 Paul Hedquist, architect. Aerial view and terminal of Stockholm-Bromma Airport, 1935-36 (terminal rebuilt 1948-49), with a Douglas DC-3 airplane.

Hamburg's terminal, built in 1929 in the modern brick style of northern Germany, is one of the earliest buildings of its type, and it set the standards for terminal architecture in general – above all in its consistent separation of functions on different levels and in its understanding of the airport as the stage for public spectacles. The terraces of the building and the adjoining grounds were supposed to provide room for up to 35,000 spectators during airshows. The photograph here shows it with the diminutive Junkers F-13 and the massive Junkers G-38 (1929-31), which flew up to thirty-four passengers on the Berlin to London route. The Hamburg terminal remained in operation until 1993 and was probably the oldest building of its type still in use at that time. The concave curve towards the airfield side can also be found in the airport at Madrid, in the small terminal built in 1936 by Luis Gutiérrez Soto, with its streamlined design. Dedicated in the same year, Bromma Airport at Stockholm was the first in Europe to be equipped with a complete system of paved runways. Paul Hedquist designed the functionalistic terminal, a construction of lightness and brightness, and an excellent example of Scandinavian modernism.

W.V.

22-23 Charles Monteith, chief engineer and designer. Boeing 247, 1933. Exterior view of a restored Boeing 247D at the Museum of Flight, Seattle, in the 1940 United Airlines livery designed by Zay Smith, with a photograph of the interior of a 247 airliner from 1933.

24 Interior view of the Boeing factory, Seattle, showing model 247 aircraft under construction, 1933.

Most historians credit the Douglas DC-3 (1935-36) as the first airplane to revolutionize modern air transport. But the slightly earlier Boeing 247 (1933) represented modern design in air travel at the time of the 1933-34 Century of Progress Exposition in Chicago, much as the streamlined Burlington Zephyr and the Union Pacific M 10,000 – both introduced at the Fair – symbolized a new era in rail travel. The Boeing 247, intended as a replacement for the trimotors of the 1920s, was the first significant lowwing American transport to feature retractable wheels within its aerodynamically shaped form. Seating ten passengers in an air-conditioned cabin, the 247 and 247D cruised at 170 and 189 mph (50 to 70 mph faster than trimotors), making a transcontinental journey in nineteen-and-a-half hours. Commissioned by United Airlines – now an offshoot of Boeing Air Transport – seventy-five 247 series planes were produced, and almost all served with that carrier. Ironically, it was Boeing's commitment to fulfilling that order that led Trans World Airlines to ask the Douglas Aircraft Company near Los Angeles to develop a similar airplane, since they could not buy any 247s from Boeing. The result of their efforts was the highly successful series of DC-1 to DC-3 aircraft.

J.Z.

25-26 Norman Bel Geddes, designer. Interior of the Pan American Airways "China Clipper," the Martin M-130, 1934-35, with a photograph of the airplane in flight over San Francisco.

The famed theater and industrial designer Norman Bel Geddes was one of the first in his profession to shape the interior space of a commercial airplane. He upholstered the spacious compartments with slipcovered seats and wall coverings that could be easily unzipped for cleaning and structural inspection. The *China Clipper*, although not the first flying boat, was probably the most famous, especially after being popularized by a 1936 Warner Brothers film of the same name starring Pat O'Brien and Humphrey Bogart. The aircraft became synonymous with luxury air travel, with a range of 2,400-3,000 miles and a normal capacity of thirty passengers (or only eighteen passengers for overnight flights) and a crew of six for daytime flights that would journey to exotic destinations across the Pacific. The brainchild of Juan Trippe of Pan American Airways and the flamboyant aviator Glenn Martin, president of the Martin Aircraft Company of Baltimore, only three of these aircraft were built for Pan American – the *China*, *Hawaii*, and *Philippine Clipper*s – with another variant sold later to the Soviet Union (the M-156).

J.Z.

27-28 Delano and Aldrich, architects.
International Air Terminal and
Dinner Key Seaplane Base,
Miami, 1934 (now the Miami
City Hall), showing Consolidated
"Commodore" and Sikorsky
S-40/S-42 "Clippers," with
an interior view of the terminal.

Throughout the late 1920s and the 1930s,
Pan American Airways repeatedly employed
the firm of Delano and Aldrich to help guide
the development of the airline's pioneering
global system of airports, inns, and crew
quarters extending across the Pacific Ocean
from San Francisco via Honolulu, Midway
Island, Wake Island, Guam, and Manila, and
to the southern hemisphere. The International
Air Terminal was the second airport terminal
that the firm designed for Pan American in
Miami. The first, which opened in 1928,
accommodated land-based aircraft. The firm
began the new terminal in 1934 exclusively
to serve the longer-range, larger, water-based
craft. The terminal stood at the center of a
small point of land, and stairways on
opposite sides of the waiting room circulated
travelers to a lower level, where two flying
boats could load or unload simultaneously.
Passengers not boarding immediately could
walk up from the main floor, eat in the
dining room, drink at the bar, or observe the
scenery from an outdoor deck.
                                        D.B.

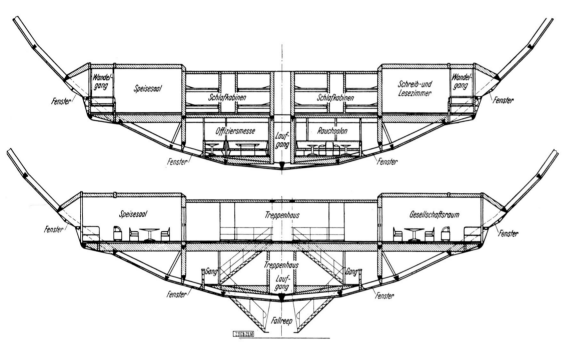

29-31 Cäsar Pinnau for Fritz Breuhaus de Groot, designer. LZ 129 Airship "Hindenburg," 1931-35, with an interior view of the dining-room (Speisesaal) from "Innen-Dekoration" (August 1936), and two cross-sections from "Zeitschrift des Vereines deutscher Ingenieure" (March 28, 1936).

In 1934, in the southwestern part of Frankfurt, the Rhein-Main Airport and airship port were laid out as the Central European junction for the most modern means of transportation. The airport was directly adjacent to the "Frankfurt Crossing," the heart of the German autobahn network, which was being constructed at the same time. In the northern section lay an oval airfield one-and-a-third miles long. At the southern end lay the airship port with two hangars for airships, completed in 1936 and 1938. These were streamlined, with movable walls that could be rolled to the side on curved rails. Starting in 1936, Frankfurt was to be the base for regularly scheduled transatlantic flights by Zeppelin airships to North and South America. The passenger deck in the fuselage of the LZ 129, the *Hindenburg,* designed for fifty travelers, was given a luxurious elegance comparable to that of an ocean liner. In order to save weight, aluminum was used for the tubular furniture in place of steel tubing. It did not help, however, as the end of this brief renaissance of the airship began with the fiery explosion of the *Hindenburg* in Lakehurst, N.J., on May 6, 1937.

W.V.

32 Frankfurt City Architect.
Terminal at Rhein-Main Airport,
Frankfurt am Main, 1936
(now demolished), with a view
of Junkers 52-3m and Heinkel
70 aircraft.

33 Seibert Company, architects.
View of the Zeppelin hangar,
Rhein-Main Airport, Frankfurt
am Main, 1937-38 (now demolished), from "Vom Werdegang
der Stahlbauwerke" (1939).

34 Virgil Borbiró and Lásaló Klárik, architects. Terminal at Budaörs Airport, Budapest, 1937 (now slightly altered), with a Junkers 52-3m and a Bloch 220 aircraft on the field.

35 Adolf Benš, architect. Terminal at Prague-Ruzyne Airport, 1933-37 (now slightly altered), with a Douglas DC-3 airplane.

36-37 J. M. Wilson and H. C. Mason, architects. Exterior and interior views of Al Basra Airport, Iraq, 1937-38.

The airports of Prague and Budapest – both built in one piece according to plan – provide good examples of the high quality that airport architecture achieved in the countries of Eastern Europe. The elegant terminal of Budaörs represents the successful attempt to organize the passenger-processing area in a rotunda, as can also be seen at Gatwick near London (1936; see pl. 92) and at Helsinki (1938; D. Englund and V. Rosendal). The land-sea airport in the Iraqi town of Basra was laid out in the 1920s on the right bank of the Shatt-El-Arab. It was an important intermediate landing station on the flight connection between Britain and its colonies in the Far East. Most of the space in the terminal was occupied by a hotel with seventy beds. The formidable-looking massive brick walls with only meager openings provided the coolness necessary in the hot Arabian climate. The colonial aristocracy who happened to be traveling through could sit and relax in the high-ceilinged waiting room, reminiscent of a baronial hall in an English country house, in spite of the modern steel tubular chairs, and a grand piano where the fireplace would otherwise be located.

W.V.

38-39 Georges Labro, architect. Aerial and ground-level views of the terminal at Le Bourget Airport, Paris, 1936-37 (now slightly altered), with Bloch 220 aircraft.

The airfield of Le Bourget, laid out in 1914 only seven-and-a-half miles north of Paris, served during World War I as a military airport. Aviation history was made at Le Bourget in 1919 when the airport was the destination of the first international air route between London and Paris, and this is also where Charles A. Lindbergh landed on May 21, 1927, after the first non-stop flight across the Atlantic. But not until 1937 did the airport receive a modern terminal that was worthy of its importance, a facility that was to become the busiest in the world until the new terminal complex at Berlin-Tempelhof became operational in 1939. The long, elegant structure still impresses today.

In 1937, on the protruding middle pylon of the façade towards the city, were mounted the coats-of-arms of the city of Paris and thirteen European cities with which an air route had been established. These were replaced after World War II with three allegorical female figures representing destinations around the globe. The building today houses the Musée de l'Air et de l'Espace.

W.V

40-41 Albert D. Jenkins, land steward and surveyor, Corporation of Liverpool. Terminal West and hangar, Liverpool Airport, Speke, 1937-38 (now slightly altered).

Liverpool Airport was the most important air junction on the British Isles in the 1930s, serving as the stopover between London's Croydon Airport and Belfast, and as a transfer station for flights to Glasgow. The Art Deco ensemble of a terminal and a hangar, completed in 1938, shows that the city was determined that its airport should not be overshadowed by the immense port of Liverpool. In its architectonic stance it is the exact opposite of Hedquist's buildings at the Stockholm airport (see pls. 20-21). Thus, the hangar, constructed out of steel but with a brick outer layer, received a decoration unprecedented in Europe – tall corner towers and a transom shaped like stylized wings. In its massing, the arrangement of its spectator terraces, and the division of its windows, the terminal, which is curved concavely towards the airfield, testifies that its model was the somewhat simpler terminal in Hamburg (see pl. 18). Rising out of the middle axis of the building at Speke is an unusually tall control tower (90 feet), which emulates a lighthouse.

W.V.

42-43 Delano and Aldrich, architects. Exterior and interior views of the Marine Air Terminal, LaGuardia Airport, New York, 1937-39 (extant).

44-45 Delano and Aldrich, architects. Administration Building and Terminal, LaGuardia Airport, New York, 1937-39 (original terminal demolished and replaced; the remainder later altered), with an aerial view of the entire airport.

Frustrated by the City of Newark's domination of air transportation to and from the New York metropolitan area, flamboyant Mayor Fiorello LaGuardia began plans in 1934 to build a new, more convenient airport, which the Federal Government would designate as an airmail terminus. Three years later the City of New York employed the local firm of Delano and Aldrich, which by this time had gained extensive experience in airport terminal design. Builders finished the airport, located on the site of an amusement park, in 1939. Almost immediately city officials renamed the Municipal Airport at North Beach after Mayor LaGuardia. Architects, civil engineers, and planners erected in effect two airports in one, since at this stage of air transportation aeronautical engineers were creating two types of aircraft. Planes with the largest capacity and the greatest range – requiring the longest distance for takeoff – operated on water, thereby eliminating the need to build lengthy, and thus costly, concrete runways. Smaller aircraft operated from land. Consequently, one set of buildings adjacent to Bowery Bay accommodated flying boats, while the other set of buildings, constructed on the east side of a runway on landfill, handled land-based airplanes. D.B.

46-47 Richard Vogt, chief engineer.
Exterior and interior views of
the Blohm and Voss flying boat,
the BV 222 "Viking," 1937-38,
shown under construction in
Hamburg-Finkenwerder.

48 Erich zu Putlitz, architect.
Interior view of the Blohm
and Voss flying boat factory
in Hamburg-Finkenwerder,
1939-40, showing the stairway
mosaic with HA 139 or BV 144
transport planes circling the
globe.

Blohm and Voss, a Hamburg shipyard with
a rich tradition, founded a subsidiary in
1933 for the construction of airplanes and
seaplanes for civil and military purposes.
A new factory was built in 1939 on the
island of Finkenwerder, in the Elbe River,
to designs by Erich zu Putlitz. Today this
is where the main works for the German
division of Airbus are located. The two-story
administration building was erected in dark
red brick in 1939-40 directly on the banks
of the Elbe. The rooms for construction and
design are still located in the 1,000-foot-long
hallways of this elongated building. The
visitor enters the building from the front
through an open hall of pillars and proceeds
by way of a stairway, decorated in marble
and stucco, whose original furnishings have
remained nearly unchanged: here are set up
various silver-colored models – in 1940 it
was a BV 222 *Viking* and other machines;
today there are Airbus models and other
planes in actual production by Daimler-Benz
Aerospace (formerly Deutscher Airbus), along
with designs for aircraft that are still in
development. On a colored mosaic image on
the back wall, HA 139 or BV 144 transport
planes orbit the earth.

W.V.

49-51 Howard Ketcham, interior design advisor, with Pan American Airways staff designers. Cutaway and interior views of the Boeing 314, 1938.

Many nations developed flying boats for passenger service in the 1930s, but probably none more successfully than America. The Sikorsky S-40/S-42 and the Martin M-130 paved the way for larger aircraft that would offer the speed of air transport, yet the luxurious spaces of sea or rail travel. One of the largest of these aircraft was the Boeing 314, which, begun in 1936 and first flown in 1938, entered service with Pan American in 1939. The 314 and 314A could carry up to seventy-four passengers (or forty in sleeper configuration) and ten crew members, with a flight range of 3,500 miles. Twelve of these flying boats were built, and all served as transports during World War II. In a drive to match American expertise in this area, the Blohm and Voss shipbuilding company designed the BV 222 *Viking* for Lufthansa in 1937, a six-engined seaplane with a crew of six and spacious lounges and other compartments for twenty-four passengers (see pls. 46-47). The beginning of World War II saw the development of the BV 222 as a transport for up to 110 troops, with thirteen of these giants built in the Hamburg-Finkenwerder factory during the war.

J.Z.

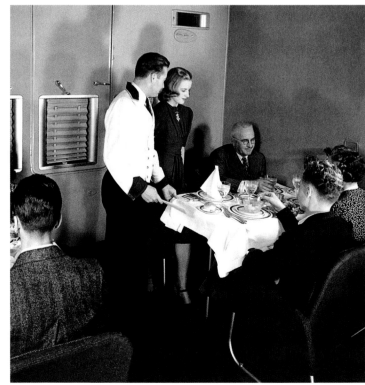

52 Anton Tedesko of Roberts and Schaefer, engineers. Seaplane hangars at North Island Naval Air Station, San Diego, 1940–41 (extant).

53–54 Dames and Moore, engineers. Airship Hangar at Tustin Marine Corps Helicopter Air Station, Santa Ana, California, 1942 (extant).

These structures constitute good examples of engineering creativity during World War II. As with some other aircraft facilities during the war, two hangars at Tustin were built of prefabricated pressure-treated lumber, a non-strategic material, within only sixty days. When finished, they were said to have been the largest clear-span wooden structures in the world, almost 300 feet wide at the base, more than 1,000 feet long, and 171 feet high. The North Island hangars, built of thin-shell concrete, have a comparable span of some 298 feet each and a depth of 240 feet, making them the largest concrete hangars in the United States when they were built. Their reinforced concrete form was duplicated by the same engineers in other structures from Dayton to Buenos Aires, the roof design being built with their patented "ZD" process. These expressively elegant concrete structures inspired other imitators even after the war, notably in hangars at Chicago's Midway Airport from 1948 by engineers Ammann and Whitney and architect Aymar Embury II.
J.Z.

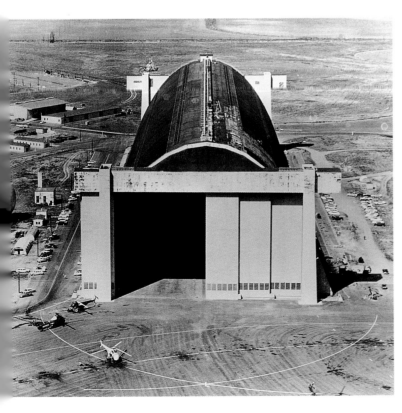

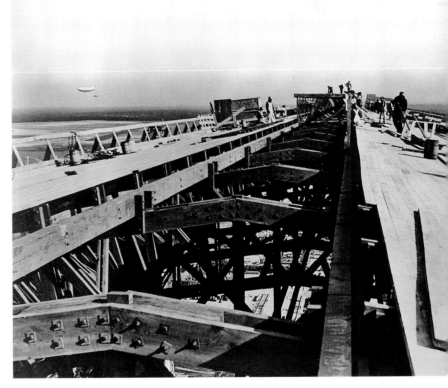

55 Albert Kahn, architect. Ford Plant
at Willow Run, Michigan, near
Detroit, 1942 (extant; now part
of General Motors).

Even before America entered World War II,
President Franklin Delano Roosevelt ad-
dressed a joint session of Congress on May
16, 1940, urging industry to produce an
astonishing 50,000 planes a year. By 1944
aircraft production went well beyond that
projection to some 9,000 per month. Albert
Kahn was perfectly poised to benefit from
this expansion because he was the most
important industrial architect in the United
States. Kahn's automobile factories in and
around Detroit were acclaimed by architects,
industrialists, and architectural critics alike.
The war saw Kahn designing new facilities,
including the Ford plant at Willow Run,
which built Consolidated B-24 bombers under
license. The Willow Run building housed
component manufacturing as well as final
assembly of the aircraft, forcing Kahn's
designers to stretch the plans for the building
to accommodate both functions. His
buildings earned a special commendation

from the U.S. Navy, announced after his
death in 1942. The firm of Albert Kahn and
Associates continued to build factories for
the duration of the war, and created aircraft
facilities well into the postwar era.
                                        J.Z.

56 Albert Kahn, architect. Interior view
of the Martin Aircraft Company
assembly factory, Baltimore, 1937,
showing Martin B-10 bombers and
an M-156 flying boat inside the
hangar.

57 Daniel Brenner, architect. Concert
Hall Project, 1946, after Ludwig
Mies van der Rohe's 1942 concert
hall design. Collage of paper,
oil, and wood veneer on photo
enlargement. Gift of Rachael,
Jon and Ariel Brenner to The Art
Institute of Chicago, 1988.33.

Daniel Brenner's collage from his days at the
Illinois Institute of Technology, similar to one
by his teacher Mies van der Rohe, represents
a proposed adaptive reuse, a common
postwar task, in which disused factories were
sold and converted to other functions,
including shopping malls. Indeed, aircraft
contracts and production plummeted at the
end of the war. When the new Martin
assembly building opened in 1937, however,
the company had just finished a stellar year,
based on export sales of some 170 B-10
bombers, as well as one flying boat sold to
the Soviet Union for $1.05 million. Although
the company's light bombers were more
profitable than its flying boats, Glenn Martin
had been infatuated with the latter since his
1912 "hydro-aeroplane" flight from Newport
Beach to Catalina Island. He even commem-
orated the twenty-fifth anniversary of that
event with a special transcontinental flight
in the *China Clipper* (see pls. 25-26). Martin
intended to use the new space to construct
flying boats with three times the capacity of
the *China Clipper*. Kahn's design satisfied the
client's demands for an enclosed space of
300 by 450 feet with no interior columns.
No wonder Mies and his modernist students
were impressed.
                                        J.Z.

58-59 Alfred and Heinrich Oeschger, architects. Aerial and ground-level views of Zurich International Airport, 1946-53 (now altered), showing mostly Douglas DC-3 and DC-4 aircraft.

Zurich International Airport has been greatly augmented in size since it opened in the early 1950s. The location of the terminal, at the southern end of a valley, backed up against a mountain, was largely determined by topography and available connections with highways to and from the city. After passing through their ticket check, passengers proceed through a spacious main concourse, before reaching the dramatic flight of stairs that will lead them to the lower level, where they assemble in one of two departure spaces. Meanwhile, their baggage is transported through the basement level. The separation of departures, arrivals, and baggage handling in three levels results in a very simple organization of the building. A four-story office building and the air traffic control tower are located in one wing; in another wing, parallel to the gates, can be found the restaurants, shops, and observation terraces. The different functional elements of the building are visible from the outside: the office block is rather austere; the main hall looks narrow at the entrance and becomes wider and brighter as one approaches the airside; and the restaurant area is dominated by glass fronts facing the field.　　K.B.

60 Roy Worden, architect, with Vincent
Fagan, associated architect, and
Frank Montana, consultant. Bendix
Field, St. Joseph's County Airport,
South Bend, Indiana, 1949 (now
demolished), with a Douglas DC-3
airplane on the field.

61 John Messmer, architect. General
Mitchell Field, Milwaukee, 1955
(now demolished).

A DC-3 aircraft awaits passengers and crew
who step out of the St. Joseph's County
Airport terminal building, in order to bring
them, before day's end, to New York or San
Francisco. South Bend and Milwaukee were
still regular ports of call on the transcontinental air route when these pictures were
taken. Their glass, brick, steel, and aluminum
buildings with well-planned pedestrian,
baggage, and aircraft circulation patterns and
ample passenger amenities, could compete
favorably with other terminals along the way,
and they show that a modern design vocabulary accompanied modern aviation into the
"fields" of the American heartland. Both
these designs also express an accommodation
to the automobile: at Bendix Field, non-
passenger visitors arriving by car were
encouraged by the architect to indulge what
he called "their honest American instinct"
and see the sights from the observation deck;
at General Mitchell Field, arriving passengers
could hail a taxi beneath the wide canopies
out front, while departing passengers entered
the lobby past a sign for Milwaukee's own
Blatz beer. Both guests and passengers with
enough time on their hands could survey the
automobiles of the coming season from a
veritable airport showroom, visible at left.

M.B.

62-64 Walter Dorwin Teague, designer. Rendering of the lower-deck lounge and views of the interior of the Boeing 377 "Stratocruiser," 1946-49.

65-66 Boeing 377 "Stratocruiser," shown in flight and under construction, 1946-47.

With the end of war in sight, manufacturers retooled their factories to produce commercial rather than military products. Boeing's entry for a postwar airliner, the *Stratocruiser*, started life as their C-97 military transport. Essentially, the *Stratocruiser* used the wings, engines, and landing gear of Boeing B-29 and B-50 bombers, attached to a fuselage whose section was doubled for increased capacity and greater strength under pressurization at high altitude. Its cruising speed of 340 mph and range of 4,200 miles made it an ideal aircraft for

transcontinental or transoceanic flights. The large interior could hold 55 to 100 passengers depending upon sleeping configurations; overhead compartments, instead of being hat racks, held sleeping berths, while the seats below could be converted to sleeping cabins. One could also descend to a luxurious lower-deck lounge, which enhanced the feeling of spaciousness. The interior configuration was the first of many that noted industrial designer Walter Dorwin Teague and his firm were to do for Boeing. The airlines ordered a total of fifty-five of these aerial behemoths, with twenty going to Pan American Airways.

J.Z.

67-68 E. Gilbert Mason and Henry
Dreyfuss of Henry Dreyfuss
Designers. Interior of the
Lockheed L-188 "Electra," 1957,
with a view of the plane in
flight.

When Capital Airlines introduced the British-
made Vickers *Viscount* to the U.S. in 1955,
American and Eastern airlines approached
the Lockheed Corporation of California to
develop a competitor to Vickers's turboprop
jet. The manufacturer responded with the
L-188. First flown in 1957, the *Electra* could
carry up to 99 people at more than 400 mph
– 30 to 40 more passengers and about 60
mph faster than the *Viscount*. Henry Dreyfuss
and E. Gilbert Mason, veterans at designing
interiors for Lockheed and Douglas, intended
the *Electra*'s space to imitate a commuter
train since most of its flights would be
relatively short. Bulkheads broke up the
fuselage into compartments, some of which
contained angled seats with end tables and
lamps in an attempt to create the atmosphere
of a living room. Built-in steps incorporated
into the sides of the aisle seats made it easier
for stewardesses to reach hat racks above,
and a curved lounge at the rear reinforced
the commuter train image. Despite a series of
five crashes in 1959-60 caused by structural

dynamic problems in the wing and engine housing, *Electras* served various commuter airlines well into the 1970s, particularly on the Eastern Airlines shuttle connecting New York, Boston, and Washington, D.C.   J.Z.

69-70 Pierre Satre, chief engineer and designer, Sud-Est Aviation. S. E. 210 "Caravelle," 1955. Interior view of the prototype and exterior view of a United Airlines "Caravelle" in the livery designed by Raymond Loewy, 1959-60.

The *Caravelle* was arguably the first jet aircraft to serve short-range markets successfully, and the first European jetliner to win international popularity. The designers at Sud-Est Aviation initiated a number of radical innovations: placing the engines near the tail, thereby providing a quiet cabin and more efficient airflow across the wings; designing windows in a distinctive triangular droplet shape; and planning an integral aft staircase. The designers also benefited from the experience of the British-made De Havilland *Comet* (1949-52), copying its graceful nose through an arrangement with De Havilland. Air France ordered the first *Caravelles* in 1956, and two airlines, SAS and Air France, initiated service in 1959, providing up to eighty passengers with 500 mph travel in quiet comfort. United Airlines ordered twenty of these planes, implementing an all-first-class service between Chicago and New York in 1961 with planes named after French cities. The Sud-Est and, later, Aerospatiale factory in Toulouse built 282 *Caravelles* and *Super Caravelles* until production ceased in 1972. The success of the *Caravelle*'s engine configuration inspired similar designs by British Aerospace (BAC 111), Fokker (F-28, F-100), McDonnell Douglas (DC-9, MD-80, MD-90, and MD-95), and Tupolev (TU-134).   J.Z.

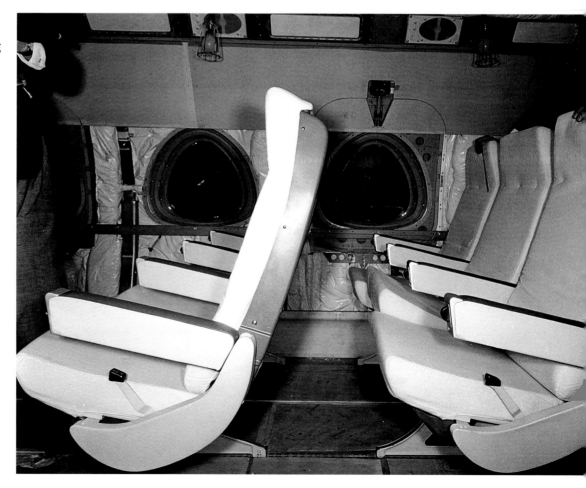

71-72 Skidmore, Owings and Merrill, architects. International Arrivals Building, John F. Kennedy International Airport, New York, 1957, and the United Airlines Terminal, 1960.

Begun in 1941 on the site of a golf course and operating by 1946, New York's Idlewild Airport – dedicated to the memory of President Kennedy following his assassination in 1963 – has long been an important international gateway. Kennedy International is really a series of interconnected semi-autonomous terminals. J. Walter Severinghaus, Charles E. Hughes, and Albert Kennerly of Skidmore, Owings and Merrill oversaw the design of the terminal for international arrivals and two connecting airline buildings. Although SOM was responsible for the overall architectural composition of the international complex and interiors for deplaning passengers, each airline had the latitude to employ its own architects or interior designers to develop the enplaning waiting and ticketing areas as well as the other terminals. Florence Knoll, for example, designed the Golden Door Restaurant, which was located in a penthouse atop the International Terminal and provided diners with a spectacular view of aircraft activity with the New York City skyline in the background. Severinghaus, Hughes, and Kennerly also created the United Airlines Terminal, with a single-level approach roadway and pier fingers for loading and unloading passengers.

D.B.

73-74 Hellmuth, Yamasaki and Leinweber, architects. Exterior and interior views of the terminal at Lambert St. Louis International Airport, 1951-56.

In 1951 the City of St. Louis employed the young firm of Hellmuth, Yamasaki and Leinweber to design a facility to replace the city's 1927 passenger terminal. St. Louis was richly rewarded, for the building that opened in 1956 was hailed as a stunning achievement. The architects designed a thin-shell concrete structure, still evident despite a host of later additions. The interior is a series of cross-vaulted spaces, enclosed by window walls and resting on a single-story, ground-level base. Although concrete was ideal for large-span structures housing aviation activity, architects and engineers ceased using it by the end of the decade. A succession of other facilities designed by the successor firm, Hellmuth, Obata and Kassabaum, then by Sverdrup and Parcel, and, most recently, again by HOK, all sprawl to the east. Begun in 1993 the East Terminal extension is expected to be finished in 1996. Like the 1951-56 structure, the eastern extension will have a dual-level automobile approach road. Unlike the original pier-finger terminal, however, this latest addition will be a hybrid of a "linear" or "gate arrival" building, with an exposed steel structure doubling as support and ornament.

D.B.

75-77 Walter Dorwin Teague, designer. Interior views of a Boeing 720 as outfitted for Pacific Northern Airlines, 1959-60.

Designed to be a military transport and aerial tanker (KC-135), fast enough to refuel jet fighters and bombers in flight, the prototype of the Boeing 707 was widened by more than a foot to accommodate the needs of the U.S. Air Force and, especially, Boeing's airline customers. Because Boeing could share tooling for military and civil applications, the 707 had an advantage over its lead competitor, the Douglas DC-8. The first 707s entered service in 1958 with Pan American. The 707 enabled airlines to carry both first- and economy-class passengers in one plane, with an initial capacity up to 181 people – 153 in the slightly shorter model 720 – at a cruising speed of some 550 mph – approximately as fast as planes travel today. When designing the 707 interior, Walter Dorwin Teague built a full-scale mockup of the plane's fuselage in a loft building in New York so that airline executives, most with offices there, could easily visit it. The mockup had spacious five-across seating for one class, but the airlines rejected this in favor of coach seating of six across and a first-class section of four across.

J.Z.

78-81 Edward Larrabee Barnes with Charles Forberg. Pan American Airways corporate imagery, 1955, with interior views of the ticket office in the Pan Am Building, New York, 1962, and proposed color scheme for ground crew uniforms with a Pan Am Boeing 707 in the background, c. 1978.

As Pan American planned to enter the jet age, it hired two young creative talents, Edward Larrabee Barnes and Charles Forberg, to phase in a new image for their new fleet. For the company's corporate symbol, Barnes and Forberg recycled the traditional Pan

American globe, representative of the airline's worldwide coverage, but they removed the attached wing, lightened the traditional navy blue to a more atmospheric sky blue, and overlaid this with a stylized map grid. This new logo, and the shortening of the company's name to its nickname "Pan Am," became the trademarks of a design that lasted through minor alterations until the airline went out of business in 1991, a victim of the 1978 Airline Deregulation Act, as were other carriers from the legendary Eastern Airlines to the upstart Midway. As part of their efforts to reshape Pan Am's identity, Barnes and Forberg created new standard ticket offices, the most famous of these being the curvilinear interior with sculpted counters inside the Pan Am Building in New York — a miniature masterpiece akin to the fluid shapes of Eero Saarinen's Trans World Airlines Terminal of the same era at New York's Kennedy Airport (see pls. 84-85).

J.Z.

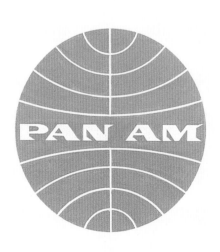

82-83 C. F. Murphy Associates, architects. O'Hare International Airport, Chicago, 1957-63.

Planning for O'Hare Airport in Chicago started in the last days of World War II. The master plan was prepared in 1948 and construction began in 1949. By 1956, however, the original scheme was found to be insufficient for the volume of anticipated air traffic, and new designers, C. F. Murphy Associates, were hired to revise the designs. Dedicated in 1963, the airport quickly became the busiest in the world, reaching capacity within five years and leading to further rounds of additions and remodelings. An airport hotel and an enormous garage were added in 1973, for example, and, starting in 1981, an extensive program of additions, consisting of the replacement of the old International Terminal with a new United Terminal by the successor firm Murphy/Jahn; the construction, outside the original area, of a new International Terminal by Perkins and Will (1989-93); and a people-mover system to convey passengers around the airport. Through it all, the tight U-shaped configuration and handsome original terminal buildings of steel and glass have continued to give good service and to set the tone for later architectural additions.

R.B.

84-85 Eero Saarinen, architect. Trans World Airlines Terminal, John F. Kennedy International Airport, New York, 1956-62, 1970.

After the Port of New York Authority selected a location for the International Arrivals Building designed by Skidmore, Owings and Merrill, the regional agency assigned construction sites to each airline on the basis of the seniority of their operation from the new airport. Trans World Airlines received one of the most coveted sites on which to build. Above all others, TWA took the greatest advantage of its location, employing Eero Saarinen and Associates, who designed the now-landmark terminal. Unlike the architects of most of the other terminals at Kennedy, Saarinen and his colleagues conceived the building as a satellite terminal, with aircraft clustered around a separate compact building rather than a long finger with airplanes parked in a line. The separate building is linked by a short corridor. TWA occupied the first satellite on the south side of the terminal in 1962. In 1967, after Saarinen's death, Kevin Roche, John Dinkeloo and Associates designed the second, larger satellite on the north to accommodate the wide-body jets; it began serving travelers in 1970.   D.B.

86-90 Alexander Girard, designer.
Braniff International Airways
corporate identity program,
1965, with views of BAC 111
and Boeing 720 exteriors,
Boeing 707 interiors, as well as
luggage and service trucks.

Alexander Girard was a noted designer
whose work ranged from the interiors of Ford
and Lincoln automobiles of the 1940s to the
interior of film director Billy Wilder's home
(1957) in Los Angeles. But he was equally
important as the head of the fabric division
of the furniture company Herman Miller.
In 1965 Dallas-based Braniff International
Airways, a maverick firm that would later
hire American sculptor Alexander Calder to
decorate their planes (1973), commissioned
Girard to create a new design program that,
in the words of Braniff president Harding L.
Lawrence, would add "sheer pleasure to the
experience of flight." Girard stripped away
non-essential forms, reducing the exterior
paint schemes of the airplanes and auxiliary
service vehicles to a fresh palette of colors,
and he created a new swept-back alphabet
that featured the simple *BI* on the aircraft
tails. He styled colorful interiors with
patterned and striped fabric for planes and
ticket offices alike, even collaborating with
fashion designer Emilio Pucci for the air
hostess uniforms. His dynamic work for
Braniff made it the envy of other carriers
and set the tone for future individualistic
expressions of identity in airline liveries
of the 1970s and 1980s.   J.Z.

91, 93 Yorke, Rosenberg and Mardall, architects. Gatwick Airport, 1958, shown with a Vickers "Viscount," and an aerial view of the entire airport site c. 1985.

92. Hoar, Marlow and Lovett, architects. Original terminal at Gatwick Airport, 1936.

Gatwick Airport is situated approximately twenty-five miles south of London, and, from the time it opened, with connections through an underground passageway, it was only a forty-minute train ride from London Bridge. The original terminal consisted of three cylinders of reinforced concrete; passengers entered on the ground level and could await their plane either in the lounge and bar or in the restaurant on the second level, from which they had a panoramic view of the airfield. A novelty at Gatwick was the use of a narrow, flexible telescope, covered with canvas, that connected the terminal's gateway with the fuselage of the aircraft. To relieve the strain on London's Heathrow airport, a new terminal was added at Gatwick in the 1950s. The boxlike terminal rises five stories above the London-Brighton highway, and a bridge from the present railway station leads to the main concourse. While the terminal is constructed of a concrete skeleton with a steel and glass exterior, the operations block is a long, one-story-high finger of all-steel construction with a glass curtain wall. A new, north terminal was opened in 1988.

K.B.

94-95 Skidmore, Owings and Merrill, architects, with Myron Goldsmith, principal designer. United Airlines jet maintenance hangar, San Francisco International Airport, 1958 (now demolished).

96 Skidmore, Owings and Merrill, architects. United Airlines hangar, Hopkins International Airport, Cleveland, 1958.

The development of jet engines during World War II led to new building types. Large new jet transports such as the Boeing 707 and the Douglas DC-8 required even larger maintenance facilities. United Airlines's hangar in San Francisco was among the most famous of such buildings. It was one of two designs by Myron Goldsmith of Skidmore, Owings and Merrill. The first, a wash hangar, was demolished in recent years. The second, demolished in 1996, was well known for its cantilevered structure, being publicized while under construction and likened in interior detailing to the work of Pier Luigi Nervi, one of Goldsmith's mentors. Though not the first dramatically cantilevered facility (see, for example, the structural work at Tempelhof Airport in Berlin, pl. 6), this span of 142 feet from the central supports made it large enough to house four of United's new DC-8s. In a 1990 interview, Goldsmith stated that he wanted to have the hangar sheathed in glass to reveal the dramatic structure within, but economic factors prevented it. Because of the extensive attention received by this work, many have overlooked SOM's equally expressive hangar built for United Airlines at Hopkins International in Cleveland the same year.

J.Z.

97 Aeroproekt, architects; with
   Ivan Zholtovsky and Lev Rudnev,
   consultants. Minsk Airport,
   1950-56.

98 Elkin, Kryukov and Lokshin,
   architects for Aeroproekt. Additions
   to Domodedovo Airport, Moscow,
   1965 (original buildings from
   early 1950s visible at right).

99 Ustinov and Smirnov, architects
   for Aeroproekt. Airport, Rostov-
   on-Don, 1978, with a Tupolev
   TU-154b partially visible.

100 Krystyna and Jan Dobrowolski,
    architects. Warsaw International
    Airport, 1967-69.

When the Soviet Union began postwar reconstruction, airports were part of their program,
under the direction of architect Lev Rudnev.
Well-known for public buildings, including
Stalinist skyscrapers from 1954-55 such as
Moscow State University and the Palace of
Culture in Warsaw, Rudnev designed classical
airport terminals, such as the one in Minsk,
that project the image of railroad stations
from a bygone era. With the death of Joseph
Stalin in 1952 and the subsequent rise of
Nikita Khrushchev came a desire to move
beyond classical forms associated with
buildings from Stalin's regime. On November
10, 1955, a government decree shifted state
style from ornamented classicism toward the
simple planes of International Style
modernism. Within a decade of mid-fifties
historicism, the architects who expanded
Moscow's Domodedovo Airport created a
modernist addition with a spectacular curtain
wall overlooking the airfield, much as architects did all over the world in the jet age,
from O'Hare in Chicago to Orly in Paris and
Itami in Osaka. Given the conditions of state-
sponsored modernism, architects throughout
the Warsaw Pact countries designed accordingly, and airports in the various Soviet
republics contained regional variants of this
officially endorsed style.

J.Z.

101   Giefer and Mäckler, architects.
       Aerial view of Terminal 1,
       Rhein–Main International
       Airport, Frankfurt am Main,
       1965–72.

102   Joos, Schulze and Krüger-
       Heyden, with O. M. Ungers and
       Perkins and Will, architects.
       Terminal 2, 1990–94.

103-04 H. G. Beckert and G. Becker,
       architects. Aircraft Maintenance
       Hangar, 1968–70, showing
       Boeing 747 aircraft.

The international airport at Frankfurt acts as
the major hub for Lufthansa Airlines and is
one of the largest freight transporters in
Europe. With immediate access to two autobahn routes, Terminal 1 accommodates a three-
story parking garage, a double-deck elliptical
road system, as well as its own underground
railway station only a few stops from Frankfurt's main railway terminal. Increases in
both passenger and freight transport required
a major extension of the entire airfield, work
on which started in the mid-1980s. Terminal 2,
which lies to the east, is over 1,800 feet
long and features a partly transparent roof.
To facilitate connection between the two
terminals, a track for magnet trains has been
constructed. This "Sky Line" runs almost
a mile in length, carrying passengers at
a maximum speed of thirty-eight mph.

K.B.

105 Skidmore, Owings and Merrill, architects. Haj Terminal, King Abdul Aziz International Airport, Jeddah, Saudi Arabia, 1976-78.

106 Hellmuth, Obata and Kassabaum, architects. King Khaled International Airport, Riyadh, Saudi Arabia, 1983-84.

One of the most interesting challenges facing Western architects working in other parts of the world is trying to find an appropriate architectural language that they and their clients find mutually expressive and satisfactory. This search for a common architectural language is particularly difficult when the building to be constructed is a vast airport terminal and there are few local examples of monumental building. Two of the boldest solutions to this problem are visible in Saudi Arabia. At the Haj Terminal in Jeddah, architects Skidmore, Owings and Merrill needed to provide a very large space that would be used approximately once a year by pilgrims to the holy city of Mecca for the period between their disembarkation from the planes and the time they boarded buses to Mecca. The architects' solution was to place all of the functional spaces of the terminal beneath a series of large tentlike structures made of fiberglass coated with Teflon, suspended with steel cables. At Riyadh, architects Hellmuth, Obata and Kassabaum used interlocking domes with clerestory lighting between them to light the interior courtyard spaces of the terminals and a single large dome for the central building, a mosque for 5,000 worshippers.

R.B.

107-09 Sundberg-Ferar, designers. Interior views of the mockup of the Lockheed L-1011 "Tri-Star," 1970, with an interior view of the lounge designed by Charles Butler Associates for TWA, 1970-72, and a view of the plane in flight.

The early 1970s witnessed increased accessibility of air travel, with airliners that could seat 300 to 500 people. The first and foremost of these aircraft was the Boeing 747 (1968-69), but airlines sought alternatives in the less costly three-engined DC-10 and L-1011 (both 1970). For the L-1011 interior, the Lockheed Corporation hired Sundberg-Ferar, an industrial design firm from Detroit. Sundberg-Ferar had already worked on Lockheed's proposal for a supersonic transport (1966), and the firm executed major transportation work in this era. Their interior design offered special racks for coat and garment storage, increased leg room, window seating with two instead of three seats, and increased storage above and adjacent to the seats. Galleys below deck and accessible via elevators served a projected 256 people in a first- and economy-class mixture, and there was additional space for a lounge area as in the larger 747. A number of their suggestions were incorporated into the final airline versions. Lockheed produced only 250 of these planes, and their relatively low sales compared with competitors may well have influenced Lockheed to abandon future commercial developments.

J.Z.

110 Kivett and Myers, architects. Kansas City International Airport, 1968–72.

111 Tippetts-Abbett-McCarthy-Stratton, architects for the initial studies; with Hellmuth, Obata and Kassabaum, architects of the executed project. Dallas-Fort Worth International Airport, 1965–73.

112 Hidroservice Engenharia de Projetos Limitada, architects. Rio de Janiero International Airport, 1974–90.

The Dallas-Fort Worth (DFW) and Tampa International airports are significant as the first facilities to be planned with light rail systems to transport passengers between terminals and parking lots, employing a people-moving system that has become standard in many subsequent airports. The planning of DFW influenced the organization of other airports around the world, from Kansas City to Rio de Janiero and, most recently, Terminal 2 at the Charles de Gaulle Airport at Roissy, outside Paris. DFW's curvilinear plan features quick and easy access from the curb to check-in and departure gates. But the airport's planners could not

have foreseen that the Airline Deregulation Act of 1978 would lead airlines to create their own hubs, through which many of their flights pass and at which passengers change from one plane to another. Situated on 2,500 acres, DFW is considered to be the world's second busiest airport after O'Hare, and nearly 50 million passengers a year travel through it. The conversion of DFW to a hub airport now makes it difficult for passengers to connect from one plane to another easily and quickly when they are located at opposite ends of the terminal.

J.Z.

114

115

116

117

113/ Aéroports de Paris, architects;
116/ Paul Andreu, chief architect.
118 Charles de Gaulle International
    Airport, Roissy-en-France:
    Terminal 1, 1967-74; Terminal 2A,
    1972-83; 2B, 1972-82; 2D,
    1985-89; 2C, 1987-94.

114 Aéroports de Paris, architects;
    Paul Andreu, chief architect.
    TGV Station, 1994, and Sheraton
    Hotel, 1995.

Lying only twelve-and-a-half miles northeast
of Paris, Charles de Gaulle International
Airport was on the planning tables by the
mid-1960s, when it became clear that neither
Le Bourget Airport nor Orly Airport could be
expanded sufficiently to accommodate the
needs of France's capital city. The whole
megastructure of Charles de Gaulle has been
designed by Aéroports de Paris. The roads,
bridges, water tower, air traffic control tower,
the terminal exteriors, and their interior
appearance have a more or less uniform
design. Terminal 1 is a composition of a
circular, nine-story main building with seven
satellites. The various stories are connected
by escalators that cross the empty core of the
terminal. The satellites, containing the gates,
are connected to the terminal by underground walkways. In contrast to Terminal 1,
Terminal 2 is linear and elliptical and axially
symmetrical, with curves and counter-curves
in the façades, and it is linked down the
middle by a service highway.   K.B.

115/ Air France, architects, with Direc-
117 tion du Frey and Groupe Acora.
Air France Cargo Facility, BOP,
Charles de Gaulle Airport, Roissy-
en-France, 1988.

Expansions at Charles de Gaulle Airport
over the past two decades, including the
connection to France's high-speed rail
network (TGV), are part of its bid to become
the hub of Europe. Integral to this competitive attempt to be the center of the
European Union in the 1990s is the success
of a facility known as BOP (Bâtiment
d'Ordonnancement des Palettes, literally,
pallet marshaling unit). Most freight facilities,
of course, have warehouses as an integral
component, and, indeed, there is a massive
220,000 square-foot warehouse within the
Air France cargo area at Roissy. But the
BOP, in anticipation of a customs-free Europe,
is a high-tech open tent of 300,000 square
feet where freight is moved, via computer
controls, between trucks and aircraft. This
sophisticated freight-moving system aids
the commercial success of the airport and
ultimately affects the nearby towns of Roissy,
LeMesnil-Amelot, and Mitry-Mory, all of
which share in the tax revenues of the
airport.

J.Z.

119-120 HNTB Corporation, architects. Nantucket Memorial Airport, Nantucket, Massachusetts, c. 1992.

You may have had another routine flight, the airports of the 1980s seem to say, but now you have landed and now you are here. And *here* is what these airports were designed to express. Each of these regional airports adopts some aspect of the immediate locality for its major design motif. The task for the architect seems to be to pick the pockets of historical design, while advancing the case of high-tech progressivism that new airports and aviation centers are to represent. Planes seem to land on the greensward of a beach-front Nantucket mansion, for example, replete with bay windows, gables, porch, and historical lighting. At Chattanooga and Roanoke, which, historically, are railroad cities nestled in the mountains, the architects refer to the masonry construction of railroad-era warehouses, though in strikingly different ways. A liberal use of red brick and pavers at Roanoke offsets a picture window affording a view out to the Blue Ridge Mountains. The scored and textured concrete exterior wall at Chattanooga imitates that city's warehouse district, while the grand, domed entry hall at the hub of the concourses bespeaks the spaciousness of a railroad waiting room as it leads the eye heavenward.

M.B.

121 The NBBJ Group, with Leo A. Daly, architects. Modernization and Expansion of Concourses B, C, and D of Sea-Tac International Airport, Seattle-Tacoma, 1992, with a view of an MD-80 aircraft.

Sea-Tac, the international airport serving both Seattle and Tacoma, Washington, opened in 1944, but it did not have its terminal built until 1947-49. By 1954 it was serving one million passengers annually. Subsequent buildings, such as the 1972 terminal and various additions, have encased the original structure. In 1992 almost 18 million passengers used these airport facil-

ities, planned to handle up to 25 million annually, its increased use having warranted almost continual improvements. The latest of these were done by Rick Zieve, project designer for the NBBJ Group, which sought to improve the image of Sea-Tac as a major gateway to the Pacific Northwest. The architects widened the concourses at various points from twelve to thirty-eight feet to create greater internal space, and they added large glass bays both to lighten the waiting areas and illuminate the building at night, thereby letting the exterior act as a welcoming beacon to arriving passengers. During the day, white metal panels unify the exterior design of the various concourses. The project architects at NBBJ believe that the next decade will witness a number of such renovations to upgrade the capacity and appearance of existing airports.

J.Z.

122 Odell Associates, architects, in association with Delta Associates. Roanoke Regional Airport, Roanoke, Virginia, 1985-89.

123 Gensler and Associates, architects, with Derthick, Henley and Wilkerson. Municipal Airport, Chattanooga, Tennessee, 1985-90.

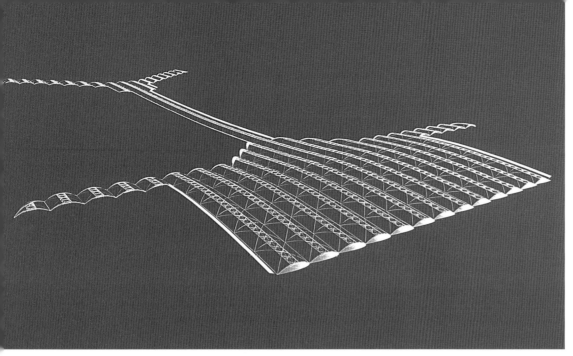

124 Norman Foster and Partners, architects, with Ove Arup and Partners, and Hellmuth, Obata and Kassabaum, master partners. Computer rendering of the roof structure at Chek Lap Kok Airport, Hong Kong, 1992-95.

125 The Richard Rogers Partnership, architects, with Ove Arup and Partners. Computer rendering of roof design and structural planning for the proposed Terminal 5, Heathrow International Airport, London, 1991-99.

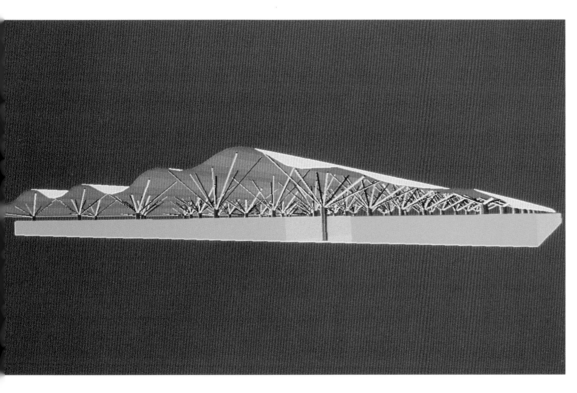

126 Ove Arup and Partners, architects. Project Dragonfly, British Airways Maintenance Facility, Cardiff, 1990-93.

Ove Arup is best known in aviation circles for the structural engineering of new terminals worldwide. But the firm also designs and builds aviation facilities such as Project Dragonfly. When first commissioned by British Airways in 1990, this base in Cardiff, Wales, was intended to be part of the airline's strategic plan to insure high-quality maintenance for its growing fleet of 747s. The solution offered by Ove Arup and Partners was constructed in consultation with the Alex Gordon Partnership for its architecture and Gillespie for its landscaping. The facility provides the carrier with a 220,000-square-foot hangar, large enough for three 747s, as well as support space for various workshops, administrative offices, and engine testing. Special features include a lifting platform that can support the loaded aircraft weight of 250 tons; smooth inner surfaces of steel that resist dust collection; acoustic linings on the thirty-two-foot-high walls where engine testing is done; and a comprehensive fire-safety system with infrared and ultraviolet detectors, foam and water sprinklers, and even special foam cannons. Construction began in May 1991 and this massive yet aesthetically attractive complex was completed in April 1993, officially entering service two months later. J.Z.

127 Ricardo Bofill, architect, with Ove Arup and Partners. Interior view of the International Terminal, Barcelona Airport, 1992.

128-29 Renzo Piano, architect for the terminal, with Ove Arup and Partners, and Paul Andreu of Aéroports de Paris, master plan. Aerial view and interior of the terminal at Kansai International Airport, Japan, 1988-94.

130   **Von Gerkan, Marg and Partners, architects. Lufthansa Technik Maintenance Center, Hamburg International Airport, 1992-94.**

131-32 **Von Gerkan, Marg and Partners, architects. Exterior and interior views of the Hamburg International Airport, 1986-94.**

In 1954 Lufthansa decided to locate its maintenance workshops at Hamburg,

and since then, a vast industrial zone has developed on the south side of the airport, with a freight terminal and a spacious lot for the carrier's aircraft. The most recent buildings are a hangar for the handling of jumbo jets and a workshop administration building, both designed by Von Gerkan, Marg and Partners (GMP). The hangar is almost 500 feet in width and some 90 feet high, and is vaulted without intermediate supports. A large, arched bridge, resting on pillars outside the hall, carries the space frame of the entire

hangar. Seen from afar, this hangar with its glass façade, is a dramatic eyecatcher for travelers. The new Hamburg International Airport itself, also designed by GMP, has already opened the first of three terminals that are to be built to replace outmoded facilities. The remaining two will be constructed once the old terminal has been pulled down. The new terminal is open and brightly lit and cleanly functional. Six pairs of heavy pillars of reinforced concrete each support four diagonal steel tubes that carry the roof.

K.B.

133 Teague Associates, designers, after a drawing by Yukie Ogaki. Whale design for an All Nippon Airways (ANA) Boeing 747-400, 1993.

134 Teague Associates, designers, after ideas developed by GSD & M. Arizona airliner design for a Southwest Airlines Boeing 737, 1994.

In addition to designing aircraft interiors for Boeing, Teague Associates has also executed a number of airline liveries for Boeing's customers. Among the more interesting of these efforts are some recent projects that recall the artistic individuality supported at Braniff in the mid-1970s when that airline chose Alexander Calder to paint some planes. As part of a promotional campaign, Southwest Airlines had Teague develop a design scheme for their 737s that featured San Diego's hugely successful Sea World, with planes painted to look like one of Sea World's most popular attractions, Shamu the killer whale. Three of their planes have also been decorated as the state flags of Arizona, California, and Texas. All Nippon Airways (ANA) held a contest in 1992 to celebrate its 500 millionth passenger. The airline asked young students to propose a color scheme for a new Boeing 747-400 aircraft that would embody their feelings about the sky. Twelve-year-old Yukie Ogaki won the competition out of 20,000 entries. Her scheme suggests that underwater animals might like to inhabit an area even larger than the sea – the sky. Teague helped translate her design into reality for aircraft in the ANA fleet.

J.Z.

135-36 Karl Dieter Köpcke, head of architecture for Daimler-Benz Aerospace Airbus; with Sellhorn, architects. Otto Lilienthal Assembly Plant for the Airbus Industrie A321 and A319 aircraft, Hamburg-Finkenwerder, 1993-94.

137-38 Claude Tran Van and Luc Tran Van, with Calvo and ARCA, architects. Clément Ader Assembly Plant for the Airbus Industrie A330 and A340 aircraft, Toulouse-Colomier, 1987-90.

When the European consortium Airbus Industrie selected assembly facilities for its A300 airplane in the early 1970s, they chose to expand existing plants operated by Aerospatiale in Toulouse, which had produced the successful *Caravelle* (see pl. 69). The new assembly plant in Toulouse-Colomier, built to construct the large, long-range A330 and A340 aircraft of the 1990s, is a virtual cathedral of the aviation industry, covering approximately 600,000 square feet on a 126-acre site. The facility was planned to be spacious enough for crews to construct seven of these large airplanes per month. The Otto Lilienthal plant in Hamburg is a much smaller assembly hall, constructed to build both the stretched and shortened versions of the A320 – the A321 and A319, respectively. Nonetheless, the Lilienthal assembly hall occupies some 300,000 square feet, capable of holding eleven aircraft under construction.
J.Z.

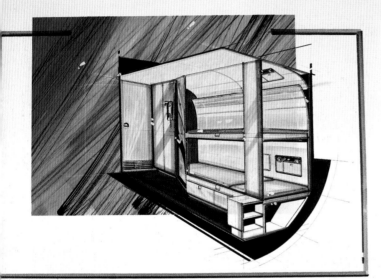

340 Lower Deck Utilization - Industrial Design Study

Flight crew compartment - short version

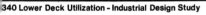

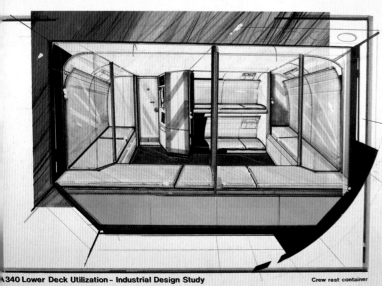

A340 Lower Deck Utilization - Industrial Design Study

Crew rest container

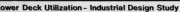

139-41 Uwe Schneider, chief of industrial design for Daimler-Benz Aerospace Airbus. Studies for the lower deck of the Airbus Industrie A340: stairs, flight crew compartment, and crew rest container, 1993-94.

142-44 Interior views of the Airbus Industrie A330-340, showing first-, business-, and coach-class sections.

145 Airbus Industrie A340, A330, and A321 in flight.

146-47 Rendering of the interior design of the A320, with a photograph of a mock-up.

Uwe Schneider, currently the head of the Daimler-Benz Aerospace industrial design group, has developed interiors for the entire Airbus fleet since the early 1970s. The large medium- and long-range A330 (1992) and A340 (1991), both designed with capacity for some 260 to 440 passengers, are two versions of the same basic aircraft with the same flight systems. Their interiors feature overhead storage units that gracefully blend with the curvature of the cabin, first- and business-class seats with personal video screens, and crew rest areas integrated within the overall design of the aircraft. The short range A320 (1987), along with the A321 (1993) and A319 (1995), is a single-aisle aircraft that seats 124 to 220 people, depending upon the model. Designed to compete with Boeing 737/757 and McDonnell Douglas MD-80 airplanes, the Airbus interiors feature passenger amenities generally available only on larger aircraft.
                                                J.Z.

148-54 Landor Associates, designers. Corporate identities for British Airways, 1983-86, applied to the Boeing 747 and "Concorde" exterior and interior, and for Japan Airlines, 1986-89, applied to the 747, crew uniforms, and graphics.

Landor Associates, the San Francisco-based firm founded by Walter Landor in 1941, has been a leader in airline corporate identity since it designed Alitalia's logo in 1967. Many of their clients from the 1980s have been major airlines, such as Japan Airlines (JAL) and British Airways (BA). Landor's work for BA ranged from redesigning the interiors and accessories of the supersonic *Concorde* to creating an overall corporate identity. The latter incorporated traditional elements that related to images of quality, such as the coat of arms and "speedwing" – a diagonally shaped form deriving from an earlier symbol for BOAC – to the emphasis on the primary red and blue found in the flag of Great Britain. Landor performed a similar service in their JAL commission, updating the carrier's image to stress the international sophistication of contemporary Japan. Landor Associates created a new graphic identity for Japan Airlines in which the traditional crane form was slightly modified and used only on the aircraft's tail, while Japan Airlines became JAL and these initials, combined with a red square and a gray stripe, were used everywhere else as part of this modernizing campaign.

J.Z.

155 Leo A. Daly, architects, with site adaptation by Holmes and Narver, architects. Prototypical high-activity air traffic control tower, O'Hare International Airport, Chicago, 1993-95.

156 Leo A. Daly, architects, with Pei Cobb Freed and Partners, program manager. FAA Control Tower, John F. Kennedy International Airport, New York, 1992-95.

157 Holmes and Narver, architects, with Kate Diamond, design architect, of Siegel-Diamond, consulting architects. Air traffic control tower, Los Angeles International Airport, 1992-95, with a view in the foreground of the 1961 Theme Building by Paul Williams, Charles Luckman, and Welton Beckett.

Prior to the 1960s, airport traffic control towers were generally modestly sized glass-walled enclosures on the tops of passenger terminals. In that decade, however, in order to improve site lines and to economize on the cost of construction, the Federal Aviation Administration (FAA) began a policy of adapting a prototypical design as an independent structure. Despite their standardization, these towers were almost always outstanding architectural forms, and they became icons of safe flight. Still, some communities preferred the development of a unique design. In 1979 the FAA commissioned the firm of Leo A. Daly, led by architect Paul E. Halverson, to develop a new generation of prototypes. Other firms could adapt the tower to address local conditions. At O'Hare International Airport, for example, Holmes and Narver adapted the prototypical high-activity control tower that the Daly team had developed. Construction began in 1993; it is expected to serve aircraft in 1996. Although programmatic requirements are similar, unique control towers were constructed at Kennedy International and Los Angeles International at approximately the same time. Currently, the control tower at the new Denver airport is the tallest in the U.S. and reflects the FAA's 300-foot standard prototype.   D.B.

158-59 Gad Shannan, designer. Interior view of the Canadair regional jet, with a view of the plane in flight, 1993.

Following a spate of accidents involving turboprop commuter planes in the early 1990s, customer surveys indicated that airline passengers prefer the increased quiet and image of greater stability projected by turbofan aircraft. This preference is part of the thinking that underlies the growing popularity of the Canadair regional jet, a 1989-93 outgrowth of the company's successful *Challenger* corporate jet. The regional jet can take fifty passengers quickly and quietly to destinations more than 1,800 miles away at a speed of 488-528 mph, or some 200 mph faster than a small turboprop. Gad Shannan, an industrial designer based in Montreal, where Canadairs are built, designed the open sculptured seats and large overhead bins to give passengers the feeling of being in an aircraft larger than a commuter jet, though the cabin is only 8′ 5″ wide. The schemes that Shannan chose for airline customers, such as Comair and Lufthansa City Line, use a cool, businesslike gray as the base color, with highlights of burgundy in Comair's case and of blue and yellow for Lufthansa.

J.Z.

160 The Austin Company, architects. Interior view of the assembly plant for the Boeing 747, Everett, Washington, 1966-67, with additions in 1978-79 for the Boeing 767 series, and in 1991-92 for the Boeing 777. Shown here are 767s under construction.

When Boeing built their new factory north of Seattle in Everett, Washington, in 1966 to construct the 747 "jumbo jet," they called upon the Austin Company, an industrial architecture firm with considerable experience in designing aircraft facilities. The manufacturing plant they created was the world's largest building in terms of volume. Boeing then expanded the facility in the late 1970s to build 767s, and the most recent additions (1992) house the assembly of their new 777s. The factory is still the largest building by volume in the world with a capacity of 472 million cubic feet of space, sitting on 96 acres. The original facility cost Boeing some $200 million, whereas their expenditures on this latest expansion have totaled about $1.5 billion. The building incorporates a number of high-tech features, including CD-ROM-controlled automated riveting machines on the 777 assembly line. More than 20,000 Boeing employees work at this site alone. Since its original construction some thirty years ago, the mammoth factory has produced over 1,100 747s and more than 300 of the 767 model, as it begins to build what will probably be an equally successful run for the 777.

J.Z.

161-65 Teague Associates, designers.
Interior views of the mockup
of the Boeing 777, 1993-94, with
views of the crew rest area and
coach-class interior with personal
video screen, and a United Airlines
777 in flight.

The 777 is the latest in a successful line of
wide-body jets created by the Boeing Company.
This aircraft was created by a team of Boeing
aeronautical engineers who worked closely with
airline representatives to shape the final product.
The 777 was first flown in June 1994, and the
first airplane was delivered to United Airlines less
than a year later. Boeing targeted the plane for
service between its larger 747 and smaller 767,
the 777 having a seating capacity of some 305 to
328 if arranged in three classes, and up to 440
seats if configured for all economy class. Teague
Associates, with almost fifty years' experience of
designing commercial airline interiors for Boeing,
designed the space here, offering extra-large
overhead storage bins in a fluid, curvilinear
cabin, with built-in amenities such as personal
video screens. One of the most significant

features here is the plane's built-in interior flexibility, allowing airlines to reconfigure the cabin quickly to adapt to changing market requirements. Some 250 orders have been placed by airlines from around the world who desire the latest in computerized flight controls, passenger amenities, and fuel efficiency for their high-density routes.

J.Z.

166-67 Teague Associates, designers. Computer rendering of the interior of the Boeing 737-700, 1994-97, with a computer-generated image of the plane in flight.

Southwest Airlines is a success story in the recession-plagued 1990s. This carrier decided against the hub-and-spoke operations of the major airlines by offering a more traditional point-to-point, short-hop service on their fleet of 737s, with few amenities but relatively low fares. Its success has been so considerable that others have copied its formula. With an expansion of its routes comes a need for a longer-range aircraft that will use the same parts. Hence Boeing is developing for Southwest the new 737-700, which will seat 128 to 149 passengers for a distance of some 3,400 miles. The interiors designed by Teague for this and the 737-600 and 737-800 will have the same curvilinear look as the new 777, with passenger amenities and flight systems upgraded to those capabilities as well. With a core of 229 Boeing 737 aircraft in 1996, Southwest has already doubled its fleet since 1990, and additional purchases of 737 models, including the 737-700, scheduled for delivery in 1997, may almost double its fleet size again within the next decade.

J.Z.

168-70 Uwe Schneider, chief industrial designer for Daimler-Benz Aerospace Airbus. Exterior and interior perspective studies of a proposed double-decker airliner, Airbus A3XX, 1994-2003.

The thought of an airliner with almost twice the passenger capacity of a current wide-body jet might horrify some travelers. Indeed, a plane that could carry up to 800 people would need a wingspan larger than many taxiways could accommodate, not to mention the need for replanned jetways and gates at terminals, larger waiting areas, and larger baggage carousels. But aircraft companies are beginning to investigate this possibility because of the potential market in Asia, where today even large 747s are used as interurban air shuttles with 550 to 569 seats in an all-economy-class configuration. Current studies by aircraft designers indicate that these aerial behemoths might harken back to the era of the flying boats of the 1930s, especially in view of the fact that there would be enough room for lounges and sleeping compartments, as well as for spaces related to contemporary lifestyles, such as a health club, self-service snack bar, conference center, and even an on-board medical unit. Even if these giant jets are never built, designers could incorporate some of these "futuristic" ideas into airliners of the near future, regardless of the size of the aircraft.

J.Z.

171-72 Uwe Schneider, chief industrial
designer for Daimler-Benz
Aerospace Airbus. Mockup of
the flight-deck interior and
perspective sketch of the cockpit
of a 100-seat aircraft, 1989-95.

The Airbus design team led by Uwe Schneider is currently planning a new 100-seat
regional airliner. In something of a departure
from convention, Schneider's team has been
given responsibility for parts of the plane
that are normally the domain of engineers at
aircraft companies: the exterior styling of
the nose and the layout of the cockpit.
Airbus has, in fact, always taken a more progressive approach to the design of aircraft
cockpits than their competitors. Their A310
(1978-83), for example, contained a cockpit
designed in consultation with the sportscar-
maker Porsche, and the A320 (1987) was the
first commercial aircraft to use fighter pilot
"joy sticks" for their advanced electronic
controls instead of the traditional steering
wheel. The shared layout and appearance of
all Airbus cockpits makes it cost effective for
an airline to train its pilots to fly the entire
Airbus family of jetliners.   J.Z.

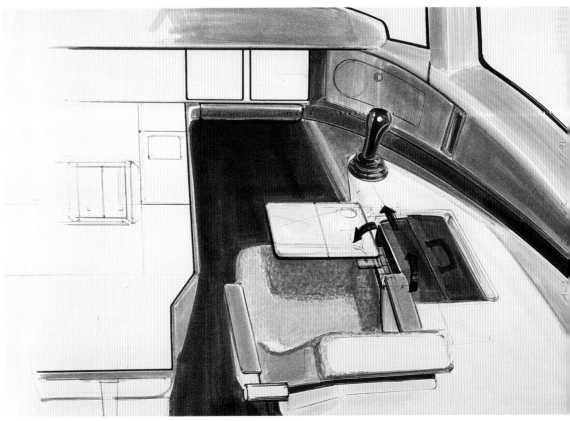

173-74 Murphy/Jahn, architects, with TAMS and ACT, associate architects. Perspective drawing and model of the proposed Second Bangkok International Airport, 1993–2000.

As is the case with many of the major cities in Southeast Asia, activity at the existing Bangkok International Airport at Don Muang has been rising at an extremely rapid pace, annually registering passenger increases of 15 percent and cargo increases of nearly 20 percent for most of the last decade. Realizing that this airport's capacity was limited, the Thai government started, as early as the 1960s, to buy land in a vast swamp area east of Bangkok for a second major airport. In the early 1990s the government assembled an international team of consultants to deal with difficult problems of drainage and aviation planning. The design of the terminals, which is the product of a joint venture team consisting of Murphy/Jahn, TAMS, and ACT, envisions a terminal consisting of a group of separate buildings all covered by an enormous roof trellis structure, giving the terminal a consistent architectural image and shading it from the intense tropical sun.

R.B.

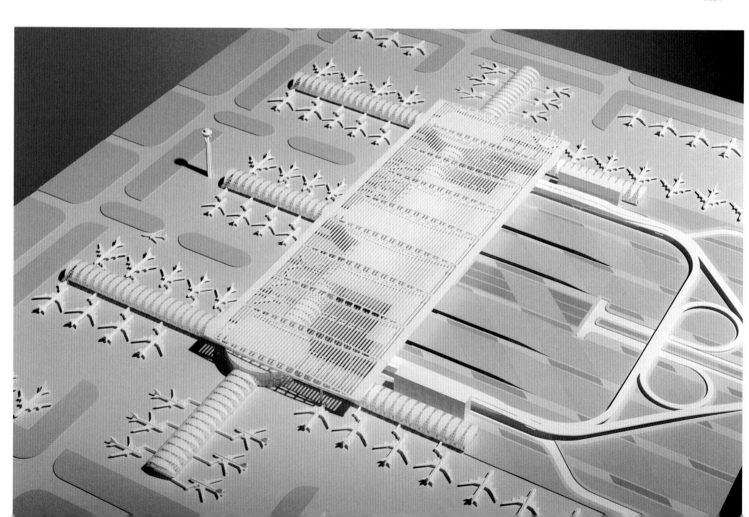

175-76 Skidmore, Owings and Merrill,
Del Campo and Maru, and
Michael Willis and Associates,
architects. Model and
perspective rendering of the
proposed International Arrivals
Building, San Francisco International Airport, 1993-99.

San Francisco constructed its first terminal in
1937 in a Spanish Mission style, a building
now demolished. The current proposal by
Skidmore, Owings and Merrill for a new
International Arrivals Building directly
opposite the present international terminal
is related to this airport's traditional role as
the "Gateway to the Pacific." Projections on
increased traffic with Pacific Rim countries
dictate the need to create additional facilities
in San Francisco. A current capacity to
accommodate eight large aircraft, mostly for
Asian travel, will be expanded to twenty with
this new building of 2 million square feet.
A new light rail system will connect this
terminal to others at the airport. The new
terminal will incorporate greater concession
space for passengers, as well as facilities like
an aquarium, a packaging design museum,
and a library for aviation memorabilia –
a library that will be based on the design
of the waiting room in the original 1937
terminal. All in all, the new facility is
intended to insure that San Francisco will be
able to handle efficiently their international
traffic, which, at 4 million people today (out
of almost 33 million total in 1993), is expected to double early in the next century.

J.Z.

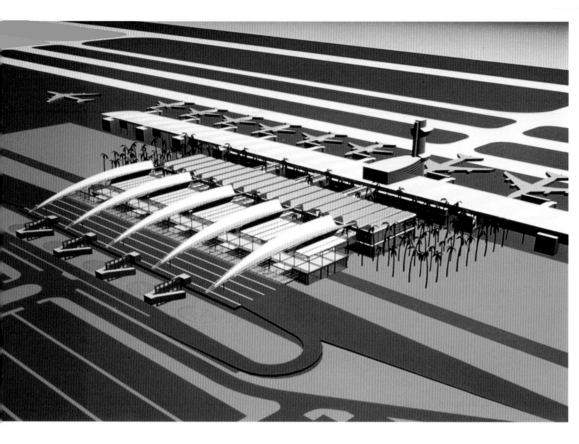

177 Hellmuth, Obata and Kassabaum, architects, with EMA – Engineers, Managers Associates. Computer projection of Cochin Airport, India, 1995-2002.

178 Hellmuth, Obata and Kassabaum, architects. Perspective view of the interior of Fukuoka International Airport, Japan, 1993-97.

Many of America's largest architectural firms have found an increasingly large percentage of their work abroad in recent years. Nowhere is this phenomenon more pronounced than in the field of airport design. At Fukuoka International Airport in Japan, the American firm of Hellmuth, Obata and Kassabaum, along with Japanese partners, has designed a new $280 million international terminal. The same architects are also part of the team responsible for a new terminal at the airport serving Cochin and the tropical Kerala region of India. Both projects include major new air facilities, hotels, and retail and office development.

R.B.

179-80 Kisho Kurokawa, architect. Perspective views of Kuala Lumpur International Airport, 1993-98.

In anticipation of Kuala Lumpur becoming one of the financial centers of Southeast Asia (and already the site of the world's tallest building), the government of Malaysia made a commitment to build a world-class airport that would become a regional hub for the next century. Situated 31 miles from the city center, the site alone will occupy about 39 square miles, while a new, 58-square-mile rain forest will separate the airport from its surroundings. Japanese architect Kisho Kurokawa, whose design philosophy integrates Asian and Western concepts, planned the architecture of the new main terminal of 1.35 million square feet to incorporate references to both traditional Islamic domes and high-tech curvilinear airfoils in the roof structure. He also employed design motifs from indigenous Malaysian wood structures, especially evident on the interior of the vaults. The large glass windows, especially in the wooded satellite atria, remind one of the rain forest outside, which is also mirrored, in image, by the tree-like internal structure of the terminals. The main terminal and its four satellites will be connected to the city and region by a high-speed train with a new main station, also designed by this architect.   J.Z.

Mark J. Bouman

Cities of the Plane: Airports in the Networked City

Near the old railroad hamlet of Sturtevant, Wisconsin, is a small, general aviation airport named "Air City." Built in the 1920s, this tiny facility was given a name that portended the sort of urban development that would, by the 1990s, engulf Sturtevant in the burgeoning Chicago-Milwaukee metropolitan corridor, which has as one anchor Milwaukee's General William Mitchell Field and as the other, "the world's busiest airport" – Chicago's O'Hare International. Many would say that this whole sprawling complex is the true "air city," and that Sturtevant's airport, if it is significant at all, is but a small knot in the global net made up of Mitchell and O'Hare and London's Heathrow and Tokyo's Narita and hundreds of others, large and small. In short, since as early as the 1940s, the term "air city" or "airport city" has summarized in one image both the web of urban forms that characterizes the modern metropolis and the international network of cities.[1] For many others – especially city officials and those who have invested in airport development – the term describes the urban world that ought to be, as when an erstwhile Aviation Commissioner for the City of Chicago summed up O'Hare's economic effects on the metropolis by using the term "airport city" – "a city in itself," he said, "and we like to talk about it."[2]

But Amtrak still stops at little Sturtevant, barely an hour's train ride north of Chicago, and its rails still drive into the heart of Chicago past both suburban sprawl and inner city industrial decay, carrying the traveler from the "air city" of today into a major metropolitan area that has already served to define several urban coinages of the past: the rail city, the canal city, the port city. Each of these terms reflects a particular era in city development, and each was used to describe not only what was, but also what those at the time thought ought to be. And the shadow of each era remains, as the "restless formation and reformation of geographical landscapes" continues.[3] This essay pauses to consider some of the transformations wrought by the "air city" on the landscape and life of the older, pre-aviation urban core in the past fifty years. The effort to assimilate the demands of a new technology into an existing urban fabric is not a new struggle, but it has taken a new shape in the aviation era. Much of what happens as a result of the creation of these new landscapes reminds us that the "air city" is not about airports alone, but, instead, involves a whole host of changes that have engulfed society and economy in the late twentieth century.

Although airports have clearly spawned suburban developments of massive extent and influence, they too need to be physically accommodated within the existing metropolitan fabric of services and transportation (see, in addition, the essay by Robert Bruegmann in this volume). Airports, the points through which cities are connected to a global network of cities, are themselves enveloped within the "networked city," and for this reason we shall look at the relation of large airports to transportation infrastructure, public utilities, land use and configuration, and open space planning. Social and economic patterns within the central city have also had to adapt to the new facilities in ways as profound as those that have touched the metropolitan periphery.

1 Charles Froesch and Walther Prokosch, *Airport Planning* (New York, 1946), p. 17. One observer likened the "air community," with its clustering of activity around decentralized airport nodes, to Ebenezer Howard's "Garden City"; Raymond S. Sleeper, "Small Airports: Economic Stimulus for Cities and Semirural Areas," in W. Stewart-Evans, ed., *Air Transportation: The Airport and the Community* (Knoxville, Tenn., 1970), pp. 33-38.

2 William E. Downes, Jr., "O'Hare International Airport: What It Means to Chicago," in *Air Transportation Conference, Proceedings* (Society of Automotive Engineers, American Institute of Aeronautics and Astronautics, American Society of Mechanical Engineers, 1972), pp. 25-31. Downes focuses entirely on economic benefit to the Chicago region as a whole and especially to communities near the airport.

3 David Harvey, *The Urbanization of Capital* (Oxford, 1985), p. 150.

Airports and Networks

When he came to the little settlement of Phocis in the second century A.D., the Greek writer Pausanias balked at calling the place a "city" since it had "no government offices or gymnasium, no theatre or agora or water flowing down to a fountain."[4] It would be easy to imagine that, if Pausanias were to stumble onto a settlement today and find no airport within easy reach of it, that settlement, too, would fail the test of being a true city. Even the smallest places with any pretension to urbanity feel the "responsibility" or "public obligation," as airport planners put it, to have airport service.[5] The United States Federal Aviation Administration counted 17,451 airports in the U.S. in 1995, of which 568 had scheduled service. These are graded hierarchically (based on the percentage of national passenger enplanements they represent), from 433 nonhub airports, to 64 small air traffic hubs, to 42 medium air traffic hubs, to 29 large air traffic hubs.[6]

The airport hierarchy is representative of the way that cities are stitched into regional, national, and international space-economies. It is common, for example, to speak of "world cities" or "global cities," places that fully participate in the international economy through, among other things, direct international air connections. New York, London, and Tokyo spring to mind as premier global cities, an impression confirmed by the amount of air traffic spawned in the multiple airports of each one.[7] Air service also connects Third World cities – usually one per country – to the international urban network, through development objectives that are often aimed more at impressing the international financial community than uplifting the lives of local residents.[8] In the more developed world, smaller metropolises also have their "international airports," cities such as Seattle (fig. 1; pl. 121), Kansas City (pl. 110), Birmingham, England, and Nagoya. Below these in size are such regional airports as South Bend (pl. 60) or Evansville. And, though they may lack scheduled air service, the ubiquity of landing strips and municipal airports near virtually every American county seat suggests a deep level of penetration of the air city to even the smallest places. In many of its rudiments, the air city presents a relatively standardized face to the world, if only because it is essential to guarantee that "an Indonesian registered, American manufactured aircraft, powered with British engines, flown by a Dutch crew, using a Swiss aircraft radio, guided by a French [instrument landing system], into a Malaysian airport [arrive] with surprises to no one and safety to all."[9]

The global network of cities has two additional features. First, it is dynamic: the sheer speed of jet travel has in turn so sped up the circulation that

4 R. E. Wycherley, *How the Greeks Built Cities*, 2nd ed. (New York, 1962), p. xix.

5 Ralph H. Burke, *Master Plan of Chicago Orchard (Douglas) Airport* (Chicago, 1948), made the quintessential American planning case: that "adequate airport facilities are primarily the concern of the community," since "any community which aspires to industrial greatness, must provide airport facilities to keep pace with the ever-increasing demands of aviation"; pp. 1-2. For the "public obligation" argument with respect to Chicago, see General Airport Company, *Comprehensive Study Relating to Aeronautical Facilities for Metropolitan Area of Chicago Projected to 1970* (Stamford, Conn., 1946), p. 66.

6 Robert Horonjeff and Francis McKelvey, *Planning and Design of Airports*, 4th ed. (New York, 1994), pp. 17-18.

7 The term "world cities," like so much apt urban terminology, was introduced by Patrick Geddes in *Cities in Evolution* in 1915 and advanced by Peter Hall in *World Cities*, 2nd ed. (New York, 1977), who wrote, "The world cities are the sites of the great international airports: Heathrow, Kennedy, Orly, Schiphol, Sheremetyevo"; p. 1. See also Jean Gottmann, "The Dynamics of City Networks in an Expanding World," *Ekistics* 350/351 (1991), pp. 277-81; Richard V. Knight and Gary Gappert, eds., *Cities in a Global Society*, Urban Affairs Annual Reviews, no. 35 (New York, 1989); and Saskia Sassen, *The Global City: New York, London, Tokyo* (Princeton, 1991).

8 See, for example, David Drakakis-Smith, *The Third World City* (London, 1987), pp. 46, 63. For the most part, the present essay focuses on airport development in the more developed world.

9 John R. Wiley, *Airport Administration and Management* (Westport, Conn., 1986), p. 32.

Fig. 1 Port of Seattle, architects. Seattle-Tacoma Airport, 1947-49 (now greatly altered, with additions by TRA Associates; photo c. 1950).

10 A point noted in virtually every local airport planning study.

11 John R. Borchert, "American Metropolitan Evolution," *Geographical Review* 57 (July 1967), pp. 301-32.

12 Roughly 85 percent of American intercity passenger traffic is airborne; James Vance, Jr., *Capturing the Horizon: The Historical Geography of Transportation since the Transportation Revolution of the Sixteenth Century* (New York, 1986), p. 592.

13 Barney Warf, "The Port Authority of New York-New Jersey," *Professional Geographer* 40, no. 3 (Aug. 1988), pp. 288-97.

14 Froesch and Prokosch (note 1), p. 7. Elsewhere the authors write: "Each airport must represent an *advance* in planning; there is no such thing as 'copying an airport design'"; p. 1. As early as 1929, a planner noted that airports provided the "first chance that history has offered to apply the modern principle of prevention to a new art and science in a big way"; George B. Ford, "The Airport and the City Plan," *American City* 40 (March 1929), p. 129; quoted in Paul Barrett, "Cities and Their Airports: Policy Formation, 1926-1952," *Journal of Urban History* 14, no. 1 (Nov. 1987), pp. 112-37. Barrett's article is an excellent overview of American airport planning issues with a detailed Chicago case study.

all points are now drawn into a tighter web than ever before. Places so closely in communication with each other must respond quickly to competitive threats emanating from other cities. Jockeying for the top spot in the hierarchy involves staying up to date on airport facilities.[10] Indeed, some places that attained a spot atop the urban hierarchy in the railroad age have now slipped back in the jet age, to be replaced by other emergent centers.[11] In the United States, a country of continental proportions, air has more firmly supplanted rail in intercity travel, so American airports are more ubiquitous and tend to be larger than in other parts of the world.[12]

The second feature of the global network of cities is that each place is tied to the whole net in its own way: each knot is its own network. Local transportation networks funnel local production and people to points of export and emigration; local public service networks ensure that basic needs are provided to the producers and the residents and are themselves drawn into regional and international grids of water, power, and light; and people circulate within and between metropolises in a ceaseless parade of human activity. Each place also has its socio-political network, the various parts of which respond differently and at times conflictingly to the prospect of so huge a public investment as an airport.[13]

Airports emerged on the urban scene long after basic networks were in place, and a way to accommodate them had to be found that differed, in some respects, from the airport-spawned development that occurred in greenfield sites. Airport development happened at a significant point in planning history. While canal, port, and railroad cities were occasionally planned in advance, specifics of urban network formation were usually left to local authorities to work out, often after some crisis of local transportation, water supply, wastewater removal, or housing provision had reared its head. By the beginning of the twentieth century, an emergent tradition of planning began to feel that metropolitan networks could be controlled and coordinated to facilitate the accumulation of capital and stave off local crises over the provision of urban services. What is striking about airports, then, is the extensive planning that goes into creating them and the effort made to graft them onto the existing metropolis. In the United States, this tendency was certainly abetted by the role delegated to municipalities by the federal government in 1926 to take responsibility for airport development (see the essay by David Brodherson in this volume). As two airport planners asserted in 1946, "[Airport] terminal plans of the future must start with the community, and be planned to take their proper place within the framework of community life."[14] But planning's "comprehensiveness" more often deals with questions of location and transportation than of economy and society, and, as we shall see, even here the task of integrating airports into the community has proven far easier in conception than in execution.

A Place for Airports

Visionary schemes for airports often willfully dismiss or disregard basic requirements so that they can idealize other possibilities. This is true of Antonio Sant'Elia's well-known 1914 sketch of a central city station for trains and airplanes, just as it is of Sergius Ruegenberg's 1948 plan for an airport to be located next to Berlin's Zoo Station. Ruegenberg in fact represents the ideal world of the airport location planner: runways are tucked neatly into the pris-

Fig. 2 Sergius Ruegenberg, architect. Project for a combined airport and railroad station, Berlin, 1948.

tine network of highways and rail lines at a point very near the heart of the city (fig. 2). Buildings are either absent or helpfully hug the ground. The reality of modern airports, of course, is vastly more demanding.

Airports are simply so large – major ones are at least four or five square miles in size – that they dwarf most other urban land uses; they are frequently larger than the downtown areas of the cities they serve.[15] The most significant landscape feature of an airport is undoubtedly its size, a fact that is most directly related to the technical requirements of the airplanes themselves; that is, adequate land for takeoff and landing, as well as buffer zones for safety and noise control, and additional space for maintenance and repair hangars must be found.[16] Runways for jets, for example, are about two miles in length and approaches need to be clear of water towers, smokestacks, and other urban obstructions, a fact that favors waterfront sites, as at Rio de Janeiro (fig. 3), or cornfield sites, such as at Indianapolis (fig. 4). Few cities have had available open space for airport development within the existing urban fabric that is not also prohibitively expensive. Those airports that are developed in a built-up zone are quickly hemmed in by competing land uses and usually cannot expand when the time comes. Multiple airports in large metropolises also cannot be sited so as to compete with each other for the same air space.

Fig. 3 Hidroservice Engenharia de Projetos Limitada, architects. Aerial view of Rio de Janeiro International Airport in the Bay of Guanabara, 1974-90.

Fig. 4 Everett I. Brown, architect. Remodeling and expansion of Indianapolis International Airport (Edward James, architect, 1954-56), 1967-74.

15 It should be pointed out that air transport is vastly more land efficient than any other mode in terms of land taken per passenger mile; see Terence Bendixson and John Whitelegg, "Assessments of Institutional Responses," in David Banister and Kenneth Button, eds., *Transport: The Environment and Sustainable Development* (London, 1993), table 4.

16 Edward Relph, *The Modern Urban Landscape* (Baltimore, 1987), p. 124.

17 Barrett (note 14), pp. 116-20.

18 For more on Chicago airport location and architecture, see David Brodherson, "'All Airplanes Lead to Chicago': Airport Planning and Design in a Midwest Metropolis," in John Zukowsky, ed., *Chicago Architecture and Design, 1923-1993: Reconfiguration of an American Metropolis* (Munich and Chicago, 1993), pp. 75-97.

19 Special Committee Representing Chicago Association of Commerce, Chicago Plan Commission, and Chicago Regional Planning Association, *Airport Program for Chicago and the Region of Chicago* (Chicago, 1941); Burke (note 5), pp. 4-8, reviews the site selection process for what would become O'Hare.

20 *Comprehensive Study* (note 5), pp. 53, 75; *Airport Program* (note 19), p. 6.

Thus, airports have tugged at the hem of the urban fabric, threatening to uncloak the urban middle. At the same time, however, the large hand of the marketplace has the urban cloak firmly in its grasp. Being in the geographic middle of the marketplace usually means serving more passengers, especially business and professional travelers working in the central business district.[17] Few passengers care to spend more time getting to the airport than they will spend in the air itself. The scramble for suitable airport sites therefore requires a balance of centrality and peripherality.

The search for an airport site that would guarantee Chicago's transportation hegemony in America is a case in point of the tension between centrality and peripherality.[18] Most studies conducted in the 1940s took a regional view of the issue. Three sites were typically weighed: expansion of the existing Municipal Airport (now Midway Airport); a site even closer to the city's Loop central business district; and a site northwest of the city then occupied by a Douglas Aircraft Company manufacturing plant. Other places that were examined from time to time included a site in Lake Michigan just off the central business district; a site in the Lake Calumet wetlands near the city's thickest concentration of heavy industry on the far South Side; and a site on the massive Clearing Industrial District railroad yards near Midway Airport.[19]

The lure of centrality was a strong factor in most of these site considerations. A 1941 study, for example, examined specific sites near the city center on a manmade island or polder in Lake Michigan; in the warehouse district of the near South Side; on stilts above existing rail yards; or in the near West Side "slum area." In 1946, a State of Illinois consultant suggested that the two-mile area south of the Loop containing 242,000 "blighted" or "near-blighted" dwelling units could be cleared for small urban air strips.[20] But the virtues of centrality were also its undoing: being close to industrial districts meant coping with smokestacks and smog; being close to the commercial district meant coping with high land costs and tall buildings; being in Lake Michigan near the Loop meant dealing with fog, spray, and tricky winds; and being close to any site of economic value meant paying exorbitant costs for land acquisition.

So the Chicago studies generally came to the same conclusion: that Midway Airport was too hemmed in by existing land use; that land near the central business district was too scarce, too costly, and fettered by adjacent

Fig. 5 C. F. Murphy Associates, architects. Rendering for a proposed airport in Lake Michigan, 1969.

obstructions to aviation; and that the Douglas site, though rather far away, presented the right combination of land availability, low acquisition cost, obstructionless approach, and potentially good ground access via a newly planned superhighway. O'Hare was, thus, constructed there (1957-63), and Midway went into a deep decline, hastened by postwar residential construction that had made the purchase of land for a buffer zone prohibitively expensive; the need for jets to have greater takeoff and landing room; and a crash into a residential neighborhood that made residents fear that jet aircraft would require an even greater buffer zone than piston aircraft.[21]

Despite the continued success of O'Hare, the lure of centrality has reared itself at least twice: once, when Mayor Richard J. Daley revived the old dike-and-polder Lake Michigan airport plan in the late 1960s (see fig. 5), and again, when his son, Mayor Richard M. Daley, renewed the old plan to site an airport in the Lake Calumet wetlands in 1990 (see Bruegmann, fig. 13). Both sites had the virtues of accessibility to the center of Chicago, but both were fraught with concerns over the cost of land assembly, the technical feasibility of what was to be attempted, and, by this time, a vocal and sophisticated opposition that raised these points and others about the impact of such a huge airport on the economic and environmental quality of life in adjacent neighborhoods.[22] The Lake Calumet site also raised the prospect of displacing a large local population, something that airports, unlike freeways and railroads, have generally not done.[23]

The failures to find new sites for a Chicago airport were by no means unique; many other areas have had "unbuilt" airports. New York City attempted for years to build a fourth major airport at Great Swamp, New Jersey; London spent so much time and money studying a third major airport location that the monumental but pointless effort has been dubbed a "Great Planning Disaster." Even sites that were selected and successfully built could be widely seen as failures, at least for a while, especially those that chose peripherality over centrality, such as Dulles International Airport, twenty-seven miles from the center of Washington, D.C., Montreal's Mirabel Airport, thirty-four miles away, or Buenos Aires International, thirty-two miles distant.[24]

In the meantime, the downtown air terminal never completely vanished from the scene. Early plans called for "airparks" to be located on railyards, floodplains, or other open spaces near the central business district. New York had several significant experiments with seaplane airports, especially at LaGuardia (see pl. 44). Even today, downtown commuter airports are rela-

21 Landrum and Brown, *Airport Master Plan Study, Data Collection and Analysis, Chicago Midway Airport* (Chicago, 1976). Despite the fact that Midway had reached a traffic saturation point in 1953, the airport's decline was far from certain when O'Hare was first opened. Even in 1957, when the new terminals were begun at O'Hare, most passengers and air carriers preferred to endure delays at Midway rather than venture out to O'Hare because of its greater distance from the Loop. See L.L. Doty, "Midway Traffic Jams Clog Entire System," *Aviation Week* (Dec. 16, 1957), pp. 38-40.

22 For a comparison of the two "third airport" proposals, see Fredrick Blum, "The Third Airport Revisited: Lessons from the Past," in Mark Bouman, ed., *Transportation and Economic Development in Illinois,* Proceedings of the Third Annual Board of Governors Public Policy Conference (Chicago, 1990), pp. 15-19. For a lucid dissenting view on the Lake Michigan airport, see Open Lands Project, *Will a Lake Airport Best Serve the Chicago Area?* (Chicago, 1968); for dissent on the Lake Calumet Airport, see the papers published by the Center for Neighborhood Technology, *Plane Basics* (Chicago, 1991).

23 On railroads, see John R. Kellett, *The Impact of Railways on Victorian Cities* (London, 1969); on the automobile, see, among many examples, Joe R. Feagin and Robert Parker, *Building American Cities: The Urban Real Estate Game,* 2nd ed. (Englewood Cliffs, N.J., 1990), pp. 153-80.

24 The actual site selection process, of course, is a long and involved one, although it varies from country to country. France, for example, spends much less time on winning public consensus than does the United States; Richard de Neufville, *Airport Systems Planning* (Cambridge, Mass., 1976), pp. 5-6, 66. On distance, see Vance (note 12), p. 598.

Fig. 6 John Carl Warnecke and Associates, architects, with Desmond and Lord, Inc. Aerial view of Boston-Logan International Airport, 1967, with later additions (photo June 1993).

Fig. 7 Nikken Sekkei and the Joint Venture Architects of the New Tokyo International Airport Authority. Aerial view of New Tokyo International Airport, Narita, Terminals 1 (1977-78) and 2 (1992).

Fig. 8 C. W. Fentress, J. H. Bradburn and Associates, architects. Denver International Airport, 1989-95.

tively common, as at Chicago's Meigs Field and St. Paul's Holman, and some large airports near the core have managed to survive, such as Boston's Logan International (fig. 6), Washington National (see Brodherson, figs. 16-17 and 32), and Berlin's Tempelhof (pls. 5-7).[25]

It is one of the air city's central ironies that the once distant airports are now hemmed in by real estate development that is the best evidence of their own success. Already, the generation of new metropolitan airports built from 1950 to 1965 in the United States was significantly farther out than the existing ones they largely replaced.[26] Most metropolitan airports are now at considerable distances from the central business districts, but, even here, development impinges. Subdivisions sprout near the far-off Dulles; apartment buildings lie at the end of runways at San Francisco International. London's Heathrow is an extreme case of urban congestion (see Lockhart, fig. 10). Suburban locations now have the disadvantages of centrality: high costs, difficult land acquisition, aviation obstacles, and politically well-organized opposition to expansion.[27] Peripherality has a new face: the present generation of large airports, as in the case of the New Tokyo International Airport in Narita (fig. 7) and the new Denver International Airport (fig. 8), have moved to exurbia.

Airports and Local Transportation

So airports have pulled away from the urban center. But the logic of centrality is still in play, and airports need good connections to the core. The farther they roam, the better the connection needs to be. Clearly, ground transportation must conform to the market demands of aviation. As historical geographer James Vance has noted, "We have become increasingly concerned not with the conditions of actual flight, which have tended to become quite standardized, but rather with the geography of airports and the access to those facilities that in some cities have taken over from the central business district as the main site of human conflux within the metropolis and certainly within its region, on any continuing basis."[28]

In the railroad era, rail and streetcar lines and major roads focused strongly on "downtown." But siting such a major traffic generator as an airport in a peripheral location was sure to alter the primacy of downtown. Not only would that location need to be connected to the center, but it would be-

25 Froesch and Prokosch (note 1), pp. 64-80, show several examples.
26 Arthur D. Little, Inc., *Airport Land Needs* (Cambridge, Mass., 1966), pp. 1-3. The *additional* distance in miles from the central business district for new airports built 1950-1965: Jacksonville (4); Honolulu (3); Chicago (11); Shreveport (6); Detroit (14.5); Jackson (6); Toledo (6); Pittsburgh (8); Houston (7); New York, Kennedy (8); Washington, D.C., Dulles (23).
27 Ibid., p. 13.
28 Vance (note 12), p. 599.

come a hub of ground transportation in its own right. As early as 1941, for example, Chicago airport planners envisioned three peripheral air terminals, all "connected with adequate express highways and each ... served by fast transportation to the central and other sections of Chicago and suburbs."[29]

Exactly how airports and downtowns would be connected was another issue. One possible method of getting passengers to peripheral locations from the central business district was to create a downtown airline terminal, where passengers might be ticketed and checked in, and then ferried by bus to the passenger terminal on the periphery. New York City was the first to try the idea, with an airlines terminal significantly located near Grand Central Station (see Brodherson, fig. 14).[30] Brussels offered rail service from center city airline terminals to the airport. While this approach made sense in some of the larger metropolises, it soon became clear that most passengers would prefer to arrive at the airport on their own, even if the airport itself continued to carry off the architectural analogy to the downtown railroad terminal.

For fifty years, ground transportation planners have taken it as axiomatic that travel times to the airport should be less than a half hour, but that wish would prove difficult to fulfill. In the early days of intercity passenger aviation, one could drive or take public transportation to the airport following local arterial streets. But the time taken to negotiate local traffic defeated the purpose of aviation, which was, after all, speed. An additional problem that American cities west of the Appalachians face is that the street network is strongly influenced by the original rectangular survey system; while some diagonal roads entered the centers of most cities, peripheral airport locations were often sited amid checkerboard fields. Chicago's perfect square mile Midway Airport was an obvious example: for many years, Midway's connection to downtown Chicago required a transfer from the Archer Avenue streetcar to the South Cicero shuttle, "a lightly patronized, single-track line."[31] Faster straight line journeys that cut these corners would have to be made.

The 1941 Chicago *Airport Program* study, for example, looked forward to the implementation of the city's newly adopted superhighway plan that would cut travel times from forty to twenty minutes. The study downplayed any positive benefits from a city proposal to connect the airport by deep subway, since many riders would make intervening stops, and for airport passengers, time was of the essence. Concern over travel time continues to be a counterforce to the peripheral tugging that airport space demands. By the mid-1960s, studies were showing that, on short-haul air journeys of up to 250 miles, well over half the total journey time was taking place on the ground.[32]

Solutions to the problem have varied, but they usually involve rapid urban rail transit, mainline rail service, and/or a superhighway in various intermodal combinations. Larger metropolises increasingly have tended to add rail to the mix. An early example of dedicated rapid transit to the airport is the Cleveland "Rapid," which connected Terminal Tower in the central business district to Hopkins International Airport in 1956 (fig. 9). Other cities, such as London, Paris, New York, Philadelphia, and Chicago, extended existing rapid transit or metro systems to the airport, in the latter case as part of an intermodal highway-rail corridor culminating in a spectacular "gateway" station under the airport parking garage. Cities with completely new metro systems, such as Atlanta and Washington, integrated airports into the route planning from the start. Munich extended its existing S-Bahn rail system when it ran a separate line out north to its new Franz Josef Strauss International Airport;

Fig. 9 Rapid transit at Hopkins International Airport (Outcalf, Guenther and Associates, architects), Cleveland, 1956 (photo 1969).

184   Mark J. Bouman

29 *Airport Program* (note 19), p. 4.
30 Froesch and Prokosch (note 1), pp. 231ff.
31 Alan R. Lind, *Chicago Surface Lines: An Illustrated History*, 3rd ed. (Park Forest, Ill., 1986), p. 431. Travelers could also take the 63rd Street line east and then transfer to a line north. Midway was sited essentially at the end of both the 63rd and South Cicero lines until after World War II.
32 Little (note 26), p. 10.
33 John Nolan, *Airports and Airways and Their Relation to City and Regional Planning* (New York, 1928), pp. 12-13; quoted in Barrett (note 14), p. 117.
34 de Neufville (note 24), p. 66.

San Francisco's failure to provide a rail link with its new International Airport (pls. 175-76) presents a significant exception to current practices.

In Europe it is common to find airports connected to the intercity railroad grid. In Amsterdam, Barcelona, Birmingham, Brussels, Dusseldorf, Frankfurt, Geneva, Pisa, Rome, Vienna, and Zurich, among others cities, mainline rail is the primary connection to the central city. In the United States, only Baltimore-Washington International is connected to Amtrak in this way. Connections are better in Japan, with the great distance between Tokyo and its new international airport in Narita making mainline rail a necessity. In many cases, of course, one can board a train heading away from the central city and into the hinterland. National rail systems have worked to integrate other cities into the rail network serving the airport. It is possible, for example, to board a train in Birmingham and ride three hours directly to Gatwick Airport (pl. 93) without having to stop at the London rail terminals. Links are now being forged between airports and the emergent European high-speed rail network, as in the recently completed TGV line that allows a bypass of central Paris from Charles de Gaulle International Airport on the northeast, through EuroDisney on the east, to the Paris-Lyons mainline on the southeast (see pl. 114).

The airport era is also the highway era, so it is not surprising that airport planners work hard to accommodate the automobile. Airport planning is frequently conjoined to freeway planning, though the two do not always proceed in lockstep. An early call for joint airport/highway planning was made in 1928, when planner John Nolan observed that "in large cities the airplane calls for improved motorways of the superhighway type."[33] Perhaps the earliest example of an airport planned in the context of freeway development is Frankfurt's Rhein-Main Airport, sited in the 1930s at the junction of two autobahns. Drawings in the 1948 O'Hare master plan also show the airport connected to the city by rapid transit as well as a sprawling new intersection of limited-access highways. A spectacular effort was made to connect Washington's Dulles International, which needed excellent accessibility to be at all usable. The solution was to create a dedicated limited-access road, now expanded and operated as a private tollroad, solely for Dulles users. The effect of such freeways was frequently to make remote locations more accessible (in terms of travel time) than central city locations.[34]

But not all air traffic is generated from downtown. At the same time that particularly strong links needed to be forged between the airport and downtown, the airport and its postwar transport sibling, the freeway, were contributing to a massive rearrangement of metropolitan space. Planners have different words for this – the galactic metropolis, the polycentered metropolis, the urban field, and so forth – but the rearrangement has had a serious effect on patterns within the central city. Now cross- and reverse-commuting turn inside out the old patterns of moving into the city by morning and back out by night as airports become hubs of ground transportation in their own right. Especially in the American Sunbelt, airports like Phoenix Sky Harbor and Dallas-Fort Worth are now squarely at the center of the expanded metropolis and it is the old railroad core that has the eccentric location. Still, few airports are connected by mass transit to the outlying areas or along the circumference.

How does the arriving passenger approach all of this? Once on the ground, the passenger has to find his or her way to the connections to the urban core. Signs point to parking or to "ground transportation," which in

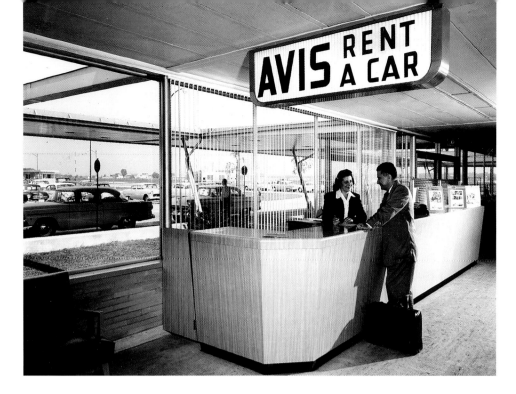

many airports is functionally separated from departing traffic. Care is taken in many airports to site car rental desks as near to baggage claim areas as possible (fig. 10). The onboard navigational systems that are now available in rental cars had their precursors in the maps and computer-generated travel instructions available at rental car desks.

Then comes the walk – or the ride – to the car. Massive parking lots and garages await; in certain instances, such as at Dallas-Fort Worth, Kansas City, and Rio de Janeiro (pls. 110-12), minimizing the walk from the car park to the terminal has been the governing principle in terminal planning and layout. Moving people from terminal to terminal, or from a remote parking lot to a terminal, has made it necessary to put on-site mass transit in place. Since an on-the-ground people-mover system was pioneered at Tampa in 1970 (fig. 11), other airports have followed, including Atlanta (fig. 12), Birmingham, Dallas-Fort Worth, Houston, Las Vegas, Gatwick, Miami, Orlando, Sea-Tac, Denver, Pittsburgh, Newark, and Chicago. At the latter, people-mover service has been fully integrated into the design of the new International Terminal at

Fig. 11 Reynolds, Smith and Hills, architects. People mover at Tampa International Airport, 1970, with transit vehicle by Westinghouse Electric Corp.

Fig. 12 Smith, Hinchman and Grylls, architects. People mover by Westinghouse at William B. Hartsfield International Airport, Atlanta, 1980.

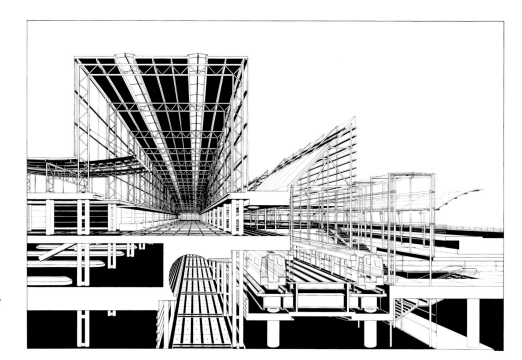

Fig. 13 Perkins and Will, architects; Ralph Johnson, designer. Cutaway perspective view of the International Terminal and people mover at O'Hare International Airport, Chicago, 1989.

O'Hare (see fig. 13). It was hoped that the high-tech gloss and functionality of people-mover systems would rub off on the downtown areas as well, and such systems were subsequently tried in Detroit, Jacksonville, and Miami.

Drawing all these methods of moving about the earth into one grand, airport-based multi-modal transportation center is now not such a far-fetched dream in the eye of planners. At Charles de Gaulle International Airport, one can now move from plane to TGV train through moving sidewalks, hamster-run escalators, and personal rapid transit (PRT). Plans are afoot to use PRT in Seattle to link the airport to local businesses, in Newark to link the airport to the Amtrak station, and in New York to link Kennedy and LaGuardia airports. Miami planners dream of linking their already well-connected International Airport via a people-mover system to a multi-modal center where a future high-speed rail line, Amtrak, commuter heavy rail, metro, bus, light rail directly to the port, and an automobile rental complex would all converge. Thus, the great interurban and intraurban transportation networks are continuing to draw together at one point.[35]

Airports, Urban Services, and the Environment

Like any facility handling large numbers of people, goods, and transportation equipment, airports require urban services. Their huge demands on gas, water, electricity, telephone lines, and sewage disposal were recognized as early as 1920 in the U.S. Army Air Service's guidelines for airport construction.[36] The construction and operation of an airport also places stress on natural environmental systems. Among these impacts are air and noise pollution; modification of water tables, river courses, and field drainage; land taken for infrastructure; and congestion generated by motor traffic entering and leaving the airport grounds.[37] While not an impact on the "natural" environment, airports also often encroach on high-quality agricultural land, as Heathrow did when it took some of the "best agricultural soil in all Britain" in the 1940s.[38]

When scheduled commercial air service in the United States began between Boston's Logan Airport and Newark in 1927, packed cinder runways

35 There are many articles on the state of the art to be found in William J. Sproule, Edward S. Neumann, and Murthy V. A. Bondada, eds., *Automated People Movers IV: Enhancing Values in Major Activity Centers*, Proceedings of the Fourth International Conference, American Society of Civil Engineers (New York, 1993); especially useful here are William J. Sproule, "An Introduction to APM Systems and Applications," pp. 22-34; L. David Shen, "The Role of APM in a Multi-Modal Transit System," pp. 230-38; and David M. Casselman and David D. Little, "Planning for Airport APM Systems: New Applications," pp. 332-43.

36 Froesch and Prokosch (note 1), p. 82.

37 This typology of environmental impacts can be found in Kenneth Button and Werner Rothengatter, "Global Environmental Degradation: The Role of Transport," in Banister and Button (note 15), pp. 22-23. It should also be pointed out here that air transport not only is the least energy efficient way to travel, it also ranks higher than other modes of transport on carbon dioxide emissions, nitrogen oxide emissions, hydrocarbons, and carbon monoxide emissions, adding up to 95,000 cubic meters of polluted air per passenger kilometer; compared to 38,000 for cars; 3,300 for buses; and 1,200 for rail; see Bendixson and Whitelegg (note 15).

38 Peter Hall, *Great Planning Disasters* (Berkeley, 1982), p. 16.

were adequate. Today's aircraft require runways roughly a foot thick with concrete, which add enormously to total construction costs and which have as their very reason for existence the swift removal of water.[39] The water must go somewhere. The first massive stage of airport construction usually involves rerouting of local transportation at the site, careful grading to accomplish proper drainage, and connection to the pre-existing grid of utilities.[40] Obviously, the flatter the site the lower the costs of grading the land, although a completely flat, low-lying site can be very expensive to pump free of water.[41] In many instances, on-site drainage ponds need to be created (see fig. 14); Chicago's manmade Lake O'Hare is now one of the largest bodies of water in the metropolitan area.

Less well known are the landscape re-designs necessary to accommodate drainage basin alterations of at least several square miles in extent and the resulting downstream impacts. Mountains have been flattened (Charleston, West Virginia), oceans and lakes have been filled (Meigs, Kansai, and Singapore), and wetlands have been drained to make way for airports (Schiphol and Kennedy). Chicago's flirtation with a third major airport in Lake Michigan involved construction of a dike four miles in diameter centered some five miles from shore. The 8,000 acres within the ring would be pumped free of water for a landing field (see fig. 5).[42] A proposed runway extension into Jamaica Bay at New York's Kennedy International Airport would have caused, according to a joint committee of the National Academy of Sciences and National Academy of Engineering, "major irreversible ecological damage."[43]

Not the least of the concerns airport managers have about wetlands is that these locations also attract landfills; and garbage attracts birds like gulls and starlings, which pose a special danger to jet engines. A fatal crash at Boston's Logan International in 1960 after a flock of starlings disabled a jet engine has led to a variety of measures. According to one scientist, "Airports should be managed as unattractive bird habitats: food sources like fruit trees and shrubs should be eliminated; grass should be kept no higher than 5-8 inches. Airport buildings should be designed so as not to provide attractive shelter, and to prevent ponding of water on rooftops. Water impoundments should be avoided. Dumps and fish processing plants which attract large flocks of birds should not be located near airports."[44] Not all airports can do this, but Kennedy Airport employs a full-time Director of the Bird Control Unit, pursuant to an FAA order to have a "dawn-to-dusk bird patrol." The unit roves about the grounds and disperses any flocks that form.[45]

Fig. 14 Kivett and Myers, architects. Aerial view of Kansas City International Airport, Kansas City, Missouri, 1968-72, showing the airport's drainage lake.

Fig. 15 Skidmore, Owings and Merrill, architects. Central heating and refrigeration plant, Idlewild Airport (now John F. Kennedy International Airport), New York, 1957.

39 Horonjeff and McKelvey (note 6), pp. 553-636.
40 Burke (note 5), p. 15.
41 Norman Ashford and Paul H. Wright, *Airport Engineering*, 2nd ed. (New York, 1984), p. 91.
42 Harza Engineering Company, *An Appraisal of a Lake Michigan Site for Chicago's Third Major Airport* (Chicago, 1967).
43 Jamaica Bay Environmental Study Group, *Jamaica Bay and Kennedy Airport: A Multi-Disciplinary Environmental Report* (New York, 1971).
44 Victor Solman, "Aircraft and Wildlife," in John H. Noyes and Donald R. Progulske, eds., *A Symposium on Wildlife in an Urbanizing Environment* (Amherst, Mass., 1973), p. 73; quoted in Annie Whiston Spirn, *The Granite Garden: Urban Nature and Human Design* (New York, 1984), p. 212.
45 James Kaplan, *The Airport: Terminal Nights and Runway Days at John F. Kennedy International Airport* (New York, 1994), pp. 26-36.
46 Ashford and Wright (note 41), p. 88.
47 Froesch and Prokosch (note 1), p. 89.
48 Ashford and Wright (note 41), p. 92; it is asserted that Kennedy Airport consumes enough electricity to "light Hartford"; see Kaplan (note 45), p. 25.

Indeed, while wetlands were once seen as "dead land," ideal for airport construction, their fundamental importance for urban areas as recreational space, wildlife habitat, aquifer storage and recharge, flood control, and pollution mitigation have made them live again in popular appreciation and the law since the 1970s. Section 404 of the U.S. Clean Water Act provides the Army Corps of Engineers with responsibility for wetlands management, and, since 1989, the government has pursued a "no-net-loss" of wetlands policy: wetland loss through construction must be "mitigated" by upgrading wetlands elsewhere. The policy proved to be of fundamental importance in derailing Chicago's Lake Calumet Airport plan, and it is likely to drive future airport construction in the U.S. to uplands locations.

More generally, airport projects in the developed world have been increasingly regulated since the late 1960s. Since 1969, American projects have required submission of an Environmental Impact Statement. Since 1979, the Airport and Airway Development Act has mandated that environmental factors be considered in both site selection and airport design. It is now recommended that airport master plans consider the following set of environmental impacts: changes in ambient noise level; displacement of significant numbers of people; aesthetic or visual intrusion; severance of communities; effect on areas of unique interest or scenic beauty; deterioration of important recreational areas; impact on the behavioral pattern of a species; other interference with wildlife; significant increase in air or water pollution; and major adverse effects on water table.[46]

Lack of a connection to the local utility grids could force construction of larger on-site facilities and greatly add to the cost of the project, a point recognized as long as fifty years ago.[47] Especially large airports with many employees incur a demand for utilities on the "scale of a new town" that offers yet another centripetal pull to the "ideal remoteness of the site to overcome environmental problems." Significant service structures were included as part of basic airport architecture (see fig. 15).[48] At O'Hare, the utility building (fig. 16; visible at the top of pls. 82 and 83) greets all automobile passengers leaving the terminal area and shows, through massive plate glass windows, the pumps and generators that support activity at this immense facility.

Perhaps the most obvious environmental consequence of aviation – with a reach far beyond the airport's boundaries – is the noise generated by aircraft. Though the noise problem has increased as engines have become more powerful, the problem is not a new one. It was compounded by the sharp rise

Fig. 16 C. F. Murphy Associates, architects. Utility building, O'Hare International Airport, Chicago, 1963.

in flights after World War II. Communities immediately adjacent to airfields where piston-powered craft landed were no strangers to airport noise. After all flights were diverted to one of LaGuardia's runways during a resurfacing project on the other one in 1951, a sharp rise in complaints from the adjacent Jackson Heights community was registered. The airlines, the FAA, and the New York Port Authority (operators of the airport) tried to cope through a variety of techniques: those runways with approaches over open or sparsely settled airways were preferred unless specific wind conditions did not allow it; runway length was extended so that a plane would be at a higher altitude in airspace over affected communities; aircraft were required to turn away from populated areas after reaching a certain specified altitude; and hangars and other buildings were used as ground screen for aircraft maintenance noise. For a time, the Port Authority proscribed jet aircraft landings without specific permission.[49]

Jets did indeed present new problems. They have more annoying high frequencies; they mask speech; they interfere with radio and TV; and their effects are cumulative – tolerance slides quickly the more overflights there are. Noise abatement techniques coalesced in four basic areas, some of which were clearly derived from the work done earlier in the 1950s. The first two techniques are applied to the manufacture and operation of aircraft, that is, to reducing the source of engine noise through technological improvement and by prescribing certain operational techniques to lessen the effects on surrounding communities. One technical improvement that some passenger and freight carriers are making is to have the engines on their planes replaced with quieter models that meet federally mandated noise reduction guidelines, while other airlines have selected to install "hushkits" on their existing fleet.[50] Operational improvements may not have lasting effect: for example, in Minnesota, traffic was rerouted away from heavily populated Richfield, Bloomington, and south Minneapolis in the 1980s to less developed areas further away, although now it turns out that those areas are becoming heavily built up and residents are feeling the effects of airport noise.[51]

The other two techniques for dealing with noise clearly reach off the grounds of the airport into the surrounding communities for solutions by prohibiting or limiting future concentrations of people and activity near the airport grounds through stiffer land-use planning controls and through architectural design. One avenue to land-use control is through zoning. But zoning variances can and frequently are granted by local authorities anxious

190   Mark J. Bouman

to capitalize on the economic development potential of sites adjacent to airports. The best way to ensure that land will not be used is to acquire it outright, though that drives up airport development costs and tends to propel airports to even more peripheral locations where such land can be found. Local and state authorities in Illinois and Minnesota, for example, now find themselves making preemptive strikes in the land market, securing an often quite peripheral site in the event – sometimes quite unlikely – that passenger demand will justify new construction.[52] In any case, both methods are more likely to be effective when planning new airports than when dealing with existing airport noise situations.

As a last resort, and as clear evidence that planning alone cannot cover all cases, communities are increasingly turning to abating existing noise levels by architecturally retrofitting structures in affected areas. Solutions include thicker glazing and insulation, additional drywall and new heating and cooling systems. While such public facilities as schools have frequently been the main beneficiaries of such retrofits in the past, airport authorities are now turning to retrofit whole residential communities, the staggering cost of which is a reminder of the difficulties of accommodating air transportation.[53]

Social and Economic Patterns

The very essence of transportation is to connect people with places and the social and economic activities that occur in them. But all too frequently airports are planned, as historian Paul Barrett puts it, as part of a "policy tradition, developed side by side with the highway planning tradition, which treated airports as transportation facilities only."[54] Many – including those deeply involved in the airport industry – have recognized the shortcomings of that view. Fifty years ago, an airport planning manual written by two Eastern Airlines engineers insisted that "the sociological relationship of air transport and airports to communities should be thoroughly explored. Too often in the past the effects which new mechanical devices might have upon people have not been thoroughly understood until it has become too late to correct serious mistakes."[55] And twenty years ago, another airport planner asserted that "airports are part of a complex economic and social system. . . . If transport planning is to be responsive to the aspirations of a country, it must be sensitive to prevailing cultural values and social desires."[56] At times, the attempt to read out the impact of airports and access to aviation on the existing urban fabric has been made explicit. Two engineers used a social systems approach in 1970 to suggest that the "idea of achieving non-economic values through transportation has much to offer." They went on in the study to see improved airport access as solving a number of "urgent problems of the community and nation," such as poverty, education, crime, racism, and safety.[57] But others have pointed out that such global accessibility has its downside, that "like free trade, good transport cuts both ways."[58]

This is a reminder that airports, as large and as influential as they are, are but a part of a larger frame of activities that have deeply transformed urban life and landscape. Sometimes airports and aviation serve to enable those changes; at other times they merely reflect them. In any case, it is worth recalling that airports, as loci of commerce, are linked to the same cycles of investment and selective disinvestment that made the canal and railroad cities. The private and public investments that made possible airport construction in

49 This and the following discussion of jet noise closely follows Wiley (note 9), pp. 125-42.

50 See "UPS to Achieve Early Stage 3 Compliance," *Airliners* 8, no. 6 (1995), p. 48; and "IAE Says V2500 Can Keep 727 Flying Past 2000," *Aviation Week and Space Technology* (Feb. 19, 1996), p. 31.

51 John S. Adams and Barbara J. VanDrasek, *Minneapolis-St. Paul: People, Place, and Public Life* (Minneapolis, 1993), p. 200.

52 Ibid., p. 201.

53 Ray Quintanilla and Ben Grove, "O'Hare Foes Deride City's Plan to Soundproof Suburban Homes," *Chicago Tribune* (Nov. 14, 1995).

54 Barrett (note 14), p. 131.

55 Froesch and Prokosch (note 1), p. 7.

56 de Neufville (note 24), p. 3.

57 Robert F. Baker and Raymond M. Wilmotte, *Technology and Decisions in Airport Access* (New York, 1970), pp. 42-43.

58 United Kingdom Civil Aviation Authority, quoted in de Neufville (note 24), pp. 150-53.

the first place was money redirected from other infrastructural and social projects in the central cities. The connections to the international economy that airports fostered have also transformed business in fundamental ways, such that large-scale factory production is increasingly giving way to "flexible production," where goods or components – especially those with high value per weight and with high sensitivity to labor costs, such as electronics – can be made at low-wage locations in the less developed world and cheaply transshipped through airport cargo terminals for distribution in the more developed world. Obviously, the grip of older urban industrial districts on manufacturing preeminence has been loosened and the "rail city's" total share of metropolitan jobs has slipped.[59]

Chicago, again, provides a typical case. The central city's share of metropolitan Chicago's total labor force slipped from about 75 percent in 1959 to less than 50 percent in 1990. This trend was getting into full swing just as another trend – the massive immigration of largely unskilled workers, many of them African American or Hispanic, to the older, "rail" city – was just passing its peak. The years 1940 to 1970, precisely when Chicago was planning and constructing the world's busiest airport, were also the years when the city's black population quadrupled.

Thus a spatial mismatch emerged, not only between the type of job and the skill level of the workers, but also between the potential worker and the location of the new jobs. The peripheral locations of Chicago's airports meant they would not only be in more affluent areas, but areas that were also more white. Militant reaction to attempts to integrate the postwar public housing development called Airport Homes, near Midway Airport, ensured that the area would remain predominantly white for a long time.[60] In 1983, 43 percent of African American households and 27 percent of Hispanic households lacked automobiles, and at that point, the extension of the rapid transit line into O'Hare itself was not yet completed.[61] The story is similar in many other American cities, although hiring goals could be harder to implement in places where the airport is not wholly owned and operated by the city, as it is in Chicago.

What is a city or metropolitan area to do? Many communities can seek engagement with these processes precisely through their airports. They can encourage flexible production by locating light industries on the airport grounds, as at Shannon, Ireland; corporate concentration can physically occur in highrise towers well-connected to the airport; internationalization of production is sped through sophisticated cargo handling facilities, as at O'Hare (see fig. 17) and Charles de Gaulle (see pls. 115, 117); and local, service-sector employees can enjoy face-to-face contact with their international counterparts through air travel or through conventions and trade shows that might be staged in their own city.

The problem is how to make the benefits of such developments reach into the older core. Often the efforts to make airports work in favor of the central city have amounted to bettering the transit links, as described above. The city can also rebuild the core to accommodate these changes. The same period in American urban history that witnessed the building of airports was marked by downtown redevelopment and its attendant convention centers, freeway access, sports stadia, and general transition to a service and entertainment-based economy. It helps if the city has jurisdiction over the airport and control over revenues and tax dollars from ancillary development, and if it can enforce agreements during construction periods, such as at O'Hare, where

59 The literature on these changes has become enormous; for a succinct description and an application to a specific urban context, see Paul L. Knox, "The Restless Urban Landscape: Economic and Sociocultural Change and the Transformation of Metropolitan Washington, DC," *Annals, Association of American Geographers* 81, no. 2 (June 1991), pp. 181-209. Surprisingly, perhaps, places such as Phoenix have become major manufacturing centers by focusing on the electronics industry: locally made parts are shipped to Asia or Latin America for assembly and are then returned for distribution – all airport-based activities; see W. McTaggart, "International Connections," in Charles Sargent, ed., *Metro Arizona* (Scottsdale, Ariz., 1988), p. 112.
60 See Arnold R. Hirsch, *Making the Second Ghetto: Race and Housing in Chicago, 1940-1960* (Cambridge, 1983).
61 Gregory D. Squires, Larry Bennett, Kathleen McCourt, and Philip Nyden, *Chicago: Race, Class, and the Response to Urban Decline* (Philadelphia, 1987), pp. 117-18, 163-66.
62 Wiley (note 9), p. 48.
63 For a review of this issue, see William Sharpe and Leonard Wallock, "From 'Great Town' to 'Nonplace Urban Realm': Reading the Modern City," in William Sharpe and Leonard Wallock, eds., *Visions of the Modern City: Essays in History, Art, and Literature* (Baltimore, 1987), pp. 1-50.

Fig. 17 William E. Brazley, architect. Cargo facilities for Lufthansa Airlines at O'Hare International Airport, Chicago, 1990-93.

firms agreed to a goal of hiring 25 percent minority workers. But the air city operates in a wider metropolitan world, especially in America, where severe political fragmentation is the rule. Roughly half the airports in metropolitan America are municipally operated.[62] Bickering over the apportionment of an airport's positive and negative effects is likely to be a part of the scene for a long time.

Air City

In the twenty-five years of architectural modernism that followed World War II, few structures were more functionally modern than the airport. For communities around the world, up and down the urban hierarchy, the mere fact of an up-to-date airport has been a point of pride and a statement that the city "belongs" in the global net of cities. Airports are a key prize to be won by urban or metropolitan growth coalitions, as they are called in the economic and sociological literature. The irony is that the very locality so celebrated in the fact of the airport's existence would be eroded by the buffetings of the international economy, by the caprice of the aviation industry in an age of deregulation, by enveloping urban sprawl, and by the interchangeability of airport design itself. Cities must swim upstream in the flow of international capital, trade, and passengers to assert their unique identity. The notion that the quality of urbanity is attached to particular places is now seriously called into question.[63]

Perhaps this is why so frequently, in the United States especially, airport names, unlike rail stations, commemorate local people: mayors and politicians, such as LaGuardia, Hartsfield, and Munich's Franz Josef Strauss; actors like John Wayne; industrialists like Bendix; and aviation heroes, such as Edward H. O'Hare and Milwaukee's Billy Mitchell. Perhaps it explains, too, why airport design is increasingly sensitive to local and regional context. In these ways at least, the city can assert its personality before it vanishes into thin air.

Robert Bruegmann   Airport City

Through the window of an airplane, the careful observer can read whole chapters in the history of transportation by studying the settlement patterns below. From the dense, pedestrian-oriented historic cores of large cities, for example, clinging tightly to the harbors or bridgeheads that provided the impetus for their birth, to the straggling tentacles of recent growth following major highways far into the surrounding countryside, the forms of the city provide eloquent testimony to the immense impact of successive means of transportation.[1]

Despite the undoubted importance air travel has had on the economies of cities, however, its influence on urban forms is surprisingly hard to discern from the air or from the ground. Certainly the major jetports loom as large as anything in the landscape. An airport such as Dallas-Fort Worth International is, in fact, as large as an entire city. Around Dallas-Fort Worth, just as around Washington, D.C.,'s Dulles International Airport and Chicago's O'Hare International Airport, there are complex districts of superhighways, parking lots, rental car agencies, hotels, distribution facilities, buildings for light manufacturing, and office parks. But many of the same activities and structures are found in other outlying business centers, and it appears that around other airports – those in Kansas City and Philadelphia, for example – there is little intense development outside the immediate airport area. Perhaps because of the difficulty in correlating specific real estate developments with the location of the airport, surprisingly little has been written on the subject.[2]

It seems, then, that while air transportation has had an enormous impact on the city, this impact so far has been more diffuse and difficult to isolate than has been the case with other kinds of transportation. Moreover, the effect of the airplane has been even more ambiguous than that of the railroad train, the streetcar, or the automobile. Like them, it has tended both to centralize the city and to decentralize it, only on a vastly larger scale. But air travel is still relatively new. It is possible, indeed likely, that it will affect the city in ways we can hardly now imagine.

Before the Jet

The advent of the railroad in the nineteenth century had a cataclysmic effect on the landscape. Tearing through both urban fabric and pristine countryside, it marked a line of division between some places and connected others that had previously been worlds apart. Its effects on the city were diverse and contradictory. On the one hand, the railroad provided the means for a vast centralization in urban form. From the entire region and distant towns, thousands of travelers came pouring into the heart of the city every day. This horde found its way from the railroad stations to nearby hotels, office buildings, lofts, and other commercial buildings that required easy access to the station. At the same time, however, the very trains that brought travelers to the city also provided the means by which these travelers could leave it, making it possible for them to live quite far from the center and still work there.

1 For their help on this essay, I would like to thank, in addition to those named in the notes that follow, Suhail al-Chalibi of the al-Chalibi Group, Chicago; Mark J. Bouman of Chicago State University; David Brodherson of New York; Robert Fairbanks of the University of Texas at Arlington; Robert Freestone of the University of New South Wales; Gregory Hise of the University of Southern California; Ruth Knack of the American Planning Association; Charles Lockwood of Los Angeles; Dennis McClendon of Chicago Cartographics, Chicago; David McCord, City of Aurora, Colorado; David NewMyer of Southern Illinois University; Douglas Robey of the New York Transit Authority; Richard Roddewig of Clarion Associates, Chicago; and Emmett Thiessen of Bennett and Kahnweiler, Chicago. John Zukowsky was especially helpful at all stages of this work.

2 The vast majority of writing about cities and airports has been about the effect air travel has had or might have on the existing hierarchy of cities. See, for example, Edward J. Taafee, "Air Transportation and United States Urban Distribution," *Geographical Review* (April 1956), pp. 219-38, or more recently, James E. Vance, *Capturing the Horizon: The Historical Geography of Transportation Since the Transportation Revolution of the Sixteenth Century* (New York, 1986). One important piece of writing that does address the relationship of airport to city is Paul Barrett, "Cities and Their Airports: Policy Formulation, 1926-1952," *Journal of Urban History* 14, no. 1 (Nov. 1987), pp. 112-37. This work provides a good deal of information about the role of city planning in the creation of airports. Barrett's main point is how engineering and aircraft-related concerns outweighed planning ideals.

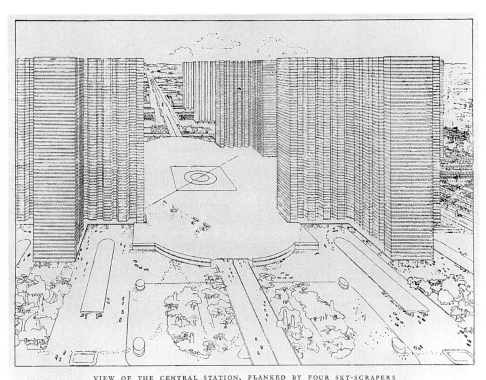

Fig. 1 Le Corbusier, architect. Scheme for a city of the future, featuring an airport amid skyscrapers; from Le Corbusier, *The City of To-morrow and Its Planning* (New York, 1929).

VIEW OF THE CENTRAL STATION, FLANKED BY FOUR SKY-SCRAPERS

The tracks for fast motor traffic pass under the aerodrome. The unobstructed and open ground-floor levels of the sky-scrapers can be seen, as can the piles or "stilts" on which they are built. Covered car-parking places can be perceived on either side. To the right are restaurants, shops, etc., set amidst trees and open spaces.

As it allowed the city to become denser at the core, the railroad simultaneously allowed it to become more diffuse at the edges. If railroad development had continued unabated, these trends might have accelerated. In cities with multiple stations near the center, each serving one or more railroads, the process of consolidation into fewer but larger "union" stations for the sake of efficiency and the conservation of valuable land would have continued. This process would have required the conversion of above-ground lines using steam locomotives to underground electric-powered operations, allowing for new urban developments above the tracks, such as those created during the interwar years in the Grand Central District in New York and in the Terminal City Complex in Cleveland. At the same time, in most cities this powerful centralizing force probably would have been matched by a continued outward growth at the edges, as trains and public transit allowed citizens to live further and further from the core and still maintain connections with it.

The appearance on the scene of the automobile and the airplane in the twentieth century suddenly altered these perspectives, but the issues of centralization and decentralization remained. During the pioneer years of air

Fig. 2 C. W. Glover, architect. Model of proposed airport plan for King's Cross, London, 1931; from *The Builder* (Dec. 25, 1931), p. 1046.

Fig. 3 Albert Speer, architect. Aerial view, looking south, of the proposed axis of Berlin, showing the location of Tempelhof Airport at left center; from Leon Krier, ed., *Albert Speer: Architecture, 1932-1942* (Brussels, 1985), p. 47.

SOUTH AERODROME

SOUTH CITY

MAIN STATION
TEMPELHOF AERODROME
TRIUMPHAL ARCH

CIRCUS
EAST-WEST AXIS

GREAT HALL

GREAT POND

NORTH STATION

3 The Corbusier scheme was published in Paris in 1924 in the architect's book *Urbanisme*, which was translated in 1929 and published as *The City of To-morrow and Its Planning*. For an excellent discussion of the genesis of this proposal, see Francesco Passanti, "The Skyscrapers of the Ville Contemporaine," *Assemblage* 4 (1987), pp. 53-65.

4 For Tempelhof's place in Hitler's schemes for Berlin, see Leon Krier, ed., *Albert Speer: Architecture, 1932-1942* (Brussels, 1985).

5 Wright's scheme was worked out over many years with many variations. He published a description in his book *The Disappearing City* (New York, 1932), and gave it a more concrete form in a series of articles starting with "Today. . . Tomorrow, American Tomorrow," *American Architect* (May 1932), pp. 14-17, 76; he developed it more fully in his books *When Democracy Builds* (Chicago, 1945) and *The Living City* (New York, 1958). On Wright's schemes, see Donald Leslie Johnson, *Frank Lloyd Wright versus America: The 1930s* (Cambridge, Mass., 1990). Wright apparently was as naive as Corbusier about air travel. He believed that airplanes would be able to land on highways as well as at small plane "stations" spaced about twenty miles apart.

6 See, for example, the comments of Lewis Mumford in his 1925 Survey Graphic, reprinted in Carol Sussman, ed., *Planning the Fourth Migration: The Neglected Vision of the Regional Planning Association of America* (Cambridge, Mass., 1976) and quoted by Greg Hise in his paper "Aviation and Western Metropolitan Development," which was presented at the Sixth National Conference on American City and Regional Planning History in Knoxville, Tennessee, in October 1995. This paper will be included in the proceedings of the conference.

travel, visionaries were quick to exploit both sides of this equation. The great Swiss architect Le Corbusier, for example, imagined a compact, rational city of the future whose center was a set of high cruciform office blocks tightly surrounding a transportation node with a railroad station and high-speed highway intersection below, and an airport on the deck above (fig. 1).[3] The airport in his scheme was literally at the center of everyday life, in fact even more dominant than the great metropolitan train station of the nineteenth century. Le Corbusier was anything but an expert on air travel when he conceived this scheme, a fact that may explain why the approach to the runways seems so harrowing, but he was able to render in concrete form the ideas of many who saw in the airplane a centralizing influence. Traces of this tendency to conceive of the city as centered on air travel can be found in many of the plans for new airports that were proposed during the interwar years (see fig. 2). Some were even built, notably Berlin's great Tempelhof Airport, conceived of as part of the monumental axis of Hitler's capital (fig. 3; see also pl. 7).[4]

At the other pole were those who believed that the new freedom of movement provided by the airplane would result in an infinitely more dispersed city or even settlement patterns with no city at all. The most potent visual realization of this was achieved by Frank Lloyd Wright in his Broadacre City project (fig. 4). Air travel was as important for Wright as it was for Le Corbusier, but in his drawings and models, Wright proposed a landscape in which air travel would lead to totally different results. He believed that the use of small airplanes, autogiros, and helicopter taxis, along with fast automobiles, would allow citizens to live in settlement patterns so decentralized that even large airports would not be necessary.[5] If this seems fanciful to us today, it is important to remember that many of the most sober planners of the interwar years thought that the plane might decentralize the city as much as the railroad or automobile had done.[6] The American designer Norman Bel Geddes, who predicted with some accuracy the shape superhighways would eventually take, believed that air travel would extend commuting time in much the

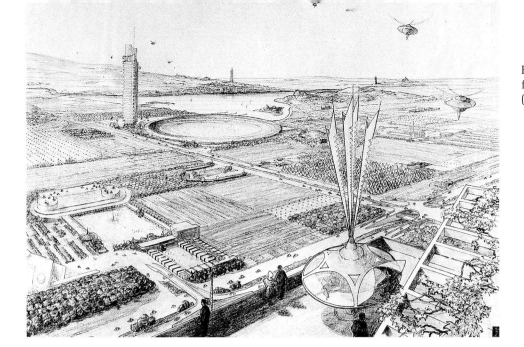

Fig. 4 Frank Lloyd Wright, architect. Design for Broadacre City; from *The Living City* (New York, 1958), p. 199.

same way as the railroad had done. "We can expect the old 5:15 to be a group of ten passenger planes arriving at minute intervals," he wrote, extending the "commuting distance from forty miles to one hundred or one hundred and fifty miles, or more."[7] Some authors even made explicit the argument, often used by advocates of the private automobile, that air travel, like the private automobile, could liberate citizens from the tyranny of the railroad and transit monopolies.[8] Many of the municipal and regional airport plans of the interwar years featured scores of airfields, all part of a vast hierarchical network.[9]

By the early post-World War II era, it had become apparent that neither Corbusier's nor Wright's model was going to be realized in the near future, but elements of both were evident, even in the names given to the places where airplanes landed. Those who looked forward to the new dispersed city, freed from the limitations of previous means of transportation, probably applauded the term "airfield." The term "airport" or a name such as "Sky Harbor" implied both a larger degree of centralization and also some connection to traditional means of transportation, in this case via water. The term that most clearly linked air travel with the dense industrial city was "air terminal," particularly in such names as "Grand Central Terminal" or "Union Terminal," which were clear references to the great rail depots of the central city.

In the early postwar years, airport planning was still quite fluid. Although the density of air travel at a given city usually reflected fairly well that city's ranking in the national hierarchy of urban places, there were many locations – for example, cities situated at halfway points along major long-distance air routes or at resort cities – where planners believed that they could build an economy based on air travel, much like the small towns whose economies were almost entirely based on servicing the railroads. Likewise, within any city, the system of airports was still evolving rapidly. Even then, the largest air terminals had become small cities unto themselves. An airport such as Chicago's Midway, originally located beyond the built-up area of the city, was soon surrounded by city fabric (fig. 5). Although most of the land around it was zoned and developed for residential uses, the airport increasingly attracted commercial activity, including motels, rental car agencies, and factories.[10] The effect of airports on the value of adjacent land was hotly debated. Some observers believed that the presence of the airport depressed land values, particularly land zoned for residential uses, but this opinion was contra-

7 Norman Bel Geddes, *Horizons* (Boston, 1932), p. 80.
8 Archibald Black, *Civil Airports and Airways* (New York, 1929), p. 5.
9 See, for example, the discussion of airports for various parts of the metropolitan area in Henry V. Hubbard, Miller McClintock, and Frank B. Williams, *Airports: Their Location, Administration, and Legal Basis* (Cambridge, Mass., 1930), which is the most important early compendium of information on the relationship between airports and planning. See also Charles Froesch and Walther Prokosch, *Airport Planning* (New

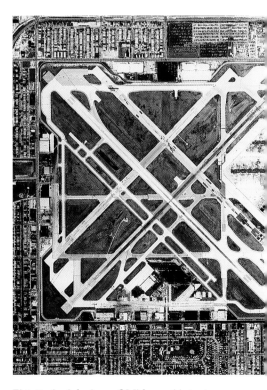

Fig. 5 Aerial view of Midway Airport, Chicago, April 1995, showing complete enclosure of airport site by residential and commercial development.

Fig. 6 Century Development Corporation. Proposed Greenway Plaza, Houston, showing STOL (short takeoff and landing) port; from H. McKinley Conway, *The Airport City: Development Concepts for the 21st Century* (Atlanta, 1980), p. 173.

York, 1946). The best source on Chicago is Eugene Carl Kirchherr, "Airport Land Use in the Chicago Metropolitan Area: A Study of Historical Development Characteristics, and Special Problems of a Land Use Type Within a Metropolitan Area" (Ph.D. diss., Northwestern University, 1959), and his article "Aviation and Airport Land Use in the Chicago Region, 1910-41," *Bulletin of the Illinois Geographical Society* (Dec. 1974), pp. 32-47. In his paper at the Conference on American Planning History in Knoxville (see note 6), Greg Hise showed that Los Angeles planners envisioned airports for virtually every settlement in the Los Angeles area. Because this area was so spread out, the number of airports was prodigious. In the San Gabriel Valley, the highways and airports element of the general plan suggested airports at one-mile intervals. County of Los Angeles, Regional Plan Commission, *A Comprehensive Report on the Regional Plan of Highways: Section 2E, San Gabriel Valley* (Los Angeles, 1929).

10 On Chicago airports, see David Brodherson, "'All Airplanes Lead to Chicago': Airport Planning and Design in a Midwest Metropolis," in John Zukowsky, ed., *Chicago Architecture and Design, 1923-1993: Reconfiguration of an American Metropolis* (Munich and Chicago, 1993), pp. 75-97.

11 There were strikingly conflicting conclusions as to the effect of airports on the immediately surrounding community. See, for example, Hubbard et al. (note 9), p. 31 and Appendix 22, for one assessment. Kirchherr (note 9), pp. 171-90, provides a summary of opinion in the late 1950s. Changing opinions in the real estate community are documented in the 1947 and 1968 editions of the Urban Land Institute's *The Community Builders Handbook*.

12 This was true, for example, at St. Louis, Long Beach, Burbank, and elsewhere.

13 The best documents on the fly-in phenomenon are the writings of H. McKinley Conway, who led a one-man crusade for the concept. The best summary is found in his book *Airport City* (Atlanta, 1980). This was actually the second edition of his book entitled *The Airport City and the Future Intermodal Transportation System* (Atlanta, 1977).

dicted by other studies, and it was becoming obvious that some industrial and commercial users might actually favor the location.[11] Needless to say, airplane manufacturers found the location useful. In fact, a large number of America's airports are located on land that the airplane manufacturers had acquired for their own use.[12] Although during these years few industrial companies made much substantial use of air freight, which remained very expensive compared to other means of shipping, the enhanced access roads required by airports made the location attractive because it facilitated truck transportation, which was fast becoming the preferred method for shipping all but the heaviest of articles.

In addition to the major airports, there were other landing fields for a wide variety of uses. Throughout the 1950s, many planners continued to envision cities with a large number of airports serving every region of the metropolitan area almost like small railroad stations. Some of these secondary airports were miniature versions of the major airport but served primarily private planes. Many observers expected that the rapid development of short takeoff and landing (STOL) airplanes would allow for small airports to dot the metropolitan area, including the central core, and there were large numbers of schemes for STOL ports in the very heart of the city (fig. 6). In other cases, the airport was built specifically to service a particular activity. For several decades, it appeared that there was a great future for fly-in facilities of all kinds. Because industrial parks typically consisted of low buildings in which the work done was not negatively affected by airport noise and because the amount of air freight was rising dramatically, the combination of airports and industrial parks promised to be extremely compatible and profitable. Enthusiasts also pointed to the first fly-in motels, golf courses, and even residential subdivisions.[13]

From Jet Age to Deregulation: 1958 to 1978

The advent of commercial jet planes brought sharp changes in the national system of airports, with the most immediate result being a rapid rise in air travel. In the decade between 1960 and 1970, air travel nearly tripled, and the impact on the major airports was overwhelming. Many older airports quickly proved to be too small and too closely hemmed in by urban development to accommodate the longer runways and noisier takeoffs and landings.[14] The result was a great wave of new airport construction lasting from the 1950s until the early 1970s. In an effort to avoid the impact of noise and to escape congestion, planners designed larger airports, such as Chicago's O'Hare, London's Heathrow, and New York's Idlewild (later renamed John F. Kennedy International Airport), and built them further from the central city than almost any previous examples. The largest and most remote of these – notably Dulles International (1958-62), Dallas-Fort Worth (1965-73), and Montreal's Mirabel (1975) – seemed to some to be ridiculously far out into the countryside. Indeed, many planners believed that the presence of the airport would render most of the land for miles around unfit for most residential purposes or for daily work. The airport was a necessity but one that seemed incompatible with urban development.[15]

These airports were nevertheless soon surrounded by developments of the same kind that had grown up near the earlier airports. The largest category of occupants was industrial, especially where railroads or waterways were adjacent to the airport. In many cases, these industrial users themselves still had little need for air transport, but by this time, the excellent highway connections were extremely important, and the presence of the airport made the land unfit for many other uses. This appears to have been the case at the Centex Industrial Park, adjacent to O'Hare Airport (see fig. 7). This development, reportedly the largest of its type in the world at the time, was actually a by-product of a large residential development scheme by the Centex company, a Texas home-building firm.[16] The industrial park was part of an attempt to secure a stable tax base and a source of jobs for the community. It also buffered the community from the airport. As more freight started to move by air, however, airports soon came to exert a positive rather than a primarily negative force on development, and land prices around the airport, including those for the industrial areas, jumped sharply upward.[17] Soon industrial complexes were planned specifically to exploit the airport, among them Rancho Conejo in Ventura County near Los Angeles or the Orlando Tradeport.[18] Another kind of business that continued to thrive near airports was the motel. Because the new airports were further from downtown and were planned for considerably more traffic, the motels came to be quite large and included conference and meeting room facilities to accommodate business needs.

Development around the major airports might have been limited to these kinds of land use but for several unforeseen occurrences. The first was the very rapid decentralization of American business in general. Although business activities, particularly industrial, had been moving out of central areas for decades, the number and type of employees involved in these moves changed after World War II. Already before the war, some corporations had moved research and development activities and corporate offices to outlying locations. After the war, this exodus accelerated dramatically. Wherever corporations building for their own use led in this development, speculative office builders soon followed. By the early 1970s, speculative office parks were sprouting up around most American cities, particularly along the superhighways that led from and around the old city.[19] The airports, usually located on these access roads, would have been highly desirable locations were it not for the noise they generated, but by the early 1970s, this problem was largely offset by technological changes, including the advent of new, quieter jet engines and new building practices, notably the use of laminated glass, improved

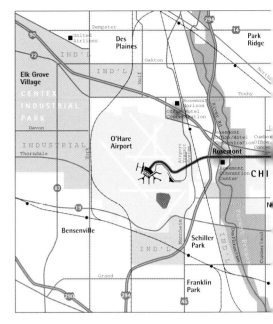

Fig. 7 Dennis McClendon, cartographer. Map of the greater O'Hare region, Chicago, 1996, showing the location of Centex Industrial Park and other major office/hotel developments.

14 The question of the effect of noise on the surrounding communities became, if anything, even more contentious after the advent of the jet plane. See, for example, the reports by Roy P. Drachman of Realty News, published in *Urban Land* (Dec. 1958), p. 2, that showed the positive effect of airports on land prices. Although much more is known about airport noise, the conclusions are still surprisingly mixed. For recent studies, see G. Pennington, N. Topham, and R. Ward, "Aircraft Noise and Residential Property Values Adjacent to Manchester International Airport," *Journal of Transport Economics and Policy* (Jan. 1990), pp. 49-59; the bibliography in Alan Collins and Alec Evans, "Aircraft Noise and Residential Property Values," *Journal of Transport Economics and Policy* (May 1994), pp. 175-97; and Terrence J. Levesque, "Modeling the Effects of Airport Noise on Residential Housing Markets," in the same issue, pp. 199-211.

15 In 1970, the Northeast Illinois Planning Commission predicted that an enormous area, including all land within five miles of O'Hare, would be unsuited for living or daily work by 1975. See Carl Condit, *Chicago, 1930-1970: Building, Planning, and Urban Technology* (Chicago, 1974), p. 263.

16 Information on Centex Industrial Park came from Louis Kahnweiler of Bennett and Kahnweiler, which was a major player in this development.

Fig. 8 Skidmore, Owings and Merrill, architects. O'Hare Plaza, Chicago, 1970-71.

17 See, for example, Albert Jedlicka, "Land Values Rise in O'Hare Area," *Chicago Daily News* (Dec. 20, 1967), p. 36.

18 On the airport and industrial park, see Leigh Fisher, "Airport Industrial Parks: Who Should Develop Them?" *Urban Land* (Feb. 1966), pp. 3-6, and the same author's "Airports Attract Industry," *Urban Land* (Oct. 1962), pp. 1-6. See also Sharon Thomason, "Industrial Parks Feather the Air Freight Nest," *Air Cargo World* (June 1986), pp. 21-25.

19 On the decentralization of businesses in American cities, see the information on Chicago in Robert Bruegmann, "Schaumburg, Oak Brook, Rosemont and the Recentering of the Chicago Metropolitan Area," in Zukowsky (note 10), pp. 159-77.

20 For information on O'Hare Plaza, I am indebted to Don Polishak of LaSalle Partners and William Bell of Rauch and Company.

sealants, and year-round forced air heating and air conditioning that masked whatever noise still affected the offices.

One of the pioneer airport office parks was O'Hare Plaza near Chicago's O'Hare International (fig. 8). Designed by Skidmore, Owings and Merrill of Chicago, this complex along the Kennedy Expressway, which leads from the Loop to the airport, was envisioned as a landscaped campus that would include a group of office buildings and a Marriott Motor Hotel. This development was targeted specifically at the sales offices of large national corporations. Not only did the employees of these offices frequently use the airport to fly to other cities, but employees from other offices often needed to come to Chicago for meetings. The marriage of office building and hotel proved to be highly advantageous. The hotel, which was least busy during the hours the offices were most used, provided retail outlets, restaurants, and conference centers for the offices during the day, and at night, when the offices were least busy, provided accommodations for the visiting businessmen and dining and night life for the adjacent residential community. So important was the airport to O'Hare Plaza that the developers' best source of advertising was the distribution of leaflets to rooms in the airport hotel.[20]

With the construction of office buildings and hotels near the airport, an increasing number of business travelers found that they could do all of their business there, making a trip downtown unnecessary and saving considerable transit time. Small meetings could be held in company offices or at airport motels. Soon the conference facilities in motels were found to be inadequate and the large, urban conference hotel made its appearance. The Hyatt Regency O'Hare, designed by John Portman, opened in 1973 with 788 rooms and extensive meeting facilities (fig. 9). It brought the number of rooms avail-

Fig. 9 John Portman, architect. Hyatt Regency O'Hare, Chicago, 1973.

able around O'Hare to 6,127, one-third of the number in the Loop. A newspaper article titled "O'Hare, Loop-area Hotels Deny Heated Competition" explained that hotel managers in both places downplayed any competition because they believed that large conventions could be held only in the Loop.[21] Within two years, however, the nearby village of Rosemont, led by an aggressively pro-business mayor, Donald Stephens, constructed a convention center and embarked on a highly successful redevelopment campaign. Expanded several times since its opening, the Rosemont Convention Center has become the tenth largest in the country.[22] In fact, the O'Hare/Rosemont area has become one of the most important office and commercial centers in the Chicago region. With 12 million square feet of office space and nearly 5,000 hotel rooms, it is an office center as large as downtown Nashville.[23]

At the Los Angeles International Airport (LAX), a low-density area built up with motels and car rental lots along Century Boulevard in the blocks nearest the entrance to the airport was transformed into a row of office buildings and hotels in the mid-1970s. There have been efforts to redevelop other areas around the airport.[24] At the John Wayne Airport in Orange County, south of Los Angeles, the effect of the airport was even more dramatic. Here the Irvine Business Complex had been planned as a vast industrial area. Most of the land had been zoned for this purpose, and many of the properties had already been developed. Because many of the industrial users also needed to accommodate research and development functions, from the beginning the Business Complex had quite a few offices. Its relatively low rents and high-quality infrastructure soon attracted office users without any production facilities. Although technically illegal, the growing number of exceptions soon made it necessary to rezone much of the area for offices. This change, together with the excellent access to the airport, made the land around the airport highly desirable for office uses, and a wall of office buildings now faces the airport.[25]

Although the evidence suggests that the airport was a powerful magnet for some businesses, there is considerable evidence that much of the office development around airports since the 1970s occurred not because of the airport but because of the superior highway access that accompanied it. This helps to explain the cases where little development followed the construction of a new or enlarged airport. Atlanta's Hartsfield International Airport, for example, certainly one of the busiest airports in the world, has had some industrial development around it, but the vast majority of office and other commercial development in the Atlanta area has continued to move north. This apparently can be explained by the fact that the city is still small enough and the superhighway system still efficient enough for air travelers to live and work in the far northern part of the metropolitan area and still be able to drive to the airport reasonably quickly. The same lack of development has characterized the Philadelphia International Airport and, until recently, the Kansas City International Airport. No airport seems to be powerful enough to overcome basic features of urban social geography. Airports that are located on the wrong side of town, that is, in a sector away from upscale housing and the trend of growth, do not seem to attract much development other than distribution facilities, some industrial uses, and the motels and rental-car agencies necessary for the operation of the airport.[26]

Perhaps the best explanation of this phenomenon is David Birch's "rubber band theory."[27] In this metaphor, a businessman planning to move or build a facility charts on a map each place where there is an urban amenity

21 Gary Washburn, "O'Hare, Loop-area Hotels Deny Heated Competition," *Chicago Tribune* (May 27, 1973), sec. 12, p. 1.

22 According to the Rosemont Convention Bureau, direct expenditures for conventions and conferences totaled nearly $500 million in 1993 and allowed Rosemont, with a population of 4,000, to host some 20,000 people per day at business meetings.

23 Information on Rosemont is from Ken Busse of Trkla, Pettigrew, Allen and Payne; see Judith Crown, "Welcome to O'Hareland," *Crain's Chicago Business* (Nov. 6, 1995), pp. 17, 19.

24 Because land for further expansion of this business center was limited and buildings were not constructed to a high standard, the area has stagnated in recent years. A major push was made in the late 1980s to redevelop it with the establishment of the LAX International Business Center, but this organization has apparently disappeared. Now the city of El Segundo is attempting to redevelop its side of the airport. Information on airport development in the Los Angeles area was supplied by Jack Kayser of the Economic Development Corporation of Los Angeles County.

25 Victor Carniglia, "Updating Industrial Zoning: The Irvine Business Complex," *Urban Land* (March 1985), pp. 15-19.

26 An interesting study of the way various airports attract quite different amounts of commercial activity can be found in a study of ten West Coast airports by Peter J. McMahon and Warren Sprague, "Local Community Benefits of a New Airport," *Urban Land* (March 1955), pp. 15-17; reprinted as "New Airports Bring Community Benefits," *Airport Technology International* (1996), pp. 55-57.

27 This theory is described in Joel Garreau, *Edge City: Life on the New Frontier* (New York, 1991), pp. 75-77.

28 This, of course, was exactly what many business leaders in each city had feared. See Stanley H. Scott and Levi H. Davis, *A Giant in Texas: A History of the Dallas-Fort Worth Regional Airport Controversy* (Dallas, 1974), and Robert B. Fairbanks, "A Clash of Priorities: The Federal Government and Dallas Airport Development, 1917-64," in Joseph F. Rishel, ed., *American Cities and Towns: Historical Perspectives* (Pittsburgh, 1992), pp. 164-84.

29 On deregulation, see James Ott and Raymond E. Neidl, *Airline Odyssey: The Airline Industry's Turbulent Flight into the Future* (New York, 1995).

to which the company or its workers will want access. For each such feature — an airport, upscale housing, downtown cultural institutions, a major university, or easy access to the beach or mountains — a peg is inserted. From each peg, a rubber band, its strength calculated in accord with the importance of the feature, is stretched to connect it to a ring. The optimum location is the place on the map where the ring comes to rest.

What is perhaps most interesting about this analogy is the way it can be used to demonstrate recent shifts in the relative importance of downtown and the airport. Whereas earlier in the century, downtown exerted an all but overwhelming force on many kinds of business, particularly the vast majority of white-collar operations, by the late twentieth century, its pull has been weakened considerably as competing business centers, some on the opposite side of the airport, have proliferated. At the same time, the pull of the airport has sharply increased. In the Dallas-Fort Worth area, for example, the old downtowns have evolved into fairly specialized centers of government, high-end finance, culture, and tourism, and the great bulk of commercial development built over the last several decades has moved steadily toward the airport. It is likely that much of this development would have occurred between the two cities, especially to the northwest of Dallas, even without the airport, but the presence of the airport greatly accelerated this trend. By the 1980s, the airport had become the effective center of gravity of the metropolitan area, and the old downtowns were psychologically, as well as physically, peripheral.[28]

From Deregulation to the Early 1990s

The great wave of jet airport construction in the United States in the postwar years was slowed considerably by the Arab oil embargo in the early 1970s and was dealt another blow by the Airline Deregulation Act of 1978, which unleashed a competitive free-for-all between old established airlines and up-start operations.[29] Even with these problems, however, air travel continued to grow, albeit less quickly than in the 1960s, but the advent of wide-body jets in the early 1970s temporarily reduced the need to expand airport capacity by cutting down sharply on the number of flights needed to move passengers. At least as important as any of these individual circumstances, however, were some fundamental uncertainties about future patterns in air travel.

One consequence of deregulation was a reinforcement of the existing hub system in which small planes feed a few hub airports from which large jets take many passengers to other hub cities. This pattern allowed the airlines considerable economies of scale and had the effect of centralizing air travel in a few cities and in a few airports. Together with the fare wars touched off by deregulation, this centralization of airports intensified the trend already apparent since the 1950s, in which air travel increasingly resembled surface mass transit, becoming a means for moving large numbers of people in the most economical way, although not always in the most comfortable or convenient fashion for passengers.

As the numbers of passengers grew at the country's largest airports, the facilities quickly reached capacity. Plans for new, larger airports, many of them long in the making — for example, New York's fourth, London's and Chicago's third, Tokyo's and Sydney's second — ran into firestorms of criticism. Because of the unsettled conditions in the air industry and increasingly hostile reaction to noise and pollution generated by the airports, only London and Tokyo have been successful to date.[30] Tokyo's new international airport in Narita took twelve years to finish and led to bloody battles between police and protesters.[31] London's third airport, which took even longer, best illustrates the problems because the British government instituted a lengthy, rational, and thoroughly documented planning process. From the volumes of testimony compiled by the Rosskill Commission, it is clear that the locations most convenient to those businesses and individuals who were likely to travel were exactly the ones in which local pressure was most capable of preventing the construction of the airport. In addition, there was a paradoxical desire to maintain the economic boost that London's airports had provided to the nation while avoiding the continued centralization of new development and business in southeast England. The final recommendation was to build an airport at the aptly named town of Foulness, the least convenient of all of the major contenders and the one least likely to produce economic development in the surrounding area. Not surprisingly, this plan was viciously attacked and soon dropped. With very little fanfare, the government decided that a new airport at Stansted would have to suffice for the moment, but even with its construction, the problem of London airport traffic has remained at a crisis level.[32]

The result of these confrontations between advocates and opponents of airport sites was an impasse and a seemingly endless set of proposals for airports to be located even further from towns, often in the desert, in swamplands, or in the middle of lakes or bays, to avoid friction with the hub city's population. These proposals usually included high-speed rail links back to the city. Some of the proposed sites included Palmdale, forty-five miles from downtown Los Angeles; Kankakee, fifty miles from the Chicago Loop; and a location in the Florida Everglades, far outside Miami. Very little came of these studies.[33]

In the late 1980s one promising method of overcoming the impasse in the construction of new airports in metropolitan areas was the "wayport." Reasoning that many people who landed at any given large airport were only using it as a hub, advocates of this concept suggested building huge new airports far from existing cities whose only function was to allow for transfers. This system, theoretically, could divert thousands of passengers away from overcrowded city hubs, and the airports could be built for a fraction of the price of expanding capacity at existing facilities because of the low price of land at places such as Burns Flat, Oklahoma, or Parchmon, Mississippi, two of the proposed sites. Although this concept has gradually faded from view, it may yet be revived, particularly if aviation develops further in the direction of centralized hubs.[34]

Beyond the immediate issues and calculations, these struggles to expand air travel capacity were based on larger questions. That air travel would probably continue to increase was usually assumed, but what would the configuration be? In many ways, this question returned planners to the basic tensions embodied in the proposals by Frank Lloyd Wright and Le Corbusier. Would airplanes continue to grow in size and the spoke-and-hub system dominate, or was the model for air travel in the future the one offered by the upstart regional carriers such as Southwest Airlines, carriers that concentrated on direct flights from smaller, often closer-in airports? Was the best course of action the creation of ever larger airports further away from cities, or would a set of smaller airports scattered throughout the metropolis better satisfy

30 There is excellent documentation on the planning of Sydney's airport in "Policy Making for Sydney's Airport Needs: A Comparative and Historical Perspective," URU Working Paper No. 20, December 1989, issued by the Urban Research Unit of the Research School of Social Sciences, Australian National University. I am grateful to Rob Freestone for sending extensive materials on Sydney's airports.

31 Edward Seidensticker, *Tokyo Rising* (New York, 1990), pp. 325-26.

32 The basic source of information on London's search for a third airport is the many volumes of the Papers and Proceedings of the Commission on the Third London Airport, published around 1970. The case for and against the proposed Foulness site can be found in Richard Layard, ed., *Cost Benefit Analysis: Selected Readings* (Harmondsworth, England, 1974). An excellent retrospective analysis can be found in Peter Hall, *Great Planning Disasters* (Berkeley, 1982), pp. 15-55.

33 A good example of this kind of proposal was Northwestern University Professor Sidney Berge's scheme for an airport at Kankakee. See his *Chicago's Next Great Airport* (Evanston, 1972).

34 On the wayport, see Transportation Research Board of the National Research Council's 1988 report "Future Development of the U.S. Airport Network." See also "Where There's a Will There's a Wayport," *Airports International* (Sept. 1989), pp. 23-24, and James Ott, "FAA Will Test Wayport Concept as Remedy to Airport Congestion," *Aviation Week and Space Technology* (Jan. 9, 1989), pp. 64-67.

customers' needs? This latter pattern was visible in a number of cities, notably in the New York metropolitan area, where, in addition to the three large airports, LaGuardia, Kennedy, and Newark, smaller airports at Islip, White Plains, and Newburgh served many citizens who lived or worked far from Manhattan. In southern California, the system was even more decentralized, with major carriers serving not just LAX but also airports at San Diego, Orange County, Long Beach, Ontario, Palm Springs, Burbank, Oxnard, and Santa Barbara. And in the future lay the possibility of radical new developments using STOL and VTOL (vertical takeoff and landing) and thus a growing number of small airports.

All these uncertainties contributed to the long hiatus in new airport construction. This, in turn, also guaranteed that existing airports would become busier, more intensively developed, and more bedeviled by opposition. To the extent that an airport was successful, it tended to act as a magnet for upscale commercial users around it, merely exacerbating the problem with increasingly affluent residents of nearby neighborhoods. Another major factor was the growing public awareness of the environmental problems caused by airports. Already by 1971, an important report on Kennedy Airport, published by the National Academy of Sciences and the National Academy of Engineers, succinctly stated the dilemma: "Kennedy Airport provides the national prototype for major jetports in the United States moving inexorably toward a confrontation between airport and community interests."[35] Large airports, such as O'Hare, Kennedy, and Heathrow, were obliged to build beside, around, and over every available parcel, reaching staggering levels of complexity, particularly at Heathrow, where the early decision to put terminal buildings in an island at the center of the runway system drastically restricted the space available (see Bosma, fig. 3; Lockhart, fig. 6).[36] The result is that the largest airports have become commercial centers as vast and complex as most traditional downtowns with working populations of over fifty thousand people at the airport itself and several times that number directly dependent on it.

In some ways, this has meant a return to earlier ideals. In the case of a number of earlier airports, the terminal served as a destination. People would drive out to the airport to watch the planes take off and land and to eat in elegant restaurants. In this way a particularly well equipped airport such as the Pittsburgh Airport of 1952, with its dining terrace, post office, bank, observation lounges, restaurants, shops, recreation center, movie theater, 500 seat night club, and 62-room hotel, continued the tradition of the great nineteenth-century railroad terminal.[37] As air travel became less exclusive, this tradition waned. Recently, however, as the airport has become more integrated with the city, it has once again started to incorporate a wider range of urban functions. This has been especially conspicuous in cases where public authorities have turned over control of the airport to private operators.[38] The most spectacular example is visible at London's Heathrow and Gatwick airports, where the privatized British Airports Authority (BAA), realizing that the large numbers of travelers and workers have made the airports cities in themselves, created vast shopping centers. Sales at Heathrow now total over $500 million, which represents some $25 for every enplaning passenger, making these airports among the largest shopping centers in the world. Airports in other cities, notably at Trillium International Terminal in Toronto, the new terminal at Pittsburgh International Airport, or Kansai International Airport in Japan, have followed suit.[39] At Pittsburgh, whose postwar airport had the most developed commercial activities to be found anywhere, BAA opened in

35 Jamaica Bay Environmental Study Group, *Jamaica Bay and Kennedy Airport: A Multi-Disciplinary Environmental Report*, vol. 2 (New York, 1971), p. 101.
36 The best source on O'Hare is Richard Paul Doherty, "The Origin and Development of Chicago-O'Hare International Airport" (Ph.D. diss., Ball State University, 1970).
37 Pittsburgh's terminal, the most comprehensive of its day, is discussed in a roundup of postwar designs in *Architectural Forum* (Nov. 1952), and in Geoffrey Arend, *Great Airports of the World* (New York, 1988) p. 620.
38 On the experience of privatization, see Norman Ashford and Clifton A. Moore, *Airport Finance* (New York, 1992), pp. 60-65.
39 On the airport as shopping center, see William J. Maher, "Retailing at Airports Lifts Off," *Urban Land* (May 1991), pp. 18-20. On retail sales at airports and other aspects of airport revenues and expenses, see Rigas Doganis, *The Airport Business* (London, 1992).

1993 a shopping center called Airmall, which has reported sales figures averaging $950 per square foot and reaching $2,100 per square foot, figures that have amazed American retailers.[40]

Another conspicuous development at airports has been the recent rise of the airport and airline lounge club, a feature that apparently dates back to 1939, when it was introduced at LaGuardia by American Airlines.[41] Facilities at these clubs have grown to include copy machines, fax machines, computers, and meeting rooms, bringing them into line with small conference centers or the office hoteling facilities that many businesses are setting up for themselves in which employees are assigned space at various locations as needed. Just as the airport hotel made it possible to avoid going downtown, these business centers and airlines lounges now make it possible for many businessmen to avoid the trip even to the airport business hotel.[42] It is possible that the airport, after drawing downtown functions to the area around it, may even absorb these functions as well. At Nashville, the center of the airport, once reserved for parking and hotels, was expanded so that it could contain industrial and office uses, effectively turning the relationship of the airport and its environs inside out.[43] New airport centers are currently being built in Munich, Berlin, and elsewhere to accommodate these business functions (see fig. 10).

Airports become more like downtowns every year, boasting new or expanded security forces, fire stations, central heating and cooling plants, hotels, medical centers, welfare organizations, restaurants, retail outlets, miniature department stores, chapels, banks, museums and other exhibition spaces, bowling alleys, sex cinemas, antique stores, and, at Milwaukee, a used book store.[44] In addition to the employees and passengers, there are activists leafleting, religious groups making conversions, pickpockets plying their trade, and a contingent of homeless people using the airport for shelter.[45] The airport, like the shopping center, is becoming the central public space of our cities today, and this perhaps explains the surprising ways in which the architectural design of large shopping centers and airport terminals is starting to converge.

The pace of change at the airport has become so rapid and the amount of income it generates so great that it has increasingly been able to serve as the testing ground for new urban ideas that could be used elsewhere. Nowhere has this been more obvious than in the area of pubic transportation, both within the airport and connecting it back to the city. As the size of airports grew, satellites appeared, and car rental, parking, and other activities had to be located further and further apart, officials were obliged to introduce new ways to carry people quickly within the airport. People movers were first used

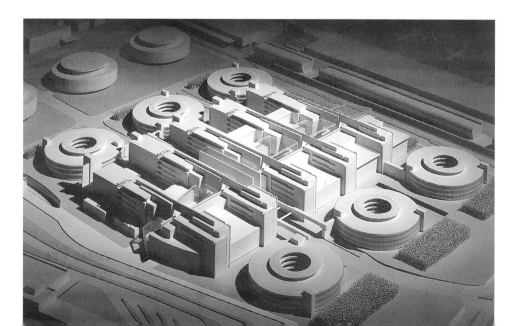

Fig. 10 Leo A. Daly, architect. Model of proposed "Airport City" business center, Berlin-Schönefeld Airport, 1996-2000.

40 Information supplied by Michael J. Caro of BAA's Pittsburgh office, June 1995.

41 Information on the American VIP lounges is from Teresa Hanson, Marketing Manager for the Admirals Club.

42 A good survey of airline lounge clubs can be found in *Consumer Reports Travel Letter* (Oct. 1994), pp. 224-27.

43 Robert Lamb Hart, "International Airport Circa 2020," *Urban Land* (May 1993), pp. 39-41.

44 Edward Robbins and Edith M. Netter, "Transit Cities," *Planning* (Sept. 1992), pp. 22-23.

45 For excellent descriptions of airports as miniature cities, see James Kaplan, *The Airport: Terminal Nights and Runway Days at John F. Kennedy International Airport* (New York, 1994), and Deyan Sudjic, *The 100 Mile City* (London, 1992).

46 The first use of people movers was apparently at the Tampa airport, according to F. K. Plous, "Just Get Me to the Plane on Time," *Planning* (Aug. 1989), pp. 20-24.

47 At Las Vegas, a monorail that currently connects the Bally's and MGM Grand hotels, is envisioned as the first stage of a transit line to the McCarran International Airport.

48 Anyone trying to travel from O'Hare's new International Terminal to a hotel in Rosemont, for example, would first have to use the airport's people mover to get to the main terminal, then ride the Chicago subway for about two miles to the River Road elevated station, where the visitor could finally board a Rosemont PRT vehicle and head off to a hotel or convention center.

49 For the New York terminal, located across 42nd Street from Grand Central Station in Midtown, see the essay in this volume by David Brodherson. For the Paris terminal, the former Gare des Invalides, see Georges Combois, "Les Liaisons entre les villes et les aérodromes,"*Œuvres et maitres d'œuvre* 2, no. 6 (Dec. 1946), pp. 24-27.

50 Karl Bremer, "Intermodalism: It's All Coming Together," *Airport Magazine* (March/April 1993), pp. 11-14.

51 For these transit links, see Plous (note 46).

52 Bremer (note 50), p. 13.

53 Sudjic (note 45), p. 156.

extensively in the early 1970s in such large decentralized airports as Dallas-Fort Worth and Atlanta.[46] In recent years, the number of such systems has greatly increased. It will be interesting to see whether these internal systems will ever be linked effectively with the public transportation systems of the cities around them. Although there are plans to do this, for example at Las Vegas, it has not yet happened.[47] Nor will an announced personal rapid transit (PRT) system in the village of Rosemont just outside O'Hare connect directly with the airport's own people mover. Instead, passengers who wish to use it will be required to use Chicago's rapid transit system and then transfer – all to reach a destination only a mile away.[48]

In most cities, the primary link is still the one that connects the airport to the historic downtown. One idea, apparently dating back at least to the 1930s, was the notion of providing terminals in the central city where passengers could check their bags and then travel to the airport on buses or by rail. In such cities as New York and Paris, these downtown terminals were quite grand (see Brodherson, fig. 13).[49] These systems were popular for a number of decades before security problems and changes in transportation made them less desirable. There are plans to revive the idea, however, for example, in Atlanta, where air passengers will be able to check baggage through to their final destination from the downtown transportation terminal. Both baggage and passenger will then ride to the airport on a MARTA train.[50] In recent years, airport bus operators in San Francisco, Dallas-Fort Worth, and several other cities have built similar airline check-in centers for outlying locations.

In addition to Atlanta's Hartsfield, many airports are connected to their central city by rail, among them London's Heathrow, Chicago's O'Hare and Midway, Washington's National, and the airports at Cleveland, St. Louis, and Philadelphia.[51] Many others, some using monorail, maglev, and other new technologies, are planned.[52] In Europe the integration of intercity air and surface travel has been a major preoccupation of planners at airports in Frankfurt (see pls. 101-02), Amsterdam, and Zurich, which have stations on intercity rail routes. The most striking example, the new station for the European TGV at Paris's Charles de Gaulle Airport (see pls. 113 and 118), promises to begin a new phase in the transformation of airports from low-density areas at the periphery of the metropolitan area to new centers of urban life. The concentration of public transportation at certain airports has already resulted in making these airports new intermodal surface transportation centers. Although statistics on this are scant, it has been estimated that at Heathrow and Gatwick as many as one in five passengers who arrive at the terminal has nothing to do with air travel.[53] The same is true at a number of American airports that are used as transfer points by bus companies.

Although there is little doubt that rail lines between the city center and the airport provide an important service in transporting people, particularly airport employees, from various parts of the city to the airport, they are very expensive both to construct and to subsidize after construction, and their value is limited by the fact that many travelers will not ride the system because of the difficulty in handling baggage and because they have to take at least one other form of transportation to get to or from their homes at the end of the train line. One of the most interesting responses to this problem has been the growth of van services like SuperShuttle. These companies are privately funded and operate at a profit so they require none of the vast initial capital expenditures and subsidies required by rail transit. Their on-demand vehicles take relatively small numbers of passengers door to door at prices

that are higher than public bus or subway fares but considerably lower than taxi fares. Begun in Los Angeles in 1982 and run by former airline employees, SuperShuttle has been a spectacular success story; it now serves fifteen airports and is expanding quickly.[54] It is in the process of constructing a national system that will operate in much the same way as the airlines, using a single national reservations center in Phoenix to operate services throughout the country. The door-to-door van system is an innovation at the airport that might well find widespread application elsewhere in the city.

As the large airports have tended to grow over the last two decades, many of the smaller general aviation airports have tended to fail, in part owing to liability problems with small planes and in part owing to the costs of land and the complaints of neighbors.[55] Several conspicuous exceptions, however, seem to point to a new role for the commercial airport and a revival of the idea of the fly-in industrial park. The most notable of these has been the Perot Group's construction of the intermodal transportation center and related real estate developments at the Alliance Airport outside Fort Worth (figs. 11 and 12).[56] Another ambitious scheme is the Global Trans Park in North Carolina.[57]

Today and Tomorrow

Even by the standards of an industry that has been marked by rapid changes throughout its history, the shifts in perspective on air travel during the last few years have been vertiginous. Airlines have come and gone, and the future of the airlines industry is less predictable than ever. Still, it is obvious that, to cope with a steadily rising demand for air travel, new planning and construction are necessary.

If one extrapolates from the period 1978 to 1990, the future would seem to lie in ever larger airports further from the old downtowns. In the United States, this has been the route followed by Denver. When it opened in early 1995, the Denver International Airport was the first wholly new major airport built in the United States since the opening of Dallas-Fort Worth International Airport (DFW) twenty years before (see Brodherson, figs. 33-34). In contrast to most American airports, where airport planning was usually divorced from larger issues of city and regional planning, at Denver, the airport was devised as part of a much larger economic development strategy. It was in-

Fig. 11 Aerial view of Alliance Airport, Fort Worth, Texas, 1995, showing from top to bottom, American Airlines maintenance center, Federal Express facility, air traffic control tower (1991), and federal Drug Enforcement Agency hangar.

Fig. 12 Artist's rendering of the Federal Express facility at Alliance Airport, Fort Worth, Texas, 1995.

54 For information on SuperShuttle, I am indebted to Ray McIntire, Vice President.

55 On the plight of general aviation, see Ruth Eckdish Knack, "Mayday, Mayday – No Place to Land," *Planning* (Nov. 1991), pp. 8-13.

56 A good recent article on Alliance is Allen R. Myerson, "This Land is My Land. . . But, Ross Perot Jr. Adds, You're Invited to Build on It," *New York Times* (Aug. 24, 1995), p. C1. See also Ashford and Moore (note 38), p. 91.

57 On the North Carolina project, see John D. Kasarda, "An Industrial/Aviation Complex for the Future," *Urban Land* (Aug. 1991), pp. 16-20, and Dennis Whitington, "Joining the Jet Set," *Planning* (Sept. 1993), pp. 22-23.

58 On planning for the Denver airport, see Ruth Knack, "Way Out Yonder, A New Airport is Taking Shape," *Planning* (Apr. 1990), pp. 20-25; and Douglas R. Porter, "Denver, Taxiing for Takeoff," *Urban Land* (Sept. 1990), pp. 32-34. For Denver, as well as for Kansai and Pittsburgh, see the excellent article by Christopher J. Duerksen, Raymond L. Reaves, and Richard Roddewig, "A Better Way to Plan Airports," *Urban Land* (March 1993), pp. 35-38. See also an earlier article by two of the same authors, Christopher J. Duerksen and Richard J. Roddewig, "Ready for Takeoff: Developing the 21st Century Airport," *Urban Land* (Nov. 1992), pp. 26-31.

Fig. 13 City of Chicago and various consultants. Bird's-eye view of proposed Lake Calumet Airport, 1991; from *Lake Calumet Airport: Crossroads of the Nation... Future of the Region* (Chicago, 1991), frontispiece.

59 The early public response to Denver has tended to support the critics' assertions. Because of the remote location and higher landing fees, many airlines and freight shippers have been using other area airports, notably the one in Colorado Springs. James Brooke, "Denver is Not Flying (At Least Yet) into the Future on Wings of Airport," *New York Times* (Oct. 22, 1995), sec. 1, p. 12.

60 See Duerksen et al., "A Better Way . . ." (note 58), pp. 35-36. Other cities have considered island airports as well; on plans for New York City, see David P. Brodherson, "Gotham City in the Air Age," paper given at the American Planning History conference, Knoxville, October 1995 (see note 6), to be included in their proceedings.

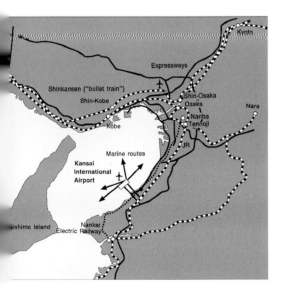

Fig. 14 Map of the area surrounding Kansai International Airport, showing the location of the airport on a manmade island and the major cities served by the airport.

tended as the nucleus for major new economic expansions.[58] Much of the negative reaction to the Denver airport has been similar to the skepticism that greeted DFW. The critics have claimed that it is too large and too far away.[59] A different line of criticism is based on the idea that the airport will, in the end, be all too successful. These critics believe that pushing airports and all the highways and infrastructure needed to service them further into the open countryside will only exacerbate what they view as sprawl, increasingly low-density settlement patterns reaching far into the countryside.

The dispute between close-in and remote sites recently resurfaced most spectacularly in Chicago during discussions about the location of a third airport. To counter proposals for locating the airport far to the south of the city, Chicago officials lined up behind a close-in site at Lake Calumet, an industrial area on the city's South Side (fig. 13). They argued that this would be an excellent way to obtain funding to solve environmental problems in the area and that it would generate much needed new development in the city's neglected South Side. On the other hand, countered aviation experts, this location would unduly restrict future expansion needs, and according to real estate professionals, it might not trigger much new development because of the many social, political, and environmental roadblocks to developing land in the city. Thus, critics have said that a new airport in this location might take jobs away from existing airports, rather than create many new ones. Ideological crossfire of this kind has resulted in an impasse in new airport construction in Chicago and many other major American cities. In the meantime, air traffic congestion and citizen complaints continue to mount.

Cities elsewhere, particularly those with a less vigorous tradition of democratic policy making, have been much more decisive, particularly in Asia. In Seoul, Hong Kong, and elsewhere, enormous new airports are planned, under construction, or already built to accommodate air travel in the fastest-growing market in the world. Virtually without exception, these cities are relying on the large, remote hub jetport. The most dramatic of these new airports to date, the $17 billion Kansai International Airport serving Osaka, Kobe, Kyoto, and surrounding cities in Japan, completed in 1994, suggests one possible scenario for the relationship of airport to city. Based on the assumption that hub airports will continue to handle large, noisy jets, this facility has been built on an artificial island in Osaka Bay even farther from the town centers than most existing airports (fig. 14; see pls. 128-29).[60] To counterbalance the remoteness of the location, the airport is connected to the urban centers by an extensive system of superhighways, rail lines, and bullet trains. The airport will also be used as the major feature in a strategy to urbanize the region around it. On the land side of the bridge that connects the island to the mainland stand the first towers of an ambitious new "aeropolis," or business center, called Rinku Town that is projected to be a twenty-four hour communications, financial, and commercial center. Further afield will be other large business centers, all tied to the transportation system serving the airport. Kansai Airport is the ultimate experiment in the application of the ideas that led to airports such as DFW but, the Japanese hope, one where strong governmental planning powers will be able to provide enough infrastructure to avoid many of the problems that have plagued American cities.[61] It is even possible that new technology, for example, new supersonic, suborbital airplanes, will make even larger, more remote airports necessary.[62]

On the other hand, the same technological and economic forces that have led to larger, more centralized airports, could, in the end, make them less dominant. It may well be that the system of large aircraft serving hubs has already started to yield to a system in which smaller airplanes will move people more directly to where they want to go.[63] If this happens, it would mirror exactly the history of surface transportation. In its initial phase, surface vehicles continually became larger in order to handle the heavy travel to very concentrated central cities. Now this has been reversed and a large percentage of the population in most countries has, whenever possible, abandoned large, mass-transit systems in favor of smaller, more private systems. In fact, the private car, in most areas, and the taxi, in congested places, have become the preferred mode of middle-class travel. There is some evidence that this is happening in air travel, with small, profitable airlines such as Southwest providing short and medium length direct flights. This trend may accelerate with the development of new small aircraft that can operate out of smaller airports.[64] Still, it is unlikely that the hubs will be displaced soon. Rather, they will probably coexist with a set of new or enlarged smaller airports in every city.

There is no inherent reason why technology should not be able to provide such a decentralized system. It would, of course, be necessary to perfect small, quiet aircraft with the capability of taking off vertically or using short runways and operating safely through greatly improved air traffic control systems or a heavier reliance on the sophisticated on-board systems that are now in place (see fig. 15).[65] Although all these technologies have been heralded for decades, they have yet to prove themselves.[66] Yet, given the importance of this kind of technology in solving what appear to be otherwise nearly insoluble land-use conflicts, it is not unreasonable to assume that the problems will be worked out. If so, this could ultimately lead to a landscape much like the one Frank Lloyd Wright imagined, with individuals using private aircraft to travel as directly as possible from one point to another.

Any predictions of this sort are completely speculative. For example, the same communications technology that has created the global market and the corresponding rise in air travel throughout the world ultimately could make such travel obsolete. In place of the meeting at an airport VIP lounge, conferences could be held in a virtual, electronic space. Teleconferencing has apparently already limited air travel to a certain extent. On the other hand, it is unlikely that this trend will seriously diminish the total number of miles flown.[67] Man is a social creature, and it seems likely that any loss in certain

61 The proposed new Chek Lap Kok airport at Hong Kong is in many ways similar to the one at Kansai. Constructed on new fill on an island far from central Hong Kong, it will be connected to the city by high-speed rail lines and highways. The Hong Kong scheme also includes a new business center, actually an entire new town, in the immediate vicinity of the airport. See Planner's Casebook, No. 7, Summer, 1973: "Port and Airport Development Strategy in Hong Kong."

62 According to Richard Tesch of the Economic Development Commission of Central Florida, Orlando is currently planning a facility, to be called Spaceport, that will accommodate these aircraft.

63 On the possibility of the demise of the hub system, see the editorial by Manfred Momberger in Airport Forum (March 1993), p. 3.

64 David NewMyer, of the Aviation Management and Flight department at Southern Illinois University, reports that a number of smaller airlines have started investing heavily in airplanes of this kind, notably the British Aerospace 146 or Bombardier's Regional Jet (RJ), which have been used quite successfully by the fast growing Comair of Cincinnati.

65 On the role of vertiports in urban development, see Erik Ferguson, "Up, Up and Away," Planning (Feb. 1992), pp. 10-13.

66 The notion that many of these technological wonders are just over the horizon has been with us for some years now. In an undated study for the redesign of Chicago's O'Hare Airport, probably completed in the 1960s, the impressive list of technical experts led the authors of the report to predict, among other things, that by 1985 VTOL would be used exclusively at O'Hare and that by this date at least one and probably two new airports would have been built. "O'Hare Airport: A Design Potential Study" in the files of the Merriam Center, now at the University of Illinois at Chicago.

67 On the effect of electronic communications on air travel, see Joan M. Feldman, "Bane of Business Travel," Air Transport World (Sept. 1993), pp. 44-49.

Fig. 15 Bell Helicopter Textron, designers. Artist's rendering of a proposed Vertiport (VTOL port) in a downtown location, 1994-95.

68 The estimate in the 1995 edition of *Aviation and Aerospace Almanac*, ed. Richard Lampl (New York, 1995), is that between 1995 and 2005 the number of passengers carried by commercial carriers will jump from 512 million to 742 million or something like 5 percent per year, which mirrors what many other forecasters have predicted over the last several years.

69 This kind of air travel has long been predicted. See, for example, the article "Jet Age," *Urban Land* (Dec. 1958), p. 5.

kinds of business travel will result in increases in travel for other reasons. Indeed, the distinctions between business and leisure activities may be blurring just as those that used to separate city and country have blurred.

Although it is impossible to predict the future of air travel, even over the next few years, several things appear to be fairly certain. One is that air travel will continue to grow rather quickly for the foreseeable future.[68] A fundamental shift in attitude has already taken place. A large number of people have learned to use the airplane just as they used the bus in an earlier era or the way they use the automobile today. Commuting by airplane has become quite common. Thousands of airline employees have taken this idea even further, not only living in one city and commuting to the airport of a distant city where they are based, but even accepting dinner invitations in still other cities, reasonably confident that they will be able to get there.[69] It seems likely that new technical innovations and high levels of competition will bring air travel to an expanding number of people in the world. Cities will probably continue to expand outward, giving an increasing number of people the advantages of space and personal mobility that were once reserved primarily for the wealthy. This means that airports, whether they centralize the city, decentralize it, or, most probably, continue to do both simultaneously, will necessarily become more complex and increasingly enmeshed in the larger urban systems. All of this presents a fascinating set of issues for planning and architectural design. Even as the stakes continue to rise, the variables multiply. In this way, planning the airport city has come to resemble planning the traditional city, the major difference being the accelerated pace of change and the costs involved with making the wrong choices.

Wood Lockhart   **A Pilot's Perspective on Airport Design**

"United Airlines announces the departure of flight 942 from Chicago to Paris." This announcement signals the beginning of a flight between two of the world's great airports. Frequently, I have been the captain of that flight – an eight-hour journey in a Boeing 767 from Terminal 1 at O'Hare International Airport to Charles de Gaulle International Airport in Roissy-en-France. As a pilot, I have seen these and many other airports from a perspective that is somewhat different from that of the typical passenger. While both pilot and passenger may recognize that the fundamental role of any airport is to function as an interface between air and surface transportation, their perceptions of that interface are probably not the same. For the passenger, the focal point of the airport is usually the terminal, which is often equated with the airport itself. For the pilot, however, the airport is defined primarily by its airside "structure" of runways, taxiways, and aprons. Seen from the air – from the pilot's perspective – this structure is the most distinctive feature of the airport, and it becomes clear that the design decisions that produced it affect all other aspects of the airport plan. The degree to which those design decisions reflect an understanding of the special requirements of the airplane largely determines the degree to which the airport can successfully fulfill its function.

My log book tells me that I first flew into O'Hare on December 31, 1959, as the copilot on a Douglas DC-3 (see Zukowsky, fig. 2). Although the venerable "Gooney Bird" was by then considered to be a relic from an earlier era, O'Hare was poised to become one of the first airports designed for the jet age. Originally built in 1943 as an assembly plant for the Douglas Aircraft Company's C-54 military transports, Orchard Field Airport was acquired by the City of Chicago in 1946 and renamed O'Hare International Airport in 1949 after World War II ace Lieutenant Commander Edward O'Hare. Over the next decade, plans were developed for the construction of new runways and a new terminal complex, but by my first visit in 1959 there was little to suggest that within ten years O'Hare would become the world's busiest airport.

Seen from the passenger's perspective in 1959, O'Hare consisted of little more than a single Y-shaped terminal – the first and only one to be completed of five such terminals that designer Ralph Burke had envisioned as projecting like fingers from a five-sided central structure located in the middle of the airport. Although the architecture at Orchard Field had been located along the periphery of the airport – an arrangement common at airports in Europe as well as in the United States – Burke's plan for O'Hare called for the terminal complex to be encircled by a system of concentric taxiways tangentially connected to as many as six sets of parallel runways (fig. 1). This runway and taxiway plan, first developed in 1948, would eventually be realized in a much modified form, but Burke's ideas for the terminal complex were abandoned following his death in 1956. Responsibility for the airport design was transferred to the architectural firm of C. F. Murphy Associates in 1957, and it became apparent then that the coming introduction of the Boeing 707 and the Douglas DC-8 jet transports would render the original design obsolete. With

Fig. 1 Ralph Burke Associates, planners. Bird's-eye view of proposed master plan for O'Hare International Airport, Chicago, 1952.

longer wing spans and the capacity to carry almost twice as many passengers as the previous generation of piston-engine airliners, the jets, which began service in 1959, required more room for maneuvering on the airside of the airport and more extensive facilities for passengers on the landside. Fortunately, by that year, only the first phase of Burke's terminal plan had been realized, and the new architects were able to radically alter his original conception. Nevertheless, the decisions made earlier for the layout of the runways and the manner in which the taxiway system would connect the runways to the terminal—decisions based upon an attempt to facilitate the movement of aircraft on the ground and in the air—would determine that the location of the terminal remained at the center of the airport. Thus, when finally dedicated on March 23, 1963, the completed airport design owed much to decisions made fifteen years before, but it would have been unrecognizable to a passenger who had seen it only four years earlier.

Despite the creation of new terminals and passenger facilities, O'Hare would not have seemed completely new to a pilot. When viewed from the air at that time, the airport retained many of the design features that had characterized it in 1959, particularly the runways and taxiways to the north of the new terminal. Essentially the same as those that had served Orchard Field, they had been augmented by a new runway parallel to the original NW-SE runway, which represented the first step in realizing Burke's parallel runway plan. As additional parallel runways were added at O'Hare, allowing simultaneous landings and takeoffs in six different directions, the original runway layout at Orchard Field became less obvious as a defining feature of the airport, but to the discerning eye it is still visible as an important element of the overall design (fig. 2).

For a pilot, the runway and taxiway layout is the most significant design element of any airport—the picture that the pilot commits to memory and that becomes the airport's identifying characteristic. Yet, the first airports of the 1920s in both Europe and the United States did not have runways or taxiways (see Voigt, figs. 6, 7, and 9). Modern jet transports have very specific requirements for runway length and orientation, and these requirements vary according to the airport's location, elevation, and prevailing winds and weather conditions. For the earliest generation of airliners, however, these re-

Fig. 2 Aerial view of O'Hare International Airport, Chicago, showing complete runway scheme (photo Aug. 1988).

quirements were minimal, and it was not until the introduction of larger and faster airplanes that runways and taxiways were commonly considered to be necessary elements of the airport design. Early European and American airports had been modeled on the omnidirectional grass fields that had been developed during World War I. At such airports, pilots simply turned their aircraft into the prevailing wind for both takeoff and landing. In Europe, where airport designers tended to focus on the architecture of terminals and hangars, this practice remained common for a longer period of time than in the United States, where the airport was treated primarily as a civil engineering problem that involved making improvements to the landing field itself. Specifications for municipal airports, developed by the Army Air Service in 1919, were very particular as to the size, shape, and marking of the landing field and also included recommendations for limiting obstacles in the path of approaching and departing airplanes. Perhaps the most interesting, as well as the most innovative, aspect of the 1919 specifications was the recommendation that the landing area be made of concrete in the shape of a cross to provide an "excellent wet weather takeoff and landing spot."[1] This new design marked the first departure from the concept of the omnidirectional grass landing field and was the initial step in the development of the hard-surfaced runway.

The world's first airport runways were built at Boston Municipal Airport in 1923.[2] Because it had been constructed on filled land, the Boston airport was not suitable for use as an omnidirectional airfield. Preparing the entire surface of the field for omnidirectional flight operations was considered too expensive, so it was decided to improve the ground only in those areas where wind conditions dictated that the majority of takeoffs and landings would be

1 "Specifications for Municipal Landing Fields," *The American City* (July 1919), p. 20.
2 The first city to take action on the Army's airport specifications of 1919 was Albany, New York, where the Quentin Roosevelt Memorial Aviation Field was established as the first municipal landing field in the United States. Other communities quickly followed suit, and by February 1920, a total of twenty-six cities boasted landing fields which met the 1919 specifications; see "Municipal Landing Fields for Air Service," *The American City* (July 1919), p. 22, and "Cities Preparing for Future Air Traffic," *The American City* (Feb. 1920), p. 107.

A Pilot's Perspective on Airport Design   215

made. Thus, as originally planned and constructed, the field was laid out in the form of a T – each axis a cinder-surfaced runway some 1,500 feet long by 200 feet wide. Boston's runway airport established a precedent in American airfield design. While omnidirectional grass fields remained common in Europe, American airport planners were discovering that, in many parts of the country, grass strong enough to withstand the wear and tear of daily aircraft operations was a rarity. In the North, the problem was compounded by heavy frosts that could cause dangerous cracks in a sod field. Accordingly, planners began to experiment with the use of artificially surfaced runways for landings and takeoffs. At Boston's airport, this surface was made of soft coal cinders rolled into place and treated with an oil dressing. Cinders were also used in 1926 in the construction of the two 1,500-foot runways at Chicago's Municipal Airport (later renamed Midway Airport), but at other fields, designers experimented with gravel, crushed rock, and even ashes. The first hard-surfaced runway, made of macadam, was built at Newark in 1928, and by 1929 the first concrete runway had been constructed at Ford Airport in Dearborn, Michigan (see pl. 10).[3] The first hard-surfaced runway in Europe was constructed at the Halle-Leipzig Airport, which was established in 1926, but this concrete surface was intended only for takeoffs. It was not until 1936 that Stockholm's new Bromma Airport became the first in Europe to utilize a complete system of hard-surfaced runways (see pl. 20).[4]

The introduction of runways and taxiways added an important new design element to the airport. Although the runway was developed to provide aircraft with a takeoff and landing surface that could be used in all weather conditions, it soon became apparent that it had major design implications for all aspects of the airport. By channeling aircraft in specific directions and separating the areas used for flying from those used for taxiing, a carefully designed runway and taxiway system could greatly increase the capacity of the airport, as well as significantly enhance the safety of flight operations. Runway layout would prove to affect decisions for terminal location, and taxiways, which connect the runways to the terminal, would come to play a part in terminal design. In the Lehigh Airports Competition of 1929, design requirements specified that airports have at least four paved runways that were not less than 100 feet in width and that these were to be an integral part of the overall airport plan. The competition drawings suggest that architects and planners were beginning to give as much thought to the design of the structure of the airfield as they were to the architecture of terminals and hangars.[5] This new emphasis on runways and taxiways began to be reflected at airports as advances were made in aircraft design. In fact, the introduction in 1933 of both the Boeing 247 and the Douglas DC-1 – the first modern airliners – led to the realization that new airports, specifically designed to meet the needs of these new aircraft, would be required. When the twenty-eight passenger Douglas DC-3 entered service in 1936, it inaugurated a new era in air transportation and served as a catalyst for the design and construction of new airports throughout the United States. New York's LaGuardia Airport (see pl. 44) and Washington, D.C.,'s National Airport (see Brodherson, figs. 16-17 and 32), opened in 1939 and 1941, respectively, were two of the first American airports to be built from comprehensive plans in which the layout of runways and taxiways was considered to be as important as the design of the terminal itself.

The advances in aircraft design during World War II brought about additional significant developments in runway and taxiway design. Not only did

3 The first building in the United States specifically designed as an air terminal was erected at the Ford Airport by Albert Kahn in 1927; by 1929, both of the original grass runways had been paved.

4 Paul Hedquist was one of six Swedish architects invited to submit entries in the Stockholm Airport Competition of 1934. Faced with a difficult site dominated by granite hills, Hedquist planned an eight-way intersecting runway system that took good advantage of the only clear flight paths to the area. This inventive solution, however, cannot be considered completely successful inasmuch as the intersecting runways precluded simultaneous operations by more than one aircraft; see John Walter Wood, *Airports: Some Elements of Design and Future Development* (New York, 1940), p. 257.

5 The Lehigh Airports Competition sought to "bring architects, engineers, and planners into public notice as the logical persons to guide the future development of American airports"; see T. S. Rogers, "Airports, the New Architectural Opportunity," *Architectural Forum* (April 1929), p. 599.

6 The Instrument Landing System (ILS) had been developed in 1930, but it was not given public support until 1940, when it was approved by the Civil Aeronautics Board and installed at six major airports throughout the United States. Comprising a localizer for lateral guidance, a glide slope for vertical guidance, and two marker beacons to pinpoint exact aircraft location, the ILS was first used at New York's LaGuardia Airport and in Chicago, Cleveland, Kansas City, Los Angeles, and Fort Worth; see "Blind Landings at Six Airports," *Scientific American* (Nov. 1940), p. 260.

7 The Army's layout was essentially two congruent triangles, which allowed two simultaneous flight operations in any of three directions. This plan not only eliminated the problem of intersecting runways and the inherent danger of collision, but also minimized the effects of possible bomb damage, which was always a consideration in wartime designs. The Army's triangular runway scheme proved extremely popular, and it was adopted, in various forms, at military and civilian airports throughout the United States.

8 See Charles Froesch and Walther Prokosch, *Airport Planning* (New York, 1946), p. 107 and fig. 18.

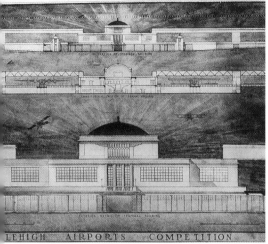

Fig. 3 Odd Nansen and Latham C. Squire, architects. Entry for the Lehigh Airports Competition, third-prize winner, 1929, showing parallel sets of runways separating takeoffs and landings; from *American Airport Designs* (New York and Chicago, 1930), p. 19.

the new four-engine transports, such as the Boeing 307, the Douglas DC-4, and the Lockheed *Constellation,* require longer runways, but their increased wing spans necessitated greater separation distances between runways, taxiways, and terminals. Additionally, planners correctly anticipated that postwar airports could handle the projected increases in air traffic only by providing for simultaneous landings and takeoffs on separate parallel runways. Although the concept of parallel runways had been advanced in 1929 by designers in the Lehigh Airports Competition, it had not been understood at that time that flight safety required a much greater separation between the runways than was suggested in their plans (see fig. 3). The introduction of the Instrument Landing System in 1940 allowed aircraft to approach the airport and land in weather conditions that previously would have precluded flight operations, but pilots believed that the safety of simultaneous instrument landings could not be assured with a parallel runway separation of less than five thousand feet.[6]

When Orchard Field was opened in Chicago in 1942, its runway layout – specifically planned to accommodate the Douglas C-54s, military versions of the postwar DC-4s, which were being built there – was based on a triangular runway design developed by the U.S. Army in 1940 (fig. 4).[7] Although this design served the airport well throughout the war years, by 1945 it had become clear that the facilities would be inadequate to accommodate the volume of air traffic that was expected if the airport were to become a new commercial airline hub for Chicago. It was a rethinking of the runway layout that became the starting point for the design decisions that would eventually recast Orchard Field as O'Hare International Airport. The tangential runway scheme advocated by Ralph Burke had first been proposed in 1944 for a new airport planned for New York City. Anticipating that a new postwar airport might have to accommodate as many as 200 landings and takeoffs per hour, the planners for Idlewild Airport (renamed John F. Kennedy International Airport in December 1963) had recommended by 1946 as many as twelve runways radiating tangentially from a system of circular taxiways, which would enclose the central terminal complex.[8] Incoming planes would be able to land on multiple runways that converged on one side of the taxiway circle, while departing planes could be taking off simultaneously on runways connected to the opposite side of the circle. Advantages of the plan included

Fig. 4 Aerial view of the Douglas Aircraft Company plant, Chicago, 1943, showing runway scheme later incorporated into O'Hare International Airport.

THREE NEW GIANTS

NEW YORK is finally underway on its $60 million "Terminal City" at Idlewild with a 24-gate International Arrivals building designed by Skidmore, Owings & Merrill under Port Authority Design Coordinator Wallace Harrison. Passengers for 17 foreign airlines enter along outer wings, mount to concourse and gates. Arrivals deplane in center "U," pass through customs at ground level. Visitors ramp up to mezzanine under arched lobby, look down on customs or ascend to rooftop restaurant. Seven smaller terminals for domestic airlines will complete oval around depressed parking for 6,000 cars.

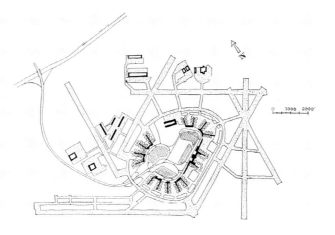

Fig. 5 Port of New York Authority, planners. Runway plan for Idlewild Airport (now John F. Kennedy International Airport), 1956, showing three sets of parallel runways and one additional runway (later extended into Jamaica Bay); from *Architectural Forum* 104 (June 1956), p. 124.

minimal taxiing distances, because there would be no backtracking after landing or before takeoff. In addition, since the runways diverged from the center of the airport, aircraft would have a greater degree of lateral separation when initiating approaches.

Objections to the tangential plan came primarily from airline pilots who, although recognizing the advantage of having multiple runways available regardless of the wind direction, pointed out that in the event of a missed approach and "go around," an aircraft would be climbing directly into the path of planes taking off from the opposite side of the circle. In a compromise solution arbitrated by the Civil Aeronautics Authority, three sets of widely spaced parallel runways were laid out tangentially around a centrally sited area for terminal construction (fig. 5). After considerable delays in the immediate postwar years, Idlewild was first opened to commercial flights on July 1, 1948. The original arrangement did not allow the number of aircraft movements initially anticipated by the planners, but it did eliminate the problems of converging air traffic. Similar modifications to the tangential runway plan were made at O'Hare, and at both airports these plans became determining factors in the overall airport designs. In 1949, a new master plan based on dual parallel runways was developed for Idlewild. This plan was realized over many years: one new runway was added (see fig. 6), but four of the original runways were later eliminated. The airport today has two sets of parallel runways aligned at 90 degrees to each other (see fig. 7).

On United's flight 942 from O'Hare to Paris, both passenger and pilot begin their journey at Terminal 1, which was designed by Helmut Jahn and opened in 1988 on the site of Ralph Burke's first terminal building at the airport (fig. 8). Quickly dubbed "the diner" by irreverent pilots and air traffic controllers, who sensed in this steel and glass structure an echo of an earlier railroad aesthetic, the building is different in both form and concept from the architecture that predates it at the airport. If it does evoke something of the great railway terminals of the nineteenth century, it is not because of a confusion of purpose, but because, like those earlier structures, it expresses an understanding of the possible relationships between transportation technology and architectural form. User friendly for both pilot and passenger, this terminal, with its remote satellite connected by an underground moving sidewalk, provides easy access to over forty aircraft, which when parked at the gate seem almost to be extensions of the architecture.

Such clarity of purpose has not always been evident in American air terminal design. Focusing primarily on the airport as a land unit having many technical requirements as to size, surroundings, surface, and the planned re-

Fig. 6 Port of New York Authority, planners. Runway plan for Idlewild Airport (now John F. Kennedy International Airport), 1961, showing placement of terminals and the addition of an eighth runway; from *Architectural Record* 130 (Sept. 1961), p. 153.

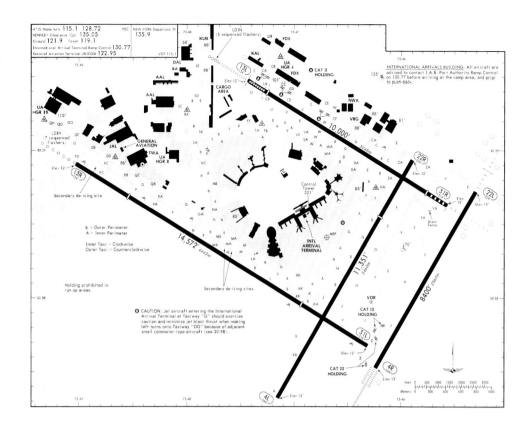

lationship to population centers and transportation routes, the first airport planners in the United States gave scant attention to air terminal architecture. In 1927, even before the completion of Berlin's Tempelhof terminal (see pl. 3; Voigt, fig. 9), Ford Airport near Dearborn, Michigan, could claim Albert Kahn's newly designed passenger terminal as the only building in the country originally conceived for that purpose. By 1928 air terminals influenced by the best European airport architecture had been built in Miami (see Brodherson, fig. 4) and at the new Hoover Airport in Washington, D.C., but at many American airports, the structures showed little evidence of a relationship between the new transportation technology and architectural form. Designers produced buildings that often displayed an eclecticism that suggests a complete misunderstanding of function, including the 1929 terminal-hangar in Los Angeles, which was designed in a pseudo Spanish Colonial Revival style, complete with bell towers and cloisters (see Brodherson, fig. 3), and the air

Fig. 8 Aerial view of O'Hare International Airport, showing location of United Airlines Terminal 1 (Murphy/Jahn, architects, 1983-88) (photo Oct. 1991).

terminal constructed in Birmingham, Alabama, in 1932 that bore more than a coincidental resemblance to George Washington's Mount Vernon. Not until the mid-1930s, after the introduction of the Boeing 247 and the Douglas DC-3 had made clear that advances in aircraft design would require an airport architecture that took into account the special needs of the airplane, did American planners and designers begin to understand that the air terminal was not just a glorified railway station that could be treated independently from the rest of the airport. The prospect of larger aircraft carrying greater numbers of passengers meant that the role and function of the terminal as well as that of the runways and taxiways must be rethought and redefined.

For the passenger departing on flight 942 to Paris, the terminal probably represents the essence of the airport. For the pilot, however, it is only when the airplane is pushed back from the gate and away from the terminal that the airport comes to life. Over the next twenty minutes, before the 767 becomes airborne, the pilot will experience the airport as an intricate arrangement of taxiways and runways, articulated by an array of lights, markings, and signs. Once known to both pilots and controllers by such names as "the stub," "the branch," "the twig," "hangar alley," and "Lake Shore Drive," the taxiways at O'Hare have recently been redesignated with standardized alphabetical terminology, but the complexity of the airfield design is such that following the assigned route to the runway can present a considerable challenge to the pilot.

"United 942, taxi to Runway 32 Right via Alpha 4, Bravo, Hotel, and Papa." Looking at the airport diagram (fig. 9) – the plan of the airport that corresponds to the airport viewed from the air – the pilot acknowledges the clearance from the ground controller and begins a slow taxi away from the terminal. Leaving the apron area at Taxiway A-4, the airplane will make a right turn on Taxiway B – the outermost of the two parallel taxiways that encircled the original complex at O'Hare. Now, however, it is not the terminal that demands the pilot's attention but rather the blue edgelights and green

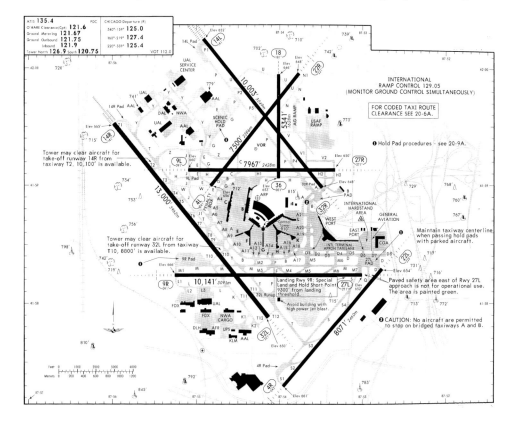

Fig. 9 Jeppesen Sanderson, Inc. Airport diagram for O'Hare International Airport, Chicago, Nov. 10, 1995. Copyright 1995 Jeppesen Sanderson, Inc. Reduced for illustrative purposes.

Fig. 10 Aerial view of Heathrow International Airport, London, showing complete runway scheme, c. 1980.

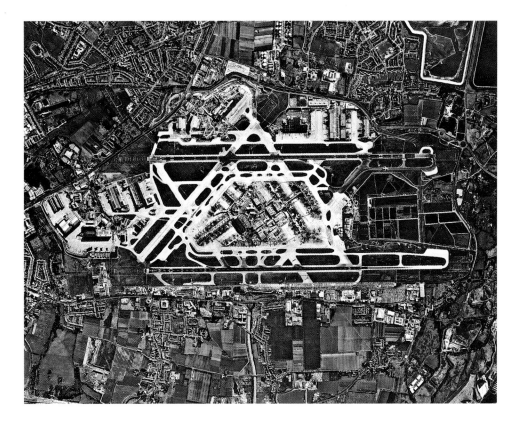

centerline lights defining the taxi route that will take the aircraft to the oldest part of the airport for takeoff on a runway that was also once part of the Orchard Field Airport. With wing tips that cannot be seen from the cockpit and that extend forty feet beyond each edge of the taxiway, the 767 can be safely maneuvered only if the route is followed precisely. After turning onto Taxiway H, flight 942 is now heading due east and paralleling Runway 9 Left – another of the original Orchard Field runways that is still in use. After a taxi distance of more than a mile, the aircraft will make another right turn onto Taxiway P and then come to a stop at the entrance to Runway 32 Right – a designation that defines it as being aligned in the direction of 320 degrees and parallel to another similarly aligned Runway 32 Left.

When cleared for takeoff, flight 942, carrying up to 206 passengers and a crew of 13, will begin a takeoff run of almost a mile and at a speed approaching two hundred miles per hour, lift off the runway, and leave O'Hare behind. Climbing to an initial cruising altitude of 33,000 feet, the flight will remain airborne for almost eight hours before landing at Roissy's Charles de Gaulle International Airport. Although the passengers on flight 942 will, in all probability, give no more thought to airports until their arrival in Paris, the pilots will be acutely aware of the major airports below them along their flight route. Those at Detroit, Toronto, Montreal, and Gander may be seen before the flight leaves the North American continent, while airports at Glasgow, Manchester, and London may be visible after crossing the North Atlantic. Seen from above, the most distinctive of these is London's Heathrow International Airport, which was originally used as a military airfield on the outskirts of London. Turned over to civilian authorities at the end of World War II and opened to commercial aviation in 1946, Heathrow's six-runway layout was composed of two triangles arranged so as to suggest a "Star of David" when seen from the air (fig. 10).[9] This runway arrangement was not based on aesthetics, but on the desire to provide for simultaneous landings and takeoffs in any of six different directions according to the prevailing wind. The

9 The "Star of David" plan was originally developed by the Austin Company of Cleveland, Ohio, in 1944.

arrangement also dictated that, as at O'Hare, the logical location for the terminal complex would be at the center of the airport. Architect Frederick Gibberd's original building program for the airport, begun in 1947, called for this central complex of structures to be surrounded by the runways and joined to the outer roadway network by a 680-yard tunnel. As the "passenger handling building" was expanded to the current complex of three separate terminals, three of the original runways were taken out of service to make room for the new facilities (see Bosma, fig. 3). Even so, the original and distinctive "Star of David" configuration is easily recognizable from the air because portions of these runways are still used as taxiways. The clarity of the design when seen from above, however, is in marked contrast to the confusing and seemingly unplanned nature of the airport from the ground-based perspective of the passenger.

Shortly after passing Heathrow, flight 942 will cross over the English Channel and receive its initial clearance for descent – the first step in the arrival process at Charles de Gaulle. When Charles de Gaulle was begun in 1967, Paris was served by two commercial airports, Orly, located to the south of the city (see Bosma, figs. 4-5), and the older Le Bourget, on the northeastern outskirts, whose facilities dated from 1936-37 (see pl. 38-39). Unlike O'Hare and Heathrow, the new airport at Roissy was, from its inception, designed for modern jet transport and was specifically intended to accommodate the Boeing 747, which was designed in 1965 and first flown in 1969. With a wing span of nearly 200 feet (65 feet greater than that of a 707), a takeoff weight of over three-quarters of a million pounds, and a seating capacity of up to 550 passengers, the 747 was the first of a new generation of jumbo jets that would not only bring about a general rethinking of terminal design at airports throughout the world, but would also require new design standards for the location and dimension of runways, taxiways, and aprons. Airports such as O'Hare had to construct new facilities to accommodate these aircraft, but the planners of Charles de Gaulle had jumbo jets in mind from the very beginning. When it opened in 1974, passengers considered its terminal to be one of the most efficient in Europe, and pilots recognized that the airside structure successfully responded to the size and handling characteristics of the new generation of wide-bodied aircraft. Originally planned with two sets of parallel east-west runways and a fifth cross-wind runway on the east side of the airfield, the airport today comprises a single pair of east-west runways separated by two terminal complexes (fig. 11). Terminal 1, the first to be completed, was opened in 1974 and is served by runway 9-27 on the northern side of the airport. Although the design concept of Terminal 1 – a circular structure surrounded by seven trapezoidal loading satellites (see Bosma, fig. 11) – was intended to be repeated in four more structures, architect Paul Andreu of Aéroports de Paris decided to create a new design for Terminal 2, the first two modules of which were completed by 1983 (see pls. 113, 116, 118). Located to the south of the first terminal, this newer structure (with additional modules opened in 1989 and 1994) is served primarily by Runway 10-28.

For the pilots of United flight 942, it is the northern part of the airport – Runway 9-27 and the taxiways leading to Terminal 1 – that becomes the focus of attention as the aircraft continues its descent. With a prevailing wind from the west, the approach is made to Runway 27, a two-mile-long ribbon of concrete, which, for the pilots, is the first identifiable feature of the airport. Touching down at a speed of approximately 140 knots (161 mph), the 767 will decelerate and then exit the runway on one of three rapid-exit taxiways con-

Fig. 11 Jeppesen Sanderson, Inc. Airport diagram for Charles de Gaulle International Airport, Roissy-en-France, Nov. 3, 1995. Copyright 1995 Jeppesen Sanderson, Inc. Reduced for illustrative purposes.

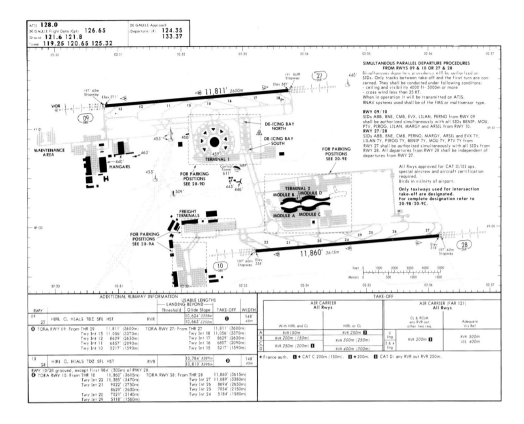

necting the runway to the taxiways leading to the terminal. Although rapid-exit taxiways are common elements in airport design, those at Charles de Gaulle diverge from the runway at a lesser angle (20 degrees) than do those at most other airports, thus allowing the pilot to use them safely at higher speeds than is usually possible. This design results in a shorter runway occupancy time for landing aircraft and has a significant effect on airport capacity. The rapid-exit taxiways lead from the runway and gently curve to join the main taxiway system, which has been designed to channel all ground movement of aircraft in a one-way flow to the terminal. At Terminal 1, where flight 942 will be completed, the taxiways loop around the central structure and pass over the underground tunnels leading to the loading satellites. This arrangement makes aircraft movement around the terminal extremely fluid, but pilots must take special care not to pass the entrance to the assigned satellite. On one of my first flights to Charles de Gaulle, I did exactly that and, because of the one-way restriction on the taxiways, was required to taxi completely around the terminal again before finally parking the aircraft at the correct gate. On that particular flight 942, the passengers were treated to an unexpected tour of the taxiway system and perhaps for the first time saw something of the airport from the pilot's perspective.

As a completely new airport, unconstrained by design decisions made during an earlier era, Charles de Gaulle is one of a relatively small number of such facilities. Although the worldwide introduction of long-range jet transport in 1958-59 generated new construction at almost every existing airport, it was only rarely that planners were given the opportunity to design and develop a new airport where none had been before. The first new civil airport designed specifically to handle jet aircraft was Dulles International, which was opened in 1962 to serve the city of Washington, D.C. (fig. 12). This was followed in 1967 by the opening of Houston Intercontinental Airport, but it was not until the 1970s that completely new airports were constructed in Dallas-Fort Worth (see pl. 111) and Tokyo and planned for Munich. At these and

other new airports, considerable attention was focused on the architectural innovations of the passenger-handling facilities, but concurrent developments in the evolution of runway layout have been equally significant. Of these, the most important has been the virtual elimination of the potentially hazardous runway intersections that were common at almost all multi-runway airports constructed in the pre-jet era. The staggered and widely spaced parallel runway schemes that have been adopted at each of these new airports have resulted in enhancements to both safety and airport capacity.

The careful consideration of the requirements of the airplane that characterize the new airports built during the 1960s and 1970s will prove to be even more necessary at airports planned to accommodate the coming generation of new large aircraft. The major aircraft manufacturers have all announced preliminary plans for the development of such airplanes, which may be as large as the 800-passenger transport envisioned by the Boeing Company. With wing spans of up to 262 feet (extended to 290 feet in the "stretch" version of the Boeing design), these aircraft may be flying as early as the year 2002 (see pls. 168-70 for the Airbus version).[10] Of all the world's airports, only a few have an airside structure of runways and taxiways designed to accommodate aircraft of such size. Among these are the Brisbane Airport, which was opened in 1988, and Denver International Airport, which was opened in 1995 (fig. 13; see Brodherson, fig. 33). The new airport under construction in Hong Kong (Chek Lap Kok) has been planned for aircraft with wing spans of 280 feet, but as yet there are no international design standards for airports planned to serve aircraft larger than the 747-400.[11]

From the pilot's perspective, the major challenge for the airport designer is to account for the advances in aircraft technology that will continue to

Fig. 12 Eero Saarinen and Associates, architects. Dulles International Airport, outside Washington, D.C., 1958-62.

10 On the status of Airbus Industrie's ultra-high-capacity transports, see Pierre Sparaco, "No Money as Yet in Airbus Jumbo Plan," *Aviation Week and Space Technology* (June 17, 1996), pp. 27-28.

11 The International Civil Aviation Organization (ICAO) specifies design criteria for airports serving aircraft with wing spans of up to 65 meters (213 feet). The largest airplane covered by these criteria is the Boeing 747-400, which has a wing span of 64.5 meters and is classified as a Code E aircraft. In 1993 ICAO established an Aerodrome Design Study Group to develop recommendations for airport design specifications for a new Code F, which will apply to future aircraft with wing spans greater than 65 meters. The Study Group (of which this author is a member) has determined that Code F will apply to aircraft with wing spans of up to 80 meters (262 feet), but it has not yet agreed upon the design guidelines for airports that will serve these new aircraft. In the United States, airport planners use the criteria developed by the Federal

Fig. 13 Jeppesen Sanderson, Inc. Airport diagram for Denver International Airport, Sept. 8, 1995. Copyright 1995 Jeppesen Sanderson, Inc. Reduced for illustrative purposes.

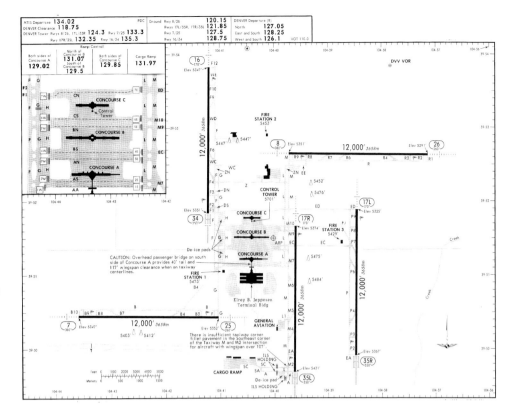

Aviation Administration. These criteria include specifications for airports intended to serve aircraft with wing spans of up to 80 meters and may prove to be the basis for the new international standards to be developed by the ICAO. On the impact of these new large aircraft on the design of Chek Lap Kok, see Michael Mecham, "Second Hong Kong Runway Prompts Superjumbo Studies," *Aviation Week and Space Technology* (June 24, 1996), pp. 35-36.

12 In the catalogue for a 1937 exhibition organized by the Royal Institute of British Architects, there appears the statement that "the new 40-seater Armstrong Whitworth monoplanes may represent, in the immediate future at any rate, the maximum practicable size for land planes." Put into service in 1938, this perceived behemoth was overtaken in size just two years later by the prototype of the Lockheed *Constellation*, which would prove to place even more stringent constraints on airports that had only recently been constructed; see Royal Institute of British Architects, *Airports and Airways*, exh. cat. (London, 1937).

characterize the development of air transportation. Architects and planners must anticipate that aircraft will inevitably grow larger and place greater demands on the airside of the airport. This would seem an obvious conclusion, yet the history of airport design is replete with examples of the failure to plan sufficiently for an ever increasing amount of traffic and larger, more complex aircraft.[12] Although the new airplanes envisioned for the first years of the twenty-first century have engendered a dialogue between planners and pilots about the design standards necessary to ensure safety and efficiency, there has as yet been little agreement about what those standards should be. From this pilot's perspective, it is clear that these standards must be based upon an understanding of the special requirements of the next generation of commercial aircraft. It will be for the pilots of tomorrow to determine if those requirements have been met.

Leonard Rau

Deregulation and Design:
The Changing Role of Identity at the Airport

The passage of the Airline Deregulation Act of 1978 removed the barriers to open competition among American airlines and caused a major shift in the way airlines used design to communicate their corporate image to the public. In order to be successful in the newly open air travel market, airlines had to take a more assertive role in marketing themselves and in creating and communicating distinctive identities, especially within increasingly complex airport systems. In Europe, with the formation of the European Union, a movement towards liberalizing airline regulations has been under way, albeit slowly. As a result, European airlines have had to redefine themselves in a physically similar, but culturally different way to their American counterparts. Design took on a greater importance, as the airlines were forced by competition to manipulate their corporate image by changing the graphic elements of their identities to reflect significant improvements in service, equipment, or other changes in the company structure, or simply to update their image. The introduction of jet aircraft in the 1950s, considered to be the beginning of the modern aviation market as we know it today, also brought major changes in the airport that have contributed to a greater emphasis by the airlines on the use of design as a marketing tool. By examining the corporate identities of three major commercial airlines – Delta Air Lines, British Airways, which was privatized in 1984, and the now defunct Pan Am – as well as briefly looking at several others, we can see the way design has been used to convey the images of these companies to the public.

Airline companies use design throughout the airport system, ranging from aircraft livery to communications, and even to the corporate-branded packaging materials for the free peanuts handed out on most flights (see figs. 1-3). Design, in a broad sense, is viewed in this work as a marketing device; it is also "a method of solving problems...and [it] has been shown to have something to do with profit."[1] Identity is viewed as a strategic business tool that helps airlines to communicate their products, values, and services to their passengers, employees, and external organizations, including financial institutions, suppliers, and competitors; this can be defined as a "process whereby the design elements of an organization are utilized to maximum effect in order to communicate what it does and how it does it."[2]

This analysis of airline identity focuses on airline products and the spaces that airlines occupy in American and European airports, including all points of visual, verbal, and physical interaction between the airline and the passenger, and between the airline and the airport authority. The role of design in the airport warrants special attention, because the airport is a negative public space (see figs. 4 and 5), in that, like a hospital or a shopping mall, it is an area where few people actually want to be; they are there to board an aircraft or to deplane, to meet or leave someone, or to go shopping. In this way, the airport is an urban environment in a non-metropolitan context, as outlined by Christopher Blow in his book *Airport Terminals*: "More often than not the airport terminal is a centre of urban-type activity (large numbers of people, public transport, commercial activity, offices, etc.) while being far removed from the metropolitan centre."[3]

1 Adrian Forty, *Objects of Desire: Design and Society, 1750-1980* (London, 1986), p. 6.
2 Alan and Isabella Livingston, *Graphic Design and Designers* (London, 1992), p. 49.
3 Christopher J. Blow, *Airport Terminals* (Oxford, 1991), p. 8.

In comparing the use of design in American and European airports, it is important to consider the social function and ownership of the airport. As one would expect, cultural differences have had an influence. In general terms, the American airport is a public place, since public access is permitted all the way to the departure gate. In Europe, the public is restricted to the check-in area, so the airport is a more private place. Being in a European airport, however, is often part of a more culturally diverse experience owing to the large number of cross-border flights and the accompanying security and customs checks, and the use of foreign currencies and languages. Another difference is that the majority of American airports are owned and operated by the Port Authority of their respective cities or states; thus they are seen as "air" ports in the traditional sense. In Europe, on the other hand, airports are usually controlled by a central government, although this, too, has been changing, as illustrated by the privatization of the British Airports Authority (BAA).[4] In both American and European airports, the relationship between the airlines and the airport authorities is that of tenant and landlord, often regulated, of course, by the national aviation authority.

Figs. 1 and 2 Landor Associates, designers. Corporate imagery for British Airways as applied to graphics standards and service vehicles, 1983-86.

4 BAA handled 72 percent of United Kingdom passenger traffic in 1994. See BAA Annual Report, 1994. See also John Heskett, *Industrial Design* (London, 1980), and Philip B. Meggs, *A History of Graphic Design* (New York, 1992) for discussions of the corporate cultural view of design. The United Kingdom is used in the present essay to represent changes taking place in Europe since it is leading the European Union in the privatization of both its domestic airlines and its airport authorities.

Fig. 3 Delta Air Lines departure area at Cincinnati International Airport (photo Jan. 1993).

Deregulation and Economic Liberalization

A visual identity has a natural life....
External conditions change continually;
internally the purpose of the identity
may also be changing.[5]

5 SampsonTyrell, *Identity Issues* (London,
   1992), p. 7.
6 See John Vickers and George Yarrow,
   Privatization: An Economic Analysis
   (Cambridge, Mass., 1988). See also Ken
   Button, ed., *Airline Deregulation: International Experiences* (New York, 1991), p. 1.
7 Vickers and Yarrow (note 6), pp. 79, 119.

Fig. 4 Smith, Hinchman and Grylls, architects. Interior view of William B. Hartsfield
International Airport, Atlanta, 1980.

Fig. 5 Murphy/Jahn, architects. Check-in
counters at United Airlines Terminal, O'Hare
International Airport, Chicago, 1983-88.

Throughout the twentieth century, transport markets have been regulated to maintain safety standards, protect passenger and worker rights, and ensure that remote, non-profitable routes have effective transport services. The deregulation of the American airline industry was based on a belief in the free market system and in the idea that increased market efficiency could be achieved by centralizing market knowledge. It encouraged competition among the airlines to ensure that "survival of the fittest" ruled the market. The Airline Deregulation Act of 1978, passed by Congress under the Carter administration as a reaction to the tightly regulated market that existed from the 1940s to the late 1970s,[6] was meant to put an end to what had become "essentially a game between government (and its agency) and the firm." "[Regulation] evolved at a time when dominant utility companies were in public ownership…the agency has greater knowledge and expertise regarding industry conditions than generalist competition can have."[7] The Airline Deregulation Act was not an isolated piece of legislation; it was followed in 1980 by the Staggers Rail Act and the Motor Carrier Act, and in 1982 by the Bus Regulatory Reform Act.

The American air travel market was deregulated overnight, while Europe's air travel system is being liberalized over a much longer period, especially as deadlines are continually pushed back. The aim of liberalization is to modify price and market entry controls in the same way as deregulation, but at a slower pace, thus altering the airlines' reaction to it. Nonetheless, liberalization will dramatically change the structure of the European air travel market in that it will allow the airlines to pick up passengers mid-route, set their own prices, operate from foreign airports, and bid for routes. For example, Air France could fly Paris-London-Dublin-Berlin-Rome-Paris, pick up passengers at any point and carry them to any other point, and set their own fares for doing so. Currently, a passenger has to change airlines in order to get to the next city or fly with Air France back to Paris in between flying to each city. Another example of the liberalized market conditions would be that Sabena, the Belgian airline headquartered in Brussels, could fly London-Paris-Geneva-Zurich, without ever having to pass through Belgium. Liberalization is

a longer process than deregulation because it involves reforming, modifying, and evolving existing legislation, thus preventing the mistakes that can occur from radical changes. But liberalization aims to break "the tradition of regulation. What has happened in recent years has been a liberalisation of attitude and something of a withdrawal of the state from this interventionist role. In North America this has been viewed as 'deregulation' although in the UK [it has been termed] 'regulatory reform' (and in a Europe wide context 'liberalisation')."[8]

It is important to note that the key difference between the American and European approaches to deregulation relates to their respective legislative cultures. America is a single country with one Congress, whereas Europe is a union of fifteen countries with several tiers of European and national legislative assemblies. The European Union is currently building consensus for new legislation, including balancing the existing individual bilateral agreements, preventing state subsidies for individual airlines, and ensuring that safety standards are maintained.[9] At present, European liberalization is projected for 1998.

In the air travel market, technological developments have had a direct influence on airline activity inside the airport. With the development of wide-bodied aircraft, such as the Boeing 747 (see pls. 133, 148, and 151) and the Lockheed L-1011 (see pls. 107-09), which can carry up to five hundred passengers each, and to a lesser extent, the new Boeing 777 (see pl. 161), greater demands have been placed on airline procedures and passenger services such as check-in and, for the airport authority, baggage handling facilities and parking areas. Deregulation has encouraged the airlines to view their passengers as customers; this also provides the airport authorities with more retail opportunities. In the airport, this new attitude is evident in the rise in the number of customer service points. The customer also faces increased visual noise and choice as competition inside the airport has intensified, a situation that is apparent in all American airports, most United Kingdom airports, and an increasing number of continental European airports.

Following deregulation in the United States and the beginning of liberalization in Europe, several key trends are developing that have a direct influ-

Fig. 6 Howard Needles Tammen and Bergendoff, architects. Interior view of Greater Rochester International Airport, showing check-in counters with airline identities of Delta Air Lines, Pan Am Express, and United Airlines, Rochester, New York, 1992.

ence on the airlines' use of identity and design as well as on the organization, operation, and ambience of the contemporary airport. First, the airlines began operating hub-and-spoke networks, causing more transfer passengers, so more services were made available for them in the airport; second, the use of information technology in the customer areas of the airport increased dramatically; and finally, the airline market became polarized through increased merger, takeover, and acquisition activity into global mega-airlines and local or regional feeder airlines. In addition, passengers have become increasingly aware of safety issues, a change that is due in part to the growing number of near collisions, what pilots and safety experts term "near midairs," that have occurred as some airlines have cut costs, including grouping flight departure and arrival slots from hub airports. Furthermore, passengers worry that lower fares will mean poorer maintenance. Running an airline in a deregulated market, especially in recessionary times, poses the question: "passenger safety vs. profits? … it's a question of consciousness."[10]

Deregulation and Design

Aviation is removing the barriers of distance and time which in the past partly isolated many lands from the rest of the world…. The airport planner must be creative and realistic in designing practical, useful, and economical landing facilities for aircraft in order to promote the welfare of society as a whole.[11]

According to airport architect Tony Gregson, the key problem facing all airports is the difficulty of moving greater numbers of people safely on and off aircraft that have been designed primarily to fly 550 mph at 35,000 feet.[12] The increased capacity of larger airplanes and grouped departures and arrivals have forced airlines to work with the airport authorities to handle as many as 400-500 passengers per flight and their "meeters and greeters," whose presence can increase the peak hour population of an airport by 62.5 percent. As airlines have appropriated space in airports around the world, they have had the opportunity to endorse and brand such products as tickets and their wallets, baggage ephemera (destination labels, address tags, and security tags), timetables, boarding cards, check-in and departure gate areas (including desks and backdrops), and staff uniforms, to name only a few. The means of delivering the message has changed but the principle has not. The solari board, for example, has been replaced by an electronic board or a bank of monitors, and advertising posters at the departure gate have been replaced by airport TV.

Prior to deregulation the airlines appeared to concentrate on using identity to build a permanent long-term image and a set of values with passengers and employees. Now, while these companies are becoming increasingly focused on satisfying their customers, they are also becoming multifaceted as they expand their route networks. Ironically, multifaceted may actually mean that the airline's image is more fragmented from a passenger's perspective; for instance, a passenger can book a ticket with British Airways, but find that he or she is flying with USAir, the outcome of the airlines' strategic alliance. Identity and values appear to have been exchanged for short-term competitive advantage. The airlines, however, need to express their identities and their values in the airport: to instruct passengers and build their confidence, and to differentiate themselves from their competitors (see fig. 6). An effectively implemented identity system will show passengers where to go and what to do inside the airport. Research has indicated that an astounding number of passengers have difficulty finding where to check in or how to get to the departure gate. Thus, the airlines need to create a feeling of confidence in passengers by expressing their corporate personalities and showing passen-

8 Button (note 6), p. 2.
9 See Sabine Cornelius and Wilhelm Pfähler, "The Liberalisation of Air Transport: Lessons from the USA," *Intereconomics* (July/Aug. 1993), pp. 183-87.
10 Jerome Lederer, *Aviation Safety Perspectives: Hindsight, Insight, Foresight* (New York, 1982).
11 Eddie Rickenbacker, foreword to Charles Froesch and Walther Prokosch, *Airport Planning* (New York, 1946), p. v.
12 Interview with T. Gregson in Reading, England, in July 1993.

gers that they are about to fly with an organized, reliable, safe, and "healthy" airline, one that warrants their trust. This image may be maintained by an airplane captain dressed in a formal uniform, by a departure gate that is kept clean and tidy, and by the use of information technology that increases the public's perception of the airline's efficiency. On the other hand, by exploiting personality, companies can move away from the bland sameness that is characterizing global airlines – the same structure, the same network, the same frequent flyer program. Virgin Atlantic Airways, for example, tries to give all passengers an ice cream during the in-flight movie and offers massage and other services to business and first-class passengers. Their lounge at London's Heathrow Airport now offers a four-hole putting green, a hydrotherapy bath, and a newly expanded bar and business center. Flexible identity systems help the airlines to communicate a consistent image during periods of rapid growth or dramatic change. Inconsistencies often undermine passenger confidence regarding safety, reliability, and technical efficiency, the criteria that customers often use in selecting their airline.

Airlines use graphic devices to appropriate space in the airport, endorsing areas such as the check-in counter, the departure gate, or the lounge to show passengers that they "own" the area. From a logistical perspective, designating a particular area for their customers also helps the airline to keep track of its passengers and thus be able to communicate with them at all times. Traditionally, most items in and around the airport have been endorsed, often with the master brand logotype (see fig. 7). Because the life span of the endorsed objects has been relatively short, from three months for a timetable to ten years for a curbside check-in sign (see fig. 8), this system should be flexible, allowing airlines to accommodate change and make cost-effective alterations as necessary. Deregulation and liberalization have encouraged the airlines to exploit identity devices as marketing tools. This function is clearly demonstrated by the current trend towards creating theme aircraft, such as Delta's Olympic sponsorship plane, the British Airways Christmas plane, or Qantas's aboriginal 747, as well as Western Pacific's advertisements for a Las Vegas casino and a television show (see Zukowsky, figs. 21 and 22; see also pls. 133-34), among others. These can work effectively, but they can also help to reinforce existing confusion regarding the relationship between the master brand and the sub-brands. For instance, a British Airways customer trav-

Fig. 7 Delta Air Lines aircraft hangar at Salt Lake City International Airport.

Fig. 8 Murphy/Jahn, architects. Curbside drop-off area at United Airlines Terminal, O'Hare International Airport, 1983-88.

eling from New York to Paris will come into contact with Club World, Club Europe, the Executive Club, the Club Lounge, and World Lounge, all subbrands of British Airways.

Airline companies, like many major corporations, must project their identity both internally and externally. Airlines, in particular, need a standardized but flexible identity system that can be used in all the airports they occupy. Implementing such a system in the deregulated market can be difficult because of cost pressures; in many cases, the less flexible the system, the cheaper it is to run. Rigid identity systems, however, can cause internal and external communication problems as procedures appear out of place away from the home airport. Few airlines, if any, have achieved this balance.

As individual airlines have increased their operation of hub-and-spoke networks, they have been encouraged to dominate hub airports (think of United Airlines, for example, at Chicago's O'Hare International Airport or Continental Airlines at Houston Intercontinental Airport). Their presence can then create a new problem relating to design control inside the airport: whether the landlord (the airport authority) or the tenant (the airline) should dictate design policy for signage in a terminal. The airline that dominates the arrival and departure slots at a particular airport is in an advantageous position to negotiate with the airport authority. British Airways at London's Heathrow and Delta Air Lines at Atlanta's Hartsfield International, for example, have developed some personalized furniture and fittings. British Airways, however, wanted to redesign the desks at Terminal 4 (their long-haul terminal) but BAA would not let them. In America some airlines have built new terminals, such as the Delta terminal at Cincinnati, but in Europe this process is only beginning. Currently BAA is seeking planning permission for a fifth terminal for Heathrow Airport, and British Airways has been involved in the initial design concept for the proposed terminal with the architect, Richard Rogers. New airport developments are rare, and only a few greenfield airports have been built in the last decade, most recently in Denver, Colorado, and Munich, Germany, and few are planned for the next decade. Increasingly, airlines will be trying to modify existing terminal structures rather than build new ones, as, for example, at the Sea-Tac International Airport in Seattle-Tacoma (see pl. 121). British Airways is trying to overcome this by flying larger aircraft on each flight; they plan to fly Boeing 757s on short-haul European routes. If an airline is unable to establish its own facilities, the company may try to attract customers by flying larger aircraft with fewer passengers, ensuring more space for each person. This spaciousness gives passengers a feeling of luxury and might influence them to choose that airline again.

When airlines have been involved in the building of new terminals, they have wanted to control the choice of fixtures, furnishings, colors, and materials, viewing this as an opportunity to reinforce their identity system. But the airport authority's interests lie in building a terminal that is dynamic and can meet changing needs. They have to plan for the possibility that another airline may occupy the terminal at some time in the future.[13] This clash of design cultures is motivated by different business concerns, and in resolving these differences, James Dunlap, operations manager at the former Stapleton International Airport in Denver, explains that the airport usually calculates the financial value of the airline based on landing fees and ground rent and then negotiates accordingly.

Since acquiring Western Airlines in December 1986, as well as many of the former Pan Am routes, Delta Air Lines has raised its profile as a global

13 Blow (note 3), p. 28.

Fig. 9 Gensler and Associates, architects. Interior view of Delta Air Lines Oasis Terminal at Los Angeles International Airport, c. 1988.

airline by increasing its presence at its hub airports. In 1988 the company built its Oasis Terminal at Los Angeles International Airport (LAX) to handle arrival and departure passengers, as well as transfer passengers. The architects of this Terminal, Gensler and Associates, designed a relaxing environment for both the businessperson and the family traveler, and the result has been quite successful. The terminal is characterized by palm trees, coffee bars, and, in certain areas, plenty of natural light (see fig. 9). Despite having built its own terminal, Delta still has to use the standard LAX gate signage system and typeface, which constantly remind visitors that they are in a standardized airport.

Building passenger loyalty has been an essential part of the airline business, and it is especially important in the deregulated market in countering price initiatives and in capturing the lucrative business market. In response, the airlines have developed complex loyalty schemes called frequent flyer programs, following the lead of American Airlines, which initiated theirs in 1981. Inside the airport, the loyal frequent flyer is entitled to a series of benefits, such as lounge facilities, priority check-in, priority stand-by, last-minute check-in, and a more personalized relationship with the airline. With some airlines, benefits include limousine pick-up from home or office, telephone check-in, and automatic upgrade. The frequent flyer programs also present a unique opportunity for the airlines to communicate directly with customers in their home or office environments, and to give something back to the customer. One drawback for business travelers who fly frequently, of course, is that the opportunity to enjoy an additional flight, even a free one, may have little appeal. The airlines have responded to this by developing other redemption schemes for miles accrued, including transferable miles, free car rental, free restaurant meals, or "miles for charity." The frequent flyer program has also helped some airlines to identify and separate occasional consumers from consistent customers. In the business travel market, however, the traveler often does not book his or her own travel. As a result, British Airways operates the Executive Secretary program, which enables members to qualify for air miles that can be redeemed for free flights, in order to build loyalty among travel organizers as part of the airline's Executive Club Frequent Flyer Scheme.

Deregulation has reduced the number of direct flights in the United States, and liberalization will do the same in Europe. The minimum transfer time between flights is forty minutes, and total journey times, on average, have doubled. According to some critics, American air travel is now characterized by "long indirect routing...hellish delays, long gate-to-gate hikes, luggage foulups, and missed connections"; as a result, the airlines have to entertain their transfer passengers.[14] In anticipation, British Airways is trying to meet some of the needs of its long-haul transfer passengers by providing dedicated

14 J. Grimwade, "The Art of Hubbing," *Traveler* (1988), p. 107.
15 Tom Mitchell, "Product as Illusion," in John Thackara, ed., *Design After Modernism: Beyond the Object* (New York, 1988), pp. 208-15.
16 SampsonTyrrell (note 5), p. 27.
17 Pan Am started flying as a mail operator in 1927: its first contract from the United States Mail Service was the route identified as FAM4.
18 R. E. G. Davies, *Pan Am: An Airline and Its Aircraft* (New York, 1987).
19 See "Pan American Expresses a New Personality for a New Kind of Travel," *Industrial Design* (March 1959), pp. 30-41. See also Franco Maria Ricci and Corinna Ferrari, *Top Symbols and Trademarks of the World* (Milan, 1973).
20 Gunn Associated was selected because their employee, David Lyotte, had worked with James Montgomery (then at Pan Am) at Dicker Raymond. Other information was gathered from a telephone interview with B. Kimura in Jan. 1994.
21 Teague Associates was selected since they had worked with Pan Am and Boeing on the development of the 747, as well as the earlier 707. See Barbara Sturken Peterson and James Glab, *Rapid Descent: Deregulation and the Shakeout in the Airlines* (New York, 1994), for an excellent analysis of Pan Am's demise.

lounges, such as the Oasis lounge in Terminal 4 at Heathrow, where passengers can sleep, or eat, or even pray, although this service is currently available only to Club World and first-class passengers. As Tom Mitchell argues in his essay "Product as Illusion," the design process shifts in relation to the "scientific" approach to products and services.[15] Prior to deregulation and liberalization, air travel was measured in empirical terms: safety, reliability, or technical efficiency. By the mid-1980s in America and the late 1980s in the UK (mainly after the privatization of British Airways), the airlines had undergone a gradual change that still continues; design was being used to promote the human aspects of flying, which have become the new measurement criteria. This cultural shift is evident in the airport with the emergence of new relationships and sub-branded products, such as shuttle services, computerized information boards, lounges, and moving walkways; all are features designed to help people understand the process and all are opportunities for the airlines to express their personalities.

Case Studies of Airline Design

Pan Am and British Airways represent two approaches to the use of design in the airport. In addition, they serve as examples of how two global airlines reacted to the changes that took place in their respective markets. It is important to remember that "A new identity never starts with a blank sheet of paper. It takes as its raw material the strengths of the company, existing associations, competitive positioning, probable uses and applications and the needs and perceptions of target audiences."[16]

An analysis of Pan Am, which was incorporated as Pan American Airways (PAA) on March 14, 1927, would not be complete without mentioning Juan Trippe, Pan Am's president for over twenty years until his retirement in 1968.[17] Responsible for driving Pan Am "almost single handedly" and credited with having had a forward vision and strong leadership skills, Trippe, unfortunately, failed to train a successor with similar abilities, and the airline subsequently went into a decline that ended in its demise.[18] In 1955, when the airline was still highly profitable, Edward Barnes was hired to redesign Pan Am's corporate identity. Initially, Barnes was commissioned to update the company's image to coincide with its introduction of new jet planes, the Boeing 707 and the DC-8. Barnes, however, believed that a complete overhaul of the identity was required and he brought in architect/designer Charles Forberg to assist him and his firm. The Barnes design firm redrew the airline's traditional symbol, a globe with wings (fig. 10), discarding the wings and superimposing a simplified map grid on the globe. This image is still recognized as the modern Pan American icon (see pl. 81).[19] The firm also shortened the Pan American name to Pan Am, modernized the typeface by returning it to a non-italicized, bold semi-serif, and changed the original navy blue to "Pan Am sky blue." All these graphic elements were displayed on a white aircraft (fig. 11). In 1973 the airline hired Gunn Associated to "modernize and soften the [Pan Am] image," which included redrawing the globe symbol and the word mark (fig. 12).[20] Pan Am then selected Teague Associates of New York to oversee the implementation of the new identity across a variety of applications.[21]

As the Pan Am management changed, so did the use of marketing companies. Identity work, it appears, was split up among a variety of advertising,

Fig. 10 Interior view of a Boeing 307 *Stratoliner*, showing corporate symbol for Pan American Airways, c. 1939.

design, and marketing firms, including their own in-house design department. The airline used design firms primarily to "maintain the identity of the airline company, rather than to create a new identity or image."[22] Deregulation forced Pan Am to compete in new markets, and it purchased National Airlines to provide a domestic connection for its international business.[23] But, unable to resurrect itself throughout the 1980s, the company recorded year upon year of loss. The year before Pan Am shut its doors, *The Economist* lamented, "Poor Pan Am. Once it was flying proud among the world's greatest airlines; now it is fluttering along, wondering where and how it will come to earth.... But few of Pan Am's problems are unique."[24]

Pan Am commissioned a new livery to communicate the internal changes that took place in the early 1980s, using the new identity to attempt a relaunch of the airline in 1983-84, after nearly fifteen years of financial problems. The new identity, probably designed in-house, centered on turning the Pan Am word mark into a supergraphic that was hung on a white fuselage, with the tailfin supporting the globe symbol (fig. 13). This further recycling of Barnes and Forberg's original design was beginning to look like a hackneyed scheme.[25] The new identity was used on the Berlin route before implementation throughout the system on a worldwide basis.

Pan Am's primary color palette incorporated two colors, blue and white, from the launch of their jet services, although the navy blue was changed to sky blue, and these colors dominated their identity system. The aircraft were characterized by a distinctive "Pan Am blue" line running the length of the

Fig. 11 Edward Larrabee Barnes with Charles Forberg, designers. Pan American Airways corporate identity, including new corporate symbol and typography; shown on a model of a Boeing 707, c. 1955.

Fig. 12 Gunn Associated, designers. Pan American Airways corporate identity, including revised corporate symbol and typography; shown on a Boeing 747, c. 1973.

22 Kimura (note 20).
23 In August 1978, under the leadership of William Seawell, Pan Am applied to the CAB to formalize their relationship with National Airlines, and after sixteen months of litigation, Pan Am gained control of National. Pan Am paid a high price for National and acquired technologically incompatible aircraft, which in the long term caused them great harm. See Peterson and Glab (note 21).
24 *The Economist* (Oct. 27, 1990).
25 David Lyotte of Gunn Associated has said that he thinks the 1983 redesign lacked a visual focus owing to its overall unprofessional appearance. He has also noted that the scheme lacked a clear visual hierarchy, which caused some customer confusion; telephone interview, January 1994.

Fig. 13 Pan American Airways corporate design department. Revised Pan American Airways corporate identity and typography as a supergraphic; shown on an Airbus A 310-222, c. 1983-85.

26 SampsonTyrrell (note 5), p. 17.

27 BOAC's identity was designed by Karl
    Gerstner of London and BEA's was
    designed by Henrion, Ludlow and
    Schmidt of London.

28 "Speedbird" is British Airways' callsign.
    The appointment of Landor to redesign
    British Airways aroused some surprise in
    the design community because the airline
    had publicized their hiring of a British
    advertising agency and then appointed an
    American design firm. Landor Associates
    has explained their intentions in using
    the identity symbols and their vision for
    the new BA identity in a 1993 pamphlet.

fuselage, and inside the airport the company used blue and white for fixtures and fittings, and brown and gray for furniture and uniforms. Two symbols represented the airline: the Pan Am globe and the Pan Am word mark – and two main typefaces were employed: one for the Pan Am word mark, the other for branded products such as Clipper Class. The company adopted an evolutionary approach to identity, developing it to the point of abstraction so that the redesigns of its corporate identity were purely rearrangements of the core visual assets. As a result, Pan Am appeared to neglect the overall impact of its identity. "Sometimes circumstances are so changed that a company is no longer adequately represented by its existing identifier. Perhaps it has changed direction, or grown by merger or acquisition; or perhaps insufficient attention has been paid to communication over the years. Then more radical solutions are appropriate."[26] Clearly, airlines have to make adjustments to their corporate identities as changes occur in management, company goals, and competition. In addition to the example of Pan Am, United and American are two airlines that have carefully redesigned their images in an evolutionary way to represent them better during their years of operation. Both companies realized the need for sleeker, more modern, and more marketable images, and their logos reflect the move toward a simplified graphic design that is highly recognizable and immediately associated with each company (see figs. 14-16).

A review of British Airways' corporate identity provides insight into the transformation of that company's image. British Airways was established in 1973 after the merger of British Overseas Airways Corporation (BOAC) and British European Airways (BEA).[27] The original identity, designed by Negus and Negus, was reinterpreted by Landor Associates in 1983-86 and launched as the current identity (see pls. 151-54). Landor's identity employs many of the same elements as its predecessor, including the stylized Union Jack on the tailfin, the clear dark/light separation of the fuselage, the word mark position, the use of a wing symbol (Negus and Negus had used BOAC's speedbird), and similar colors (see figs. 1, 2, and 17). In rising to the challenge to express British Airways' marketing promise to be "The World's Favourite Airline," Landor's solution was to create "a totally integrated design system which unifies the branding of British Airways, from baggage tags to the aircrafts themselves.... The design solution represents a change from the past for the airline, while maintaining pride in its origin."[28]

Fig. 14 Zay Smith, Raymond Loewy, and Saul Bass, designers, clockwise from upper left. Evolution of the United Airlines corporate symbol, c. 1941, c. 1959, and c. 1978.

Figs. 15 and 16 Corporate symbol for American Airlines, c. 1940, and the redesign undertaken by Henry Dreyfuss in 1971 as shown on a Boeing 767.

Fig. 17 Landor Associates, designers. Design presentation for British Airways corporate identity program, c. 1983-86.

The British Airways identity uses four primary colors – pearl gray, speedwing red, midnight blue, and silver – as well as several secondary colors. The primary colors present some problems in the design; the red is prone to fading, the blue is very formal and so dark in certain weather conditions that it seems almost sinister, and the gray can appear dull. The silver is used mainly for the coat of arms on the tailfin and for special highlighting or detailing throughout the system, such as on the *Concorde* motif on menus and other items; it can leave a weak overall impression. The airline uses two symbols in its identity, the wing and the coat of arms. The red speedwing, which arguably represents precision and technical innovation, has had implementation problems because it forms a directional arrow pointing to the right, sometimes causing confusion among passengers in the airport. The coat of arms, which was specially drawn for the airline by the College of Heraldry, incorporates the company's slogan "to fly to serve" and has provided the airline with a different, distinguished, very British element. It is used as a quality endorsement device to varying degrees of success. Several typefaces are used in the British Airways identity: Bembo for general corporate applications; Optima for department names; Univers for signage and information graphics; and what has been termed their "Special Alphabet" for the word mark, which Landor designed to express quality and traditional values. The word mark has been used as a stacked and as a linear logotype.

But the airline's identity suffers from certain distinct problems, especially in the face of the impending European liberalization. The tailfin, for example, an integral part of any airline identity, lacks focus and promotes a British imperialistic view of the world. In 1996, with the identity now over ten years old, it is evident that the system is most successful in relation to ground vehicles (see fig. 2); it clearly suffers inside the airport. British Airways has implemented its identity throughout the airport in so many different ways that it has weakened the value of the master brand, although the airline has been undeniably successful at utilizing strategic communications (rather than the concept of identity) both inside and outside the airport. British Airways has been relatively successful at building the personality of a major global player even though it is only the sixth largest airline in the world.[29]

The Future of Airline Identity

Several major issues are emerging that now confront the airlines and the way they use identity inside the airport. These include the changing competitive structure of the market, which brings increased competition and market segmentation; the future organization of the airport to cope with rising numbers of transfer passengers and changing airline types; and questions regarding the future of national identity and personality. Increased competition among the airlines has been translated into pricing strategies; competitive pricing has democratized air travel and consequently removed some of its excitement, and this trend will probably continue. As a result, airlines offering shorter flights face increased competition from other modes of transport, such as high-speed trains, especially in Europe. As the overall system is fragmented to meet the needs of individual market segments, so airline identity is becoming more fragmented to meet the new needs of the market. In this scenario, the core often gets ignored, and both internal and external communication breaks down. Fragmentation will further weaken identity because most airlines will not have enough financial and physical resources to support each brand sufficiently. British Airways' regional company British Airways Express, for example, often appears to be misunderstood by the average traveler.

In order to reap the economic benefit of having global hub-and-spoke networks, airlines will operate fewer direct flights, causing greater numbers of transfer passengers, who will need to be catered for in a more interesting way than just leaving them in a lounge for several hours. Regional airlines will feed customers into and out of global hubs and they will be linked to the global airlines through complex strategic alliances or ownership.[30] The regional airlines will take the planes to the people by utilizing local and regional airports, and they will use corporate identities that are understood locally and will hook into a global network through code sharing – two airlines using a single flight number to market a through service. For example, a passenger who travels on British Airways flight BA199 from London to Kansas City would fly from London's Gatwick Airport to Pittsburgh on British Airways and from Pittsburgh to Kansas City on USAir, but the ticket would list only London to Kansas City on British Airways.

Three types of regional airline will emerge: the cut-price, no-frills airline, which will offer a method of getting from point a to point b, especially on short direct flights; the full-service regional airline, which will provide full service on every flight; and the local airline, which will add a local flavor to the travel experience. An example of the first type of airline is Southwest Airlines, which uses identity in a nontraditional way. Its employees, for example, do not wear formal uniforms but informal ones like tan shorts and pullover shirts, and the airline does not provide food on any flights. Instead it uses the aircraft as a tool to create personality. The second type of airline could be represented by Comair. These airlines will build smaller versions of the global airlines, with similar operational and human structures. In the longer term, they may operate second division hub-and-spoke networks. The third type of company, the local carrier, will be a low-cost airline that offers limited service, and is independent, thus being able to offer its own flavor and character of service.

The airlines will also have to address the role of their national identities if they are to become truly local or global; could British Airways or Air France

29 Saatchi and Saatchi were British Airways' advertising agents until early 1995, when the airline moved the account to M&C Saatchi. See *Airline Business* (Sept. 1994). British Airways carried 30.6 million passengers from mid-1993 to mid-1994.

30 These alliances will probably be similar to the relationship between British Airways and USAir or Qantas. British Airways owns approximately 25 percent of each company.

become truly global (beyond being just international), or would their names hold them back? All the airlines will need to differentiate themselves in ways other than merely by price or service. Expressing personality will probably be the most cost effective and appropriate vehicle to do this, first because it is impossible for one company to copy another's personality, and second, because developing personality leaves a company flexible enough to grow and embrace its future needs. As Clive Barton wrote in a recent issue of *Airline Business*: "These, then, are the new realities of the airline industry ... not a decade from now, but today. The forces above are already at work, and the reconfiguration of activities ... is already underway. The time for choice is at hand."[31] Identity can be used to address these issues and to develop both physical and visual solutions to counter these problems while building company personality. Few, if any, airlines are successfully addressing all of these issues at present, although some carriers are addressing individual aspects.

It is clear that deregulation has directly affected the way American airlines present their corporate identities and the way the airport authorities behave; it is equally clear that economic liberalization will affect European airlines and airports similarly. In the short term, these economic policies have altered the use of airports by the airlines and passengers, and in the long term, they will dramatically affect the structure and organization of the airline/airport relationship. The short-term effect of deregulation in America was the prolific expansion of the number of airlines operating in an airport, a frenzy of price wars, and increased merger, acquisition, and take-over activity. These factors have forced the larger airlines to reconsider their identity programs and the methods they use to present themselves in the airport. United was redesigned by CKS Partners in 1994 to make the airline look more "global" (see pl. 161); Northwest was redesigned in 1983 by Landor Associates and the airline is at present reviewing its identity; Delta is currently being redesigned by Landor.

The impact of liberalization on the European air travel market is more difficult to assess, although it is already apparent that several major European airlines are gearing up for the changes. British Airways has built a hub at Heathrow, created British Airways Express and a complicated frequent flyer scheme, and formed alliances with airlines such as Qantas, USAir, Deutsche BA, TAT (Transport Aérien Transrégional), and, now, American to allow code sharing.[32] These factors indicate that the company is planning to operate in a liberalized market. Germany's Lufthansa and Holland's KLM have carried out similar activities. These three airlines have all moved away from being seen as national flag carriers, arguably in anticipation of impending liberalization. The airport authorities are also marketing themselves to meet future needs, following the American pattern. In London, the planning inquiry that is being conducted to establish the need for a fifth terminal at Heathrow has raised debate in the national press regarding the impact of the airport on the environment, the economy, and the country's future air travel needs. Amsterdam's Schiphol Airport is promoting itself as an integrated transport center with leisure facilities for the transfer passenger, and Frankfurt's Rhein-Main International Airport and Paris's Charles de Gaulle and Orly airports are promoting themselves as Euro hubs. These activities seem to point to a future in which airports are devoid of national identification; if a new terminal at Heathrow is not built, would British Airways, which is intended to occupy the new building, move to Paris's Charles de Gaulle Airport or another airport in order to obtain the facilities they need?

31 See Clive Barton in *Airline Business* (May 1995) on the future shape of airline networks. Barton identifies three types of network: Network managers who will "orchestrate airline traffic and take ultimate responsibility, both financially and operationally, for business with the customer"; capacity providers who will be "non-core flight operation providers – different organisations with differing capabilities for performing specific tasks.... for example, feeder/commuter carriers flying to a network manager"; and service providers who will provide "non-core functions, from cleaning to technical maintenance of a fleet."
32 British Airways also has alliances with Brymon, Manx, LoganAir, Maersk, GB Airways, and Citiflyer Express.

In general terms, deregulation has changed the role of design. Instead of using it to create an identity, airlines view it as providing a platform for cost-effective marketing initiatives. The creation of hub-and-spoke networks has increased the airlines' long-term involvement with their hub airports. Terminals built expressly for certain carriers have provided new but costly opportunities for these companies to subtly express their corporate personalities in the architectural space and detail of the airport rather than through short-term temporary objects. Delta Air Lines has done this at Los Angeles International Airport with its Oasis Terminal, but obviously this cannot be done in every airport by every airline. Identity is becoming the short-term solution; perhaps personality will become the long-term solution?

The new competitive structures of the American and European air travel markets have changed the needs that design programs must meet. There has been a shift from simply branding the aircraft and a few airline objects towards forming an identity that will work as an endorsement device flexible enough to cope with the variety of static and mobile applications in the airport; one that can be personal, intimate, and interesting for the frequent traveler but that communicates effectively to the financial world; and finally an identity that represents the core values of the airline to allow it to achieve real differentiation from the competition and yet is flexible enough to cope with brand cooperation.

Deregulation in America and liberalization in Europe have forced the airlines to reappraise their commercial situations. Maintaining and updating a corporate identity may seem expensive, but in relation to its potential return it can be cost effective. In fact, design at the airport can be used to build an identity with a visual personality to reinforce an airline's key values. The new shape of the market encourages the intangible aspects of identity to be expressed – heritage, personality, and integrity. These will undoubtedly affect the long-term success of airline identity and possibly many airlines themselves.

Appendix: Airports, Aircraft, and Related Items Represented in the Exhibition

The installation of the exhibition that this book accompanied, creatively designed by architect Helmut Jahn and constructed by Gene Young Effects, was intended to suggest an aircraft under construction and was to act as a time-tunnel through which the history of commercial aviation over the past seventy years and more would be presented. To assemble the materials presented in this exhibition, we solicited participation from over 100 airports around the world, drawing on the listing of facilities published in the annual *Airport Technology International*. The managers and directors of many of these airports responded positively to our request, and these sites have been included in the exhibition. Unfortunately, other facilities, such as Moscow's original airport buildings of 1930, exist as part of military complexes and remain inaccessible. The majority of these airports are American examples, though we have incorporated a wide range of works

around the world, noting that their inclusion, as the inclusion of all items here, is the result of the generosity and cooperation of airport authorities, architects, designers, and aircraft manufacturers.

We concentrated in this exhibition on the many realized examples of architecture and design for commercial aviation, as opposed to general aviation or utopian projects, neither having had much direct impact on the actual spaces and structures of commercial aviation. Although museums and libraries hold some of the original items that we were able to display in the exhibition, the bulk of the materials came from the offices of airports, architects, and industrial designers or from aircraft manufacturers. We discovered that only a few manufacturers have been in continuous business over a long period of time, but we were able to include a generous amount of material from their corporate archives. It actually proved to

be more difficult to secure the cooperation of some airlines, as well as many other aircraft manufacturers, who because of either firm mergers and buy-outs or a shift from commercial to military products were unable or unwilling to open their archives to us.

What follows is a two-part listing of sites and subjects, in general chronological order, that were included in the exhibition with the status of older facilities indicated when known. Most of the historic items shown in the exhibition were photographic images. It is rare for exhibitable items – striking original models or drawings of these subjects – to have survived from the 1920s through the 1960s. Very recent projects, most not yet completed, were represented in the second part of the exhibition principally by original drawings and models.

Airports, Related Facilities, and Airliners, 1915–95

Attributed to Peter Behrens, architect. AEG factory, Hennigsdorf near Berlin, 1915-16 (now demolished?).

Eugene Freyssinet, engineer. Airship hangar, Orly Airport, 1916-22 (now demolished).

Otto Firle, designer. Design for the corporate logo of Lufthansa Airlines (originally Deutsche Luft-Reederei), 1918.

Hanns Hopp, architect. Airport in Königsberg (now Kaliningrad, Russia), 1921-22 (now demolished).

City Architect Ahlhorn. Airport at Frankfurt-Rebstock, 1924-25 (now demolished).

Paul and Klaus Engler, architects. Tempelhof Airport, Berlin, 1926-29, with hangar additions by Heinrich Kosina (now demolished).

Albert Kahn, architect. Ford Airport, Dearborn, Michigan, 1927 (now partly demolished and altered).

William Mayo, chief engineer. Ford Tri-Motor, 1926-31.

Claire Egtvedt (and later Charles Monteith), chief engineer and designer. Boeing Model 80/80A, 1928.

Henry L. Gogerty, architect. Grand Central Terminal, Glendale, California, 1928 (now slightly altered).

Holden, Stott and Hutchinson, architects. Washington Airport, Washington, D.C., 1930 (now demolished).

Fritz Schumacher. Lufthansa hangar, Hamburg, 1927 (one of two; one now demolished, the other extant but altered).

Dyrssen and Averhoff, architects. Fuhlsbüttel Airport, Hamburg, 1928-29 (now altered; scheduled for demolition 1996-97).

Paul Thiersch, architect. Terminal and hangar for Halle-Leipzig Airport, at Schkeuditz, 1927, with restaurant pavilion by Hans Wittwer, 1929 (now demolished).

Behrendt and Knipping, architects. Airport in Breslau (now Wrocław, Poland), 1928 (now greatly altered; tower now demolished).

Architects of the Air Ministry. Croydon Airport near London, 1926-28 (now altered).

Army Engineers, architects; with additions by Van Riel and Jansenns. Brussels Evere Airport, 1929, with 1932 addition (now demolished?).

Indianapolis Municipal Airport, 1931.

Mitsubishi L3Y "Nippon" at Chicago, 1939.

J. Jasinski, architect. Antwerp Airport, c. 1929-30 (now demolished?).

Franz and Franzius, architects. Airport in Dortmund, c. 1927-29.

Herman Kregelius, architect. Hopkins Air Terminal, Cleveland, 1929 (now demolished).

Dirk Roosenburg, architect. Terminal and hangar, Schiphol Airport, Amsterdam, 1929, with later additions (now demolished).

Attributed to Dirk Roosenburg, architect. Fokker factory, Amsterdam, 1929 (now demolished?).

Dirk Roosenburg, architect. Twente Airport near Enschede, The Netherlands, c. 1929-30 (now demolished?).

Charles A. Smith, architect; with Ernest Herminghaus, landscape architect. Fairfax Airport, Kansas City, Kansas, 1929 (now altered).

Gable and Wyant, architects. Curtiss-Wright Depot Hangar No. 1, Mines Field, now the site of the cargo office of Los Angeles International Airport, 1929.

The Austin Company, architects. United Airport, Burbank, California, 1930 (now altered).

McGuire and Shook, architects. Indianapolis Municipal Airport, 1931 (now demolished).

Luis Gutiérrez Soto, architect. Barajas Airport, Madrid, 1929-31 (now greatly altered).

Karl Johann Mossner, architect. Hangar, 1929, and terminal of Munich Airport, Munich-Oberwiesenfeld, 1931 (now demolished).

Paul Gerhardt, Jr., architect. Chicago Municipal Airport, 1931-32 (now demolished).

Charles Monteith, chief engineer and designer. Boeing 247, 1933.

Marcelo and Milton Roberto, architects. Terminal for Santos-Dumont Airport, Rio de Janiero, 1933-38 (altered), with Pan American Airways Terminal of 1937, attributed to Delano and Aldrich, and Seaplane Station by Attilio Gorrea Lima, 1940.

Norman Bel Geddes, designer. Interiors of the Pan American Airways Martin M130 *China Clipper*, 1934-35.

Delano and Aldrich, architects. International Air Terminal and views of the Dinner Key Seaplane Base, Miami, 1934 (now the Miami City Hall), with the station designed by Delano and Aldrich, c. 1928 (now demolished).

Oliver P. Bernard, architect. Block D and Block J of Supermarine Aviation Works, Southampton, c. 1935-36 (now demolished).

Herbert Rimpl, architect. Heinkel factory for Heinkel 111 aircraft, Oranienburg, near Berlin, 1935 (now demolished).

Paul Hedquist, architect. Stockholm-Bromma Airport, 1935-36 (terminal rebuilt 1948-49).

Seibert Company, architects. Views of the Zeppelin hangar, Rhein-Main Airport, Frankfurt am Main, 1938 (now demolished).

Frankfurt City Architect. Terminal of Rhein-Main Airport, Frankfurt am Main, 1936 (now demolished).

Cäsar Pinnau for Fritz August Breuhaus de Groot, designer. Interiors of the LZ129 airship *Hindenburg*, 1931-35.

J. M. Wilson and H. C. Mason, architects. Al Basra Airport, Iraq, 1937-38 (now demolished?).

Arthur E. Raymond, designer. Douglas DC-3, 1936.

Kyunojyo Ozawa, designer. Mitsubishi MC-20, 1937-39.

Sueo Honjo, Tomio Kubo, and Nobuhiko Kuiabake, designers. Mitsubishi L3Y (G3M2), 1934-37.

Hoar, Marlow and Lovett, architects. Gatwick Airport, near London, 1936 (now slightly altered).

R. T. Russell and A. G. Wyatt, architects. Willingdon Airport (now Safdarjung Airport), New Delhi, c. 1936 (extant).

Norman and Dawbarn, architects. Jersey Airport, 1937 (now slightly altered).

Adolf Benš, architect. Original terminal of the Prague-Ruzyne Airport, 1933-37 (now slightly altered).

Virgil Borbiró and Lásaló Klárik, architects. Terminal at Budaörs Airport, Budapest, 1937 (now slightly altered).

Georges Labro, architect. Terminal at Le Bourget Airport, Paris, 1936-37 (now slightly altered).

Mehrtens, Mewes, Albert and Bartsch, architects. Butzweiler Hof Airport, Cologne, 1933-36 (now slightly altered).

Ernst Sagebiel, architect. Tempelhof Airport, Berlin, 1936-39 (now slightly altered).

Kurt Tank, chief designer. Focke-Wulf FW 200 *Condor*, 1937-38.

Ernst Sagebiel, architect. Airport, Munich-Riem, 1937-39 (now altered).

Erich zu Putlitz, architect. Blohm and Voss flying boat factory, Hamburg-Finkenwerder, 1939 (now altered; Daimler-Benz Aerospace Airbus).

Richard Vogt, chief engineer. Blohm and Voss BV222 *Viking*, 1937-38.

Gianluigi Giordani, architect. Milan-Linate Airport, 1935-37 (greatly altered later by Vittorio Gandolfi, 1958-63).

Pan American Airways Terminal, Rio de Janiero, 1937.

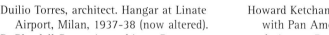

Milan-Linate Airport, 1935-37.

Mexico City Airport, c. 1940.

Duilio Torres, architect. Hangar at Linate Airport, Milan, 1937-38 (now altered).

D. Pleydell-Bouverie, architect. Ramsgate Municipal Airport, 1937 (now demolished).

Albert D. Jenkins, land steward and surveyor, Corporation of Liverpool. Liverpool Airport, terminal, and west hangar at Speke, 1937-38 (now slightly altered).

H. G. Chipier, architect. San Francisco Airport, 1937 (now demolished).

Albert Kahn, architect. United Airlines Administration Building, 5959 South Cicero Avenue, Midway Airport, Chicago, 1938 (now demolished).

Dag Englund and V. Rosendal, architects. Helsinki Airport, 1938 (now demolished?).

Norman and Dawbarn, architects. Elmdon Airport, Birmingham, 1938-39.

Delano and Aldrich, architects. LaGuardia Airport and Marine Air Terminal, New York, 1937-39 (original main terminal now demolished and replaced; the remainder later altered).

Edward Wells, designer. Boeing 307 *Stratoliner* with interiors designed by Raymond Loewy for TWA (the Pan American Airways variant was designed by Howard Ketcham), 1938-39.

Howard Ketcham, interior design advisor, with Pan American Airways staff designers. Boeing 314, 1937-39.

Vilhelm Lauritzen, architect. Terminal at Kastrup Airport, Copenhagen, 1939.

Ernest H. Blumenthal, city architect. Albuquerque Municipal Airport, New Mexico, 1939 (now altered; currently Albuquerque Junior League).

Pier Luigi Nervi, architect. Aircraft hangar, Orvieto, Italy, 1935 (now demolished).

Joseph Finger, architect. Houston Municipal Airport, now a part of Houston Hobby Airport, c. 1939-40.

Fernando Puga, architect. Mexico City Airport, c. 1940 (now demolished).

Howard Lovewell Cheney and Charles M. Goodman, architects. Washington National Airport, Washington, D.C., 1941.

Desmond Fitzgerald, architect. Dublin International Airport, 1939-41.

Attributed to John Schofield, builder. Terminal at Dorval Airport, Montreal, 1941 (now altered).

Anton Tedesko of Roberts and Schaefer, engineers, with Joe H. Lapish, associate architect. Seaplane hangars, North Island Naval Air Station, c. 1940-41.

The Austin Company, architects. Boeing Plant 2 on East Marginal Way, Seattle,

1939, and with camouflage, 1942 (now altered).

Albert Kahn, architect. Ford plant for the construction of B-24 bombers, now part of General Motors, Willow Run, Michigan, near Detroit, 1942.

Dames and Moore, engineers. Airship hangars at Tustin Marine Corps Helicopter Air Station, Santa Ana, California, 1942.

The Austin Company, architect. Douglas Aircraft plant, now the site of O'Hare International Airport, Chicago, 1943 (now largely demolished).

Keil do Amaral, architect. Lisbon International Airport, 1942-43 (now greatly altered).

Charles M. Goodman, architect. International Air Terminal for the Air Transport Command, in Washington, D.C., c. 1943-44 (now demolished).

Henry Dreyfuss, designer. Proposed conversion of a Consolidated B-24 bomber into an airliner, 1944.

Daniel Brenner, architect. Concert Hall Project, 1946, based on Albert Kahn's Martin Aircraft factory, 1937.

Paul Gerhardt, Jr., architect. Municipal Airport, later Midway Airport, Chicago, 1945-47 (now altered).

Skidmore, Owings and Merrill, architects. TWA ticket office, Chicago, 1947 (now demolished).

Aymar Embury II, architect, with Ammann and Whitney, engineers. Hangars at Midway Airport, 5035 West 55th Street, Chicago, 1948.

The Austin Company, architects. United Airlines maintenance facility, Mills Field, near San Francisco, California, 1948 (now altered).

Port of Seattle, architects. Seattle-Tacoma Airport, 1947-49 (now greatly altered, with additions by TRA Associates).

Walter Dorwin Teague, designer. Interior of the Boeing 377 *Stratocruiser*, 1946-49.

E. Gilbert Mason, designer. Interiors of the Douglas DC-6, c. 1947.

Roy Worden, architect, with Vincent Fagan, associated architect, and Frank Montana,

Dublin International Airport, 1939–41 (photo c. 1960).

consultant. Bendix Field, St. Joseph's
County Airport, South Bend, Indiana, 1949
(now demolished).

Eric Ross, architect. Bristol Aeroplane
Company factory and BOAC maintenance
center, Filton, England, 1946-49 (now
altered).

Clive Pascall and Peter Watson, architects.
Transair hangar, Gatwick Airport, c. 1950
(status unknown).

Directorate of Civil Aviation, architects. Don
Muang Airport, later Bangkok International Airport, Thailand, 1948-52, with
additions 1970.

Clarence "Kelly" Johnson, designer, and
Henry Dreyfuss, interior designer.
Lockheed *Super Constellation*, 1951.

Alfred and Heinrich Oeschger, architects.
Zurich International Airport, 1946-53
(now altered).

Frederick Gibberd and Partners, architects.
Heathrow International Airport, London,
begun 1947, with Terminal 2 (1955,
remodeled 1975 by Pascall and Watson
with Murdoch Design Associates) and later
additions of Terminals 1 (1968), 3 (1970),
and 4 (1986).

W. S. Kennedy, director of civil aviation, and
J. S. Colman, chief of civil engineering.
Salisbury Airport, Rhodesia (now Harare
Airport, Zimbabwe), 1952-56.

John Messmer, architect. General Mitchell
Field, Milwaukee, 1955 (now demolished).

José Luis Servet, chief engineer for the
airport, and Cayetano de Cabanyes, with
Alfredo Vegas, Antonio Matilla, and
engineer Pablo Lehoz, architects. New
Terminal (now National Terminal), Barajas
Airport, Madrid, 1954-65.

Rambald von Steinbüchel. Standard design
for a Lufthansa ticket office, first used in
Düsseldorf, 1955 (now demolished).

Outcalf, Guenther and Associates, architects.
Hopkins Air Terminal, Cleveland, 1956
(now altered).

Barajas Airport, Madrid, 1954-65.

Aeroproekt, architects; Ivan Zholtovsky and
Lev Rudnev, consultants to Aeroproekt.
Khabarovsk Airport, Russia, 1956.

Aeroproekt, architects; Ivan Zholtovsky and
Lev Rudnev, consultants to Aeroproekt.
Minsk Airport, Russia, 1950-56.

Augusto H. Alvarez, architect, with Carral
Icaza, Martinez Paez, Flores Villasenor,
and Peres Olagaray, architects. Mexico
City Airport, 1949-55 (now altered).

Skidmore, Owings and Merrill, architects.
International Arrivals Building, John F.
Kennedy International Airport, New York,
1957.

Ammann and Whitney, architects. Pan
American Airways hangar, John F.
Kennedy International Airport, New York,
1957-58.

George R. Edwards, chief designer. Vickers
Viscount, 1948-53, with interiors for the
North American market by Charles Butler,
1955.

E. Gilbert Mason and Henry Dreyfuss of
Henry Dreyfuss Designers. Interiors of the
Lockheed L-188 *Electra*, 1957.

Gerrit Rietveld, designer. Interior of the
Fokker F-27 *Friendship*, 1957.

Charles Butler Associates, designers. Interiors
of the Vickers *Vanguard* for Trans Canada
Airlines, 1957-60.

Walter Dorwin Teague, designer. Interiors of
the Boeing 707 mockup and Boeing 707
airliner, 1954-58. The Pan American
interiors were styled by Edward Larrabee
Barnes and Charles Forberg, with Jack
Lenor Larsen.

Tippetts-Abbett-McCarthy-Stratton, architects; Ives, Turano and Gardner associated
architects. Pan American World Airways
Terminal, John F. Kennedy International
Airport, New York, 1960 (renovated 1973;
currently the terminal for Delta Air Lines).

Skidmore, Owings and Merrill, architects.
United Airlines Terminal, John F. Kennedy
International Airport, New York, 1960.

Raymond Loewy, designer. Interior of the
United Airlines Douglas DC-7 (1956) and
DC-8 (1957-58) with view of the exterior
of the DC-8, with United's corporate
imagery, and crew uniforms designed by
Loewy, with his color scheme on their
Sud-Est *Caravelle* (1961). (Note: J. A. Graves
was chief designer for Douglas DC-8
interiors, and Pierre Satre was chief designer
for the Sud-Est Aviation *Caravelle*, 1955.)

Dorothy Draper, with Harley Earl, Inc.,
designers. Interior of the Convair 880-990
airplane, 1957-60.

C. F. Murphy Associates, architects. O'Hare
International Airport, Chicago, 1957-63.
The control tower is an FAA standard
design developed by architect I.M. Pei.
Airport graphics were done by Heyward
Blake.

Charles Eames, designer. "Tandem sling
seating," O'Hare International Airport,
Chicago, c. 1962.

Yorke, Rosenberg, and Mardall, architects.
Gatwick Airport, near London, 1958, with
later additions through the 1980s.

Károly Dávid, architect. Budapest-Ferihegy
Airport, 1954.

Hellmuth, Yamasaki and Leinweber, architects. Lambert St. Louis International
Airport, 1951-56.

Seattle-Tacoma Airport, 1947–49.

Tippetts-Abbett-McCarthy-Stratton, architects. Addition to the Mingaladon Airport of 1935, Rangoon, Burma, 1960.

Skidmore, Owings and Merrill, architects, with Outcalf, Guenther and Associates. Hangar at Hopkins Airport, Cleveland, 1958.

Skidmore, Owings and Merrill, architects; Myron Goldsmith, principal designer. United Airlines jet maintenance hangar, San Francisco International Airport, 1958 (now demolished).

Albert Kahn Associates, architect. Jet engine overhaul shop for Eastern Airlines, Miami, 1959-60.

Eero Saarinen, architect. Dulles International Airport, Washington, D. C., 1958-62.

Eero Saarinen, architect. Trans World Airlines Terminal, John F. Kennedy International Airport, New York, 1956-62, 1970.

Charles Forberg with Edward Larrabee Barnes, architects. Pan Am ticket office, Pan Am Building, New York, 1962 (later altered).

I. M. Pei, architect. National Airlines Terminal (now TWA Terminal), John F. Kennedy International Airport, New York, 1970.

Fehr and Granger, architects. Air traffic control tower and terminal, Robert Mueller Municipal Airport, Austin, Texas, 1960.

Paul R. Reddy of Reddy and Reddy, architects. FAA control tower and terminal of Denver Stapleton International Airport, 1962.

Mann and Harover, architects, with graphics by Jane Doggett and Dorothy Jackson of Architectural Graphics, Inc. Memphis Airport, 1963.

Smith, Hinchman and Grylls, architects. Metropolitan Airport Terminal, Detroit, 1966.

Everett I. Brown, architect. Remodeling and expansion of Indianapolis International Airport (1954-56) by Edward James, 1967-74, with 1987 additions by Wright, Porteous and Lowe, Browning, Day, Mullins, Dierdorf.

Karel Bubeníček, Karel Filsak, Jiří Louda, and Jan Srámek, architects. Terminal at Prague-Ruzyne Airport, 1964-68.

Gennady Elkin, Georgy Kryukov, and Lokshin, architects for Aeroproekt, Moscow. Additions to Domodedovo Airport, Moscow (early 1950s), 1965.

Urman, Neiman, and Komsky, architects for Aeroproekt, Moscow. Airport in Mineralnye Vody, 1965.

Paul Williams, in association with Charles Luckman Associates, and Welton Beckett and Associates, architects. Theme Building, Los Angeles International Airport, 1960-61.

Vilhelm Lauritzen, architect. Main Terminal, Kastrup Airport, Copenhagen, 1960 (with later additions).

John B. Parkin, architect. Lester B. Pearson International Airport, Toronto, 1961-64.

Charles Butler Associates, designers. Interiors of the Vickers VC10, 1962-64.

Charles Butler Associates, designers. Interiors of the BAC 111, 1963.

Illfley, Templeton, Archibald, LaRose and LaRose Associates, architects. Montréal International Airport-Dorval, 1956-60.

Aéroports de Paris, architects; Henri Vicariot, chief architect. International Terminal (also called Orly South, 1961) and West Terminal (or Orly West, 1971), Orly Airport, Paris.

Harrison and Abramowitz, architects. Control tower and terminal, LaGuardia Airport, New York, 1964 (modernized 1991-94).

Paul Schneider-Esleben, architect. Cologne-Bonn International Airport, 1962-70.

The Austin Company, architects. Assembly plant for the Boeing 747 in Everett, Washington, built 1966-67, with 1978-79 addition to build Boeing 767s.

Joseph Sutter, chief engineer; Teague Associates, interior designers. Boeing 747, 1968.

Teague Associates, designers. The wide-body roof and cabin look of the Boeing 747 as retrofitted to a Boeing 727 airliner (1970) with the look copied in a Soviet IL62 (1971).

Sundberg-Ferar, designers. Interiors of the mockup of the Lockheed L-1011, with TWA interior styled by Charles Butler Associates, 1970-72.

Yasui Architects' Office, architects. Itami Airport, Osaka, 1969.

Reynolds, Smith and Hills, architects. Terminal, Tampa International Airport, 1970.

Tippetts-Abbett-McCarthy-Stratton, architects for the initial studies; with Hellmuth, Obata and Kassabaum, architects of the executed project. Dallas-Fort Worth International Airport, 1965-73.

Teague Industrial Design, architects. *Airtrans System*, Dallas-Fort Worth International Airport, 1971.

Henry Dreyfuss Associates, designers. Logo, corporate image, cutlery, and aircraft interiors designed for American Airlines, 1966-89 (logo 1971, cutlery 1972).

Henry Dreyfuss Associates, designers. Graphics package for Dallas-Fort Worth International Airport, 1978.

Kivett and Myers, architects. Kansas City International Airport, 1968-72.

Hidroservice Engenharia de Projetos Limitada, architects. Rio de Janiero International Airport, 1974-90.

NACO (Netherlands Airport Consultancy) with M. Duintjer, architects. Schiphol Central Airport, The Netherlands, 1963-67. Arrival Hall Extension, 1971; Terminal Extension, Pier D, 1975, Pier C, 1982.

Otl Aicher, with Hans Roericht, Tomás Gonda, Fritz Querngässer, in association with Hans Conrad of Lufthansa, designers. Corporate identity package for Lufthansa German Airlines, 1962-63.

Giefer and Mäckler, architects. Terminal 1, Rhein-Main International Airport, Frankfurt am Main, 1965-72.

H. G Beckert and G. Becker, architects. Aircraft maintenance hangar, Rhein-Main International Airport, Frankfurt am Main, 1968-70.

Albert Kahn Associates, architect. United Airlincs hangar, O'Hare International Airport, Chicago, 1969.

Alexander Girard, designer. Braniff International Airways corporate identity program, including airplanes and interiors, 1965.

Jack Ruddle, architect. Shannon International Airport, 1971.

Krystyna and Jan Dobrowolski, architects. Warsaw International Airport, 1967-69.

Kenzo Tange, architect. Kuwait International Airport, 1967-79.

John P. Veerling, Sheldon D. Wander and George E. Ralph, architects. Newark International Airport, 1967-73.

Meinhard von Gerkan, with Volkwin Marg and Klaus Nickels, architects. Otto Lilienthal International Airport, Berlin-Tegel, 1969-74.

Uwe Schneider, chief of industrial design for Daimler-Benz Aerospace Airbus; with Eliot Noyes, Raymond Loewy, and David Ellis, design consultants; and Toshihiko Sakow, design consultant for Americanized version. Interiors of the Airbus A300, c. 1974, and Airbus A310, 1978-83.

Ernst Haas, Alfred Rieger, Ulrich Schindler, Fritz Dieter, Werner Neumann and Jochen Sänger, architects. Airport Terminal, Berlin-Schönefeld, 1974-76.

Heinz Pfaff, architect. Train station at the Berlin-Schönefeld Airport, 1983-84.

Alfredo Suarez, Felipe Montemayor, Estanislo Sekunda, Joaquin Lents and Joseba Pontesta, architects. International Terminal, Simon Bolivar Airport near Caracas, Venezuela, 1974-78. Luis Sully, architect. Main Building, 1984.

Harold Wirum and Associates, architects. FAA air traffic control tower, Anchorage International Airport, Alaska, 1977.

Yakovleva and Eksner, architects for Aeroproekt Leningrad. Kishinev Airport, Moldova, 1974.

Alexander Zhuk, architect, Aeroproekt Leningrad. Pulkovo Airport, Leningrad (now St. Petersburg), 1974.

Ivanov, Ermolaev, and Piskov, architects for Aeroproekt Moscow. Riga Airport, Latvia, 1974.

Ermolaev and Ivanov, architects for Aeroproekt Moscow. Tashkent Airport, Uzbekistan, 1975.

Cedar Homes, Inc., architects. Alaska Airlines Terminal, Gustavus, Alaska, 1979.

Skidmore, Owings and Merrill, architects. Haj Terminal, King Abdul Aziz International Airport, Jeddah, Saudi Arabia, 1976-78.

Hellmuth, Obata and Kassabaum. King Khaled International Airport, Riyadh, Saudi Arabia, 1983-84.

Nikken Sekkei and the Joint Venture Architects of the New Tokyo International Airport Authority. New Tokyo International Airport, Narita, Terminal 1 (1977-78) and 2 (1992).

Niels Diffrient, designer for the Knoll Group. Airport seating in Narita Airport, 1980.

Toyo Ito, architect. Ticket offices for Japan Air Lines in Illinois Center, Chicago, 1985 (now demolished).

Tippetts-Abbett-McCarthy-Stratton, master plan with Victor Bisharat, terminal architect, and Sir Frederick Snow, design review. Queen Alia International Airport, Jordan, c. 1973-83.

Ustinov and Smirnov, architects for Aeroproekt Moscow. Airport, Rostov-on-Don, 1978.

M. Piskov, architect for Aeroproekt Moscow. Tallinn Airport, Estonia, 1980.

Ivanov and Lokshin, architects for Aeroproekt Moscow in association with the Ruterbau and Salzgitter Concern. Sheremetievo Air Terminal 2, Moscow, 1980.

I. Artamonova, architect for Aeroproekt Moscow. Vnukovo Airport, Moscow, 1980.

M. Piskov, architect for Aeroproekt Moscow. Kazan' Airport, Tartar, 1982.

Komsky and Neiman, architects for Aeroproekt Moscow. Grozny Airport, Chechen, 1982.

Smirnov and Bezborodova, architects for Aeroproekt Moscow. Ulan-Bator Airport, Mongolia, 1982.

Smith, Hinchman and Grylls, architects. William B. Hartsfield International Airport, Atlanta, 1980.

Aéroports de Paris, architects; Paul Andreu, chief architect. Tower with Terminal 1 (1967-74), Terminal 2: modules A-B (1981-83), module D (1989), and module C (1993), TGV Station (1994), Sheraton Hotel (1995), and Terminal 2F (1995-97) of Charles de Gaulle International Airport, Roissy-en-France.

Air France, architects, with the Direction du Frey and Groupe Acora. Air France Cargo Facility, BOP (*Bâtiment d'Ordonnancement des Palettes*, "pallet marshalling unit"), Charles de Gaulle International Airport, Roissy-en-France, 1988.

Aéroports de Paris, architects; Paul Andreu, chief architect. Terminals at Abu Dhabi (1982), Dar-Es-Salaam (1984), Jakarta (1985), and Cairo (1986) international airports.

Wilke and Partner, architects. Hanover Airport, 1973 (with the addition of two modular pods, the second to open in 1999 for the Hanover Expo of 2000).

Odell Associates, architects. U.S. Air (formerly Piedmont Airlines) maintenance facility, Greensboro/High Point Airport, Greensboro, North Carolina, 1981-83.

Pierre Peersmann of the Ministry of Transportation and Infrastructure, architect. Air traffic control radar station, Bertem, Belgium, 1982.

Helmut Jahn of Murphy/Jahn, architects. Chicago Transit Authority station, 1981, and United Airlines Terminal, O'Hare International Airport, Chicago, 1983-88.

William E. Brazley, architect. Cargo facilities for Air France and Lufthansa at O'Hare International Airport, Chicago, 1990-93.

Von Busse and Partner; with Auer and Weber; and others, architects. Franz Josef Strauss International Airport, Munich, 1976-92, with airport graphics designed by Otl Aicher.

Helmut Jahn of Murphy/Jahn, architects. Munich 2 Airport Center and Kempinski Hotel, Franz Josef Strauss International Airport, Munich, 1991-94 (Airport Center to be constructed 1996-99).

John Siefert and Malcolm Elliott of the Siefert Group, architects, with Donald Butler Associates, consulting engineers for early studies. London City Airport, 1981-87.

Ervin Jaklics, with Károly Herceg, architects. Expansions of the Budapest-Ferihegy International Airport, 1985 (construction to be completed 1995-96).

Aeroproekt Architects Moscow and Far East Branch. Khabarovsk Airport, 1993.

Noel Robinson, architects, with Ove Arup and Partners. Kingsford-Smith Memorial Hangar Building, Brisbane International Airport, 1988.

Stafford Moor and Farrington, architects, with Ove Arup and Partners. Extension to Hangar 96, Kingsford-Smith Airport, Sydney, 1989.

Tierney and Associates for Aer Rianta, architects, with Ove Arup and Partners, engineers. Aeroflot maintenance hangar, for Aer Rianta, Shannon Airport, 1988-90.

Tierney and Associates for Aer Rianta, with Ove Arup and Partners, architects. Aeroflot maintenance facility, Sheremetievo Airport, Moscow, 1989-90.

Ove Arup and Partners, architects. *Project Dragonfly*, British Airways maintenance facility, Cardiff, Wales, 1990-93.

Gensler and Associates, with Leason Pomeroy and Associates, and Thompson Consultants International, architects. Thomas F. Riley Terminal, John Wayne Airport, Orange County, California, 1985-90.

Burns-Peters Group, now BPLW, architects. Albuquerque International Airport, 1985-90.

Hellmuth, Obata and Kassabaum, master plan recommendations; terminals executed by Skidmore, Owings and Merrill, architects, with Amman and Whitney. Expansion of Dulles International Airport, 1985 (master plan), 1994 (terminal expansion).

Odell Associates, architects, in association with Delta Associates. Inc. Roanoke Regional Airport, Virginia, 1985-89.

Odell Associates, architects, in association with Delta Engineering. Lynchburg Regional Airport, Virginia, 1987-90.

Odell Associates, architects. Concourse D/International Terminal (1987-90) and parking deck (1989) for the Charlotte/Douglas International Airport, Charlotte, North Carolina.

Odell Associates, architects. Patrick Henry International Airport, Newport News, Virginia, 1988-92.

Glasgow International Airport, 1966.

HNTB, architects. William Dress Terminal, Evansville Regional Airport, Indiana, 1989.

HNTB, architects. Greater Rochester International Airport, Rochester, New York, 1992.

HNTB, architects. Nantucket Memorial Airport, Massachusetts, 1992.

Sir Basil Spence, with Glover and Ferguson, architects. Original terminal (with Ove Arup and Partners, 1966); renovations, stage 1 (1989-92) and stage 2 (1992-94), Glasgow International Airport.

KHR-Knud Holscher, Svend Axelsson, and Erik Sìrenson, architects. Finger B extension of Copenhagen Airport, 1986-96.

Von Gerkan, Marg and Partners, architects. Additions to Stuttgart Airport, 1986-91.

Smith, Hinchman and Grylls, architects. Continental Airlines Terminal, Hopkins International Airport, Cleveland, 1991.

Norman Foster and Partners, architects, with Ove Arup and Partners. Stansted Airport, near London, 1988-92.

Knight Architects, Engineers, Planners, architects. Master plan for FAA Reliever Airport, Lewis University, Romeoville, Illinois, 1985-2000.

Gale Abels Associates, architects. Air traffic control tower for the FAA Reliever Airport, Centennial Airport, Arapahoe County, Colorado, 1985.

HNTB, architects. New Hanover International Airport, Wilmington, North Carolina, 1985-90.

HNTB, architects. Charleston International Airport, South Carolina, 1985.

Gensler and Associates, architects, with Derthick, Henley and Wilkersen. Municipal Airport, Chattanooga, Tennessee, 1985-92.

Richard Rogers Partnership, architects, with Ove Arup and Partners. Additions to Marseille Airport, 1988-93.

Raphael Moneo, architect. Seville International Airport, 1988-91.

Ricardo Bofill, architect, with Ove Arup and Partners. International Terminal, Barcelona Airport, 1992.

William Nicholas Bodouva and Associates, architects. U.S. Air Terminal, LaGuardia Airport, New York, 1992.

Tasso Katselas Associates with Architects for British Airports Authority. Shopping mall, Pittsburgh International Airport, 1989-92.

NACO, architects, with Benthem and Crouwel. Schiphol Airport additions and master plan to become a European Mainport, Amsterdam, 1989-2003.

NACO, architects. New control tower, Schiphol Airport, Amsterdam, 1988-91.

Leo A. Daly, architect. Site adaptation of a standard air traffic control tower (designed by Welton Becket), General Mitchell Field, Milwaukee, c. 1985-90.

Aubry Architects, with Leo A. Daly, architect of record. Air traffic control tower, Alliance Airport, Fort Worth, 1991.

McAllen Miller International Airport, McAllen, Texas, 1990-95.

Leo A. Daly, in association with Thompson Crenshaw Airport Management Consultants, architects. Terminal Two, Los Angeles International Airport, 1989.

Mario Bolullo of Harry S. Golemon, architects. Mickey Leland Terminal, Houston International Airport, 1990 (original terminal by Golemon and Rolfe, 1967-69).

Albert Speer and Partner, architect. Remodeling of Terminals A (1987-92) and C Building 183 (1986-88), Rhein-Main International Airport, Frankfurt am Main.

Joos, Schulze and Krüger-Heyden, with O. M. Ungers and Perkins and Will, architects. Terminal 2, Rhein-Main International Airport, Frankfurt am Main, 1990-94.

Renzo Piano, architect for the terminal, with Ove Arup and Partners, and Paul Andreau of ADP, master plan. Terminal for Kansai International Airport, Japan, 1988-94.

Von Gerkan, Marg and Partners, architects. Hamburg International Airport additions and alterations, 1986-94.

The NBBJ Group, with Leo A. Daly, architects. Modernization and expansion of Concourses B, C, and D for Sea-Tac International Airport, Seattle-Tacoma, 1992.

Murray Church, architect from Hochtief. Warsaw International Airport, 1992.

Von Gerkan, Marg and Partners, architects. Lufthansa Technik maintenance center, Hamburg International Airport, 1992-94.

Leo A. Daly, architect. Alaska Airlines ticket office, Seattle, 1992.

Edberg, Christiansen and Associates, architects. Alaska Airlines Terminal, Wrangell, Alaska, 1993.

C. W. Fentress, J. H. Bradburn and Associates, architects. Denver International Airport, 1989-95.

Aldo Rossi, with ITL – Italairport, architects. Remodeling of Linate International Airport, Milan, 1991-94.

ITL – Italairport, architects. Malpensa 2000 International Airport, Milan, 1987-94/95.

Gensler and Associates, with Hannon, Daniel and Dickerson, architects. Amarillo International Airport, Texas, 1989-94.

William Dale for Bell Helicopter Textron, architects. Vertiport, Dallas, 1992.

Andreé Putman, designer. Interior of the Air France *Concorde*, 1993.

Landor Associates, designer. Corporate identities for British Air, 1983-86, and Japan Air Lines, 1986-89.

Teague Associates, designers, after a drawing by Yukie Ogaki. Whale design for an All Nippon Airways Boeing 747-400, 1993.

Teague Associates, designers, after ideas developed by GSD & M. *Sea World*, *Arizona*, *California*, and *Texas* airliner designs for Boeing 737s of Southwest Airlines, 1990-95.

Gad Shannan, designers. Interior of the Canadair Regional Jet, 1993.

Leo A. Daly, architect, with Pei Cobb Freed and Partners, program manager. FAA control tower, John F. Kennedy International Airport, New York, 1992-95.

Holmes and Narver, architects, with Siegel-Diamond, consulting architects. Air traffic control tower, Los Angeles International Airport, c. 1992-95.

Leo A. Daly, architect, with site adaptation by Holmes and Narver, architects. Prototypical high-activity air traffic control tower, O'Hare International Airport, Chicago, 1993-95.

Frankfurt, Short and Bruza, architects. Maintenance center for United Airlines, Indianapolis, 1993 (with subsequent construction through 1996).

Copenhagen Airport Staff Architects. Additions to Copenhagen Airport: Pier A, 1994-95 (with additions to 1998, including an underground rail station), and International Terminal 2 (design development).

Odell Associates, architects. McAllen Miller International Airport, McAllen, Texas, 1990-95.

Tippetts-Abbett-McCarthy-Stratton, architects. Macau International Airport, 1990-95.

Teague Associates, designers. Convertible seats, designed for the Boeing 737-757, 1990-94.

Claude Tran Van and Luc Tran Van, with Calvo and ARCA, architects. Clément Ader Assembly Plant for Airbus Industrie A330 and A340 aircraft, Toulouse-Colomier, 1987-90.

Karl Dieter Köpcke, head of architecture for Daimler-Benz Aerospace Airbus; with Sellhorn, architects. Otto Lilienthal Assembly Plant for the Airbus Industrie A321 and A319 aircraft, Hamburg-Finken-werder, 1993-94.

Uwe Schneider, chief of industrial design for Daimler-Benz Aerospace Airbus. Interiors of the Airbus Industrie A320-321-319, and Airbus Industrie A330-340, 1985-95.

Tippetts-Abbett-McCarthy-Stratton, architects. Addis Ababa International Airport, 1990-98.

The Austin Company. Boeing Aircraft Company factory and office additions, Everett, Washington, 1991-92, for the construction of the Boeing 777 in 1995-96.

Skidmore, Owings and Merrill. Korean Airlines Operation and Maintenance Center, Inchon, Korea, 1992-96.

Pere Nicolau Bover, architect. "Airport City," Palma de Mallorca, 1991-96.

Cesar Pelli and Associates, architects, with Leo A. Daly. Additions to Washington National Airport, 1992-97.

Odell Associates, architects. Manassas Regional Airport, Virginia, 1991-97.

The Richard Rogers Partnership, architects, with Ove Arup and Partners. Proposed Terminal 5, Heathrow International Airport, London, 1991-99.

Norman Foster and Partners, architects, with Hellmuth, Obata, and Kassabaum, master planners, and the Ove Arup Partnership, engineers. Chek Lap Kok Airport, Hong Kong, 1992-95.

HNTB, architects. T. F. Green Airport, Warwick, Rhode Island, 1992-96.

Smith and Thompson, architects. East Hampton Airport, New York, 1989-97.

Hellmuth, Obata and Kassabaum. Expansion of the East Terminal, Lambert St. Louis International Airport, c. 1996-2000.

Santiago Calatrava, architect. New terminal, Bilbao Airport, 1991-96.

Pierre Goudiaby Atépa, architect, in association with Gamsen. Banjul International Airport, Gambia, 1994-98.

Oslo Hovedflyplass AS, architects. New airport and terminal, Olso-Gardermoen, Norway, 1993-98.

William Nicholas Bodouva and Associates, architects. International Terminal, Baltimore-Washington International Airport, 1992-97.

William Nicholas Bodouva and Associates, architects. Terminal One, John F. Kennedy International Airport, New York, 1994-98.

Skidmore, Owings and Merrill, Del Campo and Maru, and Michael Willis and Associates, architects. International Arrivals Building and light rail system, San Francisco International Airport, 1993-99.

Hellmuth, Obata and Kassabaum, architects. Sendai and Fukuoka International Airports, Japan, 1993-97.

Hellmuth, Obata and Kassabaum, architects; with Engineers and Managers Associates. Cochin Airport, India, 1995-2002.

Tippetts-Abbett-McCarthy-Stratton, architects. Zhengzhou Xuedian International Airport, Henan Province, China, 1993-97.

Kisho Kurokawa, architect. Kuala Lumpur International Airport (first phase of main terminal), 1993-98 (with additional construction 2000-2020).

C.W. Fentress, J.H. Bradburn and Associates, architects, with McClier, associate architects. Seoul International Airport, Korea, 1993-98.

Murphy/Jahn, architects. Additions to the Cologne-Bonn International Airport, 1993-98.

Kohn, Pedersen, Fox, with Cannon, and William Nicholas Bodouva and Associates,

architects. Buffalo International Airport, 1993-99.

Hellmuth, Obata and Kassabaum, architect. Studies for Concourse E and West Terminal, New Orleans International Airport, 1993-99.

Uwe Schneider, chief of industrial design, Daimler-Benz Aerospace Airbus. Proposed double-decker airliner, Airbus Industrie A3XX, 1994-2003.

Murphy/Jahn, architects, with TAMS and ACT, associate architects. Second Bangkok International Airport, 1993-2000.

HNTB, architects. New airport, Shreveport, Louisiana, 1994-98.

Teague Associates, designers. Interiors for the Boeing 777, 1993-95.

Teague Associates, designers. Interior of the Boeing 737-700, 1994-97.

C & D Interiors, designers. Overhead storage units to retrofit older DC-10 and Boeing 747 aircraft, 1993-95.

C & D Interiors, designers. Lavatory for the physically challenged, a project for American Airlines, 1994.

C & D Interiors, designers. Interior of the Embraer EMB-145 commuter jet, 1995-96.

Interactive Flight Technologies, designers. On demand video system, 1995-96.

InnoVision, designers. Corporate identity for Western Pacific Airlines "logo jets," 1996.

D'Arcy, Masius, Benton and Bowles, advertising agency and designers. Corporate identity for TWA, 1995-96.

HNTB, architects, with A. Epstein and Sons. Proposed new Midway Airport, Chicago, 1996-99.

Uwe Schneider, chief of industrial design, Daimler-Benz Aerospace Airbus. Nose, cockpit, and interiors for the proposed Airbus Industrie 100-seat regional airliner, 1989-96.

Leo A. Daly, architects. "Airport City" business center, Berlin-Schönefeld Airport, 1996-2000.

Edge Media, NYC, rendering of Buffalo Airport, 1993-99.

Zhengzhou Xuedian International Airport, China, 1993-97.

Photography Credits

Frontispiece: courtesy of Flughafen Zürich

Zukowsky
1: courtesy of Henry Ford Museum and Greenfield Village; 2, 23: courtesy of United Airlines; 3: courtesy of Lufthansa Bildarchiv; 4, 5: courtesy of Pan American World Airways, Inc., Records, Archives and Special Collections Department, University of Miami; 6, 7: courtesy of Boeing Historical Archives; 11: courtesy of Air Canada; 12: courtesy of Ronald Rhodes; 14-17: courtesy of Robert J. Price; 18-19: courtesy of Teague Associates; 20: courtesy of Daimler-Benz Aerospace Airbus; 21-22: courtesy of Western Pacific Airlines.

Voigt
3: courtesy of Australian Archives, Australian Capital Territory Regional Office; 5: courtesy of AEG Firmenarchiv; 7-9, 11, 13-17: courtesy of Lufthansa Bildarchiv.

Bosma
1, 3: courtesy of British Airports Authority; 4: DR/Duplé, courtesy of Aéroports de Paris; 6, 7, 21: courtesy of KLM Aerocarto Luchtfotografie; 8: courtesy of Air Canada; 9: courtesy of Flughafen Köln/Bonn; 10: Landesbildstelle Berlin, courtesy of Von Gerkan, Marg and Partners; 12: courtesy of Aéroports de Paris; 13: Martin Charles, courtesy of the Ove Arup Partnership; 14: courtesy of Nederlands Architectuurinstituut; 15, 16, 19: courtesy of John Zukowsky; 17, 18: courtesy of Flughafen Zürich; 20: Paul Maurer, courtesy of Aéroports de Paris; 22-23: Hans Ege, courtesy of Murphy/Jahn Architects.

Brodherson
1, 18: courtesy of the Chicago Historical Society; 3: courtesy of Los Angeles Department of Airports; 4: courtesy of the National Air and Space Museum; 5, 6, 16: courtesy of the Library of Congress; 7: courtesy of David Brodherson; 9: courtesy of the Austin Company; 10, 13, 23: courtesy of Pan American World Airways, Inc., Records, Archives and Special Collections Department, University of Miami; 11-12: courtesy of San Francisco International Airport, Bureau of Exhibitions and Cultural Education; 15, 28: courtesy of John Zukowsky; 17, 31: courtesy of United Airlines; 19: Mark Ballogg, courtesy of Steinkamp/Ballogg, Chicago; 20: Charles Eames, courtesy of Herman Miller, Inc.; 21: Aerial Photos International; 22: Ezra Stoller, courtesy of Tippetts-Abbett-McCarthy-Stratton; 24-25: courtesy of HNTB Corporation; 26: Ronald P. Sutell, courtesy of Alaska Airlines; 27: courtesy of Arapahoe County Public Airport Authority; 29: courtesy of Murphy/Jahn Architects; 30: Peter J. Schulz, courtesy of Perkins and Will; 31: Balthazar Korab; 32: courtesy of Cesar Pelli and Associates Inc.; 33: Timothy Hursley, courtesy of C. W. Fentress, J.H. Bradburn and Associates; 34: Nick Merrick, courtesy of Hedrich-Blessing.

Plates

1-5, 20, 34, 36-37, 103: courtesy of Lufthansa Bildarchiv; 6, 33: from *Vom Werdegang der Stahlbauwerk e* (1939); 7: from John Walter Wood, *Airports* (1940); 8, 45, 69, 83, 161, 163: courtesy of United Airlines; 9: courtesy of Experimental Aircraft Association; 10: courtesy of Henry Ford Museum and Greenfield Village, Dearborn, Michigan; 11, 160: courtesy of the Austin Company; 12: from John Walter Wood, *Airports* (1940); 13, 48, 95, 116, 155: courtesy of John Zukowsky; 14, 17, 22: Dennis Fleischman, courtesy of Museum of Flight, Seattle; 15-16, 49-51, 63-66, 166: courtesy of Boeing Historical Archives; 18, 25: courtesy of National Air and Space Museum (NASM), Smithsonian Institution, Washington, D.C.; 19: courtesy of the Estate of Luis Gutierrez Soto; 21: courtesy of Luftfartsverket-Swedish Civil Aviation Administration; 23-24: courtesy of Boeing Historical Archives; 26-28, 35, 42-43: courtesy of Pan American World Airways, Inc., Records, Archives, and Special Collections Department, University of Miami Library, Coral Gables, Florida; 29, 31: courtesy of Archiv der Luftschiffbau Zeppelin GmbH; 30: from *Zeitschrift des Vereines deutscher Ingenieure* (March 28, 1936); 32, 101-02: courtesy of Flughafen Frankfurt Main AG; 38-39: courtesy of Musée de l'Air et de l'Espace, Paris; 40-41: courtesy of National Monuments Record, Royal Commission on Historical Monuments, Crown copyrights; 44: courtesy of the Port Authority of New York and New Jersey; 46-47, 135, 139-47, 168-172: courtesy of Daimler-Benz Aerospace Airbus GmbH; 52: courtesy of the Naval Historical Foundation; 53-54: courtesy of the United States Marine Corps; 55, 60-61, 73-74, 82: courtesy of the Chicago Historical Society, Hedrich-Blessing Collection; 56: courtesy of Albert Kahn Associates, Architects and Engineers; 57: courtesy of The Art Institute of Chicago; 58-59: courtesy of Flughafen Zürich; 62, 75-77, 133-34, 162, 164-65, 167: courtesy of Teague Associates; 67-68, 107: courtesy of the Lockheed Corporation; 70: courtesy of Claude Lensigné; 71-72: Ezra Stoller, ESTO, courtesy Skidmore, Owings & Merrill; 78-81: courtesy of Charles Forberg; 84-85: Ezra Stoller, ESTO; 86-89: courtesy of the Girard Foundation; 90: Harvey Lloyd, courtesy of the Girard Foundation; 91: A. C. Cooper, Ltd., courtesy of the British Architectural Library, RIBA, London; 92: courtesy of Wolfgang Voigt; 93: courtesy of British Airports Authority; 94: courtesy of San Francisco International Airport, Bureau of Exhibitions, Museums, and Cultural Exchange; 96, 105, 175-76: courtesy of Skidmore, Owings & Merrill; 97-99: courtesy of Aeroproekt and Aviareklama, Moscow; 100: courtesy of the Polish National Tourist Office; 104: Werner Krüger, courtesy of Lufthansa Bildarchiv; 106: Robert Azzi, courtesy of Hellmuth, Obata & Kassabaum; 108: courtesy of Robert J. Price; 109: courtesy of Sundberg-Ferar, Inc.; 110: Commercial Photo Co., courtesy of the Aviation Department, City of Kansas City, Missouri; 111: George Silk, courtesy of Hellmuth, Obata & Kassabaum; 112: courtesy of Infraero, Empresa Brasileira de Infra-Estrutura Aeroportuária; 113-14, 118: Paul Maurer, courtesy Aéroports de Paris; 115: Valentin, courtesy of Air France; 117: courtesy of Air France; 119-120: courtesy of Howard Needles Tammen & Bergendoff; 121: courtesy of the NBBJ Group; 122: courtesy of Odell Associates, Inc.; 123: Rion Rizzo/Creative Sources, courtesy of Gensler and Associates; 124: Sir Norman Foster and Partners, courtesy of the Ove Arup Partnership; 125: Raymond Yau, courtesy of the Ove Arup Partnership; 126: Peter Mackinven, courtesy of the Ove Arup Partnership; 127: Hisao Suzuki, Archivo Eye Barcelona; 128: C. K. Hiwatashi, courtesy of the Ove Arup Partnership; 129: Phil Dilley, courtesy of the Ove Arup Partnership; 130, 132: Klaus Frahm, courtesy of Von Gerkan, Marg & Partners; 131: Michael Wortmann, courtesy of Von Gerkan, Marg & Partners; 136-38: Airbus Industrie; 148-54: courtesy of Landor Associates; 156: courtesy of Leo A. Daly; 157: courtesy of Los Angeles International Airport, City of Los Angeles, Department of Airports; 158-59: Canadair; 173-74: courtesy of Murphy/Jahn Architects; 177: Don Dedorko, courtesy of Hellmuth, Obata &

Kassabaum; 178: Michael Sechman, courtesy of Hellmuth, Obata & Kassabaum; 179-80: courtesy of Kisho Kurakawa Architect and Associates.

Bouman
1: courtesy of the Port of Seattle; 2: courtesy of Foto Marburg, LA 4727-27; 3: Infraero-Rio, courtesy of Empresa Brasileira de Infra-Estrutura Aeroportuária; 4: courtesy of Indianapolis Airport Authority; 5: courtesy of the Chicago Historical Society; 6: Aerial Photos International; 7: courtesy of New Tokyo International Airport Authority; 8: courtesy of C.W. Fentress, J.H. Bradburn and Associates; 9: courtesy of United Airlines; 10: Hedrich-Blessing, courtesy of the Chicago Historical Society; 11: Idaka, courtesy of Hillsborough County Aviation Authority; 12: Balthazar Korab, courtesy of Smith, Hinchman and Grylls Associates, Inc.; 13: courtesy of Perkins and Will; 14: Bob Askren, courtesy of the Commerical Photo Co.; 15: courtesy of Skidmore, Owings and Merrill; 16: Balthazar Korab; 17: Steinkamp/Ballogg,

courtesy of William E. Brazley and Associates, Ltd.

Bruegmann
5: Geonex/Chicago Aerial Survey; 7: courtesy of Dennis McClendon; 8: Ezra Stoller, ESTO, courtesy Skidmore, Owings & Merrill; 9: courtesy of John Zukowsky; 10: courtesy of Leo A. Daly; 11-12: courtesy of Alliance Development Company, Fort Worth; 15: courtesy of Bell Helicopter Textron.

Lockhart
1: Dave Chare Photography, courtesy of Ralph Burke Associates; 2: Geonex/Chicago Aerial Survey; 4: courtesy of McDonnell Douglas; 7, 9, 11, 13: courtesy of Jeppesen Sanderson, Inc.; 8: Lawrence Okrent, courtesy of Okrent Associates; 12: Balthazar Korab.

Rau
1-2, 17: courtesy of Landor Associates; 3, 7, 9: courtesy of Delta Air Lines; 4: Timothy Hursley, Balthazar Korab, courtesy of Smith, Hinchman and Grylls; 5, 8: courtesy of

Murphy/Jahn Architects; 6: courtesy of HNTB Corporation; 10-13: courtesy of Pan American World Airways, Inc., Records, Archives and Special Collections Department, University of Miami; 14: courtesy of United Airlines; 15: courtesy of Henry Dreyfuss Associates; 16: courtesy of John Zukowsky.

Appendix
242: courtesy of The Art Institute of Chicago; 243 top: courtesy of Mainichi Shimbun; 243 bottom: courtesy of Lufthansa Bildarchiv; 244 top left: courtesy of National Air and Space Museum, Smithsonian Institution, Washington, D.C.; 244 top right: courtesy of Pan American World Airways, Inc., Records, Archives and Special Collections Department, University of Miami; 244 bottom: courtesy of Air Rianta; 245 top: courtesy of Paisajes Españoles; 245 bottom: courtesy of Port of Seattle; 247: courtesy of BAA Scottish Airports Ltd.; 248: courtesy of Odell Associates; 249 bottom left: courtesy of Kohn Pedersen Fox Associates; 249 bottom right: courtesy of TAMS Consultants, Inc.

Contributors

Koos Bosma
is a professor of twentieth-century architecture and city planning at the Free University in Amsterdam. His doctoral dissertation covered regional planning in The Netherlands. His research interests include the history of large regional infrastructure projects, such as the TGV high-speed rail system in France, the Channel Tunnel, and similar projects that involve the cooperation of architects and engineers. His publications include *The Structural Art Works of Rijks-waterstaat.*

Mark J. Bouman
is Professor of Geography at Chicago State University. He completed his Ph.D. in 1984 at the University of Minnesota, with a dissertation on electrification and the lighting of cities. He is the author of a forthcoming volume, *City Lights: Street Lighting in Western Urban Culture.* His interest in the transportation infrastructure of airports relates closely to his ongoing research in urban geography.

David Brodherson
received his Ph.D. in the history of architecture and urban development from Cornell University, with a dissertation on the history of American airports in relation to aeronautical engineering developments, public policy, and design competitions. He is also an archi-

tectural photographer and photographic historian. He has been an NEA Research Fellow and is currently at work on a major study of American airports.

Robert Bruegmann
is Professor of Architectural and Art History at the University of Illinois at Chicago. He completed his Ph.D. in architectural history in 1976 at the University of Pennsylvania. Among his many publications are *Holabird and Roche, Holabird and Root: An Illustrated Catalog of Works, 1880-1940* and *Modernism at Mid-Century: The Architecture of the United States Air Force Academy.* He continues to research ex-urban and suburban developments in the twentieth century.

Wood Lockhart
holds a Ph.D. from Northwestern University, with a 1972 dissertation devoted to airport development and design. He has been a commercial airline pilot for more than thirty years.

Leonard Rau
is currently Design Information Manager at *SampsonTyrrell,* an identity consultancy based in London. Prior to this, he worked as a freelance design and marketing consultant in the airlines, telecommunications, and social housing sectors. He gained an M.A. in design history in 1994 from the Royal

College of Art, in a program jointly sponsored by the Victoria and Albert Museum.

Wolfgang Voigt
is a professor of architectural history at the Academy of Fine Arts in Hamburg. He received his doctorate at the University of Hanover in 1986. His publications have concentrated on architecture in Germany in the 1920s and 1930s and include *Das Bremer Haus: Wohnungsreform und Südtiebau in Bremen, 1880-1940.* His research interests include modernist architecture during the Third Reich, the emigration of architects from Germany after 1933, and the history of aviation architecture in Germany.

John Zukowsky
is Curator of Architecture at The Art Institute of Chicago. He has organized numerous exhibitions and has edited a number of publications, among them *Chicago Architecture, 1872-1922: Birth of a Metropolis* and *Chicago Architecture and Design, 1923-1993: Reconfiguration of an American Metropolis,* as well as *Karl Friedrich Schinkel, 1781-1841: The Drama of Architecture* and *The Many Faces of Modern Architecture: Building in Germany between the World Wars.* He received his Ph.D. in architectural history from the State University of New York at Binghamton.

Index

Numbers in *italics* refer to pages with illustrations